D1561779

Western Intervention in the Balkans
The Strategic Use of Emotion in Conflict

Conflicts involve powerful experiences. The residue of these experiences is captured by the concept and language of emotion. Indiscriminate killing creates fear; targeted violence produces anger and a desire for vengeance; political status reversals spawn resentment; cultural prejudices sustain ethnic contempt. These emotions can become resources for political entrepreneurs. A broad range of Western interventions are based on a view of human nature as narrowly rational. Correspondingly, intervention policy generally aims to alter material incentives ("sticks and carrots") to influence behavior. In response, poorer and weaker actors who wish to block or change this Western implemented "game" use emotions as resources. This book examines the strategic use of emotion in the conflicts and interventions occurring in the Western Balkans over a twenty-year period. The book concentrates on the conflict in Kosovo but also examines conflicts and interventions in Macedonia, Bosnia, Montenegro, and South Serbia.

Roger D. Petersen holds BA, MA, and PhD degrees in political science from the University of Chicago. Since 2001, he has taught in the Political Science Department at MIT, where he was recently named Arthur and Ruth Sloan Professor of Political Science. Petersen studies comparative politics with a special focus on conflict and violence, mainly in Eastern Europe, but also in Colombia and other regions. He is the author of *Resistance and Rebellion: Lessons from Eastern Europe* (Cambridge University Press, 2001) and *Understanding Ethnic Violence: Fear, Hatred, and Resentment in Twentieth-Century Eastern Europe* (Cambridge University Press, 2002). He also has an interest in comparative methods and has co-edited, with John Bowen, *Critical Comparisons in Politics and Culture* (Cambridge University Press, 1999). He teaches classes on civil war, ethnic politics, and civil–military relations.

"Roger Petersen unpacks the recent history of Western interventions in the Balkans to show how easily peace can be subverted by ethnic leaders who know how to appeal to anger, fear, guilt, shame, and resentment. Those who oppose peace use *jujitsu-politics:* they apply carefully calibrated violence to elicit a spiral of emotions and counterviolence that will bring them new fighters and new supporters. Petersen here extends rational choice theory to include emotions as resources no less important than money and guns; peacekeeping operations will never look the same after you have read this book."

– Clark McCauley, Bryn Mawr College

Cambridge Studies in Comparative Politics

General Editor

Margaret Levi   *University of Washington, Seattle*

Assistant General Editors

Kathleen Thelen   *Massachusetts Institute of Technology*
Erik Wibbels   *Duke University*

Associate Editors

Robert H. Bates   *Harvard University*
Stephen Hanson   *University of Washington, Seattle*
Torben Iversen   *Harvard University*
Stathis Kalyvas   *Yale University*
Peter Lange   *Duke University*
Helen Milner   *Princeton University*
Frances Rosenbluth   *Yale University*
Susan Stokes   *Yale University*
Sidney Tarrow   *Cornell University*

Other Books in the Series

David Austen-Smith, Jeffry A. Frieden, Miriam A. Golden, Karl Ove Moene,
   and Adam Przeworski, eds., *Selected Works of Michael Wallerstein: The
   Political Economy of Inequality, Unions, and Social Democracy*
Andy Baker, *The Market and the Masses in Latin America: Policy Reform
   and Consumption in Liberalizing Economies*
Lisa Baldez, *Why Women Protest? Women's Movements in Chile*
Stefano Bartolini, *The Political Mobilization of the European Left,
   1860–1980: The Class Cleavage*
Robert Bates, *When Things Fell Apart: State Failure in Late-Century Africa*
Mark Beissinger, *Nationalist Mobilization and the Collapse of the Soviet State*
Nancy Bermeo, ed., *Unemployment in the New Europe*
Carles Boix, *Democracy and Redistribution*
Carles Boix, *Political Parties, Growth, and Equality: Conservative and Social
   Democratic Economic Strategies in the World Economy*

Series list continues following the Index.

Western Intervention in the Balkans

The Strategic Use of Emotion in Conflict

ROGER D. PETERSEN

Massachusetts Institute of Technology

CAMBRIDGE UNIVERSITY PRESS
Cambridge, New York, Melbourne, Madrid, Cape Town,
Singapore, São Paulo, Delhi, Tokyo, Mexico City

Cambridge University Press
32 Avenue of the Americas, New York, NY 10013-2473, USA

www.cambridge.org
Information on this title: www.cambridge.org/9780521281263

First published 2011

Printed in the United States of America

A catalog record for this publication is available from the British Library.

Library of Congress Cataloging in Publication data

Petersen, Roger Dale, 1959–
Western intervention in the Balkans : the strategic use of emotion in conflict /
Roger D. Petersen.
   p.   cm. – (Cambridge studies in comparative politics)
Includes bibliographical references and index.
ISBN 978-1-107-01066-6 (hardback) – ISBN 978-0-521-28126-3 (pbk.)
1. Balkan Peninsula – History – 1989–   2. Balkan Peninsula – Politics and government –
1989–   3. North Atlantic Treaty Organization – Armed Forces – Balkan Peninsula.
4. Kosovo War, 1998–1999 – Participation, Foreign.   5. Kosovo War, 1998–1999 –
Psychological aspects.   6. Operation Allied Force, 1999 – Psychological aspects.
I. Title.   II. Series.
DR1319.P478   2011
949.703–dc22   2011008912

ISBN 978-1-107-01066-6 Hardback
ISBN 978-0-521-28126-3 Paperback

For Daniela

Contents

Acknowledgments

I wrote this book over the better part of a decade. In the process, I made four extensive field trips to the Western Balkans. The list of individuals who helped me along the way is very long; I can only recognize a few individuals here.

On this side of the ocean, the community centered in the MIT Political Science Department supported me in innumerable ways. In general, the MIT Political Science Department, the MIT Center for International Studies, and the MIT Security Studies Program created a rich working environment. Several MIT students made specific contributions. Evangelos Liaras and Scott Radnitz provided early research reports, Angela Kilby wrote extensive summaries of the psychological literature on emotions, Sarah Zukerman compiled background data on Kosovo, Andrew Radin gave me new insights on Bosnia, Jessica Karnis researched bombings, Sameer Lalwani produced general comments and helped write Appendix B, and Tara Maller not only provided general comments and helped write Appendix B but also did the index. My administrative assistants also furnished key support. Mike Myers helped on the art work and Scott Schnyer organized the bibliography.

Over the years, I presented parts of this project at the following forums: University of California, Berkeley, Berkeley Program in Soviet and Post-Soviet Studies; Princeton University, Program in Contemporary European Politics and Society; Yale University, Comparative Politics Seminar; Duke University; National University, Bogota, Colombia; MIT, Political Science Department; University of Virginia; International Research Seminar in Social Sciences and Politics Studies, Bogota, Colombia; MIT Counterinsurgency Workshop; Syracuse University; Serbian-American Center, Belgrade, Serbia; Watson Institute for International Studies, Colloquium for Comparative Research, Brown University; Theoretical Frontiers in Modeling Identity and Conflict, Honolulu, Hawaii; Solomon Asch Center, Bryn Mawr; Princeton's Working Group on Identity Politics; the seminar series "Limited Sovereignty and Soft Borders in Southeastern Europe and the Former Soviet States," Harriman Institute, Columbia University; Harriman Institute Balkans Lecture Series, Columbia

University; Cambridge University Press Seattle Seminar; University of Chicago, Partition Violence Conference; Fifth International Seminar of Research on Social Science and Political Studies "Politics, Hatred, and Other Emotions," Bogota, Colombia; Conference on "Emotions and Civil War," Paris, College de France; and London School of Economics, Conflict Studies Lecture Series.

In the Balkans, there are too many to name, but I was especially helped by Erol Sakiri in Macedonia and South Serbia, Joseph Kazlas in Kosovo, and Milos Solaja in Bosnia. The young scholars I interacted with in Macedonia are worthy of special mention. With few exceptions, I was treated with respect and kindness all over the region. Everywhere, individuals told me to "just write the truth." I hope I have done that in this book.

The contribution of my wife, Daniela Stojanovic, is enormous. She was present throughout the research. Fluent in Serbian and possessing a background in community psychology, she conducted many of the interviews. She was a logistical coordinator, interviewer, and translator. She read every page and, often through less than subtle criticism, greatly improved the clarity of my writing (and thinking). More than that, she often challenged my theory, bolstered my methods, and questioned my conclusions. For all extents and purposes, she is a co-author of this book.

PART I

BACKGROUND AND THEORY

I

Western Intervention in the Balkans

The Strategic Use of Emotion in Ethnic Conflict

In this book, I try to achieve multiple but connected goals. First, I wish to provide a history of ethnic conflict in the Western Balkans since the breakup of Yugoslavia. This goal is the book's substantive agenda. This history will concentrate on the role of the West, in particular the West's intervention policies. There is considerable variation in the success and failure of these policies. Understanding this variation requires some innovation in method. My second goal is to supply this innovation. This goal is the book's methodological agenda. This book has a third, less direct, aim. I hope that by developing this methodology and applying and testing it on the universe of Western Balkan cases, I will also be able to provide some understanding of Western intervention policy more broadly.

I. THE SUBSTANTIVE AGENDA

At its broadest level, this book concentrates on explaining variation in the success or failure of Western intervention in the Balkans from the collapse of communism up to the summer of 2008. With the formation of a strongly pro-EU government in Serbia in the summer of 2008, significant opposition to incorporation into Western institutions and the Western economy disappeared from the region. Not to exaggerate, but in an important sense one type of history had ended in the Balkans. Across this poor and corrupt region, nearly all looked to embrace the democracy and capitalism of the European Union and the United States. No party or leader could offer a coherent alternative. This transformation was perhaps inevitable. The combined gross domestic product of the entire Western Balkans (usually defined as the former Yugoslavia minus Slovenia but plus Albania) was dwarfed by that of its Western neighbors. In an era of globalization, these poor states could not advance outside of Europe's orbit. To be sure, significant conflicts and disputes still color the Western Balkan terrain, especially in Kosovo, Bosnia, and Macedonia. This book will chronicle the ways those conflicts are still being contested. Yet the era of massive violence and isolation appears to be over.

Although the progression of regional history was likely to reach this stage, there were a few bumps along the way. In what amounted to the bloodiest fighting in Europe since the Second World War, the Bosnian war resulted in the death and displacement of hundreds of thousands of people. Fifteen years after the Dayton Accords, progress toward the reconstruction of a functioning central state has been uneven. In Kosovo, the Milosevic regime drove over 800,000 Albanians out of their homes. In response, NATO conducted its first armed action, dropping over 26,000 bombs during a period of seventy-eight days to drive Milosevic's forces out of Kosovo.[1] The war not only changed NATO's mission, but also challenged sovereignty norms as a basic principle of the international order. Albanian guerrilla groups escalated violence in Kosovo in 1998, southern Serbia in 2000, and Macedonia in 2001. As late as 2008, radical nationalists in Serbia drew huge vote shares while their followers and sympathizers set fire to the U.S. and other foreign embassies.

Within the course of this drama, the United States and Europe made decisions about whether to intervene and how. The nature of intervention has taken a myriad of forms – informal pressure, sanctions, bombings, etc. In the years following the breakup of Yugoslavia, the United Nations conducted eight peacekeeping missions in the region, NATO carried out four different operations, and the Organization for Security and Cooperation in Europe (OSCE) worked on several assignments across the Western Balkans. Interventions took their most manifest form in brokered agreements among parties in conflict. In almost every corner of the region, the West has been involved in making these deals. In Bosnia, the Clinton Administration negotiated the 1995 Dayton Accord with special annexes for the cities of Brcko and Mostar; in Macedonia, the West mediated the Ohrid Accord and has continued to serve as arbiter in its evolving implementation; in Eastern Slavonia, the West instituted the Basic Agreement; in southern Serbia, the United States brokered the Konculj agreement; in Montenegro, the West negotiated the Belgrade Agreement and was involved in the Tuzi or Ulcinj accord; in Kosovo, the United Nations' Mission in Kosovo (UNMIK) instituted a policy of standards before status, then one of standards with status, and then transferred power to the European Union and yet another form of supervised governance in the form of the Ahtisaari Plan. The West also invested enormous resources in attempting to make these brokered agreements work. The United States spent 22 billion dollars from 1992 to 2003; the European Union spent 33 billion euros just between 2001 and 2005.[2]

---

[1] More than 38,400 sorties dropped 26,614 bombs. Iain King and Whit Mason, *Peace at Any Price: How the World Failed Kosovo* (Ithaca NY: Cornell University Press, 2006), p. 2.

[2] Elizabeth Pond, *Endgame in the Balkans: Regime Change, European Style* (Washington DC: Brookings Institution, 2006), p. 278.

The Western-brokered accords just mentioned are a primary empirical focus of this book. In each case, an accord illustrates Western goals and provides criteria for judging whether these goals were successfully reached.

Taken as a whole, these accords also illustrate the Western philosophy toward intervention. I will argue that both Western intervention practice and the social science that evaluates it are driven by a narrow sense of human nature. More specifically, individuals are seen as responding to short-term, largely economic incentives and disincentives, or perhaps to physical threats. Correspondingly, policies are formed along the lines of narrowly conceived "sticks and carrots." In the words of an American military colonel serving in Iraq, "With a heavy dose of fear and violence, and a lot of money for projects, I think we can convince these people that we are here to help them."[3] In another similar vein, interveners apply the logic of rational choice game theory, especially in the form of the "prisoners' dilemma," to the conflicts they find themselves in. As with sticks and carrots, the goal is to raise the value of rewards, or to structure penalties in such a way that the relationships among the parties in the conflict can rapidly evolve toward a new "equilibrium" with higher mutual payoffs. In an important sense, this book is an evaluation of this philosophy and the practice that follows from it.

The Western Balkans is a critical case for the study of intervention. Most factors have theoretically lined up to support successful intervention – both carrots and sticks have been abundant. In Bosnia, fourteen years after the Dayton Accords, the international community had poured more money into Bosnia per capita than into any recipient of the Marshall Plan. Under the so-called Bonn powers, international administrators could easily remove uncooperative local political actors, even from positions to which they were democratically elected. The International Criminal Tribunal has tried dozens of war criminals at the Hague. Massive security forces have kept the peace. NGOs have worked to create a strong narrative that places the blame on manipulative elites. Critically, the European Union holds out the promise of membership in exchange for compliance to its wishes. Yet the hope of developing effective central governments made only halting progress. In 2009, Richard Holbrooke, the architect of the Dayton Accord, was warning about Bosnia's possible collapse.[4] In Kosovo, the program of "standards before status" failed to create a functioning multiethnic society or to prevent massive riots in March 2004, despite having poured enormous resources into a small state of two million people. The West was pouring money into Kosovo at a rate twenty-five times greater than into Afghanistan and had helped fund troop levels at a rate fifty times greater.[5] Some regions in

---

[3] Dexter Filkins quoting Colonel Sassaman in the *New York Times*, December 7, 2003, "Tough New Tactics by U.S. Tighten Grip on Iraq Towns."

[4] Richard Holbrooke and Paddy Ashdown, "A Bosnian Powder Keg," *London Guardian*, October 22, 2009. Ashdown was writing as a former UN High Representative to Bosnia.

[5] King and Mason, *Peace at Any Price*, p. 21.

Bosnia, and arguably Macedonia, have seen more success. What explains this variation? The set of accords mentioned form a substantial field of variation from which to examine potential answers to this question.

II. THE METHODOLOGICAL AGENDA: THE STRATEGIC USE OF EMOTION IN ETHNIC CONFLICT

In terms of the substantive agenda just described, this book is a straightforward social scientific work. I develop and examine hypotheses that explain observed variation in the success or failure of Western intervention policy in one universe of cases, the Western Balkans.

At the same time, the book deviates greatly from standard practice and the conventional wisdom in political science. This deviation stems from the discrepancy that I observed over the course of several years of fieldwork in the Balkans between what actors do and the theoretical model of their behavior that underlies Western models of intervention and reconstruction. The individuals I observed had lived through violence and some of them had committed it. Many fled their homes in fear. Some would seek revenge. These individuals often hold deep historically based prejudices; they often cannot value the lives of ethnically distinct others. Many became used to being on top of the political and social hierarchy and had a hard time accustoming themselves to new political realities. In other words, the people I have observed have been through some powerful experiences. These experiences have left a residue. For those who have lived in the conflict regions of the Balkans, the residue of their experience is often as real as the guns and money that form the basis of Western social science accounts. The question is how this powerful but amorphous residue can be incorporated into social science.

The most basic underlying proposition of this book can be simply stated: *broad human experiences leave residues that affect the path of conflict.* This statement will undoubtedly seem banal to many readers. In fact, it flies in the face of the conventional wisdom of U.S. political science as it stood in the early twenty-first century. The view that broad human experience shapes the outbreak and course of conflict has been under consistent assault for much of the post–Cold War era. The current thinking comes in many different forms, and consumers of the literature will recognize the slogans and catchwords of specific versions: greed over grievance, insurgency as technology, elite manipulation, and thugs. Violence is often viewed as a matter of very small numbers of actors, either elites or criminals, making rational decisions to initiate and sustain violence to achieve narrow ends. Despite diversity in details, each of these views holds in common the idea that the daily life of members of large communities is largely irrelevant to understanding conflict.

I believe this view is wrong. The reason for the existence of this view may be that a fundamental goal of social science is to make complicated matters easier to comprehend. In the pursuit of parsimony, simplifying assumptions are necessary. Given the biases of Western society and academia, methods in the study of conflict have been based, either explicitly or implicitly, on the assumption of narrowly rational actors.[6] Perhaps unsurprisingly, both the Western practitioners of intervention and the scholars who study political violence are driven by the same assumptions. Both sometimes fail in their respective endeavors, I argue, because their overly narrow view of human nature often blinds their practices and methods.

Although civil war is not the direct subject here, recent political science literature on that subject has produced slogans and catchwords that have influenced conflict studies at large. It is worthwhile to compare the approach and essence of some of these studies with the method developed here. Consider one of the most highly influential cross-national quantitative studies of civil war and development policy.[7] Paul Collier and his collaborators conclude that civil war is overwhelmingly linked to economic variables.[8] The related slogan is "greed over grievance." They find that political grievances and social divisions, inequality, and a host of other factors are not statistically significant; rather, a simple combination of accessible natural resources and a weak state produces civil war. These correlations are then interpreted in rational choice terms. The statistically significant variables are assumed to produce the constraints and incentives that affect the rational decisions of rebels in their pursuit of narrow interests, primarily economic goods. In this view, violence is a resource that is used to grab wealth. There are two versions of this "greed" theory. In one, the existence of natural resources provides a motive for conflict and war. In the other, the focus is on the lack of opportunities for legitimate economic activity in poorer, weaker states. Both suggest that looking for explanations in grievances and nonmaterial motivations is not a productive avenue. In a passage on recruitment into rebel armies, Collier et al. address the question of noneconomic motivation with the following speculation:

The people who join rebel groups are overwhelmingly young uneducated males. For this group, objectively observed grievances might count for very little. Rather, they may be disproportionately drawn from those easily manipulated by propaganda and who find the power that comes from possession and use of a gun alluring. Social psychologists find that around 3 percent of the population has psychopathic tendencies and actually enjoys violence against others (Pinker) and this is more than is needed to equip a rebel group with recruits.[9]

---

[6] On this point, see Chaim Kaufmann, "Rational Choice and Progress in the Study of Ethnic Conflict: A Review Essay," *Security Studies* 14 (2005): 178–207.

[7] I also use quantitative studies of civil war as a primary example because they may represent the modal form of analysis among political scientists in the first years of the twenty-first century. According the APSA Task Force on Political Violence, over fifty quantitative studies of civil war appeared between 2001 and 2006 alone, more than in the previous thirty years combined. Most of these studies consider similar sets of variables.

[8] Paul Collier, V. L. Elliott, Havard Hegre, Anke Hoeffler, Marta Reynal-Querol, and Nicholas Sambanis, *Breaking the Conflict Trap: Civil War and Development Policy* (Washington D.C. and Oxford: Copublication of the World Bank and Oxford University Press, 2003).

[9] Ibid. p. 68. The Pinker citation is from S. Pinker, *The Blank Slate: The Modern Denial of Human Nature* (New York: Viking Press, 2002).

In Collier et al.'s approach, the actual everyday experiences of larger groups of people do not carry explanatory significance. Anger at violence, resentment of domination, and historically and culturally based prejudices and stigmas are not particularly relevant. Rather, violence is a matter of greedy elites operating according to structural constraints, who lead a small set of naïve or psychopathic recruits.

James Fearon and David Laitin's article on civil war and insurgency examines the onset of civil war.[10] Based on a wide reading of political science works, they develop a set of independent variables that include level of gross domestic product, income inequality, nature of terrain, population size, ethnic and religious diversity, and extent of civil liberties. They find that the variables associated with grievances and identities are statistically nonsignificant, whereas those associated with level of GDP, terrain, and population size are statistically significant. Fearon and Laitin's interpretation of these findings is that civil wars are largely a matter of insurgent technology (the related slogan is "insurgency as technology"). Rebels fight for a variety of reasons, but they do so only when they can rationally expect to avoid capture by the state. They can challenge the state if they can hide in mountains or within large populations and if the state's capabilities are weak (proxied by GDP figures).

Fearon and Laitin recognize the limits of large-n statistical studies, so they also look to case studies and qualitative treatments of civil war. However, when analyzing case studies, Fearon and Laitin seem to transfer the rationalist assumptions underlying the regression findings. In a review of a set of largely anthropological and case study works on violence, they address the puzzle of why individuals appear to participate in communal violence when it does not appear rational to do so. They solve the puzzle by concluding that "'ethnic violence' can be a cover for other motivations such as looting, land grabs, and personal revenge, and the activities of thugs sent loose by the politicians can 'tie the hands' of publics who are compelled to seek protection from the leaders who have endangered them."[11] The interpretation predictably seeks answers by positing a rational individual pursuing a constricted range of goods.

John Mueller argues that ethnic violence and war have nothing at all to do with grievances, prejudices, or history. The catchword for his explanation is "thugs." Mueller surveys the killing in recent cases and concludes, "The mechanism of violence in the former Yugoslavia and Rwanda, then, is remarkably banal. Rather than reflecting deep historic passions and hatreds, the violence seems to have been the result of a situation in which common, opportunistic, sadistic, and often distinctly nonideological marauders were recruited and permitted free rein by political authorities. Because such people are found in all societies, the events in Yugoslavia and Rwanda are not peculiar to those locales,

[10] James Fearon and David Laitin, "Ethnicity, Insurgency, and Civil War," *American Political Science Review* 97 (2003): 75–90.

[11] James Fearon and David Laitin, "Violence and the Social Construction of Identity," *International Organization* 54 (Autumn 2000): 845–77. Passage is from p. 874.

but could happen almost anywhere under the appropriate conditions."[12] For Mueller, violence is the result of a small band of power-seeking elites deciding to unleash criminals. Each of the groups pursues its narrow agenda. The broader population lie in between with their preferences, their beliefs, and their backgrounds, meaningless to the events swirling around them. Support for one's own group is only a matter of survival: "Often the choice was essentially one of being dominated by vicious bigots of one's own ethnic group or by vicious bigots of another ethnic group. Given that range of alternatives, the choice was easy."[13]

Unlike Mueller, Russell Hardin sees the process of identification as essential and worthy of exploration. Why would an individual act in favor of or support collective violence? Hardin's starting point is rational choice. As he states, "In this study, I propose to go as far as possible with a rational choice account of the reputedly primordial, moral, and irrational phenomena of ethnic and nationalist identification and action."[14] This work, like others in political science, limits its approach from the beginning. Accordingly, Hardin's consideration of norms boils down to a strategic choice represented by a coordination game. Like Mueller, Hardin posits that individuals will choose to support their own ethnic groups mainly as a matter of avoiding sanction. Individuals wish to coordinate with other individuals on a salient identity dimension. As with Mueller, the content and history of that dimension is irrelevant. Hardin's discussion is much richer than Mueller's, as it also considers the ways in which individuals' information becomes limited, both by themselves (the epistemological comforts of home) and by elites, and also raises the cognitive phenomenon of the is-ought fallacy (because a group convention exists, it should be attributed moral power). Hardin's view of group conflict, though, has little to do with broader experiences such as group stigma, status hierarchy, memory of past violence, or emotions.

For many types of conflict, most recent political science treatments seek an explanation in the form of a specific actor at a specific time making an optimizing decision based on narrow considerations of greed or power. For example, political scientists find that mass killing and genocide during war is a strategic calculation unrelated to history, identity, or politics.[15] Furthermore, security dilemma theorists hold that ethnic conflict is often the result of one specific strategic situation. When both sides are able to strike each

---

[12] John Mueller, "The Banality of 'Ethnic War,'" *International Security* 25 (1) (Summer 2000): 42–70. Passage is from p. 43.

[13] Ibid., p. 56.

[14] Russell Hardin, *One for All: The Logic of Group Conflict* (Princeton, NJ: Princeton University Press, 1995), p. 16. For a review related to the present work, see Roger Petersen, "Ethnic Conflict, Social Science, and William Butler Yeats: A Commentary on Russell Hardin's *One For All: The Logic of Group Conflict*," *European Journal of Sociology* 38 (1997): 311–23.

[15] Benjamin Valentino, Paul Huth, and Dylan Balch-Lindsay, "'Draining the Sea': Mass Killing and Guerrilla Warfare," *International Organization* 58 (2004): 375–407. Also, see Alexander Downes, *Targeting Civilians in War* (Ithaca, NY: Cornell University Press, 2008).

other and offensive and defensive actions are blurred, then it is rational to strike first rather than risk being attacked. The argument generally focuses on balances of power and the relationship between offense and defense rather than on the political and social experiences of the antagonists.[16] Relatedly, over the past three decades, many political scientists have moved away from drawing insights from psychology and history to wholeheartedly embrace economic approaches. Consider a recent economic treatment of the phenomenon of hatred. Edward Glaeser writes that hatred is a choice subject to the laws of supply and demand. Politicians supply negative stories about groups and consumers decide whether to buy these stories depending on a cost-benefit analysis of the product.[17] Clearly, this approach downplays, if not completely ignores, considerations of historical creation and momentum of identities, as well as the voluminous work on the psychology of prejudice and cognitive distortions.

As opposed to these political scientists, field researchers often do find history and collective grievances to be critical. A recent collection of studies of protracted conflict surveyed the struggle among insurgent groups and the state in eleven cases. The concluding chapter evaluated Collier's greed argument in light of the case studies evidence and produced the following statement: "None of our cases significantly support the 'supply-side explanations' of insurgent or rebel violence popularized by Professor Paul Collier of the World Bank and his colleagues, . . . ETA, GAM, Hamas, the IRA, the JKLF, the LTTE, and the PKK were formed by people influenced by nationalist and leftist doctrines, and they understood themselves to be acting in response to the repression, conquest, partition, or maltreatment of their nations."[18] Thus we see that one set of scholars finds that repression and maltreatment are central, whereas another sees them as insignificant. Why don't the findings of the case analysts show up in the treatments of political scientists? The discrepancy calls for a rethinking of how broad experiences and grievances translate into motivations and actions that precipitate and sustain conflict.

III. EMOTIONS AS THE RESIDUE OF EXPERIENCE

The approach in this book is to treat the essence of these experiences as emotions. As I will outline in detail in the following chapter, emotions can be conceived of as a package of cognitions and action tendencies, with influences on information-collection and belief-formation. Borrowing from psychology,

---

[16] Barry Posen, "The Security Dilemma and Ethnic Conflict," *Survival* 35 (1993): 27–47. Posen does recognize the influence of past violence on present calculations.

[17] Edward Glaeser, "The Political Economy of Hatred," *Quarterly Journal of Economics* 120 (2005): 45–86.

[18] Marianne Heiberg, Brendan O'Leary, and John Tirman eds., *Terror, Insurgency, and the State: Ending Protracted Conflicts* (Philadelphia: University of Pennsylvania Press, 2007), p. 400.

I will develop a conception of emotions that can be incorporated into hypotheses concerning strategic choices during conflict.

In this introduction, however, I will only discuss some common sense notions about experiences and emotions during conflict and intervention. Although many broad experiences might affect how conflict unfolds, three seem most powerful and common: the experience of violence itself, the experience of stigma and prejudice, and the experience of status reversal.

First, consider the experience of violence. People strongly react when members of their groups are killed. This statement should be uncontroversial, but its full meaning is seldom captured by analyses that employ static measures of death and hostility. These measures cannot capture the fact that the qualitative nature of violence shapes the way humans experience violence. Some types of violence create anger and a desire to strike back; other types of violence create fear and a desire to flee. If the violence targets cultural sites and specific individuals, the reaction will tend toward anger. If the killing seems indiscriminate, the reaction is likely to be fear. The emotions of anger and fear are primary resources in ongoing conflicts.

Consider a description of an actual onset of war in the city of Mostar, Bosnia:

The Muslim-Croat war for Mostar erupted one night in the early summer of 1993, climaxing months of rapidly escalating tensions. According to a Bosniac soldier, the atmosphere in the city resembled a tinderbox in those last days of 'peace', and gunmen from both sides had already taken up positions on either side of the Boulevard in anticipation of an imminent outbreak of fighting. His position on the side of the Boulevard closer to the Neretva faced Croat positions on the other side of the wide street. That night, according to his account, Croat militiamen holed up in the gymnasium building just across the Boulevard from his position brought a 17 year-old Bosniac schoolgirl abducted from west Mostar to the school. They then apparently gang-raped her before throwing her out of a top-floor window. Several years later the former Bosniac fighter recalled to me his most vivid memory of that night: the absolute stillness and silence for a few minutes after the girl's screaming ended. Then heavy firing broke out from both sides of the Boulevard.[19]

This passage illustrates the unsettling and uncomfortable realities of political violence. The passage also indicates the difficulties of treating political violence as a straightforward matter of rational calculation. The event described involved the violation of norms, the creation of memories, and, most relevant here, the triggering of emotions. It was more than some leader's calculated decision to initiate "onset." It likely left a powerful residue. Years after Dayton, and fifteen years after this event, Mostar remained an ethnically segregated city despite massive funding and Western pressure.

Next, consider the phenomenon of stigma and prejudice. As an enormous body of literature has established, members of one group often see members

---

[19] Sumantra Bose, *Bosnia after Dayton: Nationalist Partition and International Intervention* (New York: Oxford University Press, 2002), pp. 103-4.

of another group as inherently inferior. This phenomenon underlies the central case in this book, Kosovo. Julie Mertus has described the idea of an Albanian in Serbian eyes:

Kosovo was an abstraction, a set of myths in the popular imagination. Over time, the nationalism became racialized, that is, difference was framed in terms of perceived physical differences in skin, nose, ears, IQ, sexuality. In this sense, nationalism became "written on the body." Slurs against Kosovo Albanians shifted. No longer referred to as "white hats" (alluding to the hats worn by men in traditional dress), a sexualized imagery of Albanian men and women was adopted. In the mainstream Serbian and Yugoslav presses, Albanian men were declared to be rapists, although Kosovo had the lowest reported incidents of sexual violence in Yugoslavia. Albanian women were portrayed as mere baby factories, despite statistics indicating that the childbirth rates of urban Albanian women and those of other urban women in Yugoslavia were nearly identical. Accused in the past of being culturally inferior, Albanians increasingly were depicted as genetically inferior as well. This is racism of the purest sort.[20]

The existence of stigma is also evidenced by pejorative terms or slurs. The actual term used in much of Serbia is usually not "Albanian" but the pejorative "shiptar." Albanians in Kosovo have their own pejorative term for Serbs, "shkija." The presence of stigma and the belief that a group is inherently inferior are the basis of the emotions of contempt and hatred.

A third key experience is status reversal. As an abundant and well-known literature has established, humans tend to think in group terms and group hierarchies.[21] In most societies, including the United States,[22] individuals can identify which groups are "on top" and which are "on the bottom." One of the most powerful political experiences occurs when the ordering of groups in a hierarchy is transformed, when the top group is brought below a bottom one. In previous work, I found that these status reversals were a good predictor of ethnic violence across twentieth-century eastern Europe.[23] The power of status reversals, however, can be seen in a wide variety of cultural settings from Sri Lanka's postcolonial changes among Tamils and Sinhalese to Rwanda's impending changes in the wake of the Arusha Accords. Status change was wrenching for the U.S. South. It is not only the powerful who feel the force of a status reversal. Consider the description of the destruction of a friendship in Iraq following the deposing of Saddam Hussein's regime:

Shatha al-Musawi, a Shiite member of Parliament, first encountered the Sunni-Shiite divide on the day the Americans captured Saddam Hussein. Hearing the news with

[20] Julie Mertus, *How Myths and Truths Started a War* (Berkeley, CA: University of California Press, 1999), p. 8.
[21] See, for one example, James Sidanius and Felicia Pratto, *Social Dominance: An Intergroup Theory of Social Hierarchy and Oppression* (Cambridge: Cambridge University Press, 2001).
[22] See, for example, the surveys of UCLA undergraduates cited in Sidanius and Pratto, *Social Dominance*.
[23] Roger Petersen, *Understanding Ethnic Violence: Fear, Hatred, and Resentment in Twentieth Century Eastern Europe* (Cambridge: Cambridge University Press, 2002).

a close Sunni friend named Sahira, Ms. Musawi erupted like a child. "I jumped, I shouted, I came directly to Sahira and I hugged her," Ms. Musawi said. "I was crying, and I said, 'Sahira, this is the moment that we waited for.'" At least it should have been: Mr. Hussein's henchmen killed Ms. Musawi's father when she was only 13; Sahira, too, was a victim, losing her closest uncle to the Hussein government. But instead of celebrating, Sahira stood stiffly. A day later, Ms. Musawi said, Sahira's eyes were red from crying. And before long, like so many Sunnis and Shiites here, the two stopped talking.... "We were shocked, really," she (Ms. Musawi) said. "We used to have friends, neighbors. In every moment, when you met a person, you didn't think: Is he Shia or Sunni? Of course you'd notice, but it didn't matter." Then at some point, she said, it switched; sect became the defining characteristic for Iraqis. Her Sunni friends told her she did not understand. Being a Sunni used to count for something, they said.[24]

Manipulative political elites do not create the experience of status reversal. It is a widespread experience that creates the emotion of resentment. When it exists, as it did among the Sunni in Iraq, it becomes a factor, and a resource, for those wishing to change an intervener's game.

Here are the assumptions linking broad experiences and emotions that underlie this book:

(1) Violent experiences create the emotions of anger and fear.
(2) Prejudice and stigma support the emotions of contempt and hatred.
(3) The experience of status reversal can create the emotion of resentment.
(4) These emotions may have lasting effects and can come to be used as resources in conflict.

These assumptions are not an essential part of the political science approach to conflict. Because political scientists often assume that human behavior is centered on maximizing a set of limited goods, they do not consider how emotions connected with violence might produce vengeance and other nonoptimizing and self-defeating behaviors. Because political scientists often start with the assumption that narrow rationality drives outcomes, they naturally ignore the forces of prejudice, despite decades of accumulated knowledge on that issue. Because political scientists tend to concentrate on basic observable measures related to developed Western society, they do not consider, with a few prominent exceptions,[25] how domination and hierarchy can drive conflict. As evidenced in the passage about Iraq, the force that may drive or allow violence is not the denial of equality, but the loss of privilege.[26]

---

[24] Damien Cave, "Shiite's Tale: How Gulf with Sunnis Widened," *New York Times*, August 31, 2007.

[25] I have in mind here Donald Horowitz, *Ethnic Groups in Conflict* (Berkeley, CA: University of California Press, 2000) and Lars-Erik Cederman, Andreas Wimmer, and Brian Min, "Why Do Ethnic Groups Rebel? New Data and Analysis," *World Politics* 62 (2010): 87–119. Using an extensive new database with nearly 30,000 observations, the authors found very strong support for the effect of resentment of status reversals.

[26] For a treatment of grievance as denial of political rights, see Laitin and Fearon's "Ethnicity, Insurgency, and Civil War."

The assumption of rationality that pervades Western approaches seems like a convenient excuse to look away from the actual experience of protracted, violent conflict. Current methods sanitize the phenomenon. This rationalization and sanitization are problematic when one observes some basic characteristics of political violence. Violence usually takes place among groups with long-term relations that have shaped identities and prejudices. Political upheaval and violence introduce elements of domination and subordination into group relations. The repressive actions, desecrations, killings, and bombings involved with political violence are likely to produce intense experiences that disrupt normal life. The intense experiences during and after violence often trigger mechanisms that distort information collection and belief formation. Violence transforms and heightens specific preferences, in particular the desire for flight, retaliation, and vengeance. This is a nasty world in which the relationship among preferences, information collection, and belief formation is not straightforward. Some might fear the chaos of letting nonrational forces enter into their methods. But what is the cost of ignoring these forces? A central goal of this book is to show that a wider view of human nature will not necessarily lead to methodological chaos. Rather, incorporating an understanding of emotion can produce a fuller and more realistic understanding of the evolution of violent conflicts and their solutions, while still retaining rigor and parsimony.

Ronald Suny summarizes the thinking here: "I argue something that should be obvious, though not always for political scientists: emotions are key to human motivation. Indeed, we would not be human without them. They are a stimulus to action; they are fundamental to self-identification, to thinking about who 'we' are and who the 'other' is; they are involved in the social bonds that make groups, even whole societies, or nations, possible. And they are, therefore, powerful tools to explain why people do what they do politically."[27] Those engaged in case studies may be aware of the role of emotions but do not explicitly specify these emotions, how they affect action, and how they might be used strategically. Again, Suny comments, "Far too often historians and other social scientists use explanations that emphasize emotions without specifying either that they are about emotions, which emotions are at play, and what the action tendency of those emotions is likely to be."[28] This book attempts to address Suny's points by systematically linking identifiable experiences to specific emotions and further, to actions.

IV. RETURNING TO THE SUBSTANTIVE AGENDA: WHY MASSIVELY FUNDED WESTERN INTERVENTIONS SOMETIMES FAIL

What explains variation in the success and failure of Western intervention? Some explanations hold that success depends on the will of major actors and

[27] Ron Suny, "Why We Hate You: The Passions of National Identity and Ethnic Violence," *Berkeley Program in Soviet and Post-Soviet Studies*, Paper 2004_01-suny (February 1, 2004), p. 5.
[28] Ibid., p. 41.

the expenditure of sufficient resources.[29] An alternative answer provided here sees the problem in terms of asymmetric conflict, but not in the traditional terms of power asymmetries. The interveners are stepping into conflicts characterized by violence, killing, status reversals, prejudice, and ethnic stigma. These experiences breed behavior based on nonrational mechanisms, especially emotions. These emotions are the basis of provocations that alter the rationality-based strategies of the interveners. It is the existence and use of these emotions that often shape the course of intervention and its success or failure.

The answer presented here proposes that the opponents of Western intervention hold a broader view of human nature and accordingly use a broader set of resources in efforts to derail the interveners' games. Western intervention strategies imply a set of "rational" actions and norms being taught to a lesser people. They also imply a superior knowledge that allows the intervener or occupier to carefully calibrate sticks and carrots in an optimal way. In opposition, the assumption in this work is that many living under the intervention understand the desired Western norms, but they have histories and memories and emotions that drive them toward other behavior and other goals. They also understand the occupier's strategy of "calibrating the supply of sticks and carrots." In fact, they understand it so well that they develop sophisticated strategies to get around that strategy and manipulate it. Furthermore, they understand that emotions are part of the game. They even understand that the intervener's emotions are part of the game. In short, opponents of intervention are often more advanced and complex in their strategy than the interveners.

Correspondingly, in studying intervention, the focus should be placed on the actions of those wishing, and many times able, to disrupt the intervener's game. In the face of the intervener's superior structural resources, the opponent's use of provocation relies on emotions as resources. Political entrepreneurs use emotions to change the set of actors, reshape preferences, and alter the rules. They pursue a range of actions in trying to trigger emotions. These actions include: bombing to kill discriminately, bombing to kill indiscriminately, bombing property without killing, assassination, written threats, desecration of religious sites, destruction of property, creating parallel political systems, inflammatory posters and graffiti, and public demonstrations, parades, and provocations. Actors may also forego these actions and try to cooperate or simply acquiesce.

Whereas studies of interventions focus on the regime or occupier's calibration of "sticks and carrots," this work concentrates on the opponent's calibration of provocations. By examining variation in the use, or nonuse, of provocations, we can understand the connections and effects of the other elements of intervention. Provocations are the outcome of the interaction between the intervener's rational game and the spoiler's use of emotions.

---

[29] On the importance of the will of major actors, see Stephen J. Stedman, "Spoiler Problems in Peace Problems," *International Security* 22 (Fall 1997): 5–33. On the expenditure of sufficient resources, see Michael W. Doyle and Nicholas Sambanis, *Making War and Building Peace* (Princeton, NJ: Princeton University Press, 2006).

In this book, I will provide an argument that proceeds along the following steps:

(1) In many cases, broad human experiences such as prejudice and humiliation, concerns involving group status and hierarchy, memories of past violence, and reactions to present violence have left a powerful residue.
(2) The residue of these experiences is captured by the conception and language of emotion. Powerful experiences produce emotions.
(3) These emotions become resources for political entrepreneurs.
(4) A broad range of Western interventions are based on a view of human nature as narrowly rational. Correspondingly, intervention policy is applied as a matter of arranging "sticks and carrots" in the most efficient ways.
(5) During Western interventions, powerful interveners institute "games" involving economic and security-based sticks and carrots.
(6) In response, poorer and weaker actors who wish to block or change the Western-implemented game use emotions as resources. The most obvious example is the inculcation of fear through terrorism, but this is just one strategy among many. A main goal of the book is to specify other emotion-based strategies and predict when they are most likely to be employed.
(7) The course of the intervention depends on the will and resources of the intervener, but also on the more specific nature of the Western game and, crucially, the emotion resources available to opponents of the game.

Figure 1.1 represents this flow graphically. The empirical chapters will follow this outline through several cases and use it to make focused comparisons.

The primary insight and contribution of this argument is the effort to treat emotions as resources similar to guns and money. No one can deny that structural variables relating to force levels, monetary resources, and demography affect the outcome of interventions. The amount of variation explained through these common structural variables is often less than impressive. Outcomes are also affected by the agency of actors who understand how to mobilize their own populations against intervention.

V. WHAT IS TO BE EXPLAINED?

There are two dependent variables. I will call them the specific and the general dependent variables. The general dependent variable is very broad: the success or failure of an intervention as assessed by the intervener's own criteria – that is, whether the West achieved what it set out to do in each case. The second is, as labeled, more specific. It is the variation in provocations and tactics seen in the lower left box of Figure 1.1. My claim is that by adding emotions to the analysis I can explain why opponents of intervention use bombings versus boycotts, or indiscriminate killing versus discriminate killing, when they do

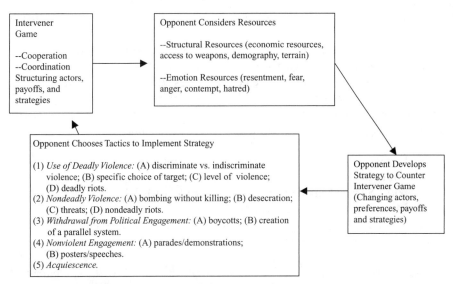

FIGURE 1.1. Western Intervention and the Nature of Its Opposition.

nothing, and so on. I will be able to explain this variation much better than existing theories with only some loss of parsimony.

The specific dependent variable is related to the larger one. The more an opponent is successful in launching effective provocations against the intervener, the better the chances that the mission will fail. However, the overall success or failure of the mission may be determined in other ways, such as the very definition of success and failure the intervener sets out for itself. The set of Western Balkan states does produce some clear cases of success and failure, though. Kosovo's "standards before status" policy is a definite failure. Some elements of the Dayton Accord are notable successes, such as preventing violence, whereas others are recognizable failures. As will become clear, the region provides substantial variation in both independent and dependent variables.

VI. THE PLAN OF THE BOOK

The book's chapters systematically follow the flow of Figure 1.1. The first section of the book develops theory and methodology. The second chapter defines emotions and provides examples of their use. The third chapter develops a framework to analyze the distribution of emotions across different situations; this chapter lays out the political entrepreneur's available emotion resources and specifies when specific emotions may be available for use. It also discusses the structural variables to be considered. The fourth chapter conceptualizes Western intervention as a type of game, fleshing out the beginning box of Figure 1.1. The fifth chapter deepens the analysis of the strategic use of emotion with illustrations from a variety of non-Balkan cases. By choosing non-Balkan cases, I hope to show the generalizability of the theory and methods. The sixth chapter concludes the first section of the book by developing and listing hypotheses.

These hypotheses are then evaluated in the second section of the work.

The seventh chapter provides necessary historical background on the region and its succession of conflicts. The next chapters cover Kosovo and the several types of interventions taking place there over the course of eighteen years. In order to avoid selection bias, I will address intervention across the entire region, examining eight different brokered agreements, including:[30]

(1) Kosovo: (a) standards before status; (b) status with standards; (c) Ahti-saari Plan
(2) South Serbia: May 2001 Accord, sometimes called the Konculj agreement
(3) Macedonia: Ohrid Accord
(4) Montenegro: (a) Belgrade Agreement; (b) Ulcinj agreement
(5) Bosnia: Dayton Accord

Each case also examines the Western role in the period before the agreements. I have not devoted a major section of the text to comparison of an emotion-based approach with other alternative explanations of intervention success/failure. This comparison can be found in Appendix B: Alternative Arguments. There, I contrast the approach taken here to that of works by Stephen Stedman, Michael Doyle and Nicholas Sambanis, Roland Paris, and Jack Snyder.

VII. WHAT IS THE VALUE ADDED OF THIS APPROACH?

As mentioned at the start of this chapter, there are two major linked explanatory goals. Refer back to Figure 1.1. My first claim is that by including emotion resources in the analysis of intervention I can explain variation in opponent tactics (the specific dependent variable) better than other approaches can. When Western interveners try to implement their "game" to structure a solution to conflict, political entrepreneurs have a wide range of options for opposing or changing that game. By specifying when certain emotions are available as resources and how actors strategically use available emotions, I will explain those choices.

The ability of political entrepreneurs to employ these tactics effectively relates to the broader explanatory goal – explaining variation in intervention outcomes (the general dependent variable). The ultimate success or failure of an intervention is determined by a broad set of factors, including the overall will and resources of the intervention force. No one variable or set of variables will provide a succinct explanation for this outcome. In studying the actual experiences and emotions of individuals living under intervention, I am identi-fying one key, and missing, factor involved in this broad outcome. Moreover,

---

[30] I am leaving out the Erdut Accord of Eastern Slavonia. I am also not covering the often-studied Special Annexes of the Dayton Accord that address Brcko (Special Mandate, Arbitral Tribunal Awards) and Mostar (Agreed Principles for the Interim Statute of the City of Mostar).

I will be explaining major puzzles, such as why interventions often go astray even when the intervener devotes enormous amounts of resources to the effort.

More specifically, the approach outlined will help explain variation in the following outcomes:

First, the method can explain the timing and nature of violent escalation during intervention. Most political scientists develop theories based on structural variables alone. By considering emotion resources, I will be able to explain cases not predicted by structure alone, while providing a more realistic sense of the strategic thinking of so-called spoilers. Furthermore, even in the presence of structural variables that support effective use of violent escalation, political entrepreneurs often eschew this tactic. Understanding the role of emotions helps explain why spoilers sometimes refrain from violence. The nature and availability of emotion resources help explain both escalation and acquiescence.

Second, the inclusion of emotions can be used to generate specific hypotheses on the nature of targeting. An understanding of emotion helps explain the level of discriminate versus indiscriminate targeting. An understanding of emotion can lead to fine-grained predictions about the calibration of violence. Why are religious targets sometimes avoided? Why do bombing strategies often target only unpopulated targets? As discussed later in detail, violent entrepreneurs hit one type of target if they wish to generate fear and another type of target if they wish to inculcate anger.

Third, the approach will help explain the spiraling dynamics of tit-for-tat violence, which often proves so destructive to both sides in conflict.

Fourth, the approach will help explain variation in less violent or nonviolent provocations. Even if the intervener's policies and force levels have closed off strategies of significant escalation of violence, the intervener's game can still be changed through low levels of violence and/or nonviolent types of provocation. If the creation of fear through indiscriminate violence is not an option, the generation of resentment through boycotts and demonstrations might become the next most desirable choice.

Fifth, the approach will provide an explanation for the rare cases of popular support for ethnic cleansing and the more common cases of strong support for partition. Sometimes peoples do not wish to live with each other; they see each other in terms of ethnic contempt. This phenomenon might be uncomfortable for some to accept, but political entrepreneurs understand that the emotions behind this position may help support certain hard-line policies.

Sixth, reference to sequences of emotion can help explain how cases can lead to massive violence even in the absence of ethnic stigma or contempt.

Seventh, emotions-based approaches help explain why the effects of violence decline over a relatively short period of time in some cases, but not in others.

VIII. THE VALUE FOR NON-BALKAN CASES AND THE FUTURE OF WESTERN INTERVENTION

Although the Western Balkans possesses unique qualities, the role of emotions, which are part of human nature, should be similar in many conflicts.

The numerous references to non-Balkan cases throughout the theory chapters illustrate the general properties of this approach. Indeed, the theory here was generated through a broad reading of case material and was heavily influenced by events in Iraq, Afghanistan, Colombia, and other cases. Chapter five develops and illustrates the theory with reference only to non-Balkan cases. The generality of the theory developed in this book is perhaps its greatest value, as it is likely that the West will continue to intervene in conflicts for the foreseeable future.

Three factors combine to make future Western intervention likely. First is the erosion of sovereignty norms. To take one prominent example, the International Crisis Group and similar groups push to establish the right to protect (R2P) as a central tenet of international relations. More broadly, an alliance of Western NGOs is working to bring human rights, freedom, transparency, accountability, and the rule of law to less developed states. These organizations often advocate the idea that sovereignty involves responsibility. If states do not respect the rights and lives of their own citizens, the international community need not respect such states' rights to sovereignty.

Second, security organizations have expanded their missions and capabilities to incorporate intervention. The Bush Administration worked to transform the role of NATO along these lines. President Bush, in a speech in Croatia immediately after the acceptance of Croatia and Albania into the NATO alliance, proclaimed, "NATO is no longer a static alliance focused on defending Europe from a Soviet tank invasion. It is now an expeditionary alliance that is sending its forces across the world to help secure a future of freedom and peace for millions."[31] Furthermore, in the economic realm, the World Bank and the International Monetary Fund are working to spread the logic of free markets and fiscal discipline across the globe. These resources are marshaled to meet ever-expanding perceptions of threat.

The erosion of constraining norms, ever more expansive definitions of threat, and more robust ability to act are all captured in the following passage from Martha Finnemore:

What used to be simple atrocities are now understood as threats to international peace and order in ways that were not true during previous eras. Consequently, intervention in these places now occurs not simply with the aim of stopping the killing, ... but instead has the mission of reconstructing entire states and societies in ways that did not occur in previous periods of history.... These interventions now involve a wide range of non-military components involving reconstruction and social services, mostly provided by international organizations, aimed at overhauling war-torn societies and remaking them in accordance with the normatively preferred liberal democratic world.[32]

---

[31] Steven Lee Myers, "Bush Supports Expansion of NATO across Europe," *New York Times*, April 6, 2008.

[32] Martha Finnemore, *The Purpose of Intervention: Changing Beliefs about the Use of Force* (Ithaca, NY: Cornell University Press, 2003), p. 136.

As the book will show, there are many people who desire Western intervention and see the spread of the Western political and economic systems as the future of the world. In July 2006, in the mountains above Budva in newly independent Montenegro, representatives from almost all of the small western Balkan states were meeting to discuss how to most quickly gain membership in NATO and other Western institutions.[33] One participant of the conference mentioned to me the possibility that European Union enlargement to the Balkans was just the start of a larger process. The European Union's enlargement process and integration of Southeastern Europe would be just one critical step in the evolution of world politics. The dominance of the new world system had spread from Western Europe to Central and Eastern Europe and was now integrating Southeastern Europe. As he proposed, the spread could continue to Russia and the Middle East and eventually the rest of the world. For this participant, it is the West and its economic and military institutional capacity that will transform the world, not the United Nations. Like other participants at this conference, he envisioned a new world emerging in the twenty-first century. In the old world of the twentieth century, nation-states exercised absolute sovereignty; in the new world, new international norms based on human rights would prevail. In the old world, the military balance of power largely determined the international order; in the new world, the role of force would dramatically decline, to be replaced by international law. Large states at the top of world and regional hierarchies dominated the old system; small states could become partners in cooperation in the new world. Nationalism pervaded twentieth century politics; multiculturalism would become the cornerstone of identity politics in the twenty-first century. Above all, the new world would be dominated by the rule of law. On one hand, Western NGOs, militaries, and economic institutions increasingly intervene in problem states and regions. On the other hand, individuals such as this Balkan political figure strongly desire that intervention and, in fact, work on strategies to help bring it about. The Western Balkans is a region where all these factors have been at work for a significant period of time.

One final note about the book's larger relevance. At its most basic level, this book serves as a warning. Consider the following excerpt from the September 2003 issue of *National Geographic Traveler*, published only a few months after the invasion in an article entitled "Traveler Q and A: Is Iraq the Next Travel Hot Spot?":

Intrepid travelers are one step closer to Iraq. While the United States government is still urging people to avoid the politically unstable, war-torn country, it recently lifted a travel ban imposed 12 years ago. Some tour operators are already planning trips to Iraq, betting the country will be the place to go once it stabilizes.[34]

[33] Center for International Relations, "International Seminar: Montenegro, Partnership for Peace, NATO," Chateau Pobore-Budva, Montenegro, July 5–9, 2006.
[34] Jaime Ciavarra, "Traveler Q and A: Is Iraq the Next Travel Hot Spot?" *National Geographic Traveler*, September 3, 2003.

Why do Westerners believe that their intervention will naturally lead to Iraq becoming the next exotic destination for their travel dollars rather than leading to tens of thousands dead? Why did so many Western policy makers, and Western academics, fail to predict such an outcome? This book hopes to show that the problems in Iraq and other cases may be the result of the asymmetric strategic game outlined here.

2

Emotions as Resources

Protracted conflict, especially when it is violent, produces powerful experiences, often connected to forces such as stigma and prejudice, the human tendency to think in terms of group hierarchy, and natural reactions to violence, victimization, and humiliation. Emotions are the residues of such experiences.

Variation in the success and failure of interventions is often related to the way that actors use, or ignore, these emotions. Western interventions are usually based on a straightforward application of "sticks and carrots." Intervention is a matter of organizing a "game," usually an iterated prisoners' dilemma (discussed in more detail later), in which players are bribed and/or constrained to make desired choices. But not everyone wishes to play the game as it is set out. Emotions become a very powerful resource that can be used to change the actors or the rules. Like weapons and money, emotions can be a strategic tool.

Before the use of emotions is discussed, it is necessary to define what they are and how they work. This chapter proceeds in two sections.

The first section defines emotions and their effects more generally. Although the theory of emotion underlying this book builds on fundamental concepts from the field of psychology, these concepts need modification to address the phenomena most central to political conflict. This section explains those modifications.

The second section identifies three categories of emotions according to the nature of cognitive antecedents. First, some emotions are about events or situations. An individual may believe that someone has committed a wrongful action or that an unjust situation or relationship exists, and then experience a reaction in the form of an emotion. Such emotions include fear, anger, and resentment. Second, some emotions are about the very nature of an object or group. An individual may believe that there is something inherently wrong with an object or group. Related emotions include contempt and hatred. Third, some emotions arise from a diversity of experiences and cannot be directly linked to specific cognitive antecedents. Rage and anxiety are examples. The section

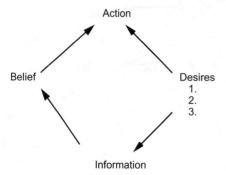

FIGURE 2.1. Action Cycle with No Reference to Emotion.

delineates these emotions, discusses the ways they differ in theoretical terms, and provides examples of how they are used as resources during conflict.

I. DEFINING EMOTIONS: GENERAL FEATURES

There is no clear consensus about how exactly to define emotion. Depending on the focus of the particular study, the social scientist will concentrate on specific features of emotion that include cognitive antecedents, physiological arousal, expression, valence, object, and action tendency. The present study concentrates on how political entrepreneurs try to use or create emotions in order to shape the actions of others. Cognitive antecedent, action tendency, and the relationship between emotions and psychological mechanisms are the most relevant features of emotion for political conflict. In this study, emotions are treated as complexes of these three features.

Consider two action cycles. Figure 2.1 represents a simple rational choice action cycle. Starting on the right side of Figure 2.1, individuals are seen as holding a short list of stable and ordered preferences or desires. For example, when buying an automobile, an individual may have the following preference order: price > safety > style. Given these desires, individuals then collect information about how best to attain their goals. The potential car buyer reads car magazines and visits Web sites to find the vehicle that best meets his or her preferences. The individual then forms a belief about the most effective means and strategies for obtaining what he or she wants. The potential car buyer forms beliefs about the best models and methods of financing. An action then results as a combination of desires and beliefs. A specific vehicle is purchased.

Figure 2.2 factors in emotion. In Figure 2.2, emotion proceeds from cognition.[1] Following many socially oriented theorists, emotion can be

---

[1] The relationship between cognition and emotion is one of the central definitional and theoretical issues in emotion theory. I discuss emotions in which emotion precedes and shapes cognition in *Understanding Ethnic Violence: Fear, Hatred, and Resentment in Twentieth Century Eastern Europe* (Cambridge: Cambridge University Press, 2002). See the discussion of "Rage" as an example; rage is also discussed below.

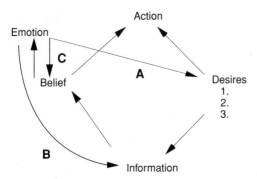

FIGURE 2.2. Action Cycle Illustrating Three Possible Effects of Emotion.

conceptualized as "thought that becomes embodied because of the intensity with which it is laced with personal self-relevancy."[2] As Ortony et al. write, "Our claims about the structure of individual emotions are always along the lines that *if* an individual conceptualizes a situation in a certain kind of way, *then* the potential for a particular type of emotion exists."[3]

In Figure 2.1, desires lead to information collection, which, in turn, leads to beliefs. In Figure 2.2, belief also leads to emotion. Three general effects of emotion may follow, marked as A, B, and C effects in Figure 2.2.

A. A Effects

First, and most fundamentally, emotions are mechanisms that can heighten the salience of a particular concern. They act as a switch among a set of basic desires. An individual may value safety, money, vengeance, and other goals, but emotion compels the individual to act on one of these desires above others. Emotion creates an urgency to act on a particular desire; the value of future payoffs on other preferences is discounted; particular issues can become obsessions. In short, emotions can act as mechanisms of preference formation and preference change. Emotions may shape preferences lexicographically, or they may operate by shaping the indifference curves between specific preferences.[4]

This aspect of emotion directly challenges the assumption of stable preferences that is at the core of rational choice theory. Economists regularly order

---

[2] This quote is from the discussion of emotion and cognition found in David D. Franks and Viktor Gecas, "Current Issues in Emotion Studies," in David D. Franks and Viktor Gecas, eds., *Social Perspectives on Emotion: A Research Annual* (Greenwich, CT: JAI Press, 1992), p. 8. Claire Armon-Jones points out that although emotion is dependent upon cognition, cognitions do not constitute emotion because the same belief could produce two different emotions. See Claire Armon-Jones, "The Thesis of Constructionism," in Rom Harre, ed., *The Social Construction of Emotions* (New York: Basil Blackwell, 1986), pp. 41–42.

[3] Andrew Ortony, Gerald Clore, and Allan Collins, *The Cognitive Structure of Emotions* (Cambridge: Cambridge University Press, 1988), p. 2.

[4] See Jon Elster, "Emotions and Economic Theory," *Journal of Economic Literature* (1998) 36: 47–64.

preferences. However, the assumption of easily ranked and unchanging preferences seems particularly inappropriate for interventions. Interventions involve
contentious and often violent events and confront individuals with choices that
they have not previously encountered. It is one thing to assume that individuals
prefer ten dollars today to twenty dollars a year from now, or to draw a curve
representing trade-offs in spending between military programs and social programs, and quite another matter to make assumptions about the relative values
of such disparate desires as revenge, safety, self-esteem, and subordination,
which are so central to political violence. In rational choice, the stability of
preferences is a simplifying assumption. Most practitioners of rational choice
would probably agree that this simplification is not always useful for every
type of human behavior. As many observers have noted, rational choice has
produced its most useful insights in iterative situations or under stable institutional environments. A proponent of rational choice, George Tsebelis, has
summarized this point: "actions taken in noniterative situations by individual
decision makers (such as in crisis situations) are not necessarily well-suited for
rational choice predictions."[5]

From another perspective, the A effect of emotion is to fill in one task that
most rational choice practitioners choose not to address. As William J. Long
and Peter Brecke summarize, "Emotions recognize challenges and opportunities
in our environment, and they identify our preferences. Rational choice tells
us that individuals pursue preferences logically, but it does not tell us, at an
individual level, what preferences are or where they come from. This void exists
because emotion is left out of the mix."[6]

Some neurobiologists would hold that evolution has hardwired A effects into
the core of our being. Antonio Damasio summarizes, "Emotional responses are
a mode of reaction of brains that are prepared by evolution to respond to certain
classes of objects and events with certain repertoires of action."[7] Damasio
and others have advanced a research program showing that emotions and
reason are inseparable. In *Descartes' Error*, Damasio argues that "Rationality
is probably shaped and modulated by body signals, even as it performs the most
sublime distinctions and acts accordingly."[8] For Damasio, emotions narrow the

---

[5] George Tsebelis, *Nested Games: Rational Choice and Comparative Politics* (Berkeley: University
  of California Press, 1990).
[6] William J. Long and Peter Brecke, *War and Reconciliation: Reason and Emotion in Conflict
  Resolution* (Cambridge, MA: MIT Press, 2003), p. 131.
[7] Antonio Damasio, "Fundamental Feelings," *Nature* (October 2001) 413: 781. In another summary statement, Damasio writes, "I see the *essence* of emotion as the collection of changes in
  body state that are induced in myriad organs by nerve cell terminals, under the control of a
  dedicated brain system, which is responding to the content of thoughts relative to a particular
  entity or event," from Damasio, *Descartes' Error: Emotion, Reason, and the Human Brain* (New
  York: Quill, 1994), p. 139.
[8] Damasio, *Descartes' Error*, p. 200. For reviews of the relationship between rationality and emotion, see Jon Elster, *Alchemies of the Mind: Rationality and Emotions* (Cambridge: Cambridge

choice set and increase the efficiency and accuracy of decision making.[9] The A effect is closely related to emotion theorists' concept of action tendency. Under the influence of a specific emotion, individuals are driven to particular actions to confront pressing problems. Fear drives individuals toward fight or flight, for example. This element of emotion clearly suggests that, contrary to many conventional views, emotion need not be seen as antithetical to reason. However, emotion can also promote mechanisms that are in conflict with rationality, as seen in B and C effects.

B. B Effects

Once in place, emotions can produce a feedback effect on information collection. Emotions lead to emotion-congruent information seeking. Emotions themselves become powerful experiential information in the appraisal of situations and objects.[10] As Gerald Clore and Karen Gasper stress, "Because emotions are directly experienced, and arise from within, the personal validity of the information they appear to convey seems self-evident to the person experiencing them. One can argue with logic, but not with feeling."[11] Similar to the well-documented confirmation bias, evidence confirming the emotion generally receives more attention and value than disconfirming evidence. For example, individuals under the influence of fear may come to obsess about the chances of catastrophe. They may concentrate only on information that stresses danger and ignore information about the lack of threat.

Psychologists discuss the related mechanism of *attentional funneling* and stress the interactive loop between emotion and biased information collection. Clore and Gasper write:

We propose that strong emotion can initiate attentional funneling, a positive feedback loop in which strong feeling narrows attention to goal-relevant information (Easterbrook, 1959). Focusing on only the most goal relevant aspects of events may then increase their apparent importance, which in turn may intensify emotional reactions to them. An increase in emotional intensity may further narrow attentional focus, making

University Press, 1999), Chapter 4; J. M. Barbalet, *Emotion, Social Theory, and Social Structure: A Macrosociological Approach* (Cambridge: Cambridge University Press, 2001), Chapter 2; Long and Brecke, *War and Reconciliation*, Chapter 4.

9 Damasio, *Descartes' Error*, p. 173. Proponents of evolutionary biology see emotions as optimizing forces in a different sense. For example, Robert Frank argues that emotions prevent humans from acting on overly narrow and suboptimal short-term interests. See Robert Frank, *Passions within Reason* (New York: W. W. Norton, 1988).

10 See the affect-as-information model in Norbert Schwarz and Gerald Clore, "Mood, Misattribution, and Judgments of Well-Being: Informative and Directive Functions of Affective States," *Journal of Personality and Social Psychology* (1983) 45: 513–23.

11 Gerald L. Clore and Karen Gasper, "Feeling Is Believing: Some Affective Influences on Belief," in Nico H. Frijda, Antony S. R. Manstead, and Sacha Bem eds., *Emotions and Beliefs: How Feelings Influence Thoughts* (Cambridge: Cambridge University Press, 2000), p. 39.

relevant events seem even more important, leading to still greater intensity, and so on in an ever-narrowing circle.[12]

The overall cycling of emotion and information supports the French saying that we come to believe what we fear.[13]

C. C Effects

Even with accurate and undistorted information, emotion can affect beliefs. The same individual with the same information may develop one belief under the sway of one emotion and a different belief under the influence of a different emotion.[14] These include the following cases:

> *Rule selection*: As William Riker has pointed out, rational individuals may operate according to several different sorts of strategies ("sincere," "avoid the worst," "average value," "sophisticated").[15] Emotions can affect which strategy becomes operative. For example, it is likely that emotions such as fear can influence a switch in the method of belief formation, perhaps to an "avoid the worst" strategy.

Other effects clearly involve irrationality or bias in belief formation.

> *Stereotyping*: Several emotions have been found to increase stereotyping of opposing groups.[16] Under negative emotions, groups are more likely to be perceived as homogeneous.[17] Emotions can reinforce the fundamental attribution error, which is the tendency to attribute others' actions to their inherent character while attributing one's own actions to one's situation and circumstances.[18]
>
> *Formation of beliefs about risk and probabilities*: As Frijda notes, "Estimates of probability, credibility and plausibility are intuitive, based on information, thought, and preference, and therefore sensitive to a variety

---

[12] Ibid, p. 11.

[13] Jon Elster mentions this saying in *Explaining Social Behavior: More Nuts and Bolts for the Social Sciences* (Cambridge: Cambridge University Press, 2007), p. 157.

[14] Also, the complete lack of emotion certainly affects information and belief formation. See the work of Damasio and others with brain-damaged patients who have lost their capacity for emotion.

[15] William H. Riker, *The Art of Political Manipulation* (New Haven, CT: Yale University Press, 1986), p. 26.

[16] See several chapters in Diane M. Mackie and David L. Hamilton eds., *Affect, Cognition, and Stereotyping: Interactive Processes in Group Perception* (San Diego: Academic Press, 1993).

[17] Steven J. Stroessner and Diane M. Mackie, "Affect and Perceived Group Variability: Implications for Stereotyping and Prejudice," in Mackie and Hamilton eds., *Affect, Cognition, and Stereotyping*, pp. 63–86.

[18] Nico H. Frijda and Batja Mesquita, "Belief through Emotions," in Frijda, Manstead, and Bem eds., *Emotions and Beliefs*, pp. 45–77.

of influences, among which are emotional ones."[19] As discussed later, fear tends to heighten perception of risk, whereas anger tends to decrease the sense of risk and the calculation of negative probabilities. This effect of emotion is central to understanding some actions undertaken during violent conflict.

Preservation of existing beliefs: Emotions can enhance attachment to an existing belief and help preserve it, even in the face of new disconfirming evidence. This effect is a form of *wishful thinking* – under the influence of emotion the desire to maintain a belief is so strong that evidence is ignored.[20]

Self-deception: Emotions can lead to the creation of new beliefs even in the face of disconfirming evidence. This effect relates to the mechanism of cognitive dissonance. The theory of cognitive dissonance, first formulated by Festinger in the 1950s, holds that having inconsistent beliefs creates a negative emotional state that drives the individual to change beliefs to relieve this discomfort. The resolution of the problem involves both the nature of cognition and the intensity of the negative emotional state. The emotion can drive individuals, in certain highly charged situations, toward adoption of new beliefs that might seem strange to outsiders but manage to solve inconsistencies for participants.[21]

The very essence of political propaganda is the shaping of beliefs through the creation of emotion. Scapegoating is one well-known example.

D. Duration and Decay of Emotions

The intensity of most emotions, particularly those based on events, will fade with time (I will address emotions that do not systematically fade later in the chapter). Social scientists currently have little knowledge about the rate of decay of emotions. One could imagine a variety of possible relationships among a specific emotion, the nature of the object of the emotion, and the rate of decline over time. Consider the emotion of anger, for example. If a child committed a blameworthy action, one could imagine a brief surge of anger toward the child followed by a swift decline in intensity. If a co-worker committed a negative action, on the other hand, the decline in intensity might be more prolonged. One study found that consumers who had suffered service failures for which they considered getting even maintained a significant level

---

[19] Ibid., p. 68.
[20] See Elster's discussion of wishful thinking and self-deception in *Explaining Social Behavior*, pp. 136–143.
[21] Eddie Harmon-Jones, "A Cognitive Dissonance Theory and Perspective on the Role of Emotion in the Maintenance and Change of Beliefs and Attitudes," in Frijda, Manstead, and Sacha Bem eds., *Emotions and Beliefs*, pp. 185–211.

of anger for several weeks.[22] If anger triggered by a service failure can last this long, then the death of a family member or acquaintance during a violent conflict should result in a much slower decay of anger.[23] Political violence is often connected to existing and long-term social group hierarchies. Combined with the intensity of the experience, emotions created through violent political conflicts must be viewed as lasting months and years instead of minutes and days. Jon Elster has discussed this effect in his work on transitional justice, pointing out that in the trials of German collaborators following the Second World War, sentences were almost invariably more severe immediately after the war than two or three years later.[24] Elster interprets this difference in terms of decay of anger measured in years.

These examples suggest systematic rates, or functions of decay. Figures 2.3–2.5 represent curves in which the intensity of the emotion, represented by the vertical axis, declines over time, represented by the horizontal axis, according to linear (Figure 2.3), exponential (Figure 2.4), and inverse exponential (Figure 2.5) functions.

E. The Treatment of Emotions in Interventions versus the Treatment in the Psychology Laboratory

Although the insights of psychologists have much to contribute to the study of political violence, many of the concepts cannot be applied without significant modification. Psychology does a good job of addressing cognitive antecedents, action tendencies, strong and obsessive preferences, and preference change produced by violence; however, most psychological treatments of anger cannot capture either the intensity of the experience of living through internal war or the rich, long-term social nature of political violence and its consequences.

This point is most clearly illustrated by the issue of duration and decay of emotion. Psychologists working in laboratories often concentrate on the physical manifestations of emotions. In laboratory settings, social psychologists usually measure the duration of emotions in seconds and minutes. Clearly, a context in which individuals are living under postconflict intervention differs

---

[22] Thomas Tripp and Robert Bies, "'Righteous' Anger and Revenge in the Workplace: The Fantasies, the Feuds, the Forgiveness," in Michael Potegal, Gerhard Stemmler, and Charles Spielberger eds., *A Handbook of Anger: Constituent and Concomitant Biological, Psychological, and Social Processes* (New York: Springer, Summer 2009).

[23] Although the subject is not well understood, there is growing research on how emotions affect memory. In a survey of recent research on fear, Daniel Gardner writes about how emotions affect the biology of the brain: "The hormones the amygdale triggers temporarily enhance memory function so the awful experience that triggered the response will be vividly encoded and remembered. Such traumatic memories last, and they are potent." See Daniel Gardner, *The Science of Fear* (New York: Dutton, 2008), p. 49.

[24] See Jon Elster, "Memory and Transitional Justice," manuscript delivered at the "Memory of War" workshop, MIT, January 2003.

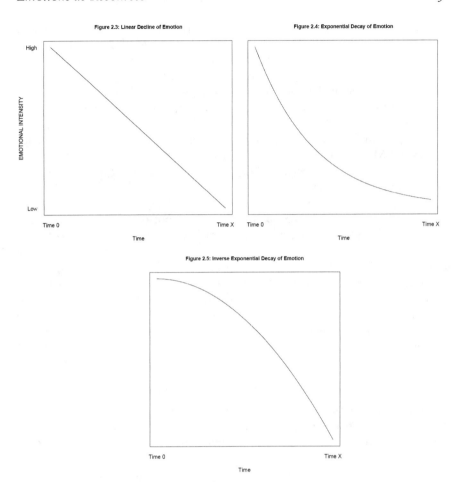

FIGURES 2.3–2.5. Decline in Emotional Intensity over Time.

drastically from one in which undergraduates play games in a one-shot laboratory experiment. The emotions of individuals living under political violence are based on repeated everyday experiences.

Consider the problem of postviolence reconciliation. David Cohen, who worked in East Timor in its reconstruction period, tells the story of a widow who could not avoid seeing, on a regular basis, her husband's killer wearing her husband's jacket.[25] Although most experiences are not so dramatic, in many instances of political violence, members of conflicting ethnic groups must intermingle in the postviolence period. Members of victim groups may have to buy something from members of perpetrator groups. Even where warring factions have been separated, groups may look across a river or a barrier and

[25] Story told at the conference "Peace and Accountability in Transitions from Armed Conflict," Bogotá, Colombia, 15–16 June 2007.

be reminded of previous atrocities. After being told that a Sunni family had moved into their family's home, a displaced Shiite responded in an interview, "I try to imagine my room and what they do in it."[26] Often, cultural symbols take on new meanings and power. In the divided city of Mitrovica in Kosovo, for instance, the Serbs have built a church high on a hill on their side of the river; the Albanians on the other side of the river cannot help but see it, and see it in light of the Serbs' previous political dominance and acts of ethnic cleansing. A similar situation exists in the divided city of Mostar, Bosnia, with Croats and Muslims erecting religious structures at the boundary lines.[27]

As Jon Elster has summarized, "(B)ecause of the power of many emotions, there are limits to what we can learn from studies of human behavior under controlled conditions. Inducing strong emotions of love, shame, and hatred in the laboratory would not only be blatantly unethical but unfeasible. And there is no presumption that what we can learn from studying the milder forms of these emotions – liking, embarrassment, or disliking – will generalize to the more urgent or virulent forms."[28] Social psychology, as Elster further notes, identifies and specifies emotion-based mechanisms. Through the specification of these mechanisms, the laboratory provides the basis for creating hypotheses to be tested with data from violent conflicts, even if the phenomena tested in the laboratory and the experiences in actual violent conflicts cannot be directly equated.[29]

F. Relationship to Other Research on Emotion

Interventions in conflict often involve an outside power getting into the middle of long-term social and political relationships among recognizable groups, which are likely to be imbued with strong overtones and experiences of

---

[26] Sabrina Tavernise, "Sectarian Toll Includes Scars to Iraq Psyche," *New York Times*, September 17, 2007.

[27] This is not to suggest that we merely rename the time axis with months and years instead of minutes and days; rather, as will be discussed below, we must reconceive the anger curves following atrocities. One way to imagine the graph would be as convex functions with survivors' anger depreciating daily (in accordance with the dominant psychological findings), but then also being reelicited daily by a combination of memories and rumination that returns the individuals' anger to elevated levels. These peak daily levels, however, would diminish over time as the original anger-provoking event faded and therefore produced weaker cognitions and ruminations that, in turn, elicit weaker emotional responses.

[28] Elster, *Alchemies*, p. 404.

[29] For an extended discussion of the relationship between the psychological and political treatment of emotions, see Roger Petersen and Sarah Zukerman, "Anger, Violence, and Political Science," in Potegal, Stemmler, and Spielberger eds., *A Handbook of Anger*. The difference between emotions and attitudes, also a focus of psychologists, should also be mentioned. Emotions differ from attitudes in that the motivational power of attitudes is unspecified. In effect, the A, B, C effects of emotions listed here are not spelled out. See Alice H. Eagly and Shelly Chaiken, *The Psychology of Attitudes* (Fort Worth: Harcourt Brace Jovanovich College Publishers, 1993). Emotion differs from mood in that mood, as in Section I.F., does not specify cognitive antecedents. Furthermore, emotions have a cognitive structure and model for a situation.

violence and domination. Under these conditions, there is usually a clear idea that "group X committed this harmful action against group Y." Beliefs will be about how "they" have come to dominate "us," how "they" killed "us," how an inferior group is receiving too much, how outsiders control things they should not. During conflict and reconstruction, individuals live every day as part of a system of "them" and "us" and with memories of what "they" did to "us." Beliefs about group-level characteristics of power, status, and group character form the cognitive basis for the emotions and strategies of emotional manipulation that pervade the conflicts that become the targets of intervention.

The treatment of emotion as an essential part of larger social groups and processes has a long, if not deep, history. Adam Smith in his *Theory of Moral Sentiments* discussed the role of sympathy, envy, and other emotions as they played out within market relations.[30] The English sociologist T. H. Marshall focused on resentment as the basis of modern class conflict. Theodore D. Kemper's work is perhaps the most influential in this vein. Kemper's *A Social Interactional Theory of Emotions* laid out a structural theory of emotion.[31] As Kemper summarizes, "A structural approach to emotions derives from the following proposition: A very large class of emotions results from real anticipated, recollected, or imagined outcomes of social relationships."[32] J. M. Barbalet, with his *Emotion, Social Theory, and Social Structure: A Macrosociological Approach*, expands on Kemper's structural approach. Following Kemper and Barbalet, the present work treats emotions as flowing from power and status relations, as well as changes in these relations.

This work's major contribution is to go beyond this general point and show how these emotions are strategically used in conflict, especially in interventions where power and status themselves are in flux. In a previous work, *Understanding Ethnic Violence: Fear, Hatred and Resentment in Twentieth Century Eastern Europe*, I addressed how the long-term social and political evolution of Eastern Europe interacted with more immediate events, many connected to the conduct and aftermath of the two world wars, to produce political outcomes. The emphasis there was on large, structural change and its effect on perception of ethnic hierarchy. That work did not focus on agency; rather, it underscored the limits of actors' ability to confront the power and momentum of structural changes. The present work might be seen as a companion or a continuance of this earlier work. In modern interventions, as the cases will illustrate, political entrepreneurs will hold theories on how to strategically use, and sometimes create, emotions as part of a game. This game is often more subtle than the situations in the earlier book. The present work attempts to capture the essence of this more subtle and complex interaction.

---

[30] For an overview of the role of emotions in sociology, see Barbalet, *Emotion, Social Theory, and Social Structure*, pp. 8–28.

[31] Theodore D. Kemper, *A Social Interactional Theory of Emotions* (New York: Wiley, 1978).

[32] Theodore D. Kemper, "A Structural Approach to Social Movement Emotions," in Jeff Goodwin, James M. Jasper, and Francesca Polletta eds., *Passionate Politics: Emotions and Social Movements* (Chicago: University of Chicago Press, 2001), p. 59.

In *The Forever War*, Dexter Filkins describes his work as a *New York Times* journalist in Iraq:

> There were always two conversations in Iraq, the one the Iraqis were having with the Americans and the one they were having among themselves. The one the Iraqis were having with us – that was positive and predictable and boring, and it made the Americans happy because it made them think they were winning. And the Iraqis kept it up because it kept the money flowing, or because it bought them a little peace. The conversation they were having with each other was the one that really mattered, of course. That conversation was the chatter of a whole other world, a parallel reality, which sometimes unfolded right next to the Americans, even right in front of them. And we almost never saw it.[33]

In my view, the parallel reality that Filkins describes is imbued with emotion and the strategic use of emotion. To understand this situation, it is necessary to further define the emotions at play, and to do so more specifically than in existing work in the social sciences.

II. SPECIFIC EMOTIONS

Political entrepreneurs use emotions as strategic resources. They use fear differently than anger; they consider how to build on or inflame resentment; they understand the limitations and opportunities presented by contempt and hatred. In short, political entrepreneurs understand the differences among emotions.

Specific emotions are commonly defined and differentiated by five characteristics: arousal, expression, feeling, cognitive antecedent, and action tendency. The last two, cognitive antecedent (belief) and action tendency (the urge to satisfy a particular desire in the preference set), are most relevant here. What follows is a catalog of emotions most connected to the experiences and politics of intervention. These are the emotions that are most fundamental to the strategies of political entrepreneurs.

Each emotion is first defined by cognitive antecedent and action tendency. Next, the salient psychological mechanisms (specific B and C effects) are noted. Third, the political use of the emotion, the method of triggering the emotion, and examples of its use are discussed in order.

This section categorizes emotion by cognitive antecedent – that is, the beliefs that trigger the emotion. The approach produces three categories: event-based emotions, object-based emotions, and emotions with no specific cognitive antecedent. There are important differences among these categories. In a point that I will expand on, object-based emotions, as opposed to event-based emotions, may not possess half-lives. Contempt and hatred, for example, are both based on cognitions about the intrinsic worth and character of an actor. Such cognitions are not easily subject to change. Once one sees an actor as inherently worthless, a change in the situation is unlikely to alter that belief rapidly.

---

[33] Dexter Filkins, *The Forever War* (New York: Alfed A. Knopf, 2008), p. 115.

For intervention, the most important emotions are event based. That is, they mainly follow from perceptions of the actions of others or one's own group. Political entrepreneurs are most able to act in ways that trigger these emotions.

A. Event-Based Emotions: Anger, Fear, and Resentment

Anger. Anger: cognition that an individual or group has committed a bad action against one's self or group; action tendency toward punishing that group.

Concerning A effects, anger heightens desire for punishment against a specific actor. Under the influence of anger, individuals become "intuitive prosecutors."[34] That is, individuals tend to specify a perpetrator and then seek retribution.

Anger's B effects distort information in predictable ways, producing attention funneling. As with other emotions, once under the influence of anger, individuals "perceive new events and objects in ways that are consistent with the original cognitive-appraisal dimensions of the emotion."[35] That is, the emotion of anger justifies the desire for punishment and pushes the individual to seek information that will further justify vengeance. Anger can create an obsession with retaliation.

Concerning C effects, the angry person lowers the threshold for attributing harmful intent. Anger enhances the fundamental attribution error – angry people blame humans, not the situation.[36] Anger also tends to produce more stereotyping.[37] Under the influence of anger, individuals lower their risk estimates and are more willing to engage in risky behavior.[38]

As defined here, anger is an event-based emotion. As an event-based emotion, it is likely to have a half-life. That is, it is likely to fade over time. In sum, anger heightens desire for punishment against a specific actor, creates a downgrading

[34] Julie H. Goldberg, Jennifer S. Lerner, and Phillip E. Tetlock, "Rage and Reason: The Psychology of the Intuitive Prosecutor," *European Journal of Social Psychology* (1999) 29: 781–95.

[35] Jennifer S. Lerner and Dacher Keltner, "Beyond Valence: Toward a Model of Emotion-Specific Influences on Judgment and Choice," *Cognition and Emotion* (2000) 14: 473–93.

[36] Dacher Keltner, Phoebe Ellsworth, and Kari Edwards, "Beyond Simple Pessimism: Effects of Sadness and Anger on Social Perception," *Journal of Personality and Social Psychology* (1993) 64 (5): 740–52. Keltner et al. studied angry subjects compared to sad subjects, asking both groups to interpret agency in an ambiguous event. Sad subjects assigned blame to the situation, angry ones to the actors.

[37] Galen Bodenhausen, Lori Sheperd, and Geoffrey Kramer, "Negative Affect and Social Judgment – The Differential Impact of Anger and Sadness," *European Journal of Social Psychology* (1994) 24 (1): 45–62.

[38] Jennifer S. Lerner and Dacher Keltner, "Fear, Anger, and Risk," *Journal of Personality and Social Psychology* (2001) 81 (1): 146–59; Dennis Gallagher and Gerald Clore, "Effects of Fear and Anger on Judgments of Risk and Evaluations of Blame," Paper presented at the Midwestern Psychological Association (May 1985); Haim Mano, "Risk-taking, Framing Effects, and Affect," *Organizational Behavior and Human Decision Processes* (1994) 57: 38–58; Jennifer S. Lerner, Roxana M. Gonzalez, Deborah A. Small, and Baruch Fischoff, "Effects of Fear and Anger on Perceived Risks of Terrorism: A National Field Experiment," *Psychological Science* (2003) 14 (2): 144–50. Lerner et al also found significant gender differences, with men more prone to anger and women more likely to experience fear.

of risk, and increases prejudice and blame, as well as selective memory.[39] Anger will, however, decrease over time.

A primary political use of anger is to provoke overreaction in an opponent. Inducing anger in a target is a form of coercion. Under the sway of anger, an opponent can be compelled toward self-destructive forms of retaliation.[40] A slogan written on a giant draping mural in Tehran provides a vivid example.[41] The caption reads, "America be angry and let that anger destroy you." Implicitly, the logic of the poster holds that the enemy, America, can be destroyed through its own emotion, an emotion that can be created by the actions of outsiders, such as the Iranian regime.

Anger is a tool for creating spiraling cycles of violence that can transform an entire conflict. As will be seen later, in the empirical sections of this work, political entrepreneurs use anger to ignite a disproportionate retaliation that serves to clarify, both to their own group and to outsiders, who is the perpetrator and who is the victim. Disproportionate reactions reveal the "true face" of the opponent. Frantz Fanon's description of the spirals that transformed the Algerian conflict is worth quoting at length:

The settler's logic is implacable and one is staggered by the counter-logic visible in the behavior of the native insofar as one has not clearly understood beforehand the mechanisms of the settler's ideas. From the moment that the native has chosen the methods of counter-violence, police reprisals automatically call forth reprisals on the side of the nationalists. However, the results are not equivalent, for machine-gunning from airplanes and bombardments from the fleet go far beyond in horror and magnitude any answer the natives can make. This recurring terror de-mystifies once and for all the most estranged members of the colonized race. They find out on the spot that all the piles of speeches on the equality of human beings do not hide the commonplace fact that the seven Frenchman killed or wounded at the Col de Sakamondy kindles the indignation of all civilized consciences, whereas the sack of the douars of Guergour and of the dechras of Djerah and the massacre of whole populations – which had merely called forth the Sakamondy ambush as reprisal – all this is not of the slightest importance. Terror, counter-terror, violence, counter-violence: that is what observers bitterly record when they describe the circle of hate, which is so tenacious and so evident in Algeria.

In all armed struggles, there exists what we might call the point of no return. Almost always it is marked off by a huge and all-inclusive repression that engulfs all sectors of the colonized people. This point was reached in Algeria in 1955 with the 12,000

---

[39] John Newhagen, "Anger, Fear and Disgust: Effects on Approach–Avoidance and Memory," *Journal of Broadcasting and Electronic Media* (1998) 42 (2): 265–76. Newhagen found that images producing anger were remembered better than those inducing fear, which in turn were remembered better than those creating disgust.

[40] One of the world's most famous incidents of "baiting" an opponent into self-destructive retaliation must be Zidane's head-butting response to taunting during a World Cup final watched by one billion people.

[41] Fotini Christia, "Walls of Martyrdom: Tehran's Propaganda Murals," *Centerpiece* (Winter 2007). The exhibit was held May 18–June 15, 2007 at the Center for Government and International Studies, Harvard University.

victims of Phillippeville, and in 1956 with Lacoste's institution of an urban and rural militia.[42]

This tactic has been employed in a wide variety of situations. The U.S. civil rights movement provoked violence, which enhanced group solidarity and increased national attention to their cause. As Doug MacAdam and Ron Aminzade write:

(t)here is the baiting of authorities into acts of official violence which tends, unless the repression is extreme, to reinforce group solidarity and the shared resolve to "fight again another day." These exercises in strategic provocation may have an additional emotional payoff for the movement. Violence by authorities that is widely perceived to be illegitimate may, as in the case of the U.S. Civil Rights Movement, anger an otherwise disinterested news media and general public, who, in turn, respond with the kind of pressure that proves decisive in producing important movement gains.[43]

Another prominent example is Ariel Sharon's visit to the Temple Mount, which many consider a blatant anger-generating provocation designed to bait Palestinians into a negotiation-ending violent response.

Anger, like other emotions, can be generated by producing the cognitive antecedents of the emotion. In the case of anger, the event must create a belief in a specific, easily defined perpetrator committing intentional negative actions against a clear target. There should be no ambiguity about the identity or purpose of the perpetrator. There must be an identified causal agent who can become a clear target for the urge to punish.[44] Ariel Sharon's provocation was successful because he undoubtedly knew how the Palestinians would perceive the event: the archenemy of the Palestinian people was going purposely to a sacred Islamic site with a clear intention to insult. An identifiable agent was intentionally committing a negative act against a specific target. As Sharon undoubtedly knew, anger would surely result. Under the influence of this emotion, violence could be expected.

When violence is not possible, political entrepreneurs can position their message in terms of "injustice frames" that clearly blame particular agents.[45] If violence is available as a means, then the violence should be *discriminate* in order to create anger rather than another emotion. The provocateur wants the target of the violence to be able to specify a target for counterviolence. By its nature, violence is very likely to produce emotional intensity. The political entrepreneur is likely to contemplate whether anger or fear is the desired reaction.

[42] Frantz Fanon, *The Wretched of the Earth* (New York: Grove Press, 1965), pp. 89–90.
[43] Ron Aminzade and Doug McAdam, "Emotions and Contentious Politics," in Ronald Aminzade, Jack Goldstone, Doug McAdam, Elizabeth Perry, William Sewell Jr., Sidney Tarrow, and Charles Tilly, eds., *Silence and Voice in the Study of Contentious Politics* (Cambridge: Cambridge University Press, 2001), pp. 14–50. Quoted passage is from p. 44.
[44] Frijda and Mesquita, "Beliefs through Emotions," p. 65.
[45] See William Gamson, *Talking Politics* (Cambridge: Cambridge University Press, 1992).

Fear. Fear: cognition of a situation of danger; an action tendency toward fight or flight.

In fear, individuals value self-preservation above all else. The A effect of fear is usually in one of two directions – fight or flight. There is some speculation that when the perception of danger comes from a belief in the deficiencies of one's own capacities, the action tendency will be flight. But, when the perception of danger comes from a belief in the other's power and one retains an ability to respond, the action tendency will be to fight.

B and C effects are key aspects of fear. As with other emotions, once under the influence of fear, individuals will process information and form beliefs to confirm the cognitive-appraisal aspects of the emotion. That is, they will privilege information about danger.[46] Fear is considered perhaps the primary mechanism for attention funneling. Events such as the 9/11 attacks heightened attention to terrorist actions. Such spectacular violent actions cause individuals to see subsequent actions through a framework of fear.[47] As John Mueller has pointed out, the number of terrorist attacks in the years after 9/11 did not increase from the preceding era, but fear and perception of danger lingered for years.[48]

The C effects of fear can be illustrated in a comparison with those of anger. Crucially, anger and fear affect beliefs about risk. However, anger and fear produce opposite effects on risk perception, with individuals under the sway of fear becoming more risk-averse. Second, unlike anger, fearful subjects have been found to have low assessments of blame.[49] Third, the effects of both anger and fear are partially determined by perceptions of the in-group. In experimental research, participants with a strong sense of in-group solidarity

---

[46] Lerner and Keltner, "Beyond Valence." Daniel Gardner surveys research that indicates that simply providing more and better information does not always counter the effects of fear. See Gardner, *The Science of Fear*, pp. 139–43.

[47] See Diego Gambetta on this point, as well as a list of other cognitive distortions (groupthink, incestuous amplification, and wishful thinking) related to terrorism and 9/11 in "Reason and Terror: Has 9/11 Made It Hard to Think Straight?" *Boston Review*, April/May 2004. On this specific point, Gambetta quotes Donald Rumsfeld on the effects of 9/11: "The coalition did not act in Iraq because we had discovered dramatic new evidence of Iraq's pursuit of weapons of mass murder. We acted because we saw the existing evidence in a new light through the prism of our experience on September 11." Rumsfeld's justification brings up the difference between a visceral emotional fear and simply prudence. No doubt Rumsfeld would claim to have been acting on rational prudence (many others would claim that his justification is a smokescreen for a political agenda). On the difference between visceral fear and prudence, see Elster, *Explaining Social Behavior*, pp. 77–8. As Elster notes, however, the fact that so many individuals altered their travel plans in the wake of 9/11 indicated the effect of visceral fear on substantial numbers of people.

[48] John Mueller, *Overblown: How Politicians and the Terrorism Industry Inflate Security Threats and Why We Believe Them* (New York: Free Press, 2006). Also, see Barry Glassner, *The Culture of Fear: Why Americans Are Afraid of the Wrong Things* (New York: Basic Books, 1999).

[49] Gallagher and Clore, "Effects of Fear and Anger on Judgments of Risk and Evaluations of Blame."

are more likely to feel anger against out-groups.[50] Likewise, fear levels can be manipulated by categorizing the victims as in-group or out-group.[51]

Like anger, fear is an event-based emotion. The intensity of fear will decline over time, although as 9/11 has shown, the half-life may have to be measured in months or years.

The primary strategic use of fear is obvious – it is usually called terrorism. Jessica Stern argues that the attempt to instill fear and dread in a target population is what distinguishes terrorism from other forms of violence.[52] In her study of religious terrorists, Stern writes that they wish to "not only frighten their victims in a physical sense, but to spread a kind of spiritual dread."[53] Louise Richardson points out that the logic of terrorism rests on its emotional power: "The whole point is for the psychological impact to be greater than the actual physical act. Terrorism is indeed a weapon of the weak."[54]

In the context of intervention, political entrepreneurs use fear to induce withdrawals of populations. They are seeking to generate fear in order to trigger the action tendency of flight. Fear is used to separate populations. Once they are separated, fear is used to prevent the return of refugees.

Political entrepreneurs can produce flight-generating fears by instilling the belief that a threat cannot be confronted. The intent is to make the target believe that he or she does not possess the capacity, or have sufficient power, to defeat the threat. Fear of disease, radiation, and sleeper cells is so powerful because such threats are invisible and create a feeling of helplessness. How can one defeat what one cannot see (or fully understand)? Political entrepreneurs can also create fear through powerful imagery, especially violent imagery. Damasio argues that humans fear air transportation more than car travel because of "availability error," which consists of allowing the image of a plane crash, with its emotional drama, to dominate the landscape of our reasoning and to generate a bias against the correct choice.[55]

As opposed to anger, political entrepreneurs create fear through *indiscriminate* violence. As Richardson and others point out, it is the seeming randomness of attacks that makes them powerful. If civilians can die as easily, or even more easily than combatants, if they can die on a bus, in a restaurant, or walking down the street, then a belief of powerlessness sets in that sets off fear and

---

[50] D. M. Mackie, T. DeVos, and E. R. Smith, "Intergroup Emotions: Explaining Offensive Action Tendencies in an Intergroup Context," *Journal of Personality and Social Psychology* (2004) 79: 602–16.

[51] M. Dumont, V. Yzerbyt, D. Wigboldus, and E. H. Gordijn, "Social Categorization and Fear Reactions to the September 11th Terrorist Attacks," *Personality and Social Psychology Bulletin* (2003) 29: 1509–1520.

[52] Jessica Stern, *Terror in the Name of God: Why Religious Militants Kill* (New York: Harper Collins, 2004), p. xx.

[53] Ibid., p. xxvii.

[54] Louise Richardson, *Terrorists: Understanding the Enemy, Containing the Threat* (New York: Random House, 2006), p. 5.

[55] Damasio, *Descartes' Error*, p. 192.

flight. When a few refugee families return to an area that was previously ethnically cleansed and one of them is attacked by unknown forces during the night, fear will almost certainly dominate that community.

Resentment. Resentment: cognition that one's group is located in an unwarranted subordinate position on a status hierarchy; an action tendency to take actions to reduce the status position of groups in a superior status.

Resentment follows from the perception that one's group is located in an unwarranted subordinate position in a status hierarchy. The conception of this emotion rests on several findings from various fields of social science. First, humans identify with groups and acquire self-esteem from group membership.[56] Second, they compare the status of their own group with that of others.[57] Third, when the comparison generates the belief that another group occupies an undeserved superior position, the emotion of resentment results.

As treated here, resentment is based on being *politically* dominated by a group that is perceived to have no right to be in a superior position. It is the everyday experience of these perceived status relations that breeds the emotion. In the day-to-day operation of government, members of ethnic groups become aware of whose group is "on top" and whose is "underneath." Status, at its core, involves an element of dominance and subordination. It is a question of who gives orders and who takes them, whose language is spoken, and whose symbols predominate.

Although status can be complex, status relations among ethnic groups are generally tied to the following indicators:

1. The language of day-to-day government
2. The composition of the bureaucracy

---

[56] This idea builds off the work of Henri Tajfel and Social Identity Theory. For a review of this theory and discussion of its findings, see Rupert Brown, "Social Identity Theory: Past Achievements, Current Problems, and Future Challenges," *European Journal of Social Psychology* (November 2000) 30 (6): 745–778.

[57] For discussions of ethnic conflict in ranked versus unranked systems, see Donald Horowitz, *Ethnic Groups in Conflict* (Berkeley: University of California Press, 1985), especially the third and fourth chapters. Social Dominance Theory, a psychological approach associated with the work of James Sidanius, is emphatic and explicit on the issue of hierarchy. In fact, Sidanius and his collaborators hold that "all human societies are inherently group-based hierarchies and inherently oppressive." See James Sidanius, "The Psychology of Group Conflict: A Social Dominance Perspective," in Shanto Iyengar and William J. McGuire, eds., *Explorations in Political Psychology* (Durham, NC: Duke University Press, 1993), pp. 183–219. Social Dominance theory deals not only with ethnic and racial groups but also with gender. For a study that compares the gender aspect across Australia, Sweden, the United States, and Russia see Jim Sidanius, Felicia Pratto, and Diana Brief, "Group Dominance and the Political Psychology of Gender: A Cross-Cultural Comparison," *Political Psychology* (1995) 16 (2): 381–96. Also see James Sidanius and Felicia Pratto, *Social Dominance: An Intergroup Theory of Social Hierarchy and Oppression* (Cambridge: Cambridge University Press, 1999) and Felicia Pratto, James Sidanius, Lisa Stallworth, and Bertram Malle, "Social Dominance Orientation: A Personality Variable Predicting Social and Political Attitudes," *Journal of Personality and Social Psychology* (1994) 67: 741–63.

3. The composition of the police
4. The composition of the officer corps
5. Symbols such as street names
6. Redistribution of land

Some ethnic groups may be wealthier than others, but when they are forced to speak the language of others in everyday business, when they are under the eye of ethnically different police, when they cannot advance in the ranks of the state bureaucracy or the military, when land is redistributed to favor another group, that is when they come to occupy a lower level on the status hierarchy. Perhaps most importantly, a belief of injustice results from status reversals. If the perception of status hierarchy is weak, beliefs about injustice and the corresponding emotion of resentment are unlikely to follow. However, if the perception of status hierarchy is deep and well established, reversals are very likely to create resentment – and the desire to reestablish the former hierarchy rapidly. After having been on top of an ethnic hierarchy, most groups come to see their dominant status as part of a natural order.

The A effect of resentment is to heighten a desire to reorder status relations by reducing the status of the out-of-place group. The most effective and rapid method of accomplishing this desire is through violence.[58] In most situations, though, the means of reordering status hierarchies will be legal and political. Resentment heightens support for policies that aim to change the visible political positions and symbols of dominance listed above.

Once in place, resentment produces attention-funneling B effects. Status hierarchy may become an obsession. Psychologists have not conducted many studies directly on the C effects of resentment as it has been conceived here, although it is not hard to imagine that the emotion might reinforce the fundamental attribution error.[59]

If the status hierarchy changes and the order of groups is "put right," then the intensity of resentment can be expected to fade quickly.

Political entrepreneurs use resentment to heighten the salience of ethnic identity. The emotion focuses attention on the unjust position of the ethnic group and helps mobilize a variety of actions. For instance, resentment is a clear motivator for riots and pogroms. If the situation allows it, violence helps put the out-of-place group back in its "proper" place quickly.[60] Donald

---

[58] For an extensive statistical analysis of related propositions, see Lars-Erik Cederman, Andreas Wimmer, and Brian Min, "Why Do Ethnic Groups Rebel? New Data and Analysis," *World Politics* (2010) 62: 87–119.

[59] Resentment, as conceived here, has been more the focus of sociologists. See Barbablet's review of the sociological literature on class and resentment in the third chapter of his *Emotion, Social Theory, and Social Structure*. Liah Greenfeld's work could also have been discussed at length here. See *Nationalism: Five Roads to Modernity* (Cambridge, MA: Harvard University Press, 1992). Greenfeld links nationalism to what she terms *ressentiment* – a psychological state resulting from suppressed feelings of envy and hatred (existential envy) and the impossibility of satisfying these feelings (p. 15).

[60] This was one of the major findings concerning violence in Petersen, *Understanding Ethnic Violence*.

Horowitz's study of hundreds of ethnic riots provides empirical support for the employment of violence as a tool to "teach them a lesson." Horowitz describes a similar phenomenon occurring in Russia, East Saint Louis, Delhi, Detroit, Sri Lanka, Nigeria, Malaysia, and other locations around the world.[61]

With resentment as an available resource, political entrepreneurs often consider the instigation of riots. They might also organize parades that raise the salience of the subordinated group's claims to justice. The U.S. Civil Rights movements and Northern Ireland provide examples here. At another level, political entrepreneurs may employ a series of posters, symbols, and rhetoric that are thoroughly built on existing political resentment.

II.B. Object-Based Emotions: Contempt and Hatred

The emotions described so far are all generated by beliefs about specific events. Individuals experience anger after they perceive that an agent has committed a negative action against them; they experience fear when they perceive that events have put them in danger; they experience resentment when changes in status hierarchy reorder group relations in a way that is perceived as unjust. If events change, the emotions will fade. If the person who committed the negative action apologizes, is punished, or pays some reparation, then anger may fade. If the threatening agent is defeated or disappears, then fear will dissipate. If status hierarchies are realigned, then resentment will dissipate.

Other emotions are based on beliefs about the nature of an object or group rather than the nature of a situation or events. In the conflicts among groups that take place during interventions, these emotions are likely to be based on history and culture.[62] Some social systems are built on emotion-laden conceptions. For example, caste systems embody strong ideas about group worth and group ability. So do apartheid systems, as in South Africa or the U.S. South under Jim Crow. These systems produce societies dominated by strong stereotypes and stigma. Political entrepreneurs can use the emotional power intrinsically linked to these stigmas as a political tool.

One key difference between event-based emotions and object-based emotions concerns decay or half-life. Emotions tied to cultural schemas do not fade with time. Rather they lie constantly, often latently, in the background. The discussion of the emotion of hatred that follows takes up on this point at length.

---

[61] Donald Horowitz, *The Deadly Ethnic Riot* (Berkeley, CA: University of California Press, 2002), pp. 368–70.

[62] The relationship between culture and emotion is a major, and controversial, issue. The position taken here is that there are some emotions common to almost all cultures. These include the event-based emotions of anger, fear, and resentment described in Section II.A. There are other emotions that are based on the contours of specific moral and cultural systems. See the treatment of spite in Section III. For an overview of the social constructivist position, see the chapters in Rom Harre ed., *The Social Construction of Emotions* (Oxford: Basil Blackwell, 1986).

Contempt. Contempt: cognition that a group or object is inherently inferior or defective; action tendency toward avoidance.

Contempt is closely related to stigma, a negative emotional reaction to some attribute of an individual, group, or object. At least some forms of racism fit here. Racists would not wish their offspring to intermarry with the racially stigmatized group or live in its neighborhood. Contempt pushes for avoidance of the stigmatized group in these key social interactions.

The sources of ethnic stigma and contempt are not always understood. Clearly, institutions such as slavery and apartheid help to create and sustain racial stigmas. In some instances, a history of conflict and cultural separation can convert ethnic difference into ethnic contempt. The empirical material of this book will provide examples, most clearly in the case of the Roma.

The A effect of contempt is avoidance. The B and C effects are the well-documented phenomena connected to prejudice. Attention funneling prevents the consideration of any positive actions of the stigmatized group. The fundamental attribution error is prominent. Stigmatized groups become a vehicle for scapegoating.

Although the stigmatized group may live quietly among other groups, the existence of the stigma is always present, even if in latent form. Contempt does not systematically decay.

With contempt as an available resource, political entrepreneurs can expect support for policies involving ethnic separation. These policies include partition and secession, as well as the building of parallel societies. Contempt can also be employed in motivating support for federal systems that institute high levels of ethnic autonomy.

Hatred. Hatred: cognition that a group is both inherently defective and dangerous; action tendency to physically eliminate the presence of that group.

Hatred involves the combination of two beliefs: first, there is something wrong with the opponent; second, the opponent is dangerous. In other words, hatred is contempt plus a belief that the other is a powerful threat. There can be no bargaining or reasoning with such an opponent – the problem is in his or her very character. Rather, the only solution is to eliminate the opponent.

Although belief in an opponent's dangerous and defective character can set off hatred, it is most likely to be triggered if the cognitive antecedents of the emotion are reinforced through a cultural schema. Hatred should not be conceived in terms of the "ancient hatreds" idea often propagated by journalists and others.[63] People simply do not live with constant hatred that invariably explodes if constraints come off. Nor should it be associated with scapegoating

---

[63] Robert Kaplan's *Balkan Ghosts: A Journey through History* (New York: St. Martin's Press, 1993) is the standard citation here. Perhaps the best survey of the literature on hatred is Edward B. Royzman, Clark McCauley, and Paul Rozin, "From Plato to Putnam: Four Ways to Think

or simple rabble-rousing. If the belief in danger is going to be strong enough to elicit this intense emotion, it will have to connect with a convincing logic that combines both of hatred's cognitive foundations.

As I have discussed elsewhere, hatred might best be conceptualized as a cultural schema.[64] The concept of a cultural schema is aptly explicated by the anthropologist Sherry Ortner:

> In effect, the cultural schema has been moved by an actor from an external to an internal position, from an abstract model of deeds done by ancient heroes and ritual participants to a personal program for understanding what is happening to one right now, and for acting upon it . . . there is a distance between actors' selves and their cultural models, in the sense that not all of a culture's repertoire of symbolic frames make sense to all actors at all times.[65]

The schema is an external, abstract model that *sometimes* informs a personal program for understanding and action. Group hatred is defined by antagonism against a group as an object; the antagonism is focused on purported innate characteristics of the opposing group. The two concepts of schema and hatred can be linked. Schemas can contain fairly constant representations of the innate nature of other ethnic groups. Some of these representations may be of a very negative nature. A culture possesses, as Ortner suggests, a repertoire of symbolic frames. At any given point a particular schema, although constantly existing as part of a repertoire, will not be guiding a large portion of the ethnocultural group. However, the external model is always available for activation. Here is the basis for a more realistic view of "ancient" hatred. The innate negative features of a group may persist within a cultural schema, but the emotive force of that schema is only seldom activated. Most of the time, individuals go about their business without the schema working to heighten any concern or guide any action. But the possibility always exists.[66] This fact

---

about Hate," in Robert J. Sternberg ed., *The Psychology of Hate* (Washington, DC: American Psychological Association, 2004), pp. 3–35.

[64] The next few paragraphs are taken from Petersen, *Understanding Ethnic Violence*.

[65] Sherry B. Ortner, "Patterns of History: Cultural Schemas in the Foundings of Sherpa Religious Institutions," in Emiko Ohnuki-Tierney ed., *Culture through Time: Anthropological Approaches* (Stanford, CA: Stanford University Press, 1990), p. 89.

[66] A primary debating point among social science disciplines concerns the "distance between the actors' selves and their cultural models." Those using a "thin rational view" posit an actor whose more immediate and personal economic or political goals dominate the murkier culture frame and push its significance into the background. Along this line of thinking, culture is more likely to be viewed as a resource than as an unconscious constraint. Culture might help produce a set of roles, but the individual is relatively free to choose among them. Others scholars see the cultural frame as heavily constraining, or even programming, the individual's choices. Roles are not chosen, but rather accepted. Ortner takes an intermediate position where "actors may internalize a schema under certain conditions and thus may be constrained by its forms, but under other conditions may reestablish a distance between themselves and the schema." Ortner, "Patterns of History," p. 84.

produces the constant, "ancient," quality that is so often sensed by journalists and travelers.[67]

The conception of cultural schema also addresses the nature of the action that the emotion triggers. The schema provides a "script" that may specify the action to be taken. In effect, a historically and culturally formed schema embodies a liturgy and the actions are specific rituals within that liturgy. When a schema is activated, the actions of one's predecessors, often involving violence, may serve as rituals to be repeated. Hatred heightens the desire for historically framed violence. The schema identifies the innate aggressive and unjust characteristics of previous enemies, the hateful characteristics, and the former violent and oppressive interactions. When hatred is activated, it becomes time to "settle old scores."

If hatred is based on the existence of certain schemas, then the schema should also shape individual actions. These actions, in turn, should help us distinguish when hatred is operative. Given the relatively unchanging scripts and rituals embodied in the schema, the justification for action should be the same across historical periods. The same innate qualities of the target group should be taken as the reason for violence and discriminatory actions. Second, the acts of violence and humiliation, the acts of vengeance, should possess ritualistic qualities. In sum, hatred predicts action against a historical target, identified in a well-known schema. Hatred also predicts that violence will be justified in a similar manner across time periods and that the action will also appear similar across time periods.

Emotion theorists, using different terminology, support the concept of schema. As Frijda and Mesquita summarize:

Temporary beliefs entailed in emotions may, however, turn into generalized long-term beliefs. When this happens, an emotion turns into a sentiment. What we call a sentiment (following Shand, 1922, and Arnold, 1960) consists of an appraisal structure that includes concern relevance of its object. Sentiments are thus dispositional emotions. They are schemas (affective schemas, Fiske, 1982) with the same structures as emotions. They consist of the latent representation of some object as being relevant to one's concerns, and suggesting what action might be desirable in relation to them. In emotion, a perception takes the place of a latent representation or a mere thought, and action readiness that of the knowledge of what action might be desirable. Sentiments turn into actual emotions when their objects are encountered with sufficient urgency or proximity. All this is part of general emotion theory.[68]

How does such a cultural schema form? At some point, cognitions about blameworthy and contemptible actions must combine coherently to form cognitions about the actor committing those actions. In other words, at some

---

[67] Rebecca West, *Black Lamb and Grey Falcon; A Journey through Yugoslavia* (New York: Penguin Books, 1995), and Robert Kaplan, *Balkan Ghosts*, provide compelling travelogues along these lines.

[68] Frijda and Mesquita, "Beliefs through Emotions," p. 55. Also see Clore and Gasper's discussion of the elaboration principle, "Feeling Is Believing," pp. 18–21.

point anger and contempt transform into hatred. Several hypotheses come to mind: the overall number of blameworthy actions could lead to hatred; the consistency of the nature of the bad acts could lead to the cognitions under-lying a hatred schema; the brutal quality of the acts would most likely lead to hatred; the rapidity of the sequence of acts might be the most important aspect.

As I have argued elsewhere, hatred is a relatively rare phenomenon.[69] First of all, political entrepreneurs cannot create a historical schema – only historical repetition of recognizably similar events can. Attempts to create such a schema will neither be convincing nor motivating, and may in fact lead to derision. Second, even if a hatred schema lies latent within a culture, elites cannot access it if unfolding events do not match those of the schema.[70] In short, I am arguing that the historical schema is generally activated by the emerging situation itself rather than by political elites. Yet political entrepreneurs will try to activate schemas to produce hate. If hatred emerges, then at least some elites are likely to try to use it.

The most detailed and sustained argument linking the emotion of hatred to political conflict and violence is Stuart Kaufman's *Modern Hatreds: The Symbolic Politics of Ethnic War*.[71] Kaufman's treatment of hatred shares some commonalities with the approach here. In both approaches, emotions can change preferences, funnel attention, and distort information processing. Kaufman's conception of "hostile myths" bears close resemblance to that of cultural schema. The two treatments also differ in key ways. First, Kaufman places emphasis on a myth–symbol complex that can be identified in school textbooks and political writings. For Kaufman, hatred is largely a cultural cre-ation. In opposition, the approach here concentrates on actual repeated events in modern history. Consistent with the overall approach, hatred is still an emo-tion connected to lived experience. Cultural schemas are far more powerful when individuals can recognize the "logic" and similarity of the schema in current events. To preview an example from the Kosovo chapter, I will argue that the Serbs do indeed possess a cultural schema capable of producing hatred toward Albanians. In my treatment, however, that schema has much less to do with the often cited Battle of Kosovo in 1389 (although that myth is not insignificant) than with the repeated and recognizably similar hostilities that have taken place between Serbs and Albanians during the twentieth century.

Second, and related, I do not believe that changing school textbooks or providing new myths and symbols is likely to erode the power of a cultural schema, at least not in the short or medium run. Yugoslavia ran a "Brotherhood

---

[69] See Petersen, *Understanding Ethnic Violence*.

[70] I have discussed the conditions under which cultural schemas are able to motivate political action at length elsewhere. See Roger Petersen, "Memory and Cultural Schema: Linking Mem-ory to Political Action," in Francesca Cappolletto ed., *Memory and Second World War: An Ethnographic Approach* (Oxford: Berg, 2005), pp. 131–53.

[71] Stuart J. Kaufman, *Modern Hatreds: The Symbolic Politics of Ethnic War* (Ithaca, NY: Cornell University Press, 2001).

and Unity" campaign for decades, but it failed to dent the cultural schema that underlay Albanian–Serbian relations. The residue of actual conflict is too powerful for these attempts at reeducation.

Third, to emphasize a previously made point, the cultural schemas that form the foundation for hatred are relatively rare. As the case studies will illustrate, there was no recognizable hatred-producing schema in Bosnia, Montenegro, or Macedonia. In those cases, emotions were at play, but not hatred.

Fourth, Kaufman's myth–symbol complex rolls several different emotions into one phenomenon.[72] The myths in his treatment involve provocation of fear, goals of ethnic dominance related to resentment, and prejudices related to contempt. In Kaufman's study, the term hatred is broad. In contrast, the approach here works to delineate specific emotions – fear, resentment, anger, contempt, and hatred. Each has separate and particular effects and uses. To be fair, Kaufman's dependent variable is ethnic war. The focus here is on the more complex political interaction taking place during intervention, which requires finer distinctions to be made.

Hatred is a tool for ethnic cleansing. If political entrepreneurs can tie their rhetoric into a schema of hatred, the emotion will provide support for a policy of cleansing or, at a minimum, demobilize opposition to such a policy.

C. Emotions without Specific Cognitive Antecedents

All of the emotions discussed so far are connected to specific cognitive antecedents. Fear arises from a belief in danger, anger from identifiable blameworthy actions, resentment from status inconsistencies, contempt from a belief about the other's character, hatred from a belief that a recognizable situation is repeating itself.

There is a long tradition in the social sciences, however, of treating emotion as preceding cognition. Perhaps the most well-known of these treatments is frustration–aggression theory and the related theory of relative deprivation.[73] In these approaches, multiple disappointments, or a general sense of not getting what one deserves, creates an underlying emotional state. Although the cognitive basis is difficult or impossible to specify, this general emotion does possess an action tendency – to lash out in order to relieve the tensions created by the emotion.

---

[72] For example, see pp. 30–31, the section on "Myths Justifying Ethnic Hostility."

[73] The literature on frustration-aggression theory is vast. John Dollard is usually credited with having developed one of the first social science treatments of the theory (John Dollard, L. Doob, N. Miller, O. Mowrer, and R. Sears, *Frustration and Aggression* (New Haven, CT: Yale University Press, 1939). See also Leonard Berkowitz, "Frustration–Aggression Hypothesis: Examination and Reformulation," *Psychological Bulletin* (1989) 106: 59–73. For the classic treatment of relative deprivation theory, see Ted Robert Gurr, *Why Men Rebel* (Princeton, NJ: Princeton University Press, 1970). For a summary and critique of the relative deprivation literature, see Barbara Salert, *Revolutions and Revolutionaries* (New York: Elsevier, 1976), especially the third chapter.

Building on several strands of social psychology, when emotion precedes cognition, distortions in information collection and belief formation may occur. Most critically, the emotion may distort the way targets are identified. The strong urge to commit violence creates the need to process available information in such a way to find an enemy (victim) and justify violence against that target. One or more of a diverse set of psychological mechanisms (for example, projection and attribution) may come into play to help with this task. With these mechanisms at work, it is likely that some groups that are attacked to relieve rage may have little to do with the actual sources of frustration. In relative deprivation theory, these are labeled as displaced or substitute targets rather than direct targets.[74] That is, if the group that is the source of frustration is unavailable for attack, another group will be found to substitute for it.

Jean-Paul Sartre's preface to Frantz Fanon's *The Wretched of the Earth* characterizes Fanon's text as an illustration of rage among colonized peoples. Sartre writes:

Read Fanon: you will learn how, in the period of their helplessness, their mad impulse to murder is the expression of the natives' collective unconscious. If this suppressed fury fails to find an outlet, it turns into a vacuum and devastates the oppressed creatures themselves. In order to free themselves they even massacre each other. The different tribes fight between themselves since they cannot face the real enemy – and you can count on colonial policy to keep up their rivalries.[75]

In previous work, I labeled the family of theories characterized by this general urge to lash out with the term "rage," and I will continue to do so in this work.[76] Political entrepreneurs cannot easily create the diverse and often complex foundations of rage. They can, however, incorporate existing rage into various strategies. Most theories of scapegoating are built on the assumption of the presence of rage. Populations wish to lash out, and elites shape the direction of that desire toward specific targets or groups. Because rage generates powerful distortions in belief formation, political elites may be able to employ the emotion flexibly toward different ends and various targets.

III. WHY ONLY THESE EMOTIONS? CULTURE AND EMOTION

Certainly, other emotions are relevant to conflict and intervention. Guilt, shame, pride, and hope come readily to mind. I have written about some of these emotions in other forums, and I will touch on them within the

---

[74] On targets, see Donald Horowitz, "Direct, Displaced, and Cumulative Ethnic Aggression," *Comparative Politics* (1973) 6: 1–16. Also see Horowitz, *The Deadly Ethnic Riot*, pp. 136–47.

[75] Jean-Paul Sartre, "Preface" to Frantz Fanon, *The Wretched of the Earth* (New York: Grove Press, 1965), p. 18.

[76] Petersen, *Understanding Ethnic Violence*, pp. 75–84.

case chapters.[77] The purpose here is to develop a general framework for studying the strategic use of emotion during intervention. Five emotions – anger, fear, resentment, contempt, and hatred – are fundamental, common, and highly relevant to the political context of intervention. The reality of and constant potential for violence means that fear and anger will be an integral part of politics. Changing status hierarchies and questions of political dominance keep resentment in play. Common prejudices basic to human nature will often bring in contempt. Hatred, as argued in Section II.B, is rarer; when present, however, its power can bring devastation. These emotions provide the basis for the strategic framework developed in the next chapter.

Analytically, there is a danger in adding emotions into the study. There can be a tendency to do so in an ad hoc manner simply to explain unusual actions. Limiting the analysis to a small but obviously relevant set of emotions maintains the level of parsimony necessary to develop a generalizable framework.

Is such parsimony desirable? Unquestionably, emotions vary across cultures.[78] Cultures create the value systems that define what is honorable, for example. In turn, what is honorable determines the operation of emotions such as shame and guilt, and may affect anger and other emotions as well. Different cultures may possess additional emotions that are especially salient to political and ethnically defined struggles. Does the quest for parsimony and generality not do damage to this reality?

I will let the reader determine the answer to this question after going through the analyses of cases. I believe that the framework here will allow the addition of emotions that are highly salient to a particular conflict.

I will give an example of one emotion that I consider as pervasive and potentially important in the Balkans – spite.

Spite: cognition that someone or some group is going to receive some undeserved good. The action tendency is to destroy that good, even at a cost to oneself.

The action tendency of spite is described by Aristotle in his *Rhetoric*. He defines spite as "thwarting another man's wishes, not to get anything for yourself, but to prevent his getting it. The slight arises just from the fact that you do not aim at something for yourself: Clearly you do not think that he can do you harm, for then you would be afraid of him instead of slighting him, nor yet that he can do you any good worth mentioning, for then you would be anxious to make friends with him."[79] Under the influence of spite, one may "cut off

---

77 See Roger Petersen with Evangelos Liaras, "Countering Fear in War: The Strategic Use of Emotion in Thucydides," *Journal of Military Ethics* (2006) 5: 317–333. Also see Roger Petersen with Sarah Zukerman, "Revenge or Reconciliation: Theory and Method of Emotions in the Context of Colombia's Peace Process," at the Forum for International Criminal and Humanitarian Law, International Peace Research Institute, Oslo (PRIO), 2009.

78 See Jon Elster, *Alchemies of the Mind*, pp. 411–12 for a general summary on emotion and culture.

79 Aristotle, *Rhetoric*, cited in Elster, *Alchemies*, p. 62.

one's nose to spite one's face," as the common expression goes. The emotion's B effect, its influence on information collection, is its defining feature. Individuals under the sway of spite focus only on preventing the opponent from achieving his or her goal, and ignore information on the costs of that action to themselves.

As Aristotle suggests in the quoted passage, other emotions, such as fear, are likely to override spite. If survival is in question, spite is unlikely to be a major factor. In actively violent conflict, anger is also likely to be more powerful. In a more stable environment, however, spite may become a useful resource. When political entrepreneurs wish to block an opponent's action, they can appeal to the wider population of their own group and ask them to sacrifice some of their own more narrow interests on behalf of the collective. Alternatively, they can imbue their group members with spite. They can create images of a happy, gloating enemy – the cognitive underpinnings of spite – that will motivate individual action to eliminate the undeserved happiness of the opponent.

Spite is commonly seen as central to social and political life in the Balkans.[80] The Serbs have a special word for a closely related phenomenon – "inat." In the words of Rasim Ljajic, Serbia and Montenegro's Minister for Human Rights and Minority Rights, "Spite is not simply an emotional factor here, it's a political factor."[81] Although I considered the inclusion of spite in the general framework I develop in the next chapters, I made a judgment call that costs of its inclusion in terms of loss of parsimony would exceed its explanatory benefits.

IV. CONCLUSIONS

This chapter has defined emotion in general terms and specified the emotions most relevant to violent conflict and intervention. Although there are many emotions, the set discussed here – anger, fear, resentment, contempt, hatred, and spite – captures the most powerful and motivating experiences of life after violence and during reconstruction. If one were to study social movements, a different set of emotions would be more relevant. In that case, one might retain anger and resentment and also include some positive emotions, such as hope and pride. The set in this book emerged from my own fieldwork; it contains those emotions that "hit me in the face," the ones that were useful for political entrepreneurs in confronting Western intervention. These are highly negative emotions, but political realities in the Western Balkans during this period were not generally of a positive nature. Bosnia and Kosovo are synonymous with

---

[80] For an example of the examination of spite in a larger context, see Ernest Fehr, Karla Hoff, and Mayuresh Kshetramade, "Spite and Development," *American Economic Review: Papers and Proceedings* (2008) 98: 494–499.

[81] From Radio Free Liberty Balkan Report, 5 December 2003.

ethnic cleansing; it would be hard to expect that negative emotions were not part of political life there. I also believe from my more limited knowledge of Iraq that this set of emotions is relevant to that country's invasion, occupation, and reconstruction.

In any given situation, only a subset of the listed emotions will be available as a resource. Often, no emotion will be available. The next chapter discusses when specific emotions will be available or unavailable. In other words, it delineates the distribution of emotions discussed in this chapter.

3

The Strategic Use of Emotions, I

The Distribution of Emotions

Recall the basic setup from the Introduction.

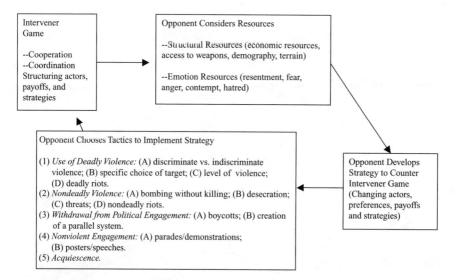

This chapter addresses the second box in the progression – "Opponent Considers Resources." The previous chapter defined emotions and provided examples of the ways they relate to political conflict. This chapter will identify when specific emotions will be available or unavailable as resources to political actors and will also consider the structural resources that serve as constraints.

As outlined in the Introduction, three experiences create the five emotions listed in Figure 1.1:

(1) Violent experiences create the emotions of anger and fear.
(2) Prejudice and stigma support the emotions of contempt and hatred.
(3) The experience of status reversal can create the emotion of resentment.

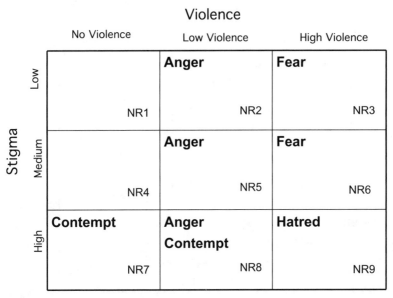

FIGURE 3.1. Distribution of Emotion Resources without Resentment (Matrix NR).

Different conflicts involve different sets of these experiences. Accordingly, conflicts will generate different distributions of emotions and different possibilities for the strategic use of emotion. For example, if a case is one of low stigma, contempt will not be an available emotion resource. If a situation does not involve a status reversal, resentment will not be available as a resource for political entrepreneurs. If there is no violence, anger and fear will not be powerful resources. The presence of these experiences will make these emotions available as resources.

The three experiences can be laid out in grid fashion with low, medium, and high values for stigma on the vertical axis and no violence, low violence, and high violence values for violence on the horizontal axis. The first matrix (Figure 3.1) addresses situations without the presence of status reversals and resentment, whereas the second matrix (Figure 3.2) includes situations with resentment. At any given time, a case will occupy one cell of either of these matrices. If a case is characterized by no violence, low stigma, and no resentment, it can be placed in the upper left box of Figure 3.1. In this instance, political entrepreneurs cannot draw on any emotion resource. If a case is one of no violence, high stigma, and no resentment, it can be placed in the bottom left box, and political actors can draw on the emotion of contempt as a resource. If a case has experienced no violence, but does exhibit high contempt and also status reversal, it can be placed in the bottom left box of Figure 3.2, and political actors will have both contempt and resentment as resources.

As a shorthand device, I will call Figure 3.1 the NR matrix (for no resentment) and label each box with a number. For example, the top left box is

Violence

		No Violence	Low Violence	High Violence
Stigma	Low	Resentment- R1	Anger Resentment- R2	Fear R3
	Medium	Resentment R4	Anger Resentment R5	Fear R6
	High	Contempt Resentment+ R7	Anger Contempt Resentment+ R8	Hatred R9

FIGURE 3.2. Distribution of Emotion Resources with Resentment (Matrix R).

designated NR1, the adjacent box on the top row is NR2, the upper right NR3. Likewise, the middle row contains boxes NR4–NR6 and the bottom row NR7–NR9.

As with the NR matrix, individual cells of the R matrix (Figure 3.2) can be signified by number, the top row containing boxes R1–R3, the middle row boxes R4–R6, and the bottom row boxes R7–R9.

The following sections explain the placement of emotions within these matrices and also develop measures of stigma, status reversal, and violence that serve to locate any case within a specific box.

I. EXPERIENCES AND EMOTIONS

For each case study, the first task will be to determine which matrix and which box represent the starting point of analysis. A consideration of political status and status reversal determines whether the resentment or nonresentment matrix will be employed; an evaluation of level of violence and level of stigma then determines the specific box within that matrix.

A. Determining the Matrix: Political Status and Resentment

Political status concerns visible positions of force and authority. As already discussed in the second chapter, individuals almost always react to the ethnic composition of visible positions of force and authority. People notice if the police are all group X or if they have to deal in bureaucracy in the language of group Y. Processes of comparison and perceptions of hierarchy are normal human phenomena. During or after the outbreak of violent conflict, such processes are greatly heightened.

Following the discussion in the previous chapter, status reversal is measured by the change in positions of visible dominance from one group to another. These include:

(1) The language of day-to-day government
(2) The composition of the bureaucracy
(3) The composition of the police
(4) The composition of the officer corps
(5) Symbols such as street names

If the state bureaucracy used to be administered in one's own language, but now is administered in another group's language, resentment arises. If the police force used to be composed of members of one's own group, but now police of another group can stop and search cars, resentment arises. Furthermore, more rapid change is also more likely to generate resentment than slower change.

When status reversal has occurred, as represented by the R matrix (Figure 3.2), the emotion of resentment will be a resource in cases of no or low violence. When violence reaches high levels, other emotions overpower resentment. For example, if killing or ethnic cleansing reaches a high level, fear or hatred is likely to crowd out concerns about group political status. I also assume that resentment varies in intensity. To become subordinated to a highly stigmatized group breeds more intense resentment than to witness the dominance of a group that one might consider equal. Correspondingly, resentment is marked with a minus sign in the low-stigma row and a plus sign in the high-stigma row.

Mitigating resentment is the basic stuff of negotiated political solutions. Shiites, Sunnis, and Kurds hammered out positions and proportions across governmental organizations, the police, and the military during the Western intervention in Iraq. One of the most influential theories of ethnic conflict prevention – consociationalism – calls for a transparent division of positions of authority that mitigates perceptions of domination. Affirmative action programs aim to create equality by evening up the numbers in these positions.

All of these political processes take time. Unlike ethnic stigmas, perceptions about political status may not take generations to change, but change will probably take years. As with contempt, political entrepreneurs can use existing resentments as a resource, but they are usually unable to create them or end them in the short term.

B. Violence, Anger, and Fear

Violence creates the emotions of anger and fear. In contrast to contempt and resentment, political entrepreneurs can change levels of violence. In this case, political actors not only employ existing emotions, but also can create new ones. Indeed, they can choose different types of targets in an effort to create either fear or anger. Two issues are at play – level of violence (high vs. low) and nature of targeting (discriminate vs. indiscriminate). High levels of violence are likely to produce fear regardless of the nature of the targeting. If multitudes of people are being killed, it is natural to become obsessed with the safety of one's own life and family. Correspondingly, fear is listed in the right-hand columns of both matrices.

With low levels of violence, the situation is more complicated. As outlined in the previous chapter, discriminate targeting, especially against leaders or symbols, is more likely to create anger than fear. Beliefs about violence are more likely to concern the injustice of the action or the sinister motivations behind the violence than beliefs about personal safety. For reasons discussed in the fifth chapter, when political entrepreneurs employ low levels of violence, they usually do so with discriminate targets. Accordingly, I have put anger in the low-level violence boxes in the matrices.

However, political actors could also use low-level indiscriminate violence to create fear. If there are seemingly random attacks, individuals may develop the belief that "anyone can be hit" and also develop fear even when the absolute numbers of victims is low. A few random attacks over a large area are unlikely to generate significant levels of fear. However, if a few random attacks are concentrated in a smaller area, political entrepreneurs may be able to imbue a limited target group with fear.

Scholars measure levels of violence in a myriad of ways, usually in terms of numbers of dead combatants and civilians. Although such measures may be relatively reliable,[1] they may not be valid measures of the connection between violence and emotion. For example, the fifty deaths in the London bombings in July 2005 and fifty deaths in Baghdad occurring at the same time cannot be coded as equivalent in emotional impact.

For the purposes here, I will discuss violence in general terms and three categories: no violence, low level of violence, and high level of violence. In Western interventions, and certainly in the Balkan interventions, violence is a "red line." The intervener is compelled to respond or otherwise risk losing credibility. Opponents of intervention will think hard about the consequences of crossing this line. Therefore, moving to any type of violent strategy is a threshold in the game. The line between low and high violence is ambiguous, but many cases can be coded into one or the other without much argument.

C. Ethnic Stigmas, Contempt, and Hatred

When a group is stigmatized, members of other groups believe that there is something inherently inferior or deficient about that group. In long-term group relations, stigmas manifest themselves both socially and culturally.

---

[1] Such figures are often not even reliable, as the Bosnian case shows. For years, everyone spoke of 200,000 dead, but further research has dropped the commonly accepted number to about half of that.

Socially, some ethnic groups develop informal rules of behavior regarding stigmatized groups. One such rule would be "do not marry into the stigmatized group." Perhaps more than any other observable measure, social scientists use intermarriage rates to assess the existence of ethnic stigma.[2] Other rules can include "do not live in a neighborhood overwhelmingly populated by members of the stigmatized group." The accompanying measure is voluntary residential self-segregation. A good example would be the massive "white flight" seen in almost every major U.S. city in previous decades. Another informal social rule associated with stigma is "do not learn the language of the stigmatized group." Speaking another group's language, and especially going to some effort to learn that language, implies and practices a measure of equality, and such equality is not the norm in relations with a stigmatized group. In some cases, these rules may also pervade the political realm. Even if political benefits seem obvious, stigma may prevent the formation of political parties that include significant numbers of the stigmatized group or prevent political coalitions with the political parties representing stigmatized groups. The power and ubiquity of such rules is obvious in many social systems. They are central to caste systems. They were also the basis of Jim Crow in the U.S. South.

Culturally, stigmas manifest themselves in language, myths, and schemas. Stigmatized groups are the target of derogatory language and slurs. Out-groups hold to and reference myths, and sometimes conspiracy theories, that incorporate the negative qualities that the stigmatized group is seen as possessing. When these cultural elements are put together into narrative form, a cultural schema may result.

Ethnic stigmas are inextricably linked to the emotion of contempt. It is this emotion, with its action tendency for avoidance, that maintains the informal rules. Thus, in the presence of stigma, we should also expect to find evidence of the psychological mechanisms related to contempt – most importantly, stereotyping and prejudice. Following Sniderman, prejudice against a stigmatized group means both that negative qualities are ascribed to that group and that positive qualities are not.[3]

As discussed previously, ethnic stigmas and the accompanying emotion of contempt can be used as a resource, especially in strategies aiming for separation and boycott. Political actors are more likely to employ these strategies, and more likely to be successful, when stigmas are stronger, and they are less likely to employ those strategies when stigmas are weaker or are in the process of erosion.

---

[2] The use of intermarriage statistics as an indicator of social integration goes back decades. See, for example, Robert K. Merton, "Intermarriage and Social Structure: Fact and Theory," *Psychiatry* 4 (1941):361–77. It is certainly a much discussed measure in the analysis of ethnic relations in the former Yugoslavia. On that issue, see Nikolai Botev, "Where East Meets West: Ethnic Intermarriage in the Former Yugoslavia, 1962 to 1989," *American Sociological Review* (June 1994) 59: 461–80.

[3] Paul Sniderman, *The Outsider: Prejudice and Politics in Italy* (Princeton, NJ: Princeton University Press, 2000).

This leads to a crucial question: How does an outsider judge the level of ethnic stigma? Following the preceding discussion, several indicators could be used to determine the strength of ethnic stigmas:

> *Social indicators*: (A) intermarriage rates; (B) residential flight (during non-violent periods); (C) declining to learn a group's language.
> *Political indicators*: (A) nonexistence of multiethnic parties that include the stigmatized group; (B) avoiding party alliances that include a party representing the stigmatized group.
> *Cultural indicators*: (A) Ubiquity of ethnic slurs; (B) the pervasiveness of myths and conspiracy theories; (C) the existence of cultural schemas that embody the perceived negative qualities underlying the stigma.
> *Psychological indicator*: Surveys and fieldwork experience indicating the clear existence of stereotyping.

Of these indicators, some are more unambiguously related to ethnic stigma than others. For instance, social indicator C, language, is often related more to political status issues than to stigma (see the discussion in the preceding section). Political indicators are also sometimes connected to factors of power and demography rather than stigma. Cultural myths and schemas are no doubt good evidence of ethnic stigma, but require some level of interpretation. Surveys on prejudice and stereotype can be used as supplementary evidence but are not common and are difficult to assess out of context. The most reliable and observable indicators that are clearly related to ethnic stigma are probably intermarriage and residential flight. Additionally, for anyone who does fieldwork in a country for months or years, there may also be little doubt as to the presence of derogatory terminology.

With these comments in mind, some rough coding rules can be articulated. Bear in mind that the matrix form of analysis only strives to classify cases into low, medium, and high categories. Correspondingly, the method employed here will proceed in two stages. First, cases of low stigma will be separated from those of significant stigma. If significant levels of stigma are clearly present, a second stage of analysis will separate medium from high designations.

> (1) *Separating cases of low stigma from medium/high stigma*: The three more valid, reliable, and observable indicators – intermarriage, voluntary residential segregation, and derogatory terms or slurs – can be used to distinguish high and medium ethnic stigmas from low ethnic stigma. If members of group X possess strong norms against intermarrying members of group Y, if members of group X flee from their neighborhoods when members of group Y move in, and if derogatory terms are everyday usage, then it can be assumed that group X stigmatizes group Y (in other words, group Y is a stigmatized group). This stigma may or may not be mutual. On the other hand, if there are significant intermarriage,

residential integration, and an absence of slurs, then the situation is one of low stigma.

(2) *Separating cases of medium stigma from cases of high stigma*: If the criteria of low intermarriage, high voluntary segregation, and derogatory terminology indicate a case of significant ethnic stigma, the other remaining indicators can then be used to determine whether the designation should be medium or high. Given the cultural and historical idiosyncrasies in interethnic group relations, this cannot be an exact science; however, the remaining factors listed in the previous discussion can be employed to make a convincing designation in most cases. If all of these factors (existence of myths, evidence of a negative cultural schema, absence of political cooperation in terms of multiethnic parties and multiethnic alliances, the shunning of the group's language, and evidence of stereotyping) line up in the ways expected in the presence of ethnic stigma, then the judgment must be that the case is one of high stigma. If these indicators run the other way, then the case can be placed in the medium category. In cases where the indicators are mixed, or ones in which the political and linguistic practices illustrate cooperation or integration, then the coding necessarily requires a judgment call, although one that can be supported through explanation and reference to field experience.

I believe that most readers could use the same methodology to code familiar cases. For example, an application of the list to the U.S. South under Jim Crow would point out that intermarriage between blacks and whites was illegal, segregation was very high, and words such as "nigger" were in common use. The case clearly indicates a significant level of stigma. The remaining indicators also provide evidence of stigma: justifications for lynching often involved pernicious myths, there was not only a lack of political cooperation but outright political exclusion, and evidence of stereotyping was abundant. The conclusion is straightforward: in terms of white attitudes, African-Americans in the Jim Crow South were a stigmatized group. Correspondingly, many whites had contempt for African-Americans and this emotion could often be mobilized as a resource.

A few final comments on ethnic stigma are in order here. First, as shown by the matrices, I assume that contempt will be a valuable and predictable resource only in cases of high stigma. Thus, contempt is only found in the bottom row.

Second, political entrepreneurs cannot change the level of stigma, at least not in the short or medium run. They cannot tell their own groups to like and respect stigmatized groups and expect rapid results. Thus, political entrepreneurs can use existing ethnic contempt, but they can neither create it nor quickly eliminate it.

Third, stigmas do erode. The massive literature on the contact hypothesis addresses the types of interaction that work to enhance and speed the erosion of stigmas.[4] Important policies have been enacted in employment and education, school busing being the most well-known, to create contact that eats away at ethnic and racial stigma. Yet both theory and practice suggest that ethnic stigmas are long-term and relatively stable phenomena.

Fourth, when high levels of violence are added to a situation of contempt, hatred is possible, especially with the presence of a cultural schema that works to confirm the dangerous and defective nature of the opponent. Hatred will only be found in the bottom right cell.

I will return to these four issues at various points.

II. AN ANALYTICAL FRAMEWORK

To summarize, the emotion of contempt will only be a resource at high levels of ethnic stigma versus an opposing group. Hatred can only occur when high levels of violence are combined with contempt.[5] Fear becomes a near certainty at high levels of violence. If a group is attacked with a low level of discriminate violence, the response is most likely to be anger. If a status reversal has occurred, the emotion of resentment will be a resource at levels of low and no violence.

I assume that political entrepreneurs know which box they are playing in. That is, they know which emotion resources are available. They must then consider a number of strategic possibilities:

(1) *Mobilization* of existing emotion: The political entrepreneur can employ a strategy that uses the emotion in the box. Sometimes that box will be empty and there will be nothing to choose; other times it will contain multiple emotion resources.

(2) *Transformation* of emotions: For the short term, political entrepreneurs can move the situation horizontally through the escalation or deescalation of violence. As has been explained, political entrepreneurs cannot change the level of stigma and changing status relations is a medium-term project. On the other hand, political entrepreneurs are often able to change the level of violence.[6]

(3) Use no emotion: The political entrepreneur always has the option of foregoing the use of the emotion.

Referring back to Figure 1.1, the opponent of intervention considers both structural resources and emotion resources before developing a strategy. The

---

[4] For an extensive review of the literature on the contact hypothesis, see H. D. Forbes, *Ethnic Conflict: Commerce, Culture, and the Contact Hypothesis* (New Haven, CT: Yale University Press, 1997).

[5] As argued previously, the emotion is clearest when an existing cultural schema combines and reinforces the cognitions of danger and defectiveness.

[6] The terms *mobilization* and *transformation* are used by Randall Collins, "Social Movements and the Focus of Emotional Attention," in Jeff Goodwin, James Jasper, and Francesca Poletta, *Passionate Politics: Emotions and Social Movements* (Chicago: University of Chicago Press, 2001), pp. 27–44; see pp. 28–31 in particular.

sixth chapter will list a series of hypotheses that link resources to choice of strategy and tactics. For this purpose, consider a couple of scenarios that illustrate the strategic position of political entrepreneurs. If an actor is operating in box NR1, the upper left cell of Figure 3.1, the situation is characterized by low stigma, low violence, and no status reversal. Without significant stigma, contempt is not available; without violence, fear and anger are absent; without status reversal there is no resentment to utilize. The actor in this situation has no powerful emotion resource to mobilize. The political entrepreneur in this case has two choices: remain in the upper left cell with no emotion resource or use violence to move the situation to the right and into the upper middle box and inject anger into the contest. By making a discriminate strike against an opposing group, the actor might be able to set off a spiral that escalates the conflict. Alternatively, if the situation is represented by the middle box of the middle row (R5) in Figure 3.2, the political entrepreneur possesses three options in terms of employing emotion resources: (1) consider escalating violence to high levels and generating fear, (2) remain in the center box and be able to mobilize anger and a medium level of resentment, or (3) deescalate violence and operate in a situation of resentment alone.

This matrix will be used to analyze intervention in the Western Balkans. To give a brief preview of the case studies, Kosovo provides a case of high stigma, status reversal, and violence ranging from none to high. In other words, the case spans the bottom row. Starting from 1991, I will show how actors transformed the case through an escalation of violence from the bottom left box (R7) across to the middle box (R8) and then the bottom right box (R9). Intervention then reduced violence and transformed the situation again, moving Kosovo again through the middle box and then back across to the bottom left box (R7), where it remained in 2009. For comparison, Bosnia is a case of low ethnic stigma, status reversal, and violence ranging from low to extremely high. In other words, Bosnia across time will illustrate movement across the top row of the matrix. The Macedonian, Montenegrin, and South Serbian cases will illustrate yet different dynamics.

It is appropriate to note that this analytical framework is straightforward and relatively simple in practice. Although there are eighteen cells, that is, eighteen possible situations, only a small, usually adjacent set of these cells will be relevant to any given case.

III. STRUCTURAL RESOURCES AND CONSTRAINTS

One of the most critical questions raised by the analysis in Section II is the ability of the entrepreneur to transform the game through escalation of violence. The first task of the intervener will probably be an effort to disarm combatants and create a state monopoly on violence. The new regime will try to identify, arrest, or isolate violent "spoilers" and then play the game with players dedicated to nonviolence. In effect, the intervention regime will try to use its resources to keep the game confined to the left row of boxes in the matrix. It can then more easily deal with the issues of political status relations and ethnic stigmas in the absence of threats and realities of violent escalation.

Thus framed, the issue becomes one of the technical capacity of intervention opponents to launch violence. Here, Fearon and Laitin's work on the technology of insurgency is most relevant.[7] In examining the onset of civil war, Fearon and Laitin concentrate on the constraints that potential rebels face. Many of these constraints are tied to state capacity – that is, the ability of the state to devote resources to identifying and pursuing opponents. A very powerful regime may be able to prevent the use of violence and thus block political entrepreneurs from initiating a strategy of violent escalation. In their work, as in many others, state capacity is proxied by GDP numbers. Fearon and Laitin also identify other variables as powerful constraints on rebels. The physical size of the state matters. Small states will not be able to provide space for maneuver, escape, and sanctuary. Population size also matters, for similar reasons; with more people there is more opportunity to blend in and hide. The scholars also find that terrain is a significant factor, again for similar reasons. Although opposition to intervention is not the same as civil war, these four variables – GDP, state size, state population, terrain – can be used to consider constraints on escalation.

Whereas Fearon and Laitin concentrate on constraints, other scholars identify different relevant resources. To launch violence, a group needs weapons. A large and active diaspora can provide weapons or the funding to buy them. As a second related factor, if ethnic kin live in a neighboring state, they can supply a retreat and possibly easy access to weapons.

As opposed to scholars putting the emphasis on the technology of escalation, Collier et al. put forward an argument based on opportunity costs.[8] In agreement with Fearon and Laitin, Collier et al. find that high GDP levels predict the absence of civil war. In opposition to Fearon and Laitin, their interpretation is not that high GDP produces states that constrain rebellion but rather that in richer states potential rebels have better and more lucrative things to do than launch violence.

In sum, here is a list of relevant structural variables and their basic logic:

Technology variables:

(1) Higher GDP – Measure of resources the state can bring to bear versus opponents
(2) Size of population: Larger population, more ability to hide
(3) Mountainous terrain: More ability to hide
(4) Physical size of state: More ability to hide

---

[7] James Fearon and David Laitin, "Ethnicity, Insurgency, and Civil War," *American Political Science Review* (2003) 97: 75–90.

[8] Paul Collier, V. L. Elliott, Havard Hegre, Anke Hoeffler, Marta Reynal-Querol, and Nicholas Sambanis, *Breaking the Conflict Trap: Civil War and Development Policy* (Washington DC and Oxford: Copublication of the World Bank and Oxford University Press, 2003).

Opportunity variables:

(1) Higher GDP: More opportunity for individuals to make money without making trouble
(2) Access to weapons
(3) Ethnic kin in neighboring state

I will apply this list of structural constraints and resources, as well as a consideration of opportunity costs, to the cases.

CONCLUSION: WHERE WE ARE HEADING

Thus far, Chapters 2 and 3 have defined what emotions are, identified what specific types of emotions are most relevant to the conflicts studied here, shown how these emotions are distributed according to political and historical experience, and discussed the structural constraints that could constrain the use of emotion resources.

Chapters 4 and 5 flesh out the remaining elements of Figure 1.1. Chapter 4 covers "intervention games." Chapter 5 examines how actors develop strategies, given their resources.

Chapter 6, the concluding theoretical chapter, then brings these elements together to generate a set of hypotheses that predict variation in the choice of tactics listed in the bottom left box of Figure 1.1, which I have termed the specific dependent variable.

4

Intervention Games

For the past fifteen years, Western foreign policy rhetoric and philosophy have been dominated by the ideas of classical liberalism.[1] In this worldview, two ideas stand out. First, there is the notion of universal progress. Humanity is making its way toward an ever better end state; in the words of President Bush, "freedom is on the march."

A second key concept is the "social contract." This idea is central to the present chapter. The primary goal of Western intervention is to design a social contract among the parties in conflict. In turn, the creation and implementation of these social contracts resembles the structure of certain rational choice "games." These games consist of a few basic elements: specification of actors, their preferences, and their possible actions. The Western approach to intervention, I argue, is to construct the "game" and its component parts with a narrow view of rationality. Opponents of the game, on the other hand, often use the emotions specified in the last chapter as resources to alter the game and its basic elements. In this competition, the strategic use of emotion and the Western intervention game are inextricably linked.

After presenting a gloss on recent applications of the social contract idea to intervention, this chapter will provide a very brief lesson on game theory and its most relevant applications to Western intervention. I employ a simple version of game theory for two largely heuristic reasons. First, it helps to specify the underlying logic of intervention policy and delineate its basic elements. Second, it will provide a shorthand for comparison and analysis in the empirical sections of the book. No technical background is needed; the reader will only need to know the basic structure of three simple games.

---

[1] For an example, see various works of Joshua Moravcik including *Exporting Democracy: Fulfilling America's Destiny* (Washington, DC: American Enterprise Institute, 1991); also, Walter Russell Mead, *Special Providence: American Foreign Policy and How It Changed the World* (New York: Routledge, 2002).

I. BROKEN STATES, WESTERN INTERVENTION, AND THE SOCIAL CONTRACT

Many states break down or fail. Those trained in political science or political philosophy often discuss the situation in terms of "anarchy" or "emerging anarchy," and immediately reference the fundamental works of Hobbes and Locke. Hobbes called for individuals to surrender power to a protective sovereign, a Leviathan, with nearly unlimited powers and unbound by constitutional or other constraints. Locke argued that a durable and just order would only take hold firmly when the ruled and rulers entered into a "social contract." Citizens would agree to concede complete freedom of action and, in return, the ruler would also agree to limitations. When accepted by both the governed and the government, the social contract would establish "rules of the game" making for a just and efficient society.

Many of the most widely read works on intervention and state reconstruction begin with references to the state of nature and Hobbes's and Locke's prescriptions on bringing order. If we look at the conventional wisdom on rebuilding states, perhaps best captured in Sambanis and Doyle's recent work *Making War and Building Peace*, a Leviathan is needed to produce short-term security, but on the whole, the intervener's world is that of Locke.[2] Sambanis and Doyle recommend a multistep program for fixing failed states. The first step is to provide security. As they explicitly state, "There must be a new sovereign Leviathan," and in some situations, a very large Leviathan. The later steps, however, should resemble the prescriptions of Locke: the rule of law and constitutional consent; the right of property; democracy and wider participation; and "genuine moral and psychological reconciliation." In effect, a short-term Leviathan should provide the time and space necessary for an international protectorate to create a Lockean social contract among factions.

Roland Paris's argument, labeled "institutionalization before liberalization," follows the same general contours.[3] He suggests a sequenced path in which interveners first establish security and then build institutions. Only after these steps have been accomplished can the intervener fully implement a liberal economic and social order. Paris believes that Hobbes and Locke have more in common than is generally recognized. As Paris argues, "Both men believed that domestic peace presupposed the existence of governmental institutions capable of defending society against internal and external threats."[4] For Paris, Locke allowed a strong executive hand in creating institutions that would develop, defend, and sustain the social contract.[5]

---

[2] Michael W. Doyle and Nicholas Sambanis, *Making War and Building Peace* (Princeton, NJ: Princeton University Press, 2006).

[3] Roland Paris, *At War's End: Building Peace after Civil Conflict* (Cambridge: Cambridge University Press, 2004).

[4] Ibid, p. 47.

[5] Many primers on intervention also employ Locke's notion of a social contract as the basis of an analytical framework. For example, see Tony Addison and S. Mansoob Murshed, "The Social

There is perhaps no more influential and consistent proponent of Western intervention than the International Crisis Group (ICG). The introductory sections of ICG reports often read as if they had been lifted out of Locke's Treatise. The opening lines of a 2003 report suggesting action in Kosovo state, "A simple but effective formula exists for peace in diverse societies. It consists of a civic contract: the government recognizes and supports special rights for minorities, and minorities acknowledge the authority of the government."[6] Along the lines of Paris's views, the ICG calls for a strong authority to implement this social contract in broken societies. In fact, for the ICG, it is often the duty of the international community, and sometimes Western interveners, to help structure this contract.

How should the social contract be implemented? The just-mentioned 2003 Kosovo report, besides addressing the key case of this book, provides examples of the basic process. In Kosovo in 2003, majority Albanians faced off against a Serbian minority under the United Nations Mission in Kosovo (UNMIK), an operation dominated by European and U.S. influence. The ICG report called for a social contract to be created among these parties. Above all, a social contract needs written rules. Accordingly, the ICG report advocated that a Charter of Rights outlining individual and group rights be added to the existing Constitutional Framework. The report urges that "Once the Charter is developed, a broad campaign should be undertaken to sensitize the public on its contents and how to address violations."[7]

Rules of interaction would be implemented through a more effective system of "sticks and carrots." As the report summarizes, "ICG proposes the creation of a real incentive structure to treat minorities as full and equal citizens, with clear penalties for bad behaviour and rewards for good behaviour."[8] This reward structure would include financial bonuses and public recognition for municipalities that followed the guidelines, and penalties, fines, loss of employment, and prosecution for those that did not. Budget allocations could be withheld from noncomplying municipalities and institutions. The report urges the construction of monitoring bodies and a strong judiciary that would serve to enforce the Charter of Rights against contrary actions by the majority-dominated legislative and executive branches.

In sum, this typical ICG report calls for explicit rules, communication of the nature of those rules, a system of punishments and rewards to encourage actors to follow those rules, and strong institutions to check erosion of that system of enforcement.

Contract and Violent Conflict," in Helen Yanacopulos and Joseph Hanlon eds., *Civil War, Civil Peace* (Athens, OH: Ohio University Press, 2006), pp. 137–63.

[6] International Crisis Group Balkans Report No. 143, "Kosovo's Ethnic Dilemma: The Need for a Civic Contract," May 28, 2003.

[7] Ibid, p. 24.

[8] Ibid, p. i.

Player 2

Cooperate   Defect

	Cooperate	Defect
Cooperate (Player 1)	R1, R2	S1, T2
Defect	T1, S2	P1, P2

FIGURE 4.1. 2 × 2 Game.

II. THREE SIMPLE GAMES IN ABSTRACT FORM

When Western states or Western-dominated organizations intervene in broken or failed states, their efforts to develop, implement, and enforce a social contract amounts to an effort to create a "game" between the groups in conflict. These games can be summarized and analyzed from the perspective of game theory. As James D. Morrow sums up in *Game Theory for Political Scientists*, "The game states what choices we believe the actors see in the situation, what they understand about their choices, what consequences they believe can follow from their decisions, and how they evaluate those consequences."[9] In interventions and occupations, the intervener tries to structure the interaction among opponents. The Western intervener will provide a circumscribed set of choices (those compatible with electoral democracy and free markets) and try to engineer the actor's strategies over those choices by arranging a system of rewards and penalties. Western interveners, along the lines of the rationality assumptions underlying game theory, believe that creating a proper incentive structure can bring previously warring sides to a situation of mutual benefit.

Games consist of a few fundamental elements: (1) actors, (2) strategies, (3) preferences, and (4) equilibria. The most basic of games can be represented in a 2 × 2 format. Figure 4.1 represents a game with two actors – Player 1 and Player 2. These actors have two strategies – *cooperate* and *defect*. The outcomes of the game are represented by the letters within the cells, with the first character in each pair representing the payoff for player 1 (row) and the second character representing the payoff for player 2 (column). In this figure, each letter has a meaning: when both players cooperate they receive the value of "reward" or R; when both defect, they receive the "penalty" or P; when one player cooperates while the other defects, the cooperating actor has been

---

[9] James D. Morrow, *Game Theory for Political Scientists* (Princeton, NJ: Princeton University Press, 1994), p. 57.

played for a "sucker" or S while the defector receives the "temptation" or T value.

The ordering of these preferences determines the nature and outcome of the game. The best-known game, and also one highly relevant to intervention, is the prisoners' dilemma (PD). In this game, the preference ordering is

$$T > R > P > S$$

Given the structure of the game and its envisioned payoffs, there are four outcomes for each player. The best outcome for any single player is to defect while the other side bears the costs of cooperation. In this case, the side defecting receives the "temptation" value while the other side is played as a "sucker," the worst outcome in the game. The second best outcome for each player is mutual cooperation (reward), whereas the third best is mutual defection (penalty). Thus, the order of payoffs is temptation > reward > penalty > sucker.

What does this game predict about an outcome? In game theoretic terms, the key issue concerns the presence/absence and nature of equilibria. Most simply defined, "For an outcome to be an equilibrium, it must be the case that if one player had chosen differently, he would have done worse."[10] Because no player has an incentive to change his or her strategy, an equilibrium predicts stability for a combination of choices. For the prisoners' dilemma, the equilibrium will be mutual defection. If either player chooses to unilaterally move toward cooperation, he or she will receive the "sucker" payoff, the worst possible outcome. In this case, defection is a dominant strategy for both players. A dominant strategy occurs when a player's choice does not depend on the choice of the opponent. In a PD, if player 1 chooses cooperation, the best strategy for player 2 is to defect and thus receive the temptation value (T > R). If player 1 chooses defection, player 2's best choice is still defection; in this case the choice is much better than being played for a sucker (P > S). The crucial insight of the prisoners' dilemma is that by choosing their dominant strategies, both players do worse than if they chose cooperation (R > P). As will be discussed, the intervener's goal is to change this game so that both sides of a conflict can confidently move to a mutual-reward payoff.

Different preference orderings produce different games and different outcomes. In the "chicken game," the players still value temptation first and reward second, but prefer the sucker value to mutual defection. The preference ordering is thus

$$T > R > S > P$$

As opposed to the PD, the chicken game produces two equilibria. If the players end up in the upper left cell, neither has an incentive to defect. For player 1, moving from cooperation to defection means changing payoffs from sucker to penalty (S > P); for player 2, moving from defection

[10] Henry Hamburger, *Games as Models of Social Phenomena* (San Francisco: W.H. Freeman, 1979), p. 45.

to cooperation produces the reward value instead of the temptation value (T > R). In the lower left cell, the same considerations apply in mirror form. In this case, there is no dominant strategy, as the choice of either player depends on the choice of the other.

Without further information, the chicken game does not predict a unique outcome. In certain situations, however, actors may be playing a more specific strategy that will help predict an outcome. For instance, if both players are trying to avoid the worst outcome, they may adopt a strategy of maximizing the minimum, or maximin. In this case, both players will choose cooperation. Although both will be choosing to forego their most preferred result (T), both will also be avoiding their worst outcomes (P). This strategy fits the stories and applications behind the chicken game. The game is named for a teenage driving game of brinkmanship. Two drivers head for one another and see who will be the first to lose nerve and swerve, thus gaining the title of "chicken." In another application, the game has been used to analyze the Cuban missile crisis. In this type of confrontation, both players wish to maintain or enhance their reputation for toughness and make the other actor "chicken out." However, the penalty for mutual defection, nuclear war for instance, is very high, certainly justifying the transformation of the payoff structure from the prisoners' dilemma.

Games may also be repeated. With a certain structure of cardinal payoffs, the iterated chicken game may suggest a specific outcome in the form of a mixed strategy.

To illustrate one such solution, consider a chicken game with the following set of values:

$$T = 8, R = 4, S = 3, P = 2$$

These values are graphically represented in Figure 4.2.

Assume that the game will be played for ten rounds. In a one-shot game, the players will find themselves either at T1, S2 or at S1, T2. In this case, over the course of the game, one player will end up with 80 points while the other will end up with 30, which would still be better than the 20 points that mutual defection would provide. If they adopt a maximin strategy, they will find themselves at R1, R2 and both end up at 40 points. In the iterated game, though, they can do better yet. If the players can coordinate their strategies and alternate taking the temptation and sucker values, their payoffs will be (1/2(8 + 2)), with each receiving 50 points over the course of the game.[11]

In situations where an intervener is dealing with two sides with divergent interests, the intervener might wish to follow the basic contours of the iterated chicken game. In effect, the intervener convinces the actors to take turns playing

[11] These payoffs and this particular solution are perhaps common to situations of divided societies and consociational government. See George Tsebelis, *Nested Games: Rational Choice and Comparative Politics* (Berkeley: University of California Press, 1990), Chapter 6. I am taking this example specifically from this chapter.

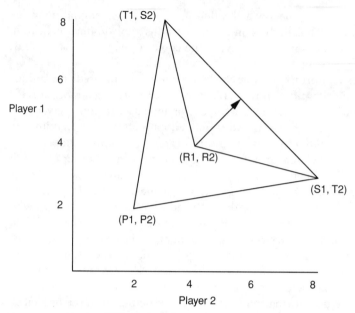

FIGURE 4.2. Iterated Chicken Game.

the other for the "sucker." One side gives in on the issue most important to the other side, while in the next turn the other player does the same.

There is one final game that is relevant to the following discussion of intervention games, usually referred to as the assurance game.[12] In the assurance game, as opposed to the prisoners' dilemma, the players value mutual reward above temptation, so the ordering is

$$R > T > P > S$$

As in PD, actors wish to avoid being suckered. As with chicken, there are two equilibria. If the players end up in the upper left cell, they are both receiving their highest payoff. If they are in the bottom right cell, neither will wish to unilaterally move to cooperation, as he or she would receive the sucker's payoff. Thus the logic of the game is that one wishes to do what the other does. The name "assurance game" derives from a lesson of the game: an actor wishes to move from defection and the P payoff to mutual reward and the R payoff, but only if he or she can be assured that the other player will also do so.

Games can also be represented in N-person forms. In this case, one actor must consider the choices of many other actors. In these games, an individual's payoff is determined by the percentage of actors choosing cooperation or defection.

---

[12] Also called Stag Hunt, after a story told by Rousseau.

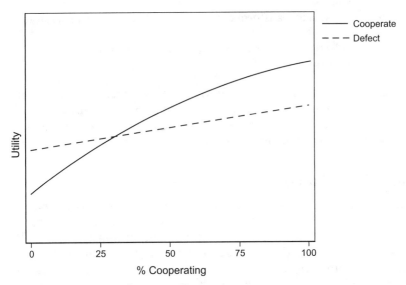

FIGURE 4.3. *N*-Person Assurance Game.

Consider Figure 4.3.[13] The solid line represents the payoff for cooperation and the dotted line for defection. In the *N*-person assurance game, the individual reward for being the first cooperator, that is, choosing cooperation at 0 percent, is very low. As the cooperation line on the figure indicates, the value of cooperation rises as the percentage of cooperation increases. At a certain point, 30 percent in the example provided here, the value of cooperation equals that for defection. This point represents an unstable equilibrium – in more colloquial terms, a "tipping point." If the number of cooperators surpasses this point, the value of cooperation outweighs that of defection. As individuals reassess the comparative values of cooperation and defection, they will choose cooperation, and rapid movement toward the 100 percent cooperation mark can be expected. In another metaphor, the *N*-person assurance game predicts "bandwagoning" effects.

III. INTERVENTION GAMES

Although many possible games can be pertinent to intervention politics, those listed here are particularly relevant. In fact, interventions usually involve a particular sequence of these games:

(1) The first task is ending an *N*-person assurance game and creating the order of a simple prisoners' dilemma.

---

[13] These figures are sometimes called Schelling diagrams from Thomas Schelling, *Micromotives and Macrobehavior* (New York: Gordon and Breach, 1985). See David Laitin, *Identity in Formation: The Russian Speaking Populations in the Near Abroad* (Ithaca, NY: Cornell University Press, 1998) for an extended application to language choice.

(2) The second goal is to transform the prisoners' dilemma into an assurance game.
(3) The third objective is to move the players of the assurance game to the optimal equilibrium.

I call this sequence the *Basic Intervention Game*. This sequence will not apply to all cases of civil violence and intervention, but elements of the game will apply to many, if not most, such cases. This basic sequence can be used as a template for comparison. I discuss the separate steps in the sequence in turn.

A. Ending N-Person Assurance Games

In a broken or failed state, centralized authority has collapsed and a level of anarchy has descended across the country. In her description of the collapse of Yugoslavia, Susan Woodward identifies a certain crucial tipping point: "The turning point in the dissolution of Yugoslavia as it affected endangered individuals, according to their own reports, was when they saw the necessity as families or localities to resort to guns in self-defense."[14] In a strong state, citizens are at the 100 percent cooperation point in Figure 4.3. They trust the state to provide security and other benefits and in return they cooperate with and participate in the state's institutions. If a state begins to unravel and can no longer provide even security, individuals begin to defect from the state and find their own way. In terms of the N-person assurance game diagram, the movement is from right to left. At a certain point, when individuals realize that the bulk of the population is moving toward defection, the "tipping point" is reached in reverse, there is flight to universal defection, and the state collapses. Under these conditions, local militias and other nonstate groups become dominant.

When an intervener enters such a situation, the first order of business is ending this anarchy. The intervention regime tries to attain security and create the belief that a competent state and central authority are coming back into existence. In terms of the assurance game, the intervener needs to generate a level of cooperation that will again pass the tipping point and drive the population toward the stable 100 percent equilibrium.

The logic of the game suggests that the intervener will be able to move individuals past a tipping point if the tipping point itself is low. Looking again at Figure 4.3, the intervention regime can do this by either lowering the value of defection, or raising the value of cooperation. Part of the game at this point is a matter of perception. The task of the intervener or occupier in this situation is one of assurance, as in the name of the game. The incoming intervention government must assure individuals that it is indeed the legitimate authority and that it will be able to provide security to those who cooperate with it. If individuals perceive the incoming regime as stable, they will raise their estimates

[14] Susan Woodward, *Balkan Tragedy* (Washington, DC: Brookings, 1995), p. 391.

of the value of cooperating with it. The intervention government often tries to accomplish this task with several tools. It can put a highly visible security presence on the streets; it can put well-known and legitimate leaders in power; it can arrest former leaders and war criminals (and those who are both) in order to show that a return to the former regime and its potential threats is not possible.

If the tipping point is lowered, a next step for the intervention regime is to convince individuals that significant numbers of others are leaning toward cooperation. The incoming regime will wish to communicate this informa-tion through focal events. One method is to hold elections quickly. If turnout in government elections is high, individuals might surmise that voters equal cooperators and the tipping point has been surpassed.[15] It may then become "common sense" that the incoming regime is legitimate and will be entrenched in the future. Rapid movement to the 100 percent cooperation equilibrium may then occur.

Opponents of intervention will, of course, develop counterstrategies to change the values of cooperation and defection, to prevent the tipping point from being reached, and thus, to maintain membership in or collaboration with local security organizations such as militias. In a few cases, control by nonstate actors becomes institutionalized within certain territories (regions of Afghanistan, for example). In other cases, the new regime struggles for a time but is eventually able to create a sense of inevitability of its control. If it needs to, the intervention regime may eventually cut bargains with opponents and draw them into the new government.

B. Moving to Games of Cooperation

When the incoming regime has gained control, the intervention will often come to resemble one of the 2 × 2 cooperation games described in Section II. Here, the task is working with representatives of the former warring sides to create and solidify a social contract. We can again turn to the basic elements of game theory to analyze this process.

1. Actors. The first question concerns the actors. After a bloody interethnic conflict, who should become the legitimate representatives of their communi-ties? In other words, who gets to play the game?

This question ties into the literature on "spoilers," defined as "leaders and parties whose vital interests are threatened by peace implementation."[16] The leading scholar on this subject, Stephen Stedman, writes:

Peace processes create spoilers.... Peace creates spoilers because it is rare in civil war for all leaders and factions to see peace as beneficial. Even if all parties come to value peace,

---

[15] There are numerous applications of this process to the fall of Communism and to cases of resistance and civil war.

[16] Sambanis and Doyle, *Making War and Building Peace*, p. 57.

they rarely do simultaneously, and they often strongly disagree over the terms of an acceptable peace. A negotiated peace often has losers: leaders and factions who do not achieve their war aims. Nor can every war find a compromise solution that addresses the demands of all the warring parties. For example, the most perfectly crafted power-sharing institutions in the world are useless if one of the parties does not want to share power.[17]

Stedman develops a typology of spoilers. "Limited" spoilers pursue recognition as legitimate political representatives, the acknowledgment of political and social grievances, and power sharing; "total" spoilers have immutable goals that cannot be altered; "greedy" spoilers fall in between, testing the limits and taking what they can get, constantly calculating risks and benefits. Stedman argues that different strategies are necessary for different types of spoilers. Applied to the argument here, only limited spoilers and some greedy spoilers are fit to be actors in games aimed at creating a social contract. The only strategy that can be used against total spoilers is coercion and elimination. Others working on intervention are in basic agreement. Sambanis and Doyle argue that such "spoilers need to be identified and marginalized to the degree possible."[18]

2. *Choices*. After the determination of who gets to play the game, the next issue is deciding what the players get to play about. In preceding discussion, the strategies were simply "cooperate" or "defect." In peace-building operations after destructive conflict, the intervener will structure a game in which players will be forced to cooperate or defect in a number of issue areas. Politically, they will be forced to consider the adoption of a new constitution outlining electoral rules and divisions of power among governmental branches. They will be compelled to negotiate forms of power sharing across territorial boundaries and across political parties. There will be discussions on the composition and competencies of the military and police. The players will need to hammer out agreements on the control of natural resources, the collection of taxes, and the flow of centrally controlled funds. Conforming to Western economic practice and pressures, actors need to settle on control of the economy, the role of private investment, and internal and external rules on trade. Eventually, the players will need to collectively consider their very relationship to the Western intervener who constructed the original game.

The intervener will not allow the players to engage with some issue areas. Building on his advocacy for forceful action against spoilers, Stedman summarizes one of his primary findings: "In this study successful management of internal conflict has resulted from the willingness of external actors to take sides as to which demands and grievances are legitimate and which are not."[19]

---

[17] Stephen John Stedman, "Spoiler Problems in Peace Processes," *International Security* (1997) 22: 5–53. Passage is from pp. 7–8.
[18] Sambanis and Doyle, *Making War and Building Peace*, p. 59.
[19] Stedman, "Spoiler Problems in Peace Processes," p. 52.

On other issues, the key question relates to the sequencing of issues. In the transition from Communism in the states north of the Balkans, the government took on a wide range of issues simultaneously. In several cases, reformers pushed for a "big bang" or some form of "shock therapy" that would prevent the possibility of sliding back into the old system. In cases characterized by higher levels of violence and ethnic diversity, "big bang" solutions are less feasible and the debate will center on the sequencing of issues.

There are several major theories about sequencing.[20] One school sees the problem as the lack of trust between the players. Accordingly, interveners should start with the least contentious issues, preferably ones that will exhibit tangible and visible results. For example, players A and B could cooperate on sewage and garbage removal. After dialogue is established and visible results are created that might bolster the actors' reputations in the eyes of their respective communities, the game can move on to more difficult issues. Eventually, with a reservoir of trust, the most problematic issues, such as the composition and jurisdiction of the police, can be put on the table. Often, this strategy is first implemented on local levels where both issues of pressing need and the possibility of quiet dialogue exist. The OSCE has long advocated and applied such practice. In Bosnia, for example, as part of its Democratization Department, the OSCE ran workshops on local governance. The workshops required locals from formerly warring groups to physically meet for the first time since the conflict ended. At this local level, the master narrative of Bosnian ethnic conflict would be less relevant to the issues at hand. As one report summarized, "As long as major Bosnian political parties are delineated by ethnicity, political competition among parties will equate to zero-sum ethnic conflict. Only through continued opportunities to build interethnic confidence sufficiently so that compromise does not mean a threat to a 'national interest' can Bosnian democracy progress."[21]

Roland Paris presents another argument on sequencing. He points out that the major elements of the Western liberal politics, democracy and capitalism, depend on competition in the form of elections, free markets, and an unfettered media. In broken states, society is not ready for this competition.[22] Paris writes in response to those urging rapid and simultaneous reforms, "But stimulating political and economic contestation in places that *already* suffer from intense societal conflicts can be dangerous, particularly if democratization spurs destructive forms of political mobilization, including 'bad civil

---

[20] For an overview of issues related to sequencing, see Edward Mansfield and Jack Snyder, "The Sequencing 'Fallacy,'" *Journal of Democracy* (2007) 18: 5–10.

[21] James S. Rogan, "Facilitating Local Multiethnic Governance in Postwar Bosnia and Hercegovina," in Nenad Dimitrijevic ed., *Managing Multiethnic Communities in the Countries of the Former Yugoslavia* (Budapest: Open Society Institute, 2000), pp. 183–206; quoted passage is from p. 200.

[22] Samuel Huntington, *Political Order in Changing Societies* (New Haven, CT: Yale University Press, 1968). Paris discusses Huntington's argument in *At War's End* on pp. 185–7.

society,' ethnic entrepreneurship, polarization, and violence."[23] Without strong institutions, the previous battles may simply be fought by the old actors in new forms – nationalist political parties, colluding monopolies and organized crime, and media spouting hate speech.[24] The solution is to build strong institutions before liberalizing (Institutions Before Liberalization or IBL, as Paris terms it). Paris's view of the dangers of societies in transition is supported by scholars both old and new. As he notes, Paris is following the outlines of Samuel Huntington's *Political Order in Changing Societies*. Huntington argued that without the development of corresponding political institutions, unfettered and newly mobilized social forces can rip developing societies apart. More recently, Jack Snyder and Edward Mansfield have made a similar argument about new democracies and war. For many of the same reasons discussed by Paris, they find that societies in transition to democracy are more likely than either stable democracies or autocracies to engage in war.

Accordingly, Paris proposes that the most competitive aspects of the intervention game be delayed until the rules of the game have been firmly established to control and properly direct that competition. The institutions that will establish the rule of law and fair play, and should be addressed immediately, are the police, the judiciary and a constitutional court, and economic regulatory bodies capable of redistributing goods to the more vulnerable segments of the population. The elements of liberal reform that should be postponed are elections, complete free speech, and free markets.

A third type of sequencing of issues has already been addressed in the form of the iterated chicken game. In situations where the parties care deeply about different issues, the intervener can attempt to arrange a "tit for tat" dynamic where the players "lose" in one round in order to "win" in the next.

3. Arranging Payoff Structures. The Western intervener will try to create a game on terms that will lead to the introduction of a desired social contract among groups and between groups and the state. As addressed in the previous two sections, the intervener will try first to limit the game to cooperative actors, and second to control the order of plays in the game. The third aspect of manipulation is about arranging the game's payoffs.

The previous analysis of games suggests a two-step process to accomplish this goal. The first step would entail transforming a PD into an assurance game. Recall that the assurance game has two equilibria – mutual defection and mutual cooperation. The second step would be ensuring that the players end up at the mutual reward equilibrium.

There are two ways that an intervener can execute the first step. Recall that the preference ordering of the PD is $T > R > P > S$ and that of the assurance game is $R > T > P > S$. In one method, the intervener can work to

---

[23] Paris, *At War's End*, p. 169

[24] Edward D. Mansfield and Jack Snyder, "Democratization and War," *Foreign Affairs* (May–June 1995) 74 (3): 79–97.

increase the value of cooperation, thus raising R above T. The intervener can achieve this change through selective financial payoffs, increased representation in government bodies, and other inducements. In a second method, the intervener can attach penalties for defection, thus lowering the value of T below R. Such penalties might be exclusion of the actor from certain government arenas, withholding of funds, or threats to charge leaders with crimes, even war crimes in some cases. In fact, many analysts of intervention see the situation as a PD and make recommendations along the lines discussed. Doyle and Sambanis write, "Multilateral peace operations can help shape the parties' incentives to cooperate in peace implementation by increasing the costs of defection from agreement through selective enforcement and by providing financial and other inducements to those who cooperate."[25]

The question still remains of how to move the players to the R, R equilibrium of the assurance game. The players might be convinced to move simultaneously. If players have reached a "hurting stalemate" in their mutual struggle, they may be ready and willing to move toward the possibility of higher rewards through mutual cooperation. In this case, all that is necessary is for the intervener to be able to assure one player that the other will also move. In other situations, the ability to provide such confidence may be absent. In that case, if one player moves to cooperation while the other remains at defection, the first-acting player will be saddled with the sucker payoff. The intervener can encourage one player to take chances by reducing the cost of exploitation. If one actor does play the other for a sucker, the intervener can provide compensation through financial or political payments.

It should be noted that the intervener's tactics toward payoffs and toward the selection of actors should not always be considered two separate steps. In Paris' sequential design, the intervener should use its control of resources and payoffs to weed out spoilers. As Paris advises:

By resisting calls for early elections, peacebuilders can allow passions to cool with the passage of time. International agencies can also use inducements and punishments – carrots and sticks – to encourage the rise of new moderate parties and leaders in the period leading up to elections. These inducements may include significant financial support to parties that publicly eschew violence and violent rhetoric and make concerted efforts to gain popular support from voters across communal lines. Punishments may include the banning of parties that preach violence or hatred from participating in elections.[26]

4. *The Eventual Transformation of the Game.* Game theorists make a distinction between two types of games – cooperation games and coordination games. In situations resembling a coordination game, no player has an incentive to deviate unilaterally and the players would prefer to coordinate on any

[25] Doyle and Sambanis, *Making War and Building Peace*, p. 45.
[26] Paris, *At War's End*, p. 189.

one common strategy rather than not to coordinate at all.[27] For interveners, the eventual goal is to reach such a point. When a social contract has been established, the players neither wish to exploit an opponent nor fear dire consequences of being exploited. Rather, they follow established rules and live in full expectation of being able to exercise rights. As Doyle and Sambanis sum up, "Truly successful contemporary peacebuilding changes not merely behavior but, more importantly, it transforms identities and institutional context. More than reforming play in an old game, it changes the game."[28]

In time, iterated structured contact or games among former enemies might create norms of behavior that rule out violence and noncooperation. In effect, the intervener, or custodian, using sticks and carrots, socializes the groups in conflict. As Stephen Stedman writes:

The strategy of socialization requires custodians to establish a set of norms for acceptable behavior by internal parties who commit to peace or external parties who seek to join a peace process. These norms then become the basis for judging the demands of the parties (are they legitimate or not?) and the behaviors of the parties (are they acceptable in the normative framework?). In turn, this strategy relies on two components to elicit normatively acceptable behavior: the material and the intellectual. The material component involves custodians carefully calibrating the supply of carrots and sticks to reward and punish the spoiler. The intellectual component emphasizes regular persuasion by custodians of the value of the desired normative behavior. Normative standards can include commitment to the rules of democratic competition and adherence to the protection of human rights.[29]

In sum, the theory behind Western intervention is based on two mechanisms of human behavior – the rational choices relating to sticks and carrots, mainly, but also an eventual role for norms.

IV. CONCLUSIONS

Despite a nod to normative mechanisms, Western theorists and practitioners alike primarily approach interventions as a matter of arranging games and manipulating sticks and carrots. Engineering reason-based social contracts is a Western tradition. Centuries ago, Locke believed that "Reason discovers God's will" and that by using reason human society could develop social contracts among factions that would preserve the lives, freedom, and property of all, as they belong to each under natural law. Important institutions today still echo those words.

Western interveners usually possess a level of wealth and force that local actors cannot match. Armed with these advantages, the intervener then establishes a "game." These games assume similar elements. First, there should

---

[27] The most commonly cited two-player coordination game is probably "Battle of the Sexes." For discussion of this game see Elster, *Explaining Social Behavior*, pp. 323–6.

[28] Doyle and Sambanis, *Making War and Building Peace*, pp. 312–13.

[29] Stedman, "Spoiler Problems in Peace Processes," p. 13.

be a legitimate, recognized set of players. These players should only be able to choose from a limited strategy set. Actors' preferences are assumed to be transparent, stable, and fairly easily ranked. In practice, Western interveners generally assume that the actors hold restricted sets of preferences centered on safety and economics.

The next chapter will illustrate how opponents work to undermine these games through the use of emotion resources. It will provide insights for hypotheses construction seen in the sixth chapter.

5

The Strategic Use of Emotions, II

*Developing Strategies; Examples
from Non-Balkan Cases*

INTRODUCTION

The previous chapter addressed the structure of the "games" set up by Western interveners. Although these games take different forms, they rest on some common assumptions about actors, preferences, and strategies. First, there should be a stable set of recognized players. Second, these players should put interests, in the form of material and political gains, before revenge or forms of identity politics. Third, the contestants in this game should choose only among a limited range of strategies determined by the intervener.

Opponents of intervention games believe that they can strategically use emotions to alter each of these three fundamental game elements. This chapter will address how opponents use emotions as resources to alter (1) preferences, (2) actors, and (3) strategies. In a fourth section, the chapter will discuss how the distribution of emotions can also serve as a constraint on action as well as a resource.

The last sections discuss one type of provocation, the planting of bombs. Bombing surely involves emotions. The examples will show how actors calculate and calibrate the emotions involved with this tactic. I will also be providing illustrations from non-Balkan cases to demonstrate the general nature of these points.

I. CHANGING PREFERENCES: WRECKING
THE BASIC INTERVENTION GAME

Recall the discussion of the Basic Intervention Game from the previous chapter. Once security in the country has been established, the game becomes a prisoners' dilemma. The intervener's goal is to transform the PD into an assurance game by raising the value of mutual reward (R) over temptation (T). This can be accomplished through changing the payoff structure of economic and political rewards for cooperation and/or lowering the value of the temptation payoff (T).

Opponents of intervention may counter by using emotions to shape preference orderings in ways that block the intervener's goals in the Basic Game. Political entrepreneurs will employ methods, often provocations, to unleash emotions that are able to disrupt the Basic Game. As will be outlined, some of these emotions raise tolerance for mutual defection, some heighten the desire to avoid being suckered, some create a strong desire to try to sucker the opponent, and some orient the player to deny an opponent a reward or a higher status. These emotions can be considered in turn.

First, the emotion of contempt raises the value of mutual defection (P). Contempt creates a desire for avoidance of a stigmatized opponent. Under the sway of contempt, the player simply does not wish to engage the opponent at all. Mutual defection is an acceptable outcome. If the situation involves a stigmatized opponent, political entrepreneurs will be able to pursue policies of separation and defection. Because contempt does not possess a half-life, political entrepreneurs can always rely on this emotion to mitigate the values of integration-oriented "carrots" offered by the intervener in the Basic Game.

Second, anger can be injected into the game to create a strong desire for retaliation. A political entrepreneur of group A can hit the opposing group B with a discriminate attack. In response, anger in group B drives demand for a counterattack. With a spiral of violence in place, both sides will devalue cooperation. Under the influence of anger, players will accept the cost of mutual defection (P); they may also relish any opportunity to gain advantage over the opponent, driving up the value of temptation (T).

Third, political entrepreneurs can create fears in opposing groups through the use of indiscriminate violence. When fear is present, individuals may come to obsess about safety. The B and C effects of fear funnel information and distort beliefs in ways that enhance fear's grip. In terms of the PD payoffs, fear creates a desire to avoid the sucker (S) payoff at all costs. The best way to do this in the context of a PD is to defect. With high levels of fear, the intervener is unlikely to be able to transform a prisoner's dilemma into an assurance game, as an obsessive concern to avoid the S payoff will still prevent movement from the lower right equilibrium to the upper left equilibrium.

Fourth, if status reversals have occurred, political actors can employ resentment to stall the Basic Game. The mutual reward payoff will often involve all sides committing to a new set of political relationships and institutions. Formerly dominant groups will likely resent their position in this new order. Political entrepreneurs will be able to build on these resentments to devalue the R payoff. In a situation of status reversal, being played for a sucker by former subordinates (S), or even cooperating with them as equals (R), may involve perceptions of unjust subordination. Imbued with resentment, actors would rather endure the costs of mutual defection (P) than cooperate.

Resentment can be compared to spite, an emotion briefly mentioned in the second chapter. With resentment, it is the relative standing of the players that matters. The formerly dominant actor wishes to maintain a superior position. Under the influence of spite, individuals simply cannot tolerate the success or happiness of an opponent. Spite is about the absolute payoff to the opponent, not relative positions. The spiteful actor desires to bring the opponent's payoff to as low a level as possible.[1] Furthermore, the spiteful players will wish to make it clear that they have denied opponents a possible reward. In either the prisoners' dilemma or the assurance game preference ordering, a spiteful actor would most wish to impose the sucker payoff on an opponent. If this is not possible, as it usually is not, then the spiteful player will wish to impose the next lowest payoff, that of penalty. In an assurance game, those filled with spite would prefer to remain at mutual defection rather than to move to the equilibrium of mutual reward, despite the rewards offered by the intervener.[2]

Game theorists base their method on a concept of rationality that assumes actors' preferences are fixed. Acting on this assumption, interveners try to change the preference orderings of players by increasing or decreasing what players already value, usually narrow economic and political goods. Opponents of the regime believe that they can change preference orderings by using or interjecting emotions into the game. Chapter 2 discussed the A effects of emotion. Perhaps the primary political aspect of emotion is its ability to heighten the saliency of a particular concern, to act as a "switch" among a set of basic desires. Intervention opponents often work to flip this switch.

II. CHANGING ACTORS

Western academic thought on identity is dominated by the idea that identities are constructed and fluid. Likewise, Western intervention practitioners often hope to construct identities in ways conducive to peace. The intervention in Rwanda provides an example. In Rwanda, references to Hutu and Tutsi are discouraged in favor of a broader common Rwandan identity. In constructing this new identity, interveners encourage the creation of a new common narrative of history that both groups can accept. In cases where new identities are impossible to construct, the intervener tries, at least, to construct or strengthen hyphenated identities – Iraqi-Shiite, Iraqi-Kurd, Iraqi-Sunni, for example – that provide common identification with the state.[3]

Opponents of intervention often believe that existing identities are rooted in powerful histories and experiences. They may see hyphenated identities as weak and exploitable.

---

[1] In *Games as Models of Social Phenomena* (San Francisco: W. H. Freeman, 1971), Henry Hamburger outlines a game entitled "spite." In this version, the spiteful actor is modeled as having a preference function of a difference maximizer. The player receives utility from the difference, not the lower absolute value for the opponent. As Hamburger notes, the game bends the notion of utility. See pp. 87–8.

[2] Spite can also be related to the Ultimatum game, although that game brings in notions of fairness that are beyond the more reactive emotion I am developing here.

[3] For a discussion of state manipulation of identities, see Daniel Byman, "Forever Enemies?: The Manipulation of Ethnic Identities to End Ethnic Wars," *Security Studies* (Spring 2000) 9: 149–90. In a comparison of four cases in the Middle East, Byman finds that identity manipulation is possible but long-term and intensive.

Consider a simple abstract case. Two ethnic groups, X and Y, exist within the state of Z. Five possible identities result. One can identify solely with an ethnic group (X or Y); one can identify with both the broader state identity and an ethnic group (XZ or YZ); one can identify with just the state (Z). Ethnic civil war implies a narrowing of the range of identities until only Xs face off against Ys. An example can be seen in the former Yugoslavia. In the late 1980s, individuals in Bosnia could identify as Yugoslavs, Bosnians, Bosnian-Muslims, Bosnian-Serbs, Bosnian-Croats, Muslims, Serbs, or Croats. Progressively, the range of identities narrowed. With the collapse of the central state, the Yugoslav identity failed to make sense. With increased polarization and voting along ethnic lines, the Bosnian identity waned. With the outbreak of violence along ethnic lines, hybrid identities were difficult to hold. In the end, "Muslim," "Serb," and "Croat" were the only viable identities in an ethnic civil war.

The question here is about changing the nature of the actors in the Western intervention game. The intervener will wish to legitimize actors identifying with the new state (the Zs) or, more realistically, work with hyphenated actors, the XZs and YZs. Such actors would represent their groups, but they would also be ready to find common ground. Given their common identification with the state, the structured interactions of the PD or assurance game might be expected to help bring such players more readily to mutual cooperation.

The opponents of intervention may develop a counterstrategy. They can use emotions to narrow the possible range of identities. If political entrepreneurs can eliminate the capacity for individuals to identify with the state, either as the primary characteristic (Z) or as a hyphenated one (XZ) or (YZ), the only actors remaining will be those who primarily identify with their own group: Xs will face off against Ys.

The most obvious strategies for accomplishing this goal would involve the generation of anger or fear. To recall from previous chapters, anger heightens the desire for punishment against a specific actor; fear may create a desire for fight that is less focused than in anger, or it may create a desire for flight from the dangerous circumstances (A effects). Anger creates a downgrading of risk; fear increases risk aversion (C effects). Anger increases prejudice and blame, as well as selective memory; fear biases information collection through overemphasis on dangers (B effects). In experimental research, participants with a strong sense of in-group are more likely to feel anger against out-groups. Likewise, fear levels can be manipulated by categorizing victims as in-group or out-group.

Let us assume that insurgent leaders possess an intuitive knowledge of the findings of social science on emotion and that they also know how to trigger emotions in their own societies. How would a leader use bombings to generate emotions to foment ethnic civil war? Referring back to the simple example already discussed, given a range of identities, X, Y, XZ, YZ, Z, who should be killed, and how, in order to create emotions that leave only identities X and Y standing in a mutual hostility? Three possibilities come to mind:

Strategy 1: From the position of an insurgent leader of X, one strategy would be to target Y (not YZ) in order to generate *anger*. Members of Y already have a clear identity and will interpret the attack as a blameworthy action of X. Under the influence of anger, Y members are more likely to think in stereotypes and more ready to blame. They will look for specific and unambiguous X targets in order to punish X. Under anger, members of Y will downgrade the risks involved in revenge attacks and will be more likely to rush to commit violence.

The X leader hopes that Y will hit some XZ targets in its response. However, even if it does not, members of X will respond, again under the influence of anger, against Y. A spiral will occur that is likely to affect the entire society. At a certain level of death, XZ and YZ may find it difficult (for reasons of interest or norms of solidarity) to maintain a common link.

Strategy 2: The insurgent leader of X will strike against YZ instead of Y. It would be easier to inflict high casualty figures against this more diffuse and less defended target. The goal is to generate *fear* in YZs. Under fear created by bombings, YZs will overestimate personal danger levels and flee to more homogeneous Y areas. Under fear, YZs will become more risk-averse, again heightening flight. There will be demographic separation of YZs from X and XZ.

Strategy 3: The insurgent leader may strike against a host of targets, not only Y and YZ, but also XZ. The strategy here attempts to develop such frustration in the population that a general level of dissatisfaction and tendency toward aggression pervade the entire social system. Under these conditions, the central government is likely to become discredited. Crucially, the very concept of a Z identity becomes delegitimated. Without a legitimate Z identity, there will not be a legitimate XZ or YZ identity, not to mention a stand-alone Z identity.

Strategy 3 aims to create *rage*. The emotion of rage, as defined earlier, differs from the other listed emotions because it has no specific cognitive antecedent. That is, there are so many negative actions occurring over an extended time period that no single specific actor or set of events can be specifically or logically blamed for one's frustrations. Instead, there is simply a desire to lash out, even more than in the fight sense of fear. There is also a tendency to try to find scapegoats. For various reasons, a society gripped by various frustrations and the resulting emotion of rage is likely to become dysfunctional and break into ethnic or regional components.

One of the best-known examples of strategy 1 is the effort by Abu Musab al-Zarqawi, the leader of al-Qaeda in Iraq, to foment civil war between Sunnis and Shiites.

Here is a description of his strategy, based largely on a captured letter of al-Zarqawi:

As Zarqawi described in his letter and subsequent broadcasts, his strategy in Iraq is to strike at the Shia – and therefore provoke a civil war. "A nation of heretics," the Shia "are the key element of change," he wrote. "If we manage to draw them onto the terrain of partisan war, it will be possible to tear the Sunnis away from their heedlessness, for they will feel the weight of the imminence of danger." Again, a strategy of provocation – which plays on an underlying reality: that Iraq sits on the crucial sectarian fault line of the Middle East and that a conflict there gains powerful momentum from the involvement of neighboring states, with Iran strongly supporting the Shia and with Saudi Arabia, Kuwait, Jordan, and Syria strongly sympathetic to the Sunnis. More and more, you can discern this outline in the chaos of the current war, with the Iranian-trained militias of the Shia Islamist parties that now control the Iraqi government battling Sunni Islamists, both Iraqi and foreign-born, and former Baathists.[4]

Although many types of killings and bombings depend on local incentives and constraints, the timing of elections, and other specific factors, al-Zarqawi's targets followed the general logic of creating anger and spiraling violence, at least in early renditions.[5] The target set included motorcades of specific Shiite political figures. Insurgents attacked the Islamic Dawa Party, car-bombed Sadr's office in the Shuala district of Baghdad, and hit police stations associated with Shiite dominance in Karada, Saydiyah, and other towns. One summary statement written in May 2005 read, "Political leaders fear that insurgents have intensified their campaign to drive a wedge between Sunnis and Shiites and that they are trying to ignite a civil war. Last month, Shiite leaders accused the largest Shiite militia force of complicity in the killing of Sunni clerics."[6] The key aspect here is the targeting of ethnic elites rather than softer, mass targets. The idea behind strategy 1 is to anger those who already have a clear ethnic identity in order to produce retaliation and begin a spiral of violence. It is the political and security elites who are most able to retaliate violently and set the spiral in motion. Several June 2005 reports of violence describe revenge killings of Sunni in response to killings of or attacks on Shiites.[7]

Certainly, the bombing of the golden dome in Samarra in February 2006 fits the strategy. The shrine was central to Shiite identity. The quotations given to reporters after the bombing are textbook responses to an anger-based strategy:

"The war could really be on now," says Abu Hassan, a Shiite street peddler who declined to give his full name. "This is something greater and more symbolic than attacks on people. This is a strike at who we are."[8]

"If I could find the people who did this, I would cut him to pieces," said Abdel Jaleel al-Sudani, a 50-year-old employee of the Health Ministry, who said he had marched in

---

[4] Mark Danner, "Taking Stock of the Forever War," *New York Times*, September 11, 2005.
[5] I am basing this judgment on data collected from my research assistant Jessica Karnis, who compiled a list of bombings based on information and descriptions from *Iraq Body Count*, the *New York Times*, and other sources.
[6] Richard Oppel and Sabrina Tavernise, with Warzer Jaff and Layla Istifan, "Car Bombings in Iraq Kill 33, with Shiites as Targets," *New York Times*, May 24, 2005.
[7] See for example, John Burns, "Three Car Bombs Leave 18 Dead and 46 Hurt in a Shiite Suburb of Baghdad," *New York Times*, June 23, 2005.
[8] Dan Murphy, "Attack Deepens Iraq's Divide," *Christian Science Monitor*, February 23, 2006.

a demonstration earlier. "I would rather hear of the death of a friend, than to hear this news."[9]

Within hours of the attack, thousands of Shiites took to the streets in protest, many of them brandishing arms. Over twenty Sunni mosques were burned in retaliation.[10]

Iraqi opponents of the insurgency recognize the emotion-based strategies of Zarqawi. After these bombings, a prominent disciple of Grand Ayatollah Ali al-Sistani told worshippers that "Submitting to one's passion and confusion will bring us to domestic sedition and eventually lead us to failure. We must go forward, be patient, and carry on building the new Iraq."[11] Likewise, political leaders such as Prime Minister Ibrahim al-Jaafari called for a "rational, political" struggle.[12] The call for rational action is accompanied by faith in the progress of political evolution and inclusion. Leaders also try to constantly frame the conflict in terms of "criminal terrorists" versus "Iraqis" in their own effort to create or solidify identities and thus prevent polarization and civil war. In the short run, the appeals seemed to fall on deaf ears.

As the general population began to protect itself through demographic separation, the bombing strategy began to change and incorporate more indiscriminate targets that would serve to heighten fear and further flight. Insurgents bombed larger groups of nonelite Shiites. The bombings were still aimed at Shiites, but the attacks were more numerous, more directed at civilians, and organized to kill larger numbers of people. As one observer summarized in September 2005, "Much of the violence is directed at Shias, the victims usually being ordinary members of the public with no particular involvement in politics."[13] In September, Zarqawi is quoted as stating, "Al-Qaeda Organization in Iraq . . . has declared war against Shi'ites in all of Iraq."[14] The statement was cited on a day when bombs killed 114 and wounded 156.

III. CHANGING STRATEGIES: PUTTING VIOLENCE BACK ON THE TABLE

Interveners will wish to restrict the strategy sets of the players to choices related to economic and political issues. Boycotts should be off the table. More importantly, there is usually a red line drawn against violent strategies. Opponents

[9] Edward Wong, "Blast Destroys Golden Dome of Sacred Shiite Shrine in Iraq," *New York Times*, February 22, 2006.

[10] The *Christian Science Monitor* put the number at 29, whereas the *New York Times* provided a number of 25 mosques "burned, taken over or attacked with a variety of weapons."

[11] The quoted passage is from Borzou Daragahi, "Sunni, Shiite Cleric Press for Calm," *Boston Globe*, September 17, 2005.

[12] "Iraq Prime Minister Condemns Bombings," Associated Press, September 14, 2005.

[13] Hussein Ali, "Sectarian Violence Rocks Al-Amiriyah," Institute for War and Peace Reporting, September 13, 2005.

[14] Reuters, September 14, 2005.

can work to provoke violence, draw actors into violent spirals, and, in the process, diminish the credibility of the interveners.

The essential resource in this strategy is the emotion of anger. One player imbues the opposing player with an emotion that essentially compels self-destructive actions. Even if the opposing player realizes the trap, anger produces such a desire for retaliation and punishment that self-constraint is not possible.

In mainstream political science, many works aim to explain these escalatory spirals. The standard approaches, unsurprisingly, leave out any reference to emotion. This section makes an extended comparison between one particular but representative rational choice account of escalation and the emotions-based approach.

Several works address the decision of extremists to initiate terrorist strategies. I will use Ethan Bueno de Mesquita and Eric Dickson's article "Propaganda of the Deed: Terrorism, Counterterrorism, and Mobilization"[15] for comparative purposes, as it explicitly addresses the idea "that terrorists use violence to provoke governments into harsh and indiscriminate responses in order to radicalize and mobilize a population."[16] Several other works could have been used.[17]

Bueno de Mesquita and Dickson's model (hereafter referred to as BD) can be broken down in terms of the rational choice cycle laid out in Figure 2.1:

Actors: In BD, there are three actors. The extremists start the game by deciding whether to play terrorism/no terrorism. The government then decides to respond with either discriminate or indiscriminate counterterrorism. The "aggrieved population," that is the population associated with the extremists, then decides whether to radicalize (support the extremists) or not to radicalize (support the moderates). Neither the population associated with the government nor the moderate leaders of the aggrieved population are actors in this model.

Preferences: Extremists want to become the leaders of their groups. The government wants to stop terrorism. There are two types of government actors, differentiated by preferences: soft-liners wish to stop terrorism, but with a minimum of suffering of the aggrieved population; hard-liners do not care much about the hardship that counterterrorism measures create for the aggrieved population. Hard-liners will not hesitate to use indiscriminate violence; soft-liners will use indiscriminate violence only when circumstances do not allow discriminate means. The aggrieved population has preferences based on economic goods (although BD recognize a range in idiosyncratic preferences for and against armed conflict).

---

[15] Ethan Bueno de Mesquita and Eric Dickson, "The Propaganda of the Deed: Terrorism, Counterterrorism, and Mobililization," *American Journal of Political Science* (April 2007) 51: pp. 364–81.

[16] Ibid, p. 364.

[17] For example, see Andrew Kydd and Barbara Walter, "Sabotaging the Peace: The Politics of Extremist Violence," *International Organization* (Spring 2002) 56: 263–96.

Information Processing and Belief Formation: As with all rational choice
models, information collection is not skewed. Actors compare the costs
and benefits of their choices and collect the proper information to do so.
There is uncertainty, however, in the BD model in that the extremists and
the aggrieved population do not know whether the government is soft-
line or hard-line. That information is only revealed after counterterrorism
methods are in place, and then only if soft-liners feel conditions allow for
discriminate means. Under some conditions, both hard-line and soft-line
governments will employ indiscriminate measures.

The Puzzles: Why does the aggrieved population decide to radicalize and
support the extremists after they initiate terrorism, even understanding
that terrorism will diminish their economic level? Why do they not act as
a brake on the terrorist violence that sets off unwanted retaliation?

There are three parts to BD's answer. All counterterrorism measures damage
the economy of the aggrieved population. Once terrorist violence has been initiated and counterterrorism measures have been instituted in response, the
economy of the aggrieved population declines significantly. At that point,
they have less to lose by supporting terrorism, due to lower opportunity
costs.

Second, given the uncertainty about the government's type assumed in the
model, the aggrieved population cannot know whether the government is soft-
line or hard-line. If the government is seen as hard-line and unconcerned with
the welfare of the aggrieved population, then refraining from violence will not
necessarily bring economic rewards. Only when the government's response
indicates that it is a soft-line actor willing to be a useful future negotiating
partner does the aggrieved population decide not to radicalize, to withhold
support, and possibly to condemn the extremist's terrorist play. In that case,
the population will see that its economic interests lie in peaceful cooperation
with the government rather than the diminished economic state under counterterrorism measures. In this case, the anticipation of future rewards from the
soft-line government will outweigh the effect of diminished opportunity costs.
There will then be a backlash against the extremists. Only if the extremists
anticipate the aforementioned outcome do they forego terrorism.

Third, there is a commitment problem. There is still the basic mystery of
these types of events – why, in most scenarios of the model, does a rational,
economically maximizing, moderate population end up supporting extremists
who diminish its economic level? Buena de Mesquita and Dickson offer a
standard rational choice answer, which is worth quoting at length:

By engaging in terrorism, the extremists have taken actions which leave the aggrieved
population strictly worse off (due to economic damage), and yet the extremists' pop-
ularity increases within that population. Why should members of the population put
up with this state of affairs rather than blaming the extremists and bolstering support
for the moderate faction instead? The answer lies in the commitment problem that the
population faces. It would be in the population's interest if individuals could commit to

punishing the extremists for sparking a cycle of violence that had a deleterious impact on the population's welfare. But they lack the means to make such a commitment. Consequently, when the time comes to decide whom to support, the diminished economic opportunities caused by the counterterrorism response make the members of the population inclined toward direct struggle against the government, leading them to support the extremist faction, even though this faction's earlier actions diminished the aggrieved population's welfare.[18]

Most fundamentally, an emotions-based alternative approach assumes that actors who escalate violence believe that bombings likely to kill noncombatants will produce an emotional response. These political entrepreneurs anticipate that response and calibrate the nature of their violence to precipitate a specific emotional effect. Based on this fundamental point, the approach here differs from the standard rational choice approaches in terms of assumptions at almost every stage of an action cycle.

First, as opposed to BD, these political entrepreneurs have more than just a binary choice between terrorism and no terrorism. It is the terrorists, in BD's terms, rather than the government, who choose among a range of discriminate or indiscriminate actions. As the cases in the next section show, there is a tremendous range in bomb-planting strategies, from highly discriminate attacks that aim to avoid killing anyone, to discriminate attacks on combatants, to indiscriminate attacks that try to maximize carnage. The political entrepreneur has at least four choices: indiscriminate violence meant to create fear; discriminate violence aimed at producing anger; highly discriminate violence aimed at affecting political outcomes with a minimum of emotion; and foregoing violence.

Second, for the emotions-based approach, one of the key actors is often the "nonaggrieved population" or the population associated with government in BD's model. For BD, this population plays no role. Political entrepreneurs will attack this population, knowing that its anger or fear will compel governments of all types to act, and often act harshly. BD wonder about the commitment problem of the aggrieved population and why they do not constrain their extremists. But the question should also be asked of the other population: why do individuals in the nonaggrieved population not restrain their leaders from engaging in counterproductive indiscriminate counterterrorism actions? Why do they not restrain them from initiating responses leading to spiraling violence? An approach based on emotion has a ready answer – the population is angry, and under the influence of anger they are driven to seek to punish. Under the influence of anger they engage in stereotyping and blame groups. Imbued with anger, they cease to collect information that differentiates moderates from extremists. They fail to consider long-term calculations and demand that their leaders respond immediately and forcefully. It is not the commitment problem at work; rather it is a problem of justice and vengeance.

---

[18] Buena de Mesquita and Dickson, "The Propaganda of the Deed," p. 375.

Third, the extremists likewise count on the emotions, especially the anger, of their own population. They anticipate that the population will react emotionally to the use of force by the government. They anticipate that their population will downgrade the value of economic goods and upgrade the desire for resistance and revenge. They predict that violence against their group will provide unity and stereotyping of the opponent. Again, the commitment problem is not what drives action; individuals themselves push for a response.

Fourth, related to this last point, preferences should not be treated as inflexible. In almost all rational choice models of escalation, there is a division between moderates and extremists. After an event of mass killing, will the preferences of these groups really be so different? Will anger or fear not shape the moderates' preference function for a violent response in a way that resembles, at least temporarily, that of nonmoderates? When a group's members become victims of a violent attack, the tendency is often for group divisions to temporarily subside. There is a power to group identity in these moments that makes treatment of "group" at least as important as treatment of the group's subdivisions.

In the study of provocation, the most analyzed case is almost certainly the Palestinian–Israeli conflict. After periods of violence in that case, polls have consistently shown support for a violent response. For instance, in a March 2004 poll, 87.4% of Palestinians backed armed attacks against Israeli soldiers, 85.8% supported hitting Israeli settlers, and 53.1% supported violent attacks against Israeli citizens inside Israel. On the other side, Israelis overwhelmingly backed targeted assassination (even if with significant collateral killing), invasion of areas designated as Palestinian in the Oslo process, and the use of heavy armor.[19] As one Palestinian observer summarizes, "it seems that for the short-term needs, high threat perception among Palestinians elicits a highly emotional and hard-line response. However, when dealing with long-term issues, rational thinking prevails among the Palestinians, even in the midst of their pain and suffering."[20] It is exactly this short-term, emotional need that political entrepreneurs count on when initiating a violent strategy. Rational choice approaches often set up a puzzle in terms of the question of why moderate populations support extremist actions.[21] The answer is that they want to, if only in the short run.

---

[19] For the Palestinian figures, see PSR poll #11, March 2004, www.pcpsr.org. For the Israeli figures, see Asher Arian, "Israeli Public Opinion on National Security," Jaffe Center for Strategic Studies. I am taking these figures, as well as the quotation in the same paragraph, from Boaz Atzilli, "Complex Spiral of Escalation: The Case of the Israeli-Palestinian Conflict," unpublished paper, 2004.

[20] Khalil Shikaki, "Palestinian Public Opinion and the al Aqsa Intifada," *Strategic Assessment* (June 2002) 5 (1): 15–20.

[21] In another oft-cited rational choice approach, Andrew Kydd and Barbara Walter also address this question, again employing the Israeli–Palestine case. Kydd and Walter's model focuses on whether the government sees the moderate leader of the aggrieved population (using BD's terminology) as a trustworthy negotiating partner. In this work, extremist violence often makes strong moderate leaders appear untrustworthy.

Finally, in the present approach, individuals do not "decide" to radicalize. Rather, powerful experiences and resulting emotions radicalize individuals. In the BD model, the individual basically compares two economic situations and decides that given the fact that the government is unsympathetic and there are few economic opportunities anyway, the best decision is to radicalize and support the extremists. The individual may recognize that the extremists have greatly diminished economic potential, but due to the commitment problem, there is nothing that can be done, so it is better to support the faction fighting the government.

Is this really the way individuals behave? Perhaps individuals believe that violence has reduced their group's dignity; or that they have lived treated as inferiors for most of their lives; or perhaps they have endured what they consider unjust subordination for years. Do such individuals simply maximize their economic welfare and decide whether to radicalize or not?

IV. EMOTIONS AS CONSTRAINTS AS WELL AS RESOURCES

A. Avoiding Backlash

The previous sections have discussed how emotions are used as resources to alter the intervener's planned game. The last two sections address these actions with reference to a particular type of provocation – planting bombs. This tactic would seem to be highly effective in transforming the strategic context of the game. However, it is not used as often as one might think. Moreover, when bombings are conducted, they are often carried out in a highly calibrated manner. Understanding the nature of this calibration illustrates how emotions are both resources and constraints.

Contrary to what one might think, political entrepreneurs who plant bombs are usually not trying to maximize casualties. Consider some examples, starting with the ETA. The Memorial Institute for the Prevention of Terrorism (MIPT) Terrorism Knowledge Base lists roughly 350 bombing incidents, as opposed to assassinations and armed attacks, associated with the Basque separatist organization ETA between 1970 and 2006.[22] These bombings caused only 37 deaths (with over 550 injured). In one remarkable string of attacks during the late 1980s and early 1990s, the MIPT data set lists dozens of bombings against economic targets without a single fatality. Banks, car dealerships, consulates, were hit one after another with no one killed. It was not that the ETA was against killing. In the period 1976–1980 alone, the ETA assassinated over 250 individuals, almost always by pistol. It has continued to use assassination as a tool throughout most of its existence. However, with a very few spectacular exceptions, the ETA has restrained itself from killing civilians with bombs.

---

[22] This data set is affiliated with RAND and the U.S. Department of Homeland Security. Some of the figures mentioned here are from an overview written by Tara Maller, MIT. Other data sets exist and list different, often higher, figures.

After all, the ETA could plant a bomb on a commuter train and slaughter tens or hundreds, as did Islamic terrorists in Madrid. But it did not.

The ultimate champion of nonlethal bombing campaigns, though, is probably found in the Front de liberation national de la Corse (FLNC) in Corsica. Since being founded in 1976, the FLNC has carried out over 5,000 bombings with less than a hundred deaths. Occasionally, political actors on the island set off dozens of bombs at the same time, a phenomenon that residents call "blue nights." Remarkably, few have ever died in these bombing campaigns.

Unlike Corsica, the conflict in Northern Ireland has been very violent, with many casualties: 39,600 shootings and 16,200 bombings.[23] Half the population has been closely associated with a victim.[24] Yet these 55,800 shootings and bombings produced only 3,600 deaths (47,500 injuries), or one death per 15 shootings/bombings. In comparison, a German air raid on Belfast killed about 750 in April 1941.[25] Northern Ireland is a case of high violence without correspondingly high numbers of deaths.[26]

Both numbers and knowledge of practice show that combatants in Northern Ireland generally avoided the use of indiscriminate deadly force. It appears that leaders of organizations wished to avoid the backlash that might have attached to killing many noncombatants. Consider the following passage from Eamon Collin's biography of his days as an IRA operative. In this passage, Collins is speaking to an interrogator from the RUC (Royal Ulster Constabulatory):

> He wanted to know whether the Provos would ever turn the families (of police officers) themselves into legitimate targets. I told them I thought they would never do that. The main reason why they would not was because the present-day IRA sought to avoid any operations which had *obviously* sectarian overtones: a policeman could be justified as a legitimate target, his non-combatant Protestant family could not. The IRA – regardless of their public utterances dismissing the condemnations of their behaviour from church and community leaders – tried to act in a way that would avoid severe censure from within the nationalist community; they knew they were operating within a sophisticated set of informal restrictions on their behaviour, no less powerful for being largely unspoken.[27]

---

[23] The numbers in this paragraph are from CAIN 2007 (http://cain.ulst.ac.uk/ni/security.htm#05) and are cited in Heather Hamill, "Identity Signaling and Mimicry in the Northern Ireland Conflict, 1966–2007," presented at the workshop "Mimicry in Civil Wars: The Strategic Use of Identity Signals, College de France, Paris, December 7–8, 2007.

[24] Hamill, "Identity Signaling and Mimicry in the Northern Ireland Conflict, 1966–2007," p. 1.

[25] Alfred McClung Lee, *Terrorism in Northern Ireland* (Bayside, NY: General Hall Inc., 1983), p. 171.

[26] As an anonymous reviewer of this manuscript pointed out, the number of deaths (3,600) is not a small number in an entity as small as Northern Ireland. As the reviewer pointed out, had the British Army not maintained a massive presence, Northern Ireland could very well have exploded into a situation as deadly as Bosnia. I agree that structural constraints prevented this case from escalating into a high-violence situation. The point here is only that the ratio of deaths to shootings/bombings – 1:15 – suggests that actors could have chosen to kill, versus wound and intimidate, much more than they did, even given their structural constraints. This ratio sets up a puzzle about motivation and calibration of violence.

[27] Eamon Collins with Mick McGovern, *Killing Rage* (London: Granta Books, 1999), p. 295.

Other conflicts witness higher deaths-to-bombing ratios. The MIPT terrorism database credits the Tamil Tigers with much higher figures, for example. In some cases, political entrepreneurs are apparently trying to maximize civilian deaths. To make a comparison, more people were killed by bombing in a single week during the height of the Iraq conflict than in all the hundreds of bombings over the years by the ETA.

There is a tremendous amount of variation in the level of discrimination in targeting among conflicts. When do some very violent organizations decide not to engage in bombing at all? When do some engage only in highly discriminate bombings? When do some organizations maximize killing?

The consideration of emotions provides an answer. In cases of low ethnic stigma, indiscriminately killing civilians will produce a backlash. If the opponent's lives are as worthy and valuable as those of your own group, killing their children brings on a reaction of disgust.

Consider the Irish case again. Northern Ireland was not a situation of high ethnic stigma; the other side was not inherently deficient. Only in low-stigma cases can the strategy of the hunger strike be at all effective. In a hunger strike, one inflicts damage on oneself as a way of striking out at the enemy. It is a method that highlights emotions relating to dignity and self-worth. In a situation where the sides hold each other in mutual contempt, such a strategy would have no hope of meeting with any positive response. For the IRA, fear-based strategies based on indiscriminate targets must be precluded. Due to resentment of British rule and Protestant political privilege, violent strategies may be accepted as a necessary strategy for putting pressure on the government. But the violence must be discriminate. It may involve angering the opponent, but above all it must emphasize a struggle against unjust dominance by targeting very clear and specific symbols of that dominance. This was a long-range war of attrition founded on the support of a population living under the sway of resentment.

In cases of high stigma, on the other hand, a backlash against the use of indiscriminate violence would not be expected. The case studies in the second section of the book will explore that hypothesis in detail.

B. Avoiding Hatred

I have argued that ethnic stigmas are long-term cultural phenomena. It follows that short-run acts and campaigns of violence do not create ethnic stigma. In my analysis, short-run violence and long-term stigma are independent of one another. However, there are situations where this might not be the case. It is possible that horrible acts of indiscriminate violence, perhaps meant to inculcate fear in an opponent, may lead to the belief that the perpetrator or perpetrating group must be inherently defective in some way in order to have committed such acts.

Following these points, it seems possible that actors who wish to be feared may become objects of contempt and hatred instead. This is of course an old insight, going back to Machiavelli. In one of the most widely noted passages in the history of political thought, Machiavelli writes on the strategic use of emotion:

Hence, on the subject of being loved or feared I will conclude that since love depends on the subjects, but the prince has it in his own hands to create fear, a wise prince will rely on what is his own, remembering at the same time that he must avoid arousing hatred, as we have said.[28]

Chapter XIX of *The Prince* is entitled "Essential to Avoid Being Hated or Despised." Machiavelli's basic point is that being hated prevents a stable political existence. No prince can achieve stable rule when the population hates the prince and wishes for his elimination. In such a situation, conspirators against the prince will come to believe, probably correctly, that killing the prince represents the popular will and acceptance of both the murder and the change in leadership. Machiavelli advises the prince to establish fear as a political tool, but by all means to avoid creating hatred.

Machiavelli's recommendation is highly relevant to the politics and conflicts of intervention. Political entrepreneurs, as pointed out in the previous chapter, can create fear through indiscriminate violent actions. These acts may, however, create a belief that the perpetrators are lacking in basic humanity – in other words, that there is something inherently defective about perpetrators. After many indiscriminate and heinous acts, the cognitions underlying hatred may develop. In effect, efforts to create fear may end up creating hatred. My speculation is that this transformation is more likely when the groups involved are political rather than ethnic. As mentioned, ethnic and racial stigmas are so deeply embedded in culture that acts of a heinous and indiscriminate nature by members of an ethnic group are unlikely to change broad emotions. On the other hand, such actions by more narrowly defined political groups may produce this transformation. These political entrepreneurs, heeding Machiavelli, will need to calculate the possibility that actions intended to generate fear will mutate into a hatred that precludes desired political possibilities.

As discussed in Chapter 2, hatred can be conceptualized as a schema. Hatred focuses on the purported innate and deficient characteristics of the opposing group. A cultural schema can embody the emotion of hatred when the schema contains a constant representation of the innate and deficient nature of an opposing group. Schemas can form if cognitions about blameworthy actions combine coherently with cognitions about the actor committing those actions. Beliefs about the other group's actions can coalesce to form beliefs about that group's basic nature. As mentioned earlier, this phenomenon could happen in several ways: a large number of blameworthy actions could lead to hatred; the similarity in the nature of the bad acts could lead to the cognitions underlying a hatred schema; the brutal quality of the acts could lead to hatred.

---

[28] Machiavelli, *The Prince*, Chapter XVII. Quotation is from *The Prince*, T. G. Bergin translator and editor (Arlington Heights, IL: Croft Classics, 1947), p. 50.

The uncertainty about the creation of hatred creates a strategic dilemma for the political entrepreneur contemplating a violent escalation. There is a set of trade-offs. On one hand, the actor will wish to inculcate anger or fear and avoid the possibility of contempt or hatred. The trade-off is most direct if a strategy of fear, based on the creation of indiscriminate violence, is at issue. Indiscriminate violence will kill bystanders and children – these are the acts most likely to generate beliefs about the inherent depravity of the violent actor. The discriminate violence behind anger is less likely to involve these targets and thus less likely to help form a negative schema.

An example from Colombia can serve to illustrate these points.[29] The case presents a particular puzzle: Why has the FARC in Colombia not engaged in more bombings in Bogota?

In February 2003, the Colombian guerrilla organization FARC planted a bomb inside the premises of the El Nogal, one of the most exclusive social clubs in all of Latin America. This club, frequented by some of the top politicians and business leaders in Colombia, was heavily guarded. Casualties included twenty dead and more than one hundred injured. If FARC could penetrate this target, it certainly had the capabilities to place bombs on buses, kill dozens many times over, and spread fear throughout the population. At that time, the Colombian state did not possess the capabilities to consistently thwart such action.[30] Yet the El Nogal bombing remained an isolated event; it seems that purposeful attacks on civilians in Bogota were avoided.

It would seem that in recent years the FARC would have had incentives to engage in strategies involving civilian deaths. As of 2008, the FARC was an insurgent group losing power relative to the regime. The regime had gained new technological military capabilities and had dislodged the insurgents from much of their territory. The insurgents, as well as the key figures in the regime, anticipate that at some point some bargain will be made to end the conflict. Given their deteriorating position, the insurgents may wish to enter into bargaining. How might the insurgents quickly enhance their bargaining position?

One common tactic might involve killing civilians in bombing attacks. Many political scientists see targeting civilians as a way to raise costs and display resolve.[31] The regime, seeing the lengths to which the insurgents are willing to

---

[29] One reason that I am including the case of the FARC in Colombia is that I have had the opportunity to discuss it with some of the actors there. See Roger Petersen, "The Strategic Use of Emotion in Conflict: Emotion and Interest in the Reconstruction of Multiethnic States," in *Argumentacion, negociacion, racional y acuerdos* (Bogota); also, see Roger Petersen with Vanda Felbab-Brown, "United States Social Science and Counter-Insurgency Policy in Colombia," in Freddy Cante and Luisa Ortiz eds., *Nonviolent Political Action in Colombia* (Bogota: Universidad del Rosario, 2005).

[30] The security situation in Bogota dramatically improved from 2003 to later years in the decade. The Colombian state under Uribe was able to eliminate the FARC's presence and power in the Bogota suburbs.

[31] For a recent treatment of the logic of suicide bombings, see Robert Pape, *Dying to Win: The Strategic Logic of Suicide Terrorism* (New York: Random House, 2005).

go, will be more likely to engage in negotiations and even make concessions in order to avoid these high future costs. The question is, how do bombings specifically increase costs? Among other things, bombings create fears in the general population that in turn create "costs" for the regime. Under the influence of fear, the general population may pressure the leadership to end the conflict despite current regime military advances. The insurgents want the population to be so concerned for their personal safety that they push the government to make a deal, even on less than favorable terms. However, hitting the indiscriminate civilian targets that create fear may also help develop the foundation for contempt and hatred.

If insurgents really wish to enter into negotiations that will hold in the long run, then they will certainly wish to avoid actions that generate hatred. The emotion of hatred is defined by cognition that a group is both inherently defective and dangerous; the action tendency is to physically eliminate the presence of that group. If insurgents believe that they are hated by society, or hated by its most powerful elements, they should have little faith that negotiations will hold. Even though the insurgents may be able to force a deal, in the presence of hatred they should have little confidence that the deal will be honored over the long run. Given the possibility of the emergence of hatred with its action tendency toward physical elimination, insurgents might be better off not entering into negotiations in the first place.

The FARC could also decide to hit symbolic or leadership targets, but this strategy not only will fail to generate fear, but will also create unwanted anger. Given their position, FARC insurgents do not wish to create anger. As discussed, the action tendency of anger is toward retribution. In anger, individuals assign specific blame and accept higher risk. Under the influence of anger, the population will push the government to continue to fight insurgents despite possible high costs. With massive anger, the likelihood of negotiations, especially negotiations on terms favorable to the insurgents, will fade.

Given their situation, neither an anger-based nor a fear-based strategy clearly furthered FARC's goals. The remaining choice, not to escalate violence in Bogota at all, was the one chosen.[32]

CONCLUSION

This chapter has illustrated the ways in which emotions serve as resources, and sometimes constraints, for political actors challenging an intervention or a government. It has specified how emotions can be strategically used to shape preferences, actors, and strategies. The insights gleaned from this exercise take the form of hypotheses in the next chapter.

---

[32] If FARC faced total elimination, which seemed possible at the time of this writing, that strategy could certainly change.

6

The Strategic Use of Emotions, III

Generating Hypotheses

Opponents of intervention possess a list of tactics that can be employed in responding to the strategy of the intervener. This list, comprising what I have termed the specific dependent variable, formed the lower left box in Figure 1.1 and is reprinted here:

(1) *Use of Deadly Violence:* (A) discriminate vs. indiscriminate violence; (B) specific choice of target; (C) level of violence; (D) deadly riots.
(2) *Nondeadly Violence:* (A) bombing without killing; (B) desecration; (C) threats; (D) nondeadly riots.
(3) *Withdrawal from Political Engagement:* (A) boycotts; (B) creation of a parallel system.
(4) *Nonviolent Engagement:* (A) parades/demonstrations; (B) posters/speeches.
(5) *Acquiescence.*

A basic goal of this book is to explain why and when political opponents of intervention choose one of these tactics rather than another. This chapter combines elements from the previous chapters to help provide this explanation. Furthermore, using knowledge of emotions, the chapter generates predictions about the use of these tactics.

Of particular interest is the question of the escalation or deescalation of violence. Following the examples in the previous chapter, the political entrepreneur has the choice to remain in the present box and mobilize the resources there or to attempt to transform the game through the control of violence. In all cases, the player will consider the available resources (both structural resources and emotion resources), constraints on violence, and possibilities for a desired political solution. In some cases, the intervener or government simply has too many resources for the opponent to consider escalation of violence. In this chapter, I will mainly address cases in which structural constraints are insufficient to prevent the consideration of violent options.

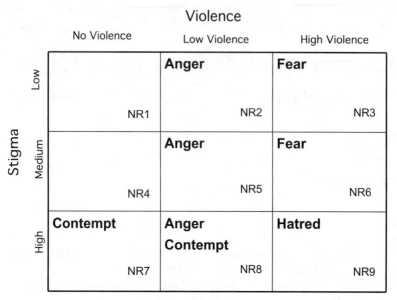

FIGURE 6.1. Distribution of Emotions in a Situation without Resentment (NR).

The past chapters have defined emotions, discussed their political uses, and developed the matrices reproduced in this chapter to capture their distributions. These matrices can be used as analytical devices to systematically develop hypotheses. Recall that for shorthand purposes Figure 6.1 is referred to as NR for no resentment and Figure 6.2 is referred to as R because resentment is present.

As the matrices illustrate, a key feature is the existence of contempt as a resource under conditions of high stigma. It is this difference that will frame much of the analysis and that appropriately serves as a starting point.

I. CASES OF LOW ETHNIC STIGMA

I begin the analysis by considering cases of low ethnic stigma, represented by the top rows of each figure (boxes NR1–NR3 and R1–R3). As a resource, the emotion of contempt allows political actors to pursue the politics of separation through boycotts and even the creation of a parallel society. In the situations represented by the upper rows of both matrices, this emotion is *not* available as a resource, leading to the following prediction:

> *Prediction 1*: In cases of low stigma, political actors will not pursue polices of boycott or parallel society.

A second major aspect of ethnic stigma and contempt is that it allows killing of civilians of the opposing group. Their lives are simply not valued as much as one's own group's lives. On the other hand, the absence of contempt will

Stigma		Violence		
		No Violence	Low Violence	High Violence
	Low	Resentment- R1	Anger Resentment- R2	Fear R3
	Medium	Resentment R4	Anger Resentment R5	Fear R6
	High	Contempt Resentment+ R7	Anger Contempt Resentment+ R8	Hatred R9

FIGURE 6.2. Distribution of Emotions with Resentment (R).

not provide this freedom to commit indiscriminate violence. In the absence of out-group contempt, any political actor who indiscriminately kills civilians is likely to suffer a backlash from his or her own population. These points lead to a second prediction and two corollaries:

> *Prediction 2*: In cases where contempt does not exist, political actors employing indiscriminate killing of civilians can expect a backlash from members of their own group.
> 2A: In these cases, we will more likely see the tactic of bombing without killing.
> 2B: We should also fail to see desecration of religious sites.

In cases without contempt as a resource, violence is likely to be used as part of pressure politics rather than to change demographics or create everescalating and deadly spirals. It is meant to keep pressure on the intervener or government to change its policies rather than to create partition or initiate civil war. In this situation, political actors are likely to hit regime officials and symbols occasionally in order to produce a controlled level of anger and retaliation that maintains enmity and wears down the intervener. The contest is likely to vacillate between R1 and R2 through the use of highly calibrated violence. This leads to a corollary of prediction 2:

> *Prediction 3*: If violence is used in cases of no contempt, it is likely to be low-level and highly discriminate, with attacks against police and regime officials, not civilians.

Predictions 1–3 apply to cases both with and without resentment (both the NR and R matrices). Consideration of the presence or absence of resentment will yield additional hypotheses. The presence of resentment can be a powerful force that justifies the use of violence. Given the presence of grievances associated with resentment, the player's own population may accept violence as a necessary evil. Without resentment, violence is much more difficult to defend. To take this analysis one step further, in the case of box NR1 – no resentment, no contempt, no violence – we are likely to see acquiescence to intervener policy. Even moving to NR2 is likely to create a backlash. In box R1, on the other hand, we will be more likely to see highly calibrated violence used as a justifiable political tool. This logic leads to the following prediction:

> *Prediction 4*: We are more likely to see the use of violence in cases of resentment than cases without resentment.
> *4A*: The case of NR1 should see the highest chance of acquiescence.

Additionally, we should expect that the nonviolent forms of politics played within cells NR1 and R1 can be expected to differ. Resentment produces excessive concern with political status and political actors will tailor their nonviolent tactics accordingly.

> *Prediction 5*: Given the presence of resentment, parades and demonstrations that highlight grievances about political status should be expected in box R1, but not NR1.

A more general expectation follows from these predictions. In situations of low stigma, the politics of redistribution should have a relatively good chance of success. If the intervener can successfully assuage status concerns, it can reduce resentment and transform R1 to NR1. Following prediction 4, we should expect less chance of violence; following prediction 5, we should see less confrontational forms of nonviolent politics. The field of political science has produced many theories about redistribution of political power and status, most famously in the form of consociationalism and theories of electoral engineering. In situations of low stigma, the resentment-reducing logic behind these theories would seem to have a chance to play out. Cases of high stigma, on the other hand, present a different set of issues.

II. CASES OF HIGH ETHNIC STIGMA

Consideration of the bottom rows of both matrices (NR7–NR9 and R7–R9) will yield a different set of hypotheses. In the presence of contempt, the political entrepreneur can be more confident that followers will be willing to bear the high costs of boycotts or even the more radical step of building a parallel society. They will also be more likely to see violence, even indiscriminate violence against civilians, as legitimate, even necessary.

A series of predictions correspond to the first two predictions in the preceding section:

Prediction 6: In NR7 and R7, political entrepreneurs are most likely to initiate the politics of boycott and the creation of parallel systems.

Prediction 7: Under conditions of contempt, players who initiate violence will suffer little backlash from their own population.

The emotion of contempt also frees the political entrepreneur to consider a broader range of strategies. Prediction 3 hypothesized that the lack of ethnic contempt would limit the range of violent strategies: low-level and highly discriminate, with attacks against police and regime officials, not civilians. With the resource of contempt, political actors do not need to fear a backlash from their own group. They can consider both hitting indiscriminate targets and hitting discriminate targets with higher frequency.

Prediction 8: If violence is used in a case with contempt, the nature of that violence is likely to be more severe than in cases without contempt. We are likely to observe a higher frequency of targeted attacks and the inclusion of more indiscriminate targets.

Along the logic laid out here, the presence of resentment acts to increase the motivation and justification for violence. In box R7, not only does a population holding an opposing group in contempt, but also it is being politically dominated by that group. Following from prediction 8:

Prediction 9: We are more likely to see escalation of violence in R7 than in NR7.

If the game does not escalate and remains in boxes NR7 and R7, we will again expect to see a difference in the nature of nonviolent politics:

Prediction 10: With contempt, nonviolent provocations such as speeches and posters will highlight the perceived inherent negative qualities of the other side. With resentment, these provocations will emphasize current changes in status relations. In situations of both contempt and resentment, both types of provocations should be observed.

If violence escalates to a high level in conjunction with contempt, we are more likely to witness popularly supported ethnic cleansing than in any other situation. In such cases, high levels of killing and cleansing are justified against an opponent who is both defective and dangerous, – in other words, hated.

Prediction 11: In a situation of hatred, strategies of ethnic cleansing will find widespread support. This phenomenon is likely only in boxes NR9 and R9.

This outcome is most likely to occur when a cultural schema supports the cognitive antecedents underlying hatred, that is, if a specific and repeated historical narrative of violence appears to be repeating itself in the present.

III. OTHER BOXES, MORE PREDICTIONS

In a couple of situations, so many resources are available that it is nearly impossible to generate a specific prediction. Of all the boxes in both matrices, R8 provides the most opportunities for political entrepreneurs. If they have the ability to control the level of violence, political actors can choose to escalate or deescalate to the boxes either to the right or left. With R8, they can use discriminate targeting to set off spirals of violence, they can use indiscriminate violence to inculcate fears, they can mobilize resentment, and they can pursue policies of separation. Essentially, whatever an intervener develops as policy, the opponent is likely to have sufficient resources to develop an effective counterstrategy. All that can be done here is to form a very general prediction:

Prediction 12: If the situation is characterized by box R8, a broad set of strategies are likely to be employed.

When the game is primarily played without violence or contempt (boxes NR1, R1 and NR4, R4), players have reasons to escalate violence occasionally and then return to nonviolent politics. If the situation moves into constant low-level violence, as represented by the middle columns of the matrices, the players may have other options to consider. As with R8, they can deescalate violence and return to nonviolence, but they can also transform the game by escalating violence to high levels. If constraints are low, political entrepreneurs can begin killing and burning indiscriminately.

Initiating high levels of indiscriminate violence essentially amounts to "blowing up the game." Recalling the third chapter, the goal of the player here is to transform the game from a structured cooperation game into an N-person assurance game. Without the assurance of safety from either the state or their own elites, individuals will be forced to look out for their own safety; they will essentially "defect" from any sort of engagement and escape to whatever sanctuary they can find. Usually, that sanctuary will be behind a territorial line that physically separates one group from the other.

Prediction 13: Players will employ high levels of indiscriminate violence in the middle boxes of the matrices if their strategies call for violent ethnic separation.

This prediction of course raises the question of when and why actors wish to blow up the game. Most basically, if there is no possibility of an acceptable (in the actor's own estimation) political solution, constraints on indiscriminate killing will be low. Moving the game into a high-violence cell generally means that there is no going back to previous forms of bargaining. Only actors who have little interest in the old game will move to this level of violence. Second, if the group's strength and position in the long run do not seem secure, it may seem more promising to try to "blow up the game" as much as possible and take one's chances in the new circumstances. Those who do move to this level have a good chance of being seen as war criminals, as well as becoming the focus of hatred not only from the opponent, but possibly from their own group as well.

IV. COMPARISONS AND CONCLUSIONS

These hypotheses predict the types of strategies that are most likely to arise from the situation represented by each box. They are based on the types of emotion resources available. The actual strategies chosen will also depend on the specific game chosen by the intervener. The case studies that form the second part of this book will examine the combination of these two elements in detail. For each case, I will first specify the starting position for analysis by examining the presence or absence of status reversals, the level of stigma, and the level of violence.

As mentioned earlier, this framework for analysis may seem complex, but in practice it is relatively straightforward when applied to actual cases. As discussed, political entrepreneurs cannot change the level of ethnic stigma, so each case is played within one horizontal row. Neither can political entrepreneurs easily change status relations (although we will indeed observe this change in two of the case studies), so we are generally analyzing a case within only one of the matrices. For any given case, only a limited number of cells will be relevant.

The major case in this book is Kosovo over the years stretching from the late 1980s to 2008. This case represents constant high ethnic stigma and an ever-present concern with status reversals and resentment. It will exhibit several changes in the level of violence, from no violence to the highest level of violence imaginable. Accordingly, only the bottom row of the Resentment matrix is relevant to the analysis. As the cases will lay out in great detail, the Kosovo case moves across this row – from R7 to R8 to R9, back to R8, and finally back to R7. This dynamic provides a series of comparisons within the Kosovo case. As emotion resources change over the course of the case, we should observe political entrepreneurs making different decisions corresponding to these changes.

When applied to the entire set of Western Balkan cases, the framework will help generate several controlled comparisons that isolate the effect of specific emotion resources. One comparison will involve South Serbia and Macedonia. These cases resemble each other in many key respects. Both play out in the Resentment matrix and both involve an escalation to a low level of violence before returning to a nonviolent status quo. They differ, I argue, in levels of ethnic stigma. As in Kosovo, there is high mutual ethnic stigma in South Serbia; in Macedonia, ethnic stigmas are at the medium level. Accordingly, the progression for South Serbia is R7–R8–R7; the progression for Macedonia is R4–R5–R4. Juxtaposing these two cases allows comparison of a case with high levels of ethnic stigma to one with medium levels. Correspondingly, it provides a focused test of the hypotheses relating to the emotion of contempt (predictions 1–3 in particular).

Another comparison will juxtapose Bosnia and Montenegro. Both cases begin in a benign position – no strong stigma, no violence, and no resentment. In terms of the matrices, they begin in NR1 (the upper left cell of the No Resentment matrix). In both cases, political resentment will arise and the case will progress to R1. However, that is where the similarities will stop. Whereas the Montenegrin case will remain nonviolent (its progression will be NR1–R1), Bosnia will descend into the worst European violence since the Second World War (its progression is NR1–R1–R2–R3–R1). The comparison highlights what happens in the R1 cell. Why does Bosnia, starting from a similarly benign position, differ so wildly from Montenegro?

In the study of conflict and intervention, certain questions are fundamental. When should we see violent escalation and why? Why do we see variation in the nature of violence? What explains variation in the tactics used by opponents of intervention? The first section of this book has worked to produce the testable hypotheses listed in this chapter. The rest of the book aims to provide a wealth of materials and sets of comparisons to test these predictions.

PART 2

CASES AND TESTS

7

Background to Western Intervention in the Balkans

By the early years of the twenty-first century, the United States and Western Europe (collectively referred to as "the West" in this book) were deeply involved in interventions across almost every region of the Western Balkans. They were carrying out the Dayton Agreement and its special annexes in Bosnia, conducting an occupation of Kosovo, supervising the Ohrid Accord in Macedonia, brokering an agreement in South Serbia, temporarily keeping Serbia and Montenegro together with the Belgrade Agreement, and assisting with other accords in Montenegro. Despite major differences in the scope and nature of these interventions, they had a common approach based in Western rationality. The West had developed an intervention style with features similar to the "games" in academic game theory. That game style approach is the subject of Chapter 3. The purpose of this chapter is to describe the evolution of Western–Balkan interactions that led to that approach.

First, a brief historical background of the former Yugoslavia, necessary for understanding crucial aspects of Western intervention, is provided. The empirical sections of the book will supply more detailed background for each specific case. Second, the period from 1990 to 2005 is treated in three stages, each marking significant transformations in the West's approach to the region.

I. SOME ESSENTIAL HISTORICAL BACKGROUND ON THE FORMER YUGOSLAVIA

The former Yugoslavia was created from the decay and collapse of multiethnic empires. For centuries, the Ottoman Empire faced off against its European rivals on the territory of what became Yugoslavia. By the end of the First World War, both the Ottoman Empire and the Austro-Hungarian Empire would be gone. The first Yugoslavia (called the Kingdom of Serbs, Croats, and Slovenes until 1929) was formed from the remnants of both empires. Essentially, the first Yugoslavia was composed of three elements: former Austro-Hungarian regions; Serbia, which had been independent for four decades; and regions to the south of Serbia, recently unfettered from the Ottomans. It is important to understand this history because when a second Yugoslavia collapsed in the early 1990s, it did so in two stages. The wealthier and Slavic-speaking regions that were formerly part of the Austro-Hungarian Empire seceded first and precipitated three wars. The poorer regions in the south that were formerly part of the Ottoman Empire became the focus of a second round of clashes. Basically, Yugoslavia generated two different subsystems of conflict, with Serbia in the middle and the main protagonist in each. These two subsystems exhibited different dynamics and experienced different types of Western intervention.

A. The Southern Subsystem

First, consider the background of the southern subsystem. The Ottoman Empire slowly decayed, leaving new nation-states in the wake of its retreat. After the Serbian uprisings of 1876–8, the Treaty of Berlin in 1878 recognized the complete independence of Serbia, Montenegro, and Romania, as well as the autonomy of Bulgaria. It also transferred the Ottoman provinces of Bosnia-Hercegovina to Austro-Hungarian occupation, although the provinces remained formally a part of the Ottoman Empire.

The Ottoman decline continued. In 1908, Bulgaria declared independence and Austria-Hungary announced its formal annexation of Bosnia-Hercegovina. In 1912, Albanians were in revolt and the young states of the Balkans felt sufficiently powerful to send the Ottomans out of the region. In October 1912, Serbia, Montenegro, and Bulgaria, followed by Greece, declared war on the Ottomans and drove them out of the Western Balkans, including what is today Kosovo and Macedonia.

For the Serbs, the war was a chance to incorporate territories prominent in the nation's historical imagination. It is easy to exaggerate the importance of the myth of Kosovo, but it would be wrong to dismiss it as well. Regardless of the impact of poems and myths, Kosovo is the home of many of Serbia's most important religious sites. The rebellions of 1876–7 involved mass expulsions;[1] the Balkan Wars served to reinforce patterns and policies of torching of villages, killing, and displacement. Already, some traditions and schemas were being established. The 1913 Carnegie Endowment report describes the Serbian advance into Kosovo in the following fashion:

Houses and whole villages reduced to ashes, unarmed and innocent populations massacred *en masse*, incredible acts of violence, pillage and brutality of every kind – such were the means which were employed and are still being employed by the Serbo-Montenegrin soldiery, with a view to the entire transformation of the ethnic character of regions inhabited exclusively by Albanians.

We thus arrive at the second characteristic feature of the Balkan wars, a feature which is a necessary correlative of the first. Since the population of the countries about to be

---

[1] Iain King and Whit Mason, *Peace at Any Price: How the World Failed Kosovo* (Ithaca, NY: Cornell University Press, 2006), pp. 29–30.

occupied knew, by tradition, instinct, and experience, what they had to expect from the armies of the enemy and from the neighboring countries from which these armies belonged, they did not await their arrival, but fled. Thus, generally speaking, the army of the enemy found on its way nothing but villages which were either half deserted or entirely abandoned.... All along the railways interminable trains of carts drawn by oxen followed one another; behind them came emigrant families and, in the neighborhoods of the big towns, bodies of refugees were found encamped.[2]

Leon Trotsky was a correspondent covering the Balkan wars for the Ukrainian newspaper *Kievskaia Mysl*. Trotsky was convinced that a demographic project lay at the root of the atrocities he witnessed: "The Serbs in Old Serbia, in their national endeavour to correct data in the ethnographical statistics that are not quite favourable to them, are engaged quite simply in systematic extermination of the Muslim population."[3]

The demographic issue was important in perhaps an even more crucial sense: the wars and their aftermath left at least one-third of Albanians out of the new Albanian state. Nearly 100 years later, the issue of the fate and political rights and privileges of this Albanian diaspora still dominate the region's politics and are the central focus of Western intervention.

The southern subsystem was marked by several characteristics that would separate it from the northern subsystem. First, it was born in violence, with overtones of ethnic cleansing. Second, the antagonists differed in language. Albanian is not a Slavic language and is seldom known by Slavs. Third, the religious differences were wider. Rather than Orthodox Christians facing off against Catholics, as in the north, Christians competed with Muslims in the south. Fourth, the south was always considerably poorer. Fifth, historical and cultural connections to Europe were very weak.

B. The Northern Subsystem

The northern subsystem emerged from the disappearance of Austria-Hungary at the conclusion of the First World War. All of a sudden, residents of the Slovenian and Croatian regions of that empire found themselves citizens of a new state. Unlike the peoples of the south (Macedonians, Montenegrins, and Albanians), the northern groups were recognized in the name of the new entity: the Kingdom of Serbs, Croats, and Slovenes.

Although the three northern, Slavic, and Christian groups all were listed in the new state's name, the Serbs were the preeminent group among them. For many Serbs, the first Yugoslavia was and rightfully should have been an extension of the Serbian state.[4] In their reckoning, one-fifth of the Serbian nation had perished during the First World War and this sacrifice helped

---

[2] Carnegie Endowment for International Peace, *The Other Balkan Wars: A 1913 Carnegie Endowment Inquiry in Retrospect* (Washington, DC: Carnegie Endowment for Peace, 1993), p. 151.

[3] Quoted by Noel Malcolm, *Kosovo: A Short History* (New York: New York University Press, 1999), p. 253.

[4] This paragraph is from Petersen, *Understanding Ethnic Violence*, pp. 212–13.

liberate their fellow south Slavs. Serbs expected a measure of gratitude as well as the right to build the new state on the government, bureaucracy, and military of prewar Serbia. Combined with an ideology of a unitary state and centralized governance, this reliance on the foundations of the prewar Serbian state was a recipe for Serbian dominance. For Serbs, it was only natural that the king of the new state would come from the Serbian dynasty. Having possessed a state for decades, ethnic Serbs easily transferred their position from the old Serbian state to the new kingdom's bureaucracy and military.[5] The following figures illustrate the extent of interwar Serbian dominance in high-status positions, even nearly two decades after the new state's birth.[6] On the eve of the Second World War, 161 of 165 Yugoslav generals were Serbian, 2 were Croats, and 2 were Slovenes. These numbers are even more astounding when it is taken into account that Croats composed 15 percent of the Austro-Hungarian Empire's generals and admirals. Moreover, these figures were not about to change radically, as 1,300 of 1,500 military cadets were Serbs. Serbian dominance among senior permanent functionaries was nearly as pronounced. In 1939, Serbs held all 13 positions in the Office of the Premier, 30 of 31 in the Royal Court, 113 of 127 in the Ministry of the Interior, 180 of 219 in the Ministry of Foreign Affairs, 150 of 156 in the Ministry of Education, 116 of 137 in the Justice Ministry, 15 of 26 in the Transportation Ministry, and 196 of 200 in the State Mortgage Bank. In short, Serbs controlled all visible levers of force and power of the interwar state, despite the Croats' and Slovenes' previous experience in the Austro-Hungarian Empire.

Having lived as second-class citizens under Austria-Hungary, Croats were not ready to accept a similar status under the less developed Serbs. Joseph Rothschild sums up the relationship between Serbs and Croats when they were first joined in the interwar state:

(T)he former subjects of the late "Central European" Habsburg Empire considered themselves more advanced, in terms of all such cultural and socioeconomic criteria, than the "Balkan" Serbs to the south, by whom they were politically dominated to their lasting ire. The Serbs of the prewar Serbian Kingdom, in turn, repudiated the cultural pretensions of the northerners and dismissed their political legacies as Austrophile, formalistic, and irresponsible. They viewed themselves as "doers" and these others as "carpers."[7]

In sum, the northern subsystem differed greatly from the southern. It was always wealthier and more developed. It was not incorporated during a fit of

---

[5] Ivo Banac embeds his analysis of the founding of the Yugoslav state and its subsequent nationality problems in the differences among national ideologies. See *The National Question in Yugoslavia: Origins, History, Politics* (Ithaca, NY: Cornell University Press, 1984). He comes back to this theme in "The Fearful Asymmetry of War: The Causes and Consequences of Yugoslavia's Demise," *Daedalus* (1992) 121: 141–75.

[6] All of these figures are from Joseph Rothschild, *East Central Europe between the Two World Wars* (Seattle: University of Washington Press, 1974), pp. 278–9.

[7] Rothschild, *East Central Europe*, p. 209.

ethnic cleansing and triumphalism. Furthermore, its members all spoke similar Slavic languages, the difference between the Serbs and Croats being little more than a dialect difference. There was a religious difference; in fact, religion is the defining characteristic distinguishing between Serbs and Croats, the former being Orthodox and the latter Catholic. Finally, the northern subsystem was connected historically and culturally to central Europe. This difference would come to play a significant role during the state's final breakup, with central European and primarily Catholic states offering early and constant support for Slovenian and Croatian independence.

II. A HISTORY OF REFORM AND EXPERIMENTATION

From its inception, the Kingdom of Yugoslavia was forced to find ways to keep its disparate elements under control. In 1929, King Alexander initiated a serious experiment in ethnic engineering, basically a test of postmodern identity theory. Shortly after the assassination of Stjepan Radic (a major Croatian political leader) on the floor of Parliament, King Alexander changed the name of the country to Yugoslavia, roughly translated as "South Slav Land."[8] He also created new administrative units cutting across historical and ethnic boundaries. These units were called banovinas, an ancient Croatian term, in order to pacify Croats, and they were named after rivers, to avoid any ethnic or national favoritism. Serbian and Croatian national symbols were to have no connection to the government.

King Alexander's reforms did not bear fruit. The Ustasha, a Croatian political and terrorist organization, managed to assassinate the king in 1934. Calls for explicit recognition of Croatian autonomy became louder. In response, Prince (Regent) Paul again recognized Croatian authority in the form of an agreement called the Sporazum. This agreement ceded to Zagreb a variety of budgetary and administrative powers. After signing the reform, the Prince Regent visited Zagreb. This was the first time the Royal House had paid a visit there in over ten years.

This reform never had a chance to be tested. Despite the efforts at deethnification, Yugoslavia witnessed horrendous killing during the Second World War. The postwar Communist regime set a figure of 1.7 million total dead, or about ten percent of the population. Other researchers put the figure lower, but still at astounding levels.[9] Multiple types of violence permeated the region

---

[8] See Appendix 1 for a list of the evolution of names relating to "Yugoslavia" and Serbia.

[9] As is common in such matters, the numbers are a point of contention. Bogoljub Kocovic, using analysis of the 1921, 1938, and 1948 censuses along with 1.1 percent annual growth, concludes that 1,014,000 individuals perished, including 487,000 Serbs. See *Zrtve Drugog Svetskog Rata u Jugoslaviji* [Casualties of WWII in Yugoslavia] (London: Veritas Press Foundation, 1985). This study is cited by many internationals, including the International Crisis Group's Christopher Bennett (see "Serbia's War with History" in the *Greek Helsinki Monitor*, 21 April 1999). Johan Wuscht provides a similar figure (1,100,000) in *Population Losses in Yugoslavia during World War II* (Bonn: Edition Atlantic Forum, 1963).

as Nazis and other occupiers fought to maintain their hold at the same time as civil wars consumed much of the former state. Perhaps most important for later events, the Ustasha Nazi-puppet Croatian state committed brutal atrocities that Serbs would recall in the early 1990s. The goals and achievements of the Ustasha regime are well known: a particular solution to the Serbian "problem" (one-third to be killed, one-third deported, and one-third converted),[10] tens of thousands of Serbs, Jews, and Roma killed at Jasenovac death camp,[11] and countless massacres, many of a primitive and horrific nature.[12]

The incoming postwar Communist regime, based on Josip Broz's (Tito's) Partisan guerrilla movement, then took its turn at solving the national and ethnic question in a second Yugoslavia. Tito's solution involved both ruthlessness and measures of pacification. The first thing the Communist regime did was kill thousands of people, including many nationalists, in the months following the war. Noel Malcolm puts the number at 250,000.[13] Lower figures put the number in the tens of thousands.[14] On the other hand, Tito's regime recognized aspirations for national expression by forming an ethnofederal state. Following the Soviet model, the major nationalities would each receive their own republic (see Figure 7.1). There were six such republics – Slovenia, Croatia, Bosnia-Hercegovina, Serbia, Macedonia, and Montenegro. Two autonomous republics, federal units with lesser powers, lay within the Serbian Republic. These were Voydodina, representing the needs of a Hungarian minority, and Kosovo, representing a largely Albanian region.

Again following the Soviets, the republics were nationalist in form, but socialist (meaning centralized party control) in content.[15] Twenty years after

[10]   Reported statement of Mile Budak, the NDH Minister of Education, June 22, 1941.
[11]   The numbers killed at Jasenovac are even more contentious than most other war figures. Franjo Tudjman puts the number killed in all camps at 56,639. Scholarly sources and Nazi officials usually put the figures much higher. Aleksa Djilas succinctly summarizes the debate over numbers killed in *The Contested Country: Yugoslav Unity and Communist Revolution 1919–1953* (Cambridge, MA: Harvard University Press, 1991), pp. 125–7. Ivo Banac, however, argues that the Ustasha crimes have been greatly exaggerated and supports a figure of 60,000 to 80,000. See "The Fearful Asymmetries of War," pp. 153–5. Christopher Bennett, citing the figures of Vladimir Zerjavic, supports a figure of 85,000. See *Yugoslavia's Bloody Collapse*, p. 46. The Simon Wiesenthal Center provided a figure of 500,000 in the late 1990s.
[12]   The Nazis themselves were often shocked and disturbed by Ustasha excesses. See Paul Hehn, *The German Struggle against Yugoslav Guerrillas in World War II: German Counter-insurgency in Yugoslavia, 1941–1943* (Boulder, CO: East European Quarterly, distributed by Columbia University Press, 1979).
[13]   Noel Malcolm, *Bosnia: A Short History* (New York: New York University Press, 1994), p. 193.
[14]   Mark Mazower lists a figure of 60,000 in *Dark Continent*; John Lampe provides a figure of 100,000 in *Yugoslavia as History* (1995).
[15]   Stevan Pavlowitch sums up the Yugoslav version of Communist nationality policy that emerged in the immediate postwar years: "It substituted ideological integration for ethnic integration, capping federalism with a unitarism of power and ideology. Ethnic pluralism and federal forms were meant as lightning conductors for national emotions until Communism had managed to do away with them." See *The Improbable Survivor: Yugoslavia and Its Problems, 1918–1988* (Columbus, OH: Ohio State University Press, 1988), p. 71.

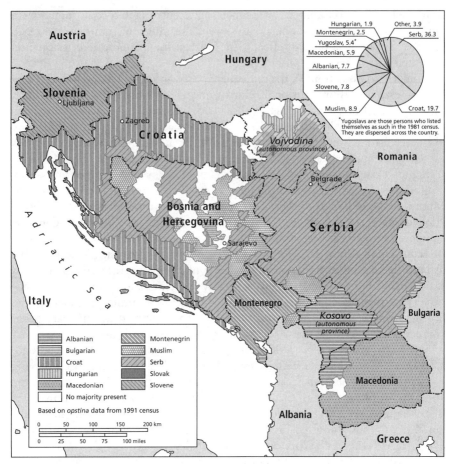

FIGURE 7.1. Yugoslavia's Republics and Ethnic Distribution.

the establishment of the ethnofederal system, the nationalist form began to take on substantial and threatening content. The first two decades of Communist rule witnessed dramatically uneven economic development. Despite socialist theory and rhetoric, the wealth gap between the northern and southern sub-systems actually increased. At the same time, the practice of enterprise self-management eroded the Party's grip over day-to-day economic and social life. The Brioni Plenum of 1966 marked a significant change in the Yugoslav system. The Party was still in command, but the locus of its power would be regional rather than federal. Given local economic autonomy, strong political bosses emerged at lower levels. Also at the Brioni Plenum, the hard-line Rankovic, then Vice President of Yugoslavia and the highest-ranking Serb Communist, was stripped of all his powers, including control of the secret police. The ouster of Rankovic, the most powerful opponent of political decentralization, combined with economic reform, unleashed centrifugal forces, including a renewal of Croatian nationalism. By 1969, the taboo on nationalist speech in Croatia was no longer in effect. The opinion that Croatia had become an exploited nation became commonplace.

Similarly to his actions in the immediate postwar years, Tito combined ruthless repression with institutional reforms meant to pacify ethnic and national aspirations. After purging tens of thousands of nationalists who "had gone too far,"[16] Tito further decentralized the Yugoslav political system. Not only did the existing Republics gain more power, but also the two autonomous republics within Serbia essentially gained republic-level powers. The Yugoslav system quickly evolved over time into a confederal system of eight units – six republics (Slovenia, Croatia, Bosnia and Hercegovina, Serbia, Montenegro, and Macedonia) and two autonomous republics lying within the borders of Serbia (Voyvodina and Kosovo). As Sabrina Ramet has argued, Yugoslavia could be compared to a classic international balance of power system.[17]

After Tito's death in 1980, the system began to unravel. No longer able to reap the economic and political benefits of a neutral state during the cold war, Yugoslavia was under pressure to pay off debts and adapt to new realities. These problems put the Serbs at odds with the wealthier members of the northern political subsystem. Slovenes and Croats pressed for an even looser confederation, whereas many Serbs championed recentralization.

Serbs also used the period to bring up long-standing, but silently held, grievances. One of these was Kosovo. For decades, Serbs had been leaving Kosovo, in most Serbian views, because of intimidation. On top of that, the 1974 constitution gave the Kosovo Autonomous Region de facto powers of a full-fledged republic. Moreover, the new constitution allowed the internal Autonomous Republic of Kosovo to veto legislation at the Republic of Serbia level, whereas Serbia could not veto legislation at the lower federal level. Serbs railed against the political and social changes occurring in Kosovo in the wake of the 1974 constitution. The percentage of Albanian employees in the social sector rose from 58.2 percent in 1974 to 83 percent in 1978 and to 92 percent in 1980. The figures for Serb employment for the same years show a decline from 31 percent to 9.3 percent to 5 percent.[18] In essence, Serbs went from gross overrepresentation to underrepresentation in a matter of six years. For the Albanians, reforms had still not gone far enough. They asked why Montenegrins, with a population of only about half a million, should have

---

[16] Fifty thousand members of the Croatian League of Communists lost their party cards; up to five thousand were imprisoned; fifty thousand students were identified as "class enemies." The imprisoned included Franjo Tudjman, who would emerge later as independent Croatia's first president. See Sabrina Ramet, *Nationalism and Federalism in Yugoslavia 1962–1991* (Bloomington: University of Indiana Press, 1984), p. 202.

[17] See Sabrina Ramet, *Nationalism and Federalism in Yugoslavia 1962–1991*, for a full argument along these lines.

[18] Ibid, pp. 192–3.

a republic whereas two million Kosovar Albanians did not. Riots swept over impoverished Kosovo in 1981.

In the mid-1980s, Serbs increasingly accused Albanians of intimidating and committing violence against Serbs as part of a plan of "genocide."[19] On January 21, 1986, a collection of 216 Belgrade intellectuals connected with the Serbian Academy of Sciences sent a document to both the Serbian and Yugoslav assemblies lamenting the mistreatment and abandonment of Kosovo's Serbs. It appealed to the assemblies to respond to the petition of the Kosovo Serbs and implied that ignoring their demands would be no less than an act of treason complicit in genocide. The document went further, though. It painted Serbia as the constant victim of Tito's policies, especially those embodied in the 1974 Constitution.

Slobodan Milosevic rode to power on a wave of discontent, using the Kosovo issue. Previously a faceless bureaucrat, Milosevic firmly established his public image as the defender of the Serbian people at a mass rally in Kosovo one night in late April 1987. After a clash between Serbian demonstrators and predominately Albanian Kosovar police, Milosevic was reported to declare, "No one shall beat these people." The phrase was taken as a guarantee that Albanians would not be allowed to persecute Serbs under his watch. The crowd exploded with chants of "Slobo! Slobo!" As Noel Malcolm has described, "With a skill which he had never displayed before, Milosevic made an eloquent extempore speech in defence of the sacred rights of the Serbs. From that day, his nature as a politician changed; it was as if a powerful new drug had entered his veins."[20] Meanwhile, alarm bells were sounding in Yugoslavia's northern republics.

While Europe was starting down a path of integration, Yugoslavia was deep in the throes of disintegration. Through strong-arm tactics, Milosevic had taken control of four of the eight federal units by 1989. In Kosovo, Milosevic mobilized mass demonstrations that put Serbs in power; Voyvodina was majority Serbian and easy to take over; Montenegro was a traditional ally with close cultural ties. With four of eight votes, Milosevic could block any political initiatives of other actors. The wealthier of Yugoslavia's federal units, Croatia and Slovenia, pushed for decentralization, whereas the most populous unit, Serbia, pushed for recentralization of the state and increased power in Belgrade. Rather than fighting it out within the existing system, increasingly dominated by Milosevic and the Serbs, Slovenia and Croatia began a process of withdrawal.

Few people could predict just how violent Yugoslavia's disintegration would become. Certainly, few in the West were ready to play an intrusive role in the affairs of what had been considered a successful multiethnic state. The following sections outline the process of Yugoslavia's unraveling and the West's increasing involvement.

---

[19] This paragraph is from Petersen, *Understanding Ethnic Violence*.
[20] Malcom, *A Short History of Kosovo*, pp. 341–2.

III. PERIOD ONE: FROM THE COLLAPSE OF COMMUNISM TO THE SIGNING OF THE DAYTON AGREEMENT

For over forty years the United States and Western Europe created organizations and spent untold billions of dollars to contain Communism. And then there was no more Communism to contain. In November 1989, the Berlin Wall came down. Massive peaceful demonstrations brought down hard-line regimes in East Germany, Czechoslovakia, Poland, and Hungary. Democracy and freedom were on the march. Containment had seemingly worked better than anyone could have imagined. Western containment had stalled Communist expansion and isolated states with one-party systems and socialist economies. The policy froze the expansion of Communism while providing time for its internal contradictions and lack of human rights to rot the system from within. It seemed that a triumphant West needed only to provide guidance, and maybe some capital, to complete Eastern Europe's transformation.

But then there was Yugoslavia. Not that long ago, political commentators praised Yugoslavia as a political and economic success story. Many commentators viewed Yugoslavia as a "third way" between capitalism and communism. In an influential and widely read volume published in 1977, *Politics and Markets*, Yale professor Charles Lindblom extolled the economic and political virtues of Tito's Yugoslavia.[21] On the ethnic issue, as late as 1989, the *American Political Science Review* published an article based on survey research that concluded, "These findings support an interpretation of Yugoslav identity as evidence of diffuse support for the existence of a shared political community."[22] In contrast to the hard-line communist states of Eastern Europe, skilled industrial workers had been commuting or migrating to Western Europe as *gastarbeiter* for decades. With these connections to the West, along with a relatively developed civil society, it may have seemed that Yugoslavia would have been the best poised state in Eastern Europe to adapt to the changes brought on by the collapse of Communism. Western Europeans and the United States were, understandably, not able to imagine the catastrophe that would unfold with the demise of Yugoslavia.

A. The Basic Dilemma

The peaceful demise of Communism in Northern and Central Europe in the late 1980s seemed to bode well for Southeastern Europe as well. The situation in Yugoslavia was not comparable to that of its northern neighbors. Most critically, its demography was different. See Figure 7.1.

---

[21] Charles Lindblom, *Politics and Markets: The World's Political–Economic Systems* (New York: Basic, 1977). See the appendix in particular.

[22] From the abstract of Steven L. Burg and Michael L. Berbaum, "Community, Integration, and Stability in Multinational Yugoslavia," *American Political Science Review* (1989) 83: 535–54.

Serbs were spread throughout Yugoslavia's federal units. According to the 1981 Yugoslav census, Serbs composed 11.5 percent of Croatia, 32 percent of Bosnia, and 13 percent of Kosovo. These Serbian populations were long established and, in the case of Kosovo, possessed a cultural and political coherence and significance beyond those 1981 census figures. If Yugoslavia dissolved along republic boundaries, the new states would find a titular majority facing off against a significant Serbian minority. A second issue concerned force. If they wanted to, these new Serbian minorities could produce violence disproportionate to their numbers, especially when supported by Serbia proper. Some analysts have summed up the dilemma of the breakup of multiethnic states by formulating the issue in terms of the following question: why should I be a minority in your state when you can be a minority in mine? But in the Yugoslav case, the essential question could be phrased differently: Why should a Serb, with access to superior force, be willing to become a minority to weaker peoples?

The non-Serbs possessed an answer to this question: Serbs will become a minority because the rich and powerful states of the West will recognize the new states as legitimate and give Serbs little choice in the matter. In other words, the imbalance of power favoring the Serbs in the region would be countered by Western recognition and implicit, if not explicit, guarantees of support accompanying that recognition. Attempts to draw in the West to counter Serbian power and threats would repeatedly play out in different forms over the course of the 1990s in the former Yugoslavia.

To draw out a major implication of this book, the West was a primary actor from the first stages of Yugoslavia's dissolution. Balkan actors were incorporating estimates of Western intervention into their strategic calculations from the beginning stages of Yugoslavia's collapse. Accordingly, the starting point of this work on Western intervention must go back to these early stages.

The non-Serbs were playing a dangerous game. First of all, "the West" was hardly a coherent actor in the early 1990s. Until 1993, Europe, as a political entity, existed in the form of the European Economic Community. As an organization, it did not possess a recognizable foreign policy or the ability to intervene in conflicts. Things changed with the Treaty on the European Union, signed in Maastricht in February 1992 and put into force on November 1, 1993. The Treaty introduced new forms of cooperation among the member states, including the area of defense. The EU's "three pillars" were designed to expand the organization's mission into the political as well as the economic realm. However, at the beginning stages of Yugoslavia's disintegration, such pillars did not exist and would take years to become established. In fact, the continual crises and wars emerging from the Balkans provided the impetus for this expansion of Europe's capacity and policy. As far as the United States was concerned, its role was even more ambiguous. As Communism collapsed, the United States turned its attention to Iraq, fighting a major war to reverse Saddam Hussein's invasion of Kuwait. As some Balkan actors would find out, it would be difficult to predict whether the United States saw that they "had a dog" in any particular Balkan fight.[23]

In short, it is not clear that during the early stages of the Yugoslav wars, Western leaders and politicians fully understood the situation and what their role should or could be. Leaders of the emerging states still placed their hopes on "the West" and tried to bring it in.

B. Slovenia

After walking out of the 1990 League of Communists of Yugoslavia Congress, the Slovenes and Croatians prepared for secession. In December 1990, Bosnia held its first multiparty elections and elected Alia Izetbegovic as President. As the Slovenes, Croats, Muslims (as they were called then), and Macedonians prepared for independence, the Serbs, including members of the Serbian minorities within non-Serbian republics, prepared for war. In Bosnia, Radovan Karadzic ascended to the leadership of the hard-line Serbian Democratic Party. Zeljko Raznatovic, better known as Arkan, formed his Tigers, one of a number of Serbian paramilitary forces. Within the Yugoslav National Army (JNA), some members made moves that would allow the transfer of weapons and soldiers to a new Serbian force.

As discussed in Section A, if Yugoslavia collapsed, severe imbalances of power in favor of the Serbs would result. For the non-Serbs, the hope was that Western recognition and Western pressure would deter or persuade Serbs to accept the new political realities and the new territorial boundaries. At first, it seemed that such hopes might be well founded. The Slovenes were the first to act, holding a plebiscite in late December 1990 in which 88 percent voted for independence. On June 25, 1991, the Slovenian Assembly declared independence. A ten-day war then followed. By most standards of war, it was a half-hearted engagement by the Serbs. The military command did not have a coherent plan,[24] JNA soldiers fought with low morale, and the political leadership did not seem to care about the ethnically homogenous Slovenian republic. Under these favorable circumstances, the European Community sent mediators to end the fighting. After three trips by the EC "troika" (the foreign minister of the state currently holding the EC presidency, as well as his or her predecessor and scheduled successor), the foundation was laid for the Brioni Accord, which successfully ended the war. All told, about sixty combatants lost their lives. The JNA withdrew peacefully. Although not officially recognized by either the European Community or the United States, the Slovenes had gained full control over their territory.

---

[23] This is a famous phrase attributed to U.S. Secretary of State James Baker.

[24] On one side, Colonel-General Blagoje Adzic, the JNA Chief of Staff, advocated an all out military operation to remove the Slovenian government. He was opposed by Veljko Kadijevic, the Yugoslav Defence Minister General of the Army, who wanted to move more cautiously to simply convince the Slovenian government to back down on its declaration of independence.

C. Croatia

The Slovenian experience would not be repeated. There were differences in the nature of the conflict in Croatia even before the war began. The Serbs reawakened images from the Second World War and spread predictions about the resurrection of the Ustasha regime. The Croatians provided fuel for this fire. In July 1990 they replaced the red star emblem of the Yugoslav flag in July 1990 with the sahovnica, the traditional red and white checkerboard symbol of Croatia, which Serbs identify with the Ustasha. Streets and public places named for Second World War victims were renamed for figures associated with the pro-Hitler Pavelic regime. In December 1990, the constitutional status of the Croatian Serbian minority was downgraded from "constituent nation" to "national minority."[25] Furthermore, in early 1991, Serbs were expunged from the police force, from educational and medical institutions, and even from some private firms. In effect, Serbs were eliminated from most positions of day-to-day authority.

In May 1991, twelve Croatian policemen were killed and reportedly mutilated in Borovo Selo, near the eastern Croatian city of Vukovar. When Croatia declared independence,[26] a serious war soon broke out. Serbs, making up more than 12 percent of the population[27] (many concentrated in the Krajina region and eastern Slavonia), rapidly mobilized for war. One of the first casualties was the city of Vukovar, just across the river from Serbia. The previously wealthy and integrated city was under siege for eighty-seven days from August until November of 1991. The Serbs were victorious, but only after 90 percent of the city's buildings were destroyed. Across Croatia, six thousand people lost their lives and over half a million were displaced.[28] Serbian forces gained control over one-fourth of the Croatian territory in Krajina and eastern Croatia before a stable front line was established at the end of 1991.

With a lull in the fighting, the Europeans were left with a key political decision – whether to grant official recognition to Slovenia and Croatia. The problem was that there were no "Europeans" at this point, just individual states. Austria, Germany (especially parties and factions based in Bavaria), and the Vatican all supported independence and lobbied for recognition. Hungary supported continuation of Yugoslavia publicly, but secretly sold tens of thousands of Kalashnikovs to the Croatian government in 1990.[29] Other states, most notably France and Great Britain, were far more reticent about recognizing Slovenia and Croatia. In fact, James Baker, enunciating U.S. policy, stated

---

[25] See Hayden, *Blueprints for a House Divided*, pp. 69–71 for a discussion of the Croatian constitution of December 1990.

[26] Croatia declared independence on the same day as Slovenia.

[27] According to the 1991 census, Serbs composed 12.2 percent of Croatia's population.

[28] Elizabeth Pond, *Endgame in the Balkans: Regime Change, European Style* (Washington, DC: Brookings Institution, 2006), pp. 18.

[29] Woodward, *Balkan Tragedy*, p. 149.

that secession would be illegal. In the end, Germany forced the other EC members' hands by announcing its plan to unilaterally recognize both Slovenia and Croatia, which it did on December 23, 1991. Arguing that recognition would prove to be an effective deterrent, Helmut Kohl provided little opportunity for resisting Germany's decision. The Vatican followed on January 13.

Yugoslavia was now dead. If one republic had the right to secede, so did the others. However, for members of Serbian minorities in these states, Europe's action was cited as justification of the principle of self-determination. If Croats had the right to secede from Yugoslavia, then Serbs should have the right to secede from Croatia.

D. Bosnia

Both Germany and the United States viewed Serbian aggression as the primary threat to peace in the region. Germany's use of recognition as a deterrence strategy eliminated any chance for the preservation of Yugoslavia in anything resembling its past form. Although the Germans' special relationship to the Croats was implicitly acknowledged, the Americans took the lead on Bosnia. The U.S. leadership believed at the time that the best hope for preserving peace was to follow the Germans' lead. The United States supported a referendum followed by quick recognition of a Bosnian state. U.S. Ambassador Warren Zimmerman has written:

I believed that early Western recognition, right after the expected referendum majority for independence, might present Milosevic and Karadzic with a *fait accompli* difficult for them to overturn. Milosevic wanted to avoid economic sanctions and to win recognition for Serbia and Montenegro as successors to Yugoslavia; we could offer him that recognition in exchange for the recognition of the territorial integrity of the four other republics, including Bosnia. I conceded drawbacks to my proposal. In the understatement of the year, I said, "I don't deny that there is some chance of violence if Bosnia wins recognition," but added my belief that "there is a much greater chance of violence if the Serbian game plan proceeds unimpeded.[30]

Izetbegovic had recognized the dangers of early recognition but, after the EC's move to recognize Slovenia and Croatia, he changed his position. Bosnia held a referendum on independence on February 29/March 1 of 1992. With Serbs boycotting, the result was 63.4 percent turnout with 99.7 percent voting yes. Fighting broke out in March. The EC recognized Bosnia on April 6 and the United States followed the next day.

Recognition did not stop the further descent into war. In fact, April saw an escalation as forces entered eastern Bosnia from Serbia proper. The numbers of dead, wounded, and displaced would come to dwarf anything previously imagined. At least 97,500 individuals died during the conflict. The majority of

---

[30] From Warren Zimmerman, *Origins of a Catastrophe: Yugoslavia and Its Destroyers* (New York: Random House, 1999), p. 192.

civilians were killed in the early period between May and August 1992, the period of ethnic cleansing by Serbian forces.[31] Of that total, 40,000 were civilians (33,000 Bosniaks, 4,100 Serbs, 2,200 Croats). Serbian forces took two-thirds of Bosnian territory and set up 400 detention centers. Hundreds of thousands became refugees or internally displaced. Rape was commonplace and may have been used as a weapon.[32] Serbs laid siege to Sarajevo with indiscriminate violence – snipers targeting civilians and mortar shells hitting the marketplace.[33] The fighting involved not only battles with and against Serbs, but also between Croats and Muslims. At one point, Croat forces launched more than 1,000 shells a day into the eastern half of Mostar, the Muslim section of the city.[34]

While the bodies piled up, the West introduced a series of peace plans, each plan proposing devolution of powers and a demarcation of territory. In February 1992, before the main Bosnian fighting had broken out, the European Community held a peace conference that resulted in the Carrington–Cutliero (or Lisbon) peace plan. It was signed by representatives of all three communities before Izetbegovic withdrew his signature on March 28.[35] In January 1993 came the Vance–Owen plan, which stalled in May of the same year. It was rejected by the Bosnian Serb assembly and declared "dead" by Lord Owen in June. Lord Owen then helped engineer the Owen–Stoltenberg plan, which the Bosniaks rejected on August 29, 1993.

In February 1994, five powerful states came together to form the Contact Group (United States, Russia, France, Great Britain, and Germany). The Contact Group made steady progress toward an agreement. Violent events also helped push toward a final agreement. A mortar shelling of the Sarajevo marketplace helped galvanize Western opinion supporting more forceful efforts. The balance of force, once overwhelmingly in favor of the Serbs, evened up, with help from the United States and others. The Muslims and Croats were now able to reverse some of the Serbian territorial gains.

[31] The most authoritative numbers come from Mirsad Tokaca, "Human Losses in Bosnia-Herzegovina 1991–1995," better know as "The Bosnian Book of the Dead." Tokaca's database sorts the victims by name, place, and circumstances of death. The other figures in this paragraph also come from this source.
[32] Alexandra Stiglmayer, *Mass Rape: The War against Women in Bosnia-Hercegovina* (Lincoln: University of Nebraska Press, 1994).
[33] Pond provides figures of 10,000 civilians killed and 56,000 wounded. See *Balkan Endgame*, p. 27.
[34] Misha Glenny, *The Balkans: Nationalism, War and the Great Powers, 1804–1999* (New York: Viking, 2000), p. 641.
[35] Izetbegovic withdrew his signature after meeting with U.S. Ambassador Zimmermann. As Zimmermann reported after discussing the plan with Izetbegovic, "He said he [Izetbegovic] didn't like it. I told him if he didn't like it, why sign it?" Later, after tens of thousands of deaths, Zimmermann said that in retrospect "the Lisbon agreement wasn't bad at all." See David Binder, "U.S. Policymakers on Bosnia Admit Errors in Opposing Partition in 1992," *New York Times*, August 29, 1993.

One of the main stumbling blocks to a final agreement in Bosnia was the existence of two minority pockets. In Croatia proper, the Serbian-held Krajina region provided connections and support for the Serbs in southern Bosnia. In eastern Bosnia, the pockets of Srebrenica and Gorazde disrupted the unity of Serb-held territory. Both of these areas would be dealt with ruthlessly in July 1995. In that month, Croatian forces swept through Krajina, resulting in the flight of almost the entire Serbian population. By this time, the United States had lost patience and was ready to sanction brute force to end the conflict. As the Croats prepared Operation Storm, U.S. and other policy makers anticipated what amounted to an ethnic cleansing operation by Croat forces against Serbs. Bob Frasure, a top aide to Richard Holbrooke, the architect of U.S. policy in the region, wrote Holbrooke the following note: "We 'hired' these guys to be our junkyard dogs because we were desperate. We need to try to 'control' them. But this is no time to get squeamish about things. This is the first time the Serb wave has been reversed. That is essential for us to get stability, so we can get out."[36] The Europeans were not quite on the same page at this time. Carl Bildt, the European Union mediator at the time, asked, "If we accept that it is alright for Tudjman to cleanse Croatia of its Serbs, then how on earth can we object if one day Milosevic sends his army to clean out the Albanians from Kosovo?"[37] In fact, three of the Croatian generals leading the three-month operation, Ante Gotovina, Ivan Cermak, and Mladen Markac, would go on trial at the Hague in March 2008 on charges of war crimes and crimes against humanity, including persecution, murder, and plunder.

The Serbs dealt with Srebrenica in an even more ruthless fashion.[38] By 1993, Muslim refugees swelled Srebrenica's population from a sleepy mixed town of 6,000 to a teeming homogenously Muslim camp of 30,000. They survived under the watch of a Dutch-administered UN protection force (UNPROFOR). Despite the idea of Srebrenica as a safe haven, skirmishes continued between Serbian and Bosnian forces around the town. The Serbs would not give up their heavier weapons and the Muslims would not give up their lighter ones. The asymmetry in weapons led Bosnian General Naser Oric toward a specific strategy. As Elizabeth Pond summarizes, "Like many other Bosniaks who saw their only salvation in eliciting international help, he hoped that his periodic forays into the surrounding Serb-held territory might provoke the Serbs into retaliation with sufficiently publicized savagery to prod the West into intervening."[39] As it turned out, the Serbs engaged in savagery but there was no Western intervention.

On July 6, Serbs began a bombardment of Srebrenica and the Drina corps advanced on the town; roughly 20,000 Bosniaks gathered near the Dutch compound; the Serbs also took Dutch personnel hostage. On July 11, General

---

[36] Richard Holbrooke, *To End a War* (New York: Random House, 1999), p. 73.

[37] Quoted by Misha Glenny, *The Balkans*, p. 650.

[38] On Srebrenica, see Jan Willem Honig and Norbert Both, *Srebrenica: Record of a War Crime* (New York: Penguin Books, 1996).

[39] Pond, *Balkan Endgame*, p. 28.

Ratko Mladic entered the town, claiming it for Serbia. On July 12, 23,000 women and children were bused out. On the following day, peacekeepers handed over 5,000 males and received back the Dutch hostages. Then Serb forces engaged in a five-day slaughter of roughly 7,000–8,000 Bosniaks. In the long run, this event would help transform how the West intervened in the region, and to a significant extent, in the world at large. In the short run, along with the cleansing of Krajina, it helped create homogenous territories that eased the path toward the Dayton accord.

A second shelling of the Sarajevo marketplace on August 28, 1995 helped to launch Operation Deliberate Force, a ratcheted-up NATO bombing campaign designed to bring the Serbs to the bargaining table. By the fall of 1995 all of the elements necessary for the Dayton agreement were in place. The most serious demographic impediments had disappeared; the balance of force had evened out; the Croats and Muslims had agreed to work together in a future federation; the Contact Group had gained acceptance of a 51:49 territorial split between the Muslim–Croat Federation and a Serbian entity; Milosevic was willing to accept an agreement in return for an end to sanctions.

The Dayton General Framework Agreement for Peace was signed in November 1995. The specifics of the accord are discussed in many works.[40] Suffice it to say that the agreement established a very weak central government, essentially creating a bifurcated state.

Western involvement throughout this period was marked by hesitation, ambivalence, and incoherence. Susan Woodward has summed up the West's reactions in the early stages of violence:

> The longer the agony and horrors went on, the more inevitable and immune to outside intervention the wars seemed. Outsiders labeled them alternatively civil wars (ascribed to ancient hatreds and a history of conflict in the region) and wars of Serbian aggression. They asked whether they should intervene and what interests would justify their engagement, as if they were not already actively involved. Critics of Western governments denounced the ineffectiveness of their diplomacy to stop the fighting with the charge, which began to circulate near the end of 1991, that the crisis was a result of too little, too late. They failed to appreciate that they had been internal players in the story all along.[41]

The West's confusion and hesitant involvement was understandable. The United States had just fought a major war in Iraq, and interests in the Middle East were more vital than those in the Balkans. The Europeans were focused on their own process of integration. Moreover, European states' loyalties were divided; Serbia was not the clear "bad guy" at the beginning of the collapse,

---

[40] See, among others, Sumantra Bose, *Bosnia after Dayton: Nationalist Partition and International Intervention* (New York: Oxford University Press, 2002). Sabrina Ramet reviews works on the Dayton Accord in the eighth chapter of *Thinking about Yugoslavia: Scholarly Debates about the Yugoslav Breakup and the Wars in Bosnia and Kosovo* (Cambridge: Cambridge University Press, 2005).

[41] Susan Woodward, *Balkan Tragedy*, p. 147.

especially in some French and British circles. German sympathies, and Catholic sympathies more generally, lay with the Croats and Slovenes.

By the end of 1995, however, a more consistent and coherent approach had crystallized with the help of several events. First, after four attempts, the West brokered a major accord in Bosnia, as well as the Erdut Accord in Croatia. The West was now in the Balkan accord business. Second, the international community established the International Criminal Tribunal for the Former Yugoslavia. When first established in 1993, this court was neither particularly Western nor very serious – its first annual budget was $276,000. Combined with ever-increasing shame over the European failure at Srebrenica, the court would help galvanize Western opinion on intervention. Third, a threshold for the use of violence had been crossed with the tacit approval of the Croats' Operation Storm and the NATO bombing campaign Deliberate Force. These forces would create the conditions for a deepening of Western intervention during the next period.

IV. PERIOD TWO: GESTATION

While the northern republics witnessed a series of wars, the southern subsystem was on hold. This period of calm fit the agendas of the three primary actors involved. The West had all it could handle and more in dealing with the wars to the north. Likewise, Milosevic knew that his forces could not handle all threats at once and he was a master at arranging his fights sequentially. The Albanian actors – the majority in Kosovo and the minorities in Macedonia and South Serbia – were willing to wait for the opportune moment when the West could come in on their side versus the Serbs. This moment certainly was not the early 1990s.

The West was a major actor in the southern subsystem even while it tried to limit its active engagement. On December 24, 1992, President Bush sent what became known as the "Christmas warning" to Milosevic, which read, "In the event of conflict in Kosovo caused by Serbian actions, the U.S. will be prepared to employ military force against Serbians in Kosovo and Serbia proper."[42] The message gave Kosovo's Albanian leaders hope that the West, and especially the United States, would eventually come in on their side and support their declaration of independence of September 21, 1991.

The Albanians, led by Ibrahim Rugova, could not plausibly develop a violent resistance strategy against the Serbs during the early 1990s. Instead, Rugova and his followers adopted a strategy of nonviolence and developed a completely separate and parallel social and political system. Eventually, it was hoped, the West would recognize the legitimacy of Kosovo's claims and there would be a state in place to take on the mantle of independence. I focus extensively on the logic and operation of this strategy in the case material.

---

[42] Cited in Tim Judah, *Kosovo: What Everyone Needs to Know* (Oxford: Oxford University Press, 2008), p. 71.

Meanwhile, the international community took important steps to head off conflict in Macedonia. The United Nations sent a UN preventive deployment force to keep the peace and deter would-be threats to Macedonia's security.

In summary, during the years of northern subsystem wars, the southern subsystem maintained something of an equilibrium, one that put important problems on hold. This equilibrium would endure until 1998. Despite an appearance of inaction, major changes were occurring that would help impel the West into massive engagement in the Balkans by 1999.

First, Western shame over failure to prevent atrocities in Europe increased over time. Human rights activists convincingly argued that the claim of "never again" had been exposed as hypocrisy by the massacre at Srebrenica. Activists had the International Criminal Tribunal for Yugoslavia (ICTY) at their disposal to pursue perpetrators and keep the issue on the front pages. For many commentators, the emotional legacy of the northern subsystem wars was the primary factor leading to intervention in the southern subsystem. As Cristina Churruca Muguruza leads off in an article explaining the 1999 Kosovo intervention, "The sense of shame over past inaction in the first four years of atrocious wars in the former Yugoslavia (1991–1995) remains the main explanation for the European Union and its member states' engagement in the humanitarian intervention in Kosovo."[43] With the rise of Tony Blair, Europe gained a strong voice supporting intervention.

The United States, and Europe to a lesser extent, "codified" some lessons from the northern conflicts – more specifically, that force needs to back up diplomacy. As former Ambassador Zimmermann writes in his memoirs:

For three years of the Bosnian war, the Western countries had attempted to rebuff the Serbian aggressors, bloated by their use of force, without making them fear that force would in turn be used against them. Western diplomacy was reduced to a kind of cynical theater, a pretence of useful activity, a way of disguising a lack of will. Diplomacy without force became an unloaded weapon, impotent and ridiculous.[44]

This lesson applied especially well to Milosevic. There was anger in the international community over having to deal with Milosevic as a legitimate bargaining partner and the belief that he had gotten off easily. Many Western actors, especially Madeleine Albright, were more than willing to apply the lesson of the necessity of force toward Milosevic and Serbia.

In the international realm, the Right to Protect (R2P) movement picked up momentum. Srebrenica and the ICTY undoubtedly propelled the movement, whereas the movement helped support and legitimize the ICTY.

Finally, the West had been involved not only in brokering Dayton, but also in administering the Erdut Agreement (which was expanded into the Basic

---

43 Cristina Churruca Muguruza, "The European Union and Humanitarian Intervention in Kosovo: A Test for the Common Foreign Policy," in Florian Bieber and Zhidas Daskalovski, *Understanding the War in Kosovo* (London: Frank Cass, 2003), p. 237.
44 Zimmermann, *Origins of a Catastrophe*, pp. 230–31.

Agreement in the eastern Slavonian region of Croatia). Signed in the fall of 1995, the United Nations Transitional Administration for Eastern Slavonia, Baranja, and Western Sirmium transferred control of eastern Slavonia from Serbian hands to Croatian. The mission was designed to demilitarize the region, conduct elections, and create the conditions for the return of Serbian refugees. On the whole, the mission went well.

By 1999, the West was operating under the shame of Srebrenica, anger at Milosevic, and the confidence produced by the implementation of the Basic Agreement in Slavonia. In comparison to the early 1990s, the West was more willing, and ready, to intervene in the troubles of the Western Balkans that were to emerge in the southern subsystem.

V. PERIOD THREE: THE WEST GOES ALL IN

The empirical chapters in the second section of this book cover period three in depth, so I will simply provide the reader with a brief overview here.

Kosovo's Albanians were clearly disappointed by the Dayton Accords because Kosovo was not mentioned in them at all. Moreover, two years after Dayton, Kosovo had fallen off of the West's radar screen. The 1997 U.S. Congress made only two references to Kosovo, as opposed to nearly sixty in 1992.[45] Many Albanians came to see Rugova's "Gandhi" strategy as a clear failure.

By the mid-1990s, the Kosovo Liberation Army (KLA), formed mainly in exile, had broken from Rugova and decided that violence was the only way to get the West's attention. As summed up by Henry Perritt:

By 1997 the KLA single-mindedly defined its strategy according to its perception of what would make international intervention most likely. Once it had that objective clearly in mind, the KLA adopted and refined an interrelated set of initiatives aimed at inducing the "right" kind of intervention. The KLA recognized that international fears of a bloodbath in Kosovo could be strengthened only by objective facts reifying the fears. There actually had to be some violence. Even before Dayton, the most obvious difference between Croatia and Bosnia, where the international community was heavily engaged, and Kosovo, where it was not, was that there was a war in Bosnia and there was none in Kosovo. The KLA intended to erase that difference.[46]

By 1998, Kosovo was at war.[47] Two hundred thousand Albanians were fleeing the Serbian army's crackdown and sweep operations.[48] In response, the West

---

[45] Henry Perritt Jr., *Kosovo Liberation Army: The Inside Story of an Insurgency* (Urbana and Chicago: University of Illinois Press, 2008); see Figure 1, p. 139.

[46] Ibid., p. 143. I am quoting Perritt here not only because of his extensive book on the KLA, but also because of his clear sympathies with the KLA. There is not much dispute that this passage captures the KLA overall strategy, as the case material will also show.

[47] To pick up on the previous mention of Congressional attention, the U.S. Congress made 185 references to Kosovo in 1998.

[48] Figure from the UN High Commissioner for Refugees.

first replicated its actions from the northern subsystem. In September 1998, NATO presented Milosevic with an ultimatum to halt the crackdown; the UN passed Resolution 1199 in the same month, calling for a cessation of hostilities; the OSCE then deployed 1,800 monitors to observe a ceasefire. Despite these efforts, violence continued. As in previous cases, a massacre galvanized a more forceful Western response. A massacre at Racak led to the Rambouillet Talks in February 1999 and another ultimatum to Milosevic. After Milosevic rejected the ultimatum, NATO commenced bombing on March 24, 1999. The Serbian regime responded with increased violence and the effective ethnic cleansing of Kosovo.

These events led to a decisive moment for the West: how should they respond to another round of ethnic cleansing. The answer would soon become clear. The West would go all in on the Balkans – they would devote incredible amounts of military, economic, and political capital to ending the region's trouble and menace. The Kosovo air campaign became nothing less than an exercise in redefining NATO after the Cold War.

At the onset of the bombing, the EU met and decided that military action must be matched and coordinated with bold political action. Accordingly, the EU announced its goal in the Western Balkans to be nothing less than "the fullest possible integration of the countries of the region into the political and economic mainstream of Europe."[49] Two months later, with bombs still falling, the EU began an initiative to create a process to systematically bring the states of the region into the EU. The *Stability Pact for South Eastern Europe* was concluded on June 10, 1999. The pact was envisioned as a preventive long-term strategy of inclusion that would eliminate the underlying sources of conflict and instability in the region. Through official Stabilization and Association Agreements (SAAs), the EU would gradually align the polities and economies of the states of the Western Balkans with those of the EU. There would be a detailed process of "sticks and carrots" in each fundamental area: human rights, democracy, and market economy. Under the principle of conditionality, when states behaved well and met standards, they would be given certain privileges (e.g., relaxed visa requirements for travel) or rewarded with funds.

Correspondingly, the EU took the lead in reconstructing the economy of the region, and Kosovo in particular. The EU set up the European Agency for Reconstruction, which provided seventy percent of Kosovo's economic assistance; it also doled out more than 500 million Euros to offset the costs of the Kosovo intervention incurred by neighboring countries.[50] The EU budgeted tens of billions of dollars over the next decade in their effort to integrate the Western Balkans.

After nearly a decade of wars and upheaval, and a flood of refugees into Western Europe (including a significant criminal element), the EU decided to

---

[49] Lisbon European Council, March 23–24, Presidency Conclusions, *Bulletin*. UE 3–2000, I. Cited in Muguruza, "The European Union and Humanitarian Intervention in Kosovo," p. 243.

[50] Muguruza, "The European Union and Humanitarian Intervention in Kosovo," p. 245.

make the Western Balkan states an offer they could not refuse. In the words of the International Commission on the Balkans, "In security, economic and political terms, the Balkans are faced with a clear choice: to be part of the European Union or to be part of a marginalized ghetto."[51]

VI. FURTHER ESCALATION BY BALKAN GROUPS

Although the support of the EU was aimed at long-term stabilization in the region, the intervention in Kosovo, and the West's active engagement, also provided the impetus for two further escalations of violence. Violence brought in the West into Kosovo; why not elsewhere?

In late 2000, the Liberation Army of Presevo–Medvede–Bujanovac launched a guerrilla war based in the new demilitarized zone between Kosovo and Serbia. After a ceasefire in South Serbia, new fighting broke out in neighboring Macedonia in March 2001. In this case, the National Liberation Army (NLA) occupied significant swaths of territory and faced off against the Macedonian military. In both cases, the groups launching the violence were composed of Albanians hoping to bring in the West to help settle their grievances with their Slavic neighbors. There had been no violence in Macedonia since the state's inception in 1991, but the West's new active role in the region changed actors' decision calculus. Even commentators with strong pro-Albanian sympathies did not dispute the strategy of Albanian armed political groups. As Michael O'Hanlon summed it up at the outbreak of the Macedonian fighting:

I still worry that the ethnic Albanians extremists, many of them former KLA, deep down really think we'll take their side. They really think that if they cause trouble and this leads to essentially shelling of ethnic Albanian villages in Macedonia, at the end of the day we'll come to their aid militarily the same way we did in Kosovo. I think there is a fundamental assumption of U.S. friendship, which is both our greatest strength and leverage in one sense, but also potential danger here to the extent that ethnic Albanians feel emboldened to keep on going.[52]

In comparison to the early 1990s, the West immediately intervened to end these violent conflicts before they escalated. In South Serbia, the United States brokered the Konculj agreement, which reintroduced Serbian administrative control in exchange for political and economic concessions to the Albanian population. In Macedonia, the West essentially forced the Ohrid Accord on the parties.

By the first years of the new century, the West had become deeply involved with every region in the southern subsystem. By the end of the decade, Kosovo would experience at least four different types of international and Western administration. The West would still be a decisive actor in a drawn-out implementation of the Ohrid Accord in Macedonia. The EU would take over the

[51] International Commission on the Balkans, *The Balkans in Europe's Future*, p. 28.
[52] Brookings Press Briefing, "Macedonia: The Next Balkans War," March 27, 2001.

continuing mission in Bosnia. The West would still monitor the situation in eastern Slavonia, southern Serbia, and Montenegro. The West, a reluctant intervener in 1991, was to some extent intervening everywhere in the Western Balkans a dozen years later.

CONCLUSION

The following chapters apply a similar method to each case. Following Figure 1.1, they specify the nature of the intervention game. Each chapter then addresses the nature of structural and emotion resources available to opponents of that game. To use the analytical framework developed in the theoretical section of the book, I will specify the level of ethnic stigma, the nature of status relations, and the level of violence in a beginning section or chapter. This exercise will specify the matrix (R or NR) and the cell of that matrix that establishes the starting point for analysis of the case. Each chapter will then examine movement across boxes, or lack of movement, within the matrix. At the end of each case, the predictions developed in Chapter 6 will be evaluated. I will also assess the general dependent variable, that is, whether the West accomplished what it set out to do in the intervention.

Kosovo is the major case. After a brief chapter addressing Kosovo's Roma population, the next five chapters are devoted to Kosovo's story over the years from 1991 to mid-2009.

8

The Case of the Roma in Kosovo

I begin the empirical section with a brief account of the Roma in Kosovo. Although the Roma case in Kosovo is a depressing one and significant on its own merits, the Roma in Kosovo were not a large group, nor were they the primary players in the conflict there. Given the desire to avoid the ethnic stigma involved with being a Rom and the incentives not to declare oneself a Rom in the census, it is difficult to get a good estimate of how many Roma have lived in Kosovo. In the last reliable prewar census of Kosovo in 1981, Roma tallied 34,126 out of a population of approximately 1.5 million. NGOs and Roma organizations have produced numbers of up to 200,000.[1] The OSCE and Save the Children give a figure of 100,000 to 150,000 for Roma, Ashkali, and Egyptians combined.[2] These numbers are not high, and the Roma case is an outlier in some ways. However, outlier cases sometimes illustrate social and political phenomena in a stark way. I begin with the Roma case to isolate the workings of contempt and hatred, which will be seen in more complexity and detail in the Albanian–Serb case that follows. In addition, the case highlights the West's problems in dealing with these emotions.

I. CIGANSKA MAHALA, MITROVICA

In August of 2006, an NGO representative took me on a tour of what used to be Ciganska Mahala, or the Roma quarter of Mitrovica.[3] I say "used to

---

[1] See the discussion of these numbers in "Ensuring Romani Interests in the Kosovo Status Negotiations Process," European Roma and Travellers Forum, Council of Europe.

[2] Kosovo Roma Oral History Project (http://www.csdbalkans.org/roma/castes_clans.shtml). On the issue of Egyptians, see Roger Petersen and Mila Dragojević, "Who's Fooling Who? Mimicry, International Norms, and (Self) Deception," Paper prepared for the workshop "Mimicry in Civil Wars: The Strategic Use of Identity Signals," College de France, Paris, December 7–8, 2007. In this paper, we discuss strategies of ethnic mimicry used to avoid the ramifications of ethnic stigma.

[3] BY 8/25/06.

be" because there was absolutely nothing left of the old district. Prior to the summer of 1999, more than 8,000 Roma were official residents of a compact neighborhood on the south bank of the Ibar River.[4] It was one of the largest, most stable and least poor Roma communities in all of Europe and covered no less than 10–12 hectares of land. The mahala contained large family compounds as well as lesser dwellings. In 2006, only a few skeleton-like remains of some brick chimneys dotted the landscape, the rest destroyed in the aftermath of the 1999 NATO bombing campaign.[5]

After Milosevic capitulated and Serbian forces withdrew in June 1999, French KFOR units arrived in Mitrovica accompanied by elements of the Kosovo Liberation Army (KLA). With NATO troops present in Mitrovica, armed Albanians entered the Ciganska Mahala and threatened the population, giving them an ultimatum to leave or face severe consequences. Many Roma had already anticipated what was coming and left without needing to hear the threat. Some remained and were beaten. As all observers agree (including the former KLA officers that I interviewed), the perpetrators were a collection of different Albanian elements.[6] Certainly, uniformed KLA members participated, both those who had been in the organization for some time and late-joiners, and some "post-war heroes." There was no resistance to the action, either from the Roma or from the KFOR. The UN Regional Press Secretary in Mitrovica, Gyorgy Kakuk, described the events in the following words:

Right after KFOR's arrival the members, or so-called members of the Albanian guerrilla army the KLA, appeared on the streets of the *Ciganska Mahala*. They openly told to the Romas: better to leave, if they want to live. The intimidation worked. The Romas took off, fled towards the North. A few of them stayed in order to guard theirs and the neighbors' properties. The thugs beat them up as a special method of conviction, and then the party time started. The Albanians looted the houses, what was followed by the full and deliberate destruction of the entire neighborhood. No help arrived. Finally the Albanians burned the *Mahala*. The flames had been seen in every part of the city, for seven days and seven nights. The Albanians' *raison d'etre*, or self-justification was as always in similar cases: they (i.e. the Romas) were collaborators.[7]

---

4 The last reliable official Yugoslav census listed the figure at 8,516. Others estimate that perhaps 6,500 Roma actually were living in the neighborhood before the bombing of 1999.

5 I had also viewed the Mahala from across the river in 2002. Some changes have occurred since then. In 2006, the international community, led by efforts of the OSCE, began to rebuild housing for Roma in one section of Ciganska Mahala. By the summer of 2008, 56 houses and a few apartment buildings existed within the still mostly deserted area. An OSCE official provided me a number of 540 returnees. This effort would serve to house far less than 10 percent of the pre-1999 number.

6 I am basing much of this discussion from interviews BY/8/23/06, BY/8/25/06, ZT/7/4/08, FJ/7/6/08, EM/7/16/02, EM/8/1/08, HM/8/3/08, YJ/8/1/08, and KC/8/5/08. I also have some familiarity with the fate of the Roma in Mitrovica, because I lived across the street from a Roma IDP camp in North Mitrovica for two weeks in the summer of 2006.

7 Gyorgy Kakuk, "Unwanted People." Kakuk gave me this unpublished version in 2002. It was his original draft of an article heavily edited and eventually published in the UNMIK journal *Focus Kosovo* under the title "In Search of Home" in the February 2002 volume. I will

As several individuals related to me, the dismantling of the Roma Mahala took place in stages: first threats and beatings, then looting and burning, and eventually carting away of bricks and other salvageable materials. During the burning stage, Serbs and other non-Albanians stood on the opposite side of the Ibar River and watched. When they implored the French KFOR to respond they were met with the reply, "Soldiers are not firefighters."[8] Needless to say, the events did not bolster confidence in the ability of the international community to maintain security and institute the rule of law. Perhaps not surprisingly, the Ibar River would become the dividing line in the "frozen conflict" that persisted into 2010 (the time of this writing).

The action was apparently highly popular throughout the Albanian community. Bajram Rexhepi was the former Kosovo Prime Minister and a favorite of the West, credited with helping end the March 2004 anti-Serb riots. Yet, tellingly, when I interviewed Rexhepi as Mayor of South Mitrovica in 2008 and asked him about the Roma, his narrative was harsh, unsympathetic, and the same as I had heard in all my other interviews with Albanians.[9] According to Rexhepi, the Roma were serious collaborators. They participated in Serbian paramilitaries; they burnt properties; they killed Albanians. The Albanian population was very angry with them and as a result, complete destruction followed. Rexhepi stated that the Roma, as a small people, should have remained neutral in the Albanian–Serbian conflict, but they did not. Given their collaboration, emotions could not be controlled. This was the logic of the conflict. I heard this same narrative from a well-known Albanian proponent of human rights. In fact, I never heard any other narrative from Albanians.

It is undoubtedly true that some Roma sided with Serbs during the 1990s; some were engaged in looting along with Serb forces. However, the Roma would likely have been given only small and dirty jobs. They would have had no chance at higher responsibilities.[10] As for looting, "the Serbs would take all the good stuff and the Roma would be left with the peanuts."[11]

In any event, Roma across Kosovo, a significant percentage of the population, suffered the same fate as the Roma in Mitrovica. As in Mitrovica, Albanians in other localities burned out Roma neighborhoods and forced Roma to flee, many to Serbia, some to Western Europe.

II. CONTEMPT AND HATRED, SEPARATION AND ETHNIC CLEANSING

By any objective indicator, the Roma are a stigmatized ethnic group. The three indicators of intermarriage rates, residential patterns, and derogatory names

---

compare this passage from the unedited version to the UNMIK sanctioned version later in this chapter.

[8] EM/8/1/08.

[9] Interview with Bajram Rexhepi in Mayor's Office, South Mitrovica, summer of 2008.

[10] BY/6/30/08.

[11] EM/7/1/08.

all register extreme values. For the Roma, intermarriage rates are near zero. It is nearly inconceivable that an Albanian or Serb would marry a Roma. Roma live in highly segregated communities, both in a physical and in a social sense. Albanians often refer to Roma as "Madjupi," a derogatory term in Albanian for Roma. Sani Rifati, a President of "Voice of Roma" from Kosovo, translated the term "Madjupi" as "lower than garbage."[12] As seen in the discussion that follows, highly negative cultural schemas of the Roma pervade Balkan culture, and all of Eastern Europe, for that matter. In the case of the Roma, there is no question that there is high ethnic stigma.

The assumption of the existence of ethnic contempt as a powerful force that shapes the nature of conflict is fundamental to this book. The existence and level of ethnic contempt place a case within the bottom row in the matrices developed within the theoretical sections and help form the predictions outlined in Chapter 6. How does the previous analysis apply to the Roma case?

Regarding political status, some Roma may have cooperated with the Serbs and taken some previously Albanian jobs during the time of Albanian boycotts and parallel society. However, Roma certainly did not take visible positions of authority in the police, military, or bureaucracy. The Roma's language did not take on a different role in society. The Roma were still a stigmatized group, just one with opportunities to play off of Serbian actions. In effect, before the violence of the late 1990s, the Roma occupied box NR7: no violence, no resentment, high stigma.

This box predicts the highest likelihood of separation either in terms of boycott or in other, severe cases of a parallel society. Certainly, this was the reality of Roma social and political life. The Roma case is different from others in its outlier qualities of stigma. Here, ethnic difference and stigma created a centuries-old system of separation and parallel society. The extreme level of ethnic contempt makes this case less one of strategic decision and more one of the overpowering forces of history and culture.

The more interesting puzzle here is the outbreak of popularly supported Albanian violence, which completely eliminated the Roma from long-held neighborhoods. To walk through Ciganska Mahala in 2006 was to witness the complete elimination of a group of people.[13] There was hardly a brick standing on another in some sections. Clearly, there was something more going on than greedy looters seeing an opportunity for easy pickings, although that motivation was surely present. In this case, even Prime Ministers, human rights advocates, and others who might abhor looting saw the case as "normal" and part of the "logic of the conflict."

One might argue that the perpetrators were driven by resentment. In this case, they would be motivated "to put the Roma back in their place," and

---

[12] See Sani Rifati, "The Roma and 'Humanitarian' Ethnic Cleaning in Kosovo," *Dissident Voice*, October 13, 2002.
[13] See footnote 5 on the situation in 2008.

violence would be the clearest and quickest way to do that. As argued previously, this is not a case of status-driven action. Roma never rose much in an overall status hierarchy. In fact, they constantly occupied the bottom rung. Furthermore, when resentment is the driving force, a humiliating pogrom will usually satisfy the goal. The elimination of an entire neighborhood does not fit the resentment explanation.

Rather than greed or resentment, the popularly supported actions against the Roma are best explained as acts of hatred. Recall the basic definition of hatred: cognition that a group is both inherently defective and dangerous; action tendency to physically eliminate the presence of that group. The matrix analysis suggests that the most common path to hatred is from box 7 to box 9. That is, starting from a level of high contempt and moving to a situation of high contempt and high violence can create the combination of perceptions that create hatred and popular support for ethnic cleansing. As outlined in the second chapter, hatred is more likely if these perceptions fit a historical schema that reinforces the perceptions of perpetrator and victim.

By 1998, Kosovo had moved into a situation of high violence. After the NATO bombing began, and the Milosevic regime moved to a policy of massive ethnic cleansing, the situation could only be characterized as one of extreme levels of violence. From the Albanian perspective, Serbs were dangerous and clearly inherently deficient in their relationship to Albanians. Recalling Rexhepi's words, the Roma should have remained neutral, but they decided to serve with the Serbs to kill Albanians and burn Albanian homes. The Roma merged their fate with that of the Serbs, and they would have to suffer the same fate as the Serbs in the midsummer countercleansings that occurred in the wake of NATO's entrance into Kosovo. Ciganska Mahala, with its concentrated population and defenseless position on the south side of the Ibar, would become the starkest symbol of the cleansings of Serbs and Roma that occurred across Kosovo.

Although the actions against Roma were a sideshow in the larger struggle between Serbs and Albanians, historical perceptions of the Roma as collaborators reinforced a cultural schema justifying their cleansing. In fact, one of the most famous scenes in all of Balkan literature involves the Roma as ruthless collaborators. In *The Bridge on the Drina*, published in 1945, Nobel Prize Laureate Ivo Andric portrays a ruthless sixteenth-century local Turkish ruler in Bosnia who tortures and then impales a Serbian peasant rebel. The torturer is, of course, a gypsy. The scene, one of the most excruciating in all of world literature, goes on for several pages. The gypsy wraps red-hot chains around the Serb's body and pulls out his toenails. Then, in a long description filled with anatomic detail, the gypsy shoves a long white stake through the Serb's body in a way that avoids crucial organs. The impaled Serb is then vertically displayed as a deterrent to other Serbs. This passage, read by every Serbian schoolchild, may resonate in part with its connection with the crucifixion, although it is the crucifixion of the Serbian people rather than Christ. The gypsy is also charged with feeding the corpse to wild dogs. Local Serbs gather money to bribe the gypsy so they can take the body and give it a proper burial. The gypsy drives a hard bargain. During the negotiation for the body, Andric portrays the Serb's thought process:

The peasant was troubled, frowned and thought to himself: "He is a gipsy, a thing without cross or soul, one cannot call him either friend nor brother, and one cannot take his word by anything in either heaven or earth."[14]

In Andric's modern fictional account of long ago events, or in the Albanians' view of Roma in the 1990s, the Roma are consistently seen as doing the dirtiest work for a ruthless occupying regime. The roles were set and current events confirmed them. Any action against the Roma would be justified.

As violence ebbed after 1999, the perception of Roma as dangerous disappeared. The emotion of hatred likewise dissipated. Under the protection of the international community, some Roma have returned to Kosovo. Those who remained or returned have returned to life as it existed before the war. The Roma are again an isolated and stigmatized group living in a parallel society.

III. THE WEST, CONTEMPT, AND HATRED

I began with the Roma case because it seems indisputable that stigma, contempt, and hatred were important forces in determining the outcome. Many in the West are uncomfortable with these phenomena. They wish to believe that these ugly forces are isolated and strange, perhaps applicable to the Roma or the Jews during the Holocaust, but surely few others. In contrast, I have made ethnic contempt a key part of my general analytical framework. I claim that hatred exists (although rare) and provide an explanation of a process that shows how it comes about. The next chapters cover the Serbian–Albanian conflict in Kosovo. That case will again move across the lower row of the matrix and back (R7–R8–R9–R8–R7), although in a much more complicated fashion. I will argue that this set of outcomes cannot be adequately explained without reference to contempt and hatred.

Clearly, the Western forces that entered Mitrovica in the summer of 1999 were incapable of imagining the ethnic cleansing that would take place, let alone having an understanding of the forces that drive such actions. The French KFOR could not tell the difference between Roma and Albanians, and perhaps even Serbs. They simply watched the burnings as they went on for a week. The West stepped into a situation where contempt and hatred drove common people to support ethnic cleansing and it stood by helplessly.

Western discomfort with contempt and stigma also shows up in Western international publications. Earlier, I produced a passage from the UN regional press secretary describing the destruction of Ciganska Mahala. That description was from his draft copy. The published copy of the article went through

---

[14] Ivo Andric, *The Bridge on the Drina*, translated from the Serbo-Croatian by Lovett F. Edwards (Chicago: University of Chicago Press, 1977, originally published 1945), p. 56.

a process of sanitization. The title changed from "Unwanted People," implying a stigmatized group, to "In Search of Home." The voice changed from active to passive. The phrase "the Albanians looted the houses" was changed to "the houses were looted," a construction that avoids assigning blame or responsibility to a specific actor or group.

Most tellingly, the entire last section of the unpublished draft was completely omitted. It was entitled, "Who Will Face Justice?" The author cited a U.S. State Department document defining ethnic cleansing: "The term 'ethnic cleansing' generally entails the systematic and forced removal of members of an ethnic group from their communities to change the ethnic composition of a region." What happened in Ciganska Mahala was clearly ethnic cleansing, but not a cleansing that the international community wanted to deal with. Certainly the United States, then closely allied with the KLA, did not wish to bring it up. Ethnic cleansing was something that Milosevic and his associated thugs would be tried for at the ICTY. The nature of what happened on the south bank of the Ibar River in 1999, in the presence of NATO, was inconvenient for the Western narrative.

9

Background to Kosovo

On Sunday, February 17, 2008, the Kosovo Parliament declared independence. Firecrackers exploded on the streets of Pristina[1] and other Kosovar cities. The red and black Albanian flag, adorned with its two-headed eagle, was everywhere – draped on storefronts, waved on the streets, flying out of car windows. For almost every Kosovar Albanian, a dream held across generations had come true. Prime Minister Hasim Thaci, in his speech to Parliament, stated, "I feel the heartbeat of our ancestors." For other Albanians who had suffered under Serbian oppression, it was less a dream come true and more an end to a nightmare. In the words of one Albanian who endured Serbian neighbors killing two of her relatives in 1999, "Independence is a catharsis. Things won't change overnight and we cannot forget the past, but maybe I will feel safe now and my nightmares will finally go away."[2]

Relations between Serbs and Albanians had never been good. The relationship embodies every negative experience studied in this book: high levels of mutual ethnic contempt, status reversals, and antagonistic historical schemas connected to periodic bouts of violence and ethnic cleansing. The last such violent episode occurred only a few years earlier (in 1999) and was marked by the Serbian killing of an estimated 10,000 Albanians and the ethnic cleansing of perhaps 800,000 more. Many in Kosovo mark the 1981 riots as the date of a fundamental shift in Kosovo. Since then, the battle over Kosovo's political status has always been high intensity. The Yugoslav government imprisoned thousands of Albanians in the early 1980s; the Milosevic regime purged tens of thousands in the late 1980s and early 1990s; Albanian leaders created a parallel society; the Kosovo Liberation Army conducted violent attacks that

---

[1] Following Tim Judah in *Kosovo: What Everyone Needs to Know* (Oxford: Oxford University Press, 2008), I am using the more commonly used international spellings for Kosovo cities. This usage is changing. Likewise, I use the name Kosovo, not Kosova, for the same reasons.

[2] Dan Bilefsky, "Kosovo Declares Its Independence from Serbia," *New York Times*, February 18, 2008.

precipitated a civil war; NATO dropped tens of thousands of bombs; Albanians cleansed thousands of Serbs and launched a massive pogrom in 2004. For at least twenty-seven years, Kosovo was the site of a tumultuous and nearly never-ending struggle between Serbs and Albanians.

Now that struggle was over. A walk through Pristina in the weeks following independence emphatically illustrated the thoroughness of the Albanian victory. Along Nena Thereza Street, one first encounters a statue of Skanderbeg, the Albanian national hero, standing guard in front of UNMIK headquarters. In a smaller form down the street, Mother Theresa holds out her arms to the impoverished. Going farther, in the form of a children's action toy, Zahir Q. Pajaziti, a KLA guerrilla fighter, overlooks the street. On a large sheet draped from the Iliria Hotel, the silhouette of the martyr Adam Jashiri looks down. The caption reads "Bac, u kry!" meaning "respected uncle, it is over." Street names honor Bill Clinton, Madeleine Albright, and other Western allies. Even more striking, every trace of Slavic history and culture had been wiped clean from the major thoroughfares. The frame of a gutted Serbian Orthodox church hovered at the edge of Pristina's major park and university area. Its ghostlike appearance was fittingly symbolic.

I. WHAT IS TO BE EXPLAINED?

A. The General Outcome

Although Kosovo's independence was a clear victory for Albanians, the outcome for the West left much to be desired. The Standards before Status policy listed eight goals: (1) functioning democratic institutions, (2) the rule of law, (3) freedom of movement, (4) returns and reintegration, (5) a market economy with privatized assets, (6) property rights, (7) normal dialogue with Belgrade and other neighboring states, and (8) development of a scaled-down and multiethnic Kosovo Protection Corps that would help integrate combatants into a civilian organization. Did the West accomplish what it set out to do in Kosovo?

The record is mixed in some areas and is of outright failure on others. As of 2009, after independence, the economy was weak and criminal networks were still pervasive. Regarding the rule of law, it is important to note the conditionality of Kosovo's independence. In 2008, the EU would need to send in a "rule of law" mission to oversee Kosovo's judicial and police institutions. Kosovo was constitutionally bound to obey a Western blueprint, the Ahtisaari plan, which dictated many policies. Even after nearly a decade of oversight and tens of billions spent, the West did not see Kosovo as quite fit to rule itself. Given that massive anti-Serbian riots had broken out across Kosovo in March 2004, the West's caution seemed warranted.

Although relations with most neighboring countries could be considered normal, Belgrade labeled Kosovo a "false state" and normal relations did not exist between the two states. Additionally, more than a year after independence, only 56 of 192 UN members recognized the new state.[3] A quick analysis of these numbers shows just how much the case had become a Western project. Of the Western states (the EU plus the United States and Canada), twenty-four of twenty-nine recognized Kosovo (Spain, Romania, Slovakia, Cyprus, and Greece had not). Eighty percent of the rest of the world did not recognize Kosovo, including Russia, Brazil, India, and China.

The most glaring Western failure was returns and reintegration. This goal went beyond simply one of eight standards. Kosovo was supposed to be a test case for creating multiethnic democracy. Especially for the Europeans, Kosovo was to illustrate how virulent nationalism could be overcome through tolerance and reason. In the words of Michael Steiner, former Special Representative of the UN Secretary General (SRSG), "We came to Kosovo to protect human rights and we cannot allow this country to become monoethnic."[4] As others have summarized, "Until Kosovo welcomes back its own people, Brussels has made it clear that Kosovo has scant chance of being welcomed into the European family."[5]

United Nations High Commission for Refugees (UNHCR) data report that 230,000 Serbs were driven out of Kosovo after the 1999 war.[6] Ten years after NATO's arrival, only about 5 percent of all displaced Serbs had returned to Kosovo. In 2009, Western states were still committing significant funds to try to bring people back. For example, the British government was devoting a quarter of a million Euros to a project to build houses for ten Serb families in the Klina district. This small number is typical and indicates that the great bulk of the displaced will never return.

Even those numbers do not do justice to the monoethnic reality of Kosovo. For a state to have a true multiethnic society, it cannot be one in which minorities lack any presence in every urban area, where they have been driven out and choose not to return. But that is exactly what has happened in Kosovo. At the time of independence, not only Pristina, but also all of the major cities south of the Ibar River were essentially monoethnic. Pristina had about 30,000 Serbs on its voter rolls in 2008, but only a couple hundred Serbs resided there. Prizren was left with a couple of dozen Serbs. Podujevo had no Serbs at all, the last two elderly women driven out in the early 2000s. There is not a single major Kosovo city where Serbs play any significant political, social, or cultural role.

One city that has not been listed, Mitrovica e Kosoves/Kosovska Mitrovica,[7] is split by the Ibar River and has become the site of one of the world's "frozen conflicts." Neither side crosses the main bridge. There is no interaction. North

---

3 These numbers are from March 9, 2009.
4 (http://www.unmikonline.org/press/2002/mon/july/lmm120702.htm#1) 12 July 2002.
5 Whitney Mason, BCR No. 463, 08-Oct-03 (http://www.iwpr.net/index.pl?archive/bcr3/bcr3_200310-463-4-eng.txt).
6 Like many other figures, this one is widely debated.
7 I will simply use Mitrovica hereafter.

of the Ibar, Serbs essentially live in Serbia. They use the Serbian dinar as currency, collect wages and payments from Belgrade, and refuse to recognize the Kosovo government.

In the countryside south of the Ibar, Serbs live in impoverished subsistence communities, staying alive through subsidies from Serbia proper. International peacekeepers still stand guard. At the time of independence, approximately 14,000 military personnel were still needed to keep the peace in this small state. Whether their fears were justified or not, while traveling in 2008 I encountered many Serbs in the southern enclaves who did not feel free to travel within Kosovo.

Ironically, at the time of independence, Serbs were following a strategy of developing a parallel society. The Serbs in North Mitrovica and north of the Ibar River, as well as those living in the southern enclaves, existed within educational, health, and support systems disconnected from the Kosovo state. During the early 1990s, it was the Albanian population living in a parallel world. Now the system had come full circle. Given the existence of parallel systems, as of 2009 Kosovo obviously could not claim to have established the rule of law and functioning democracy over its entire territory.

In their 2006 book, *Peace at Any Price: How the World Failed Kosovo*, Iain King and Whit Mason evaluate progress on each of the eight standards.[8] They conclude their evaluative chapter with the following passage:

Where the international protectorate almost completely failed was in changing the way people thought and behaved. Unfortunately for would be nation-builders, it is this human factor that determines the character of a society, not its physical or institutional infrastructure. After six years of unprecedented international support, Kosovo remained a place where the strong bullied the weak, where might made right and where there remained an extraordinary lack of public spirit.

This is less than Western Democracies hoped for when they intervened to stop barbarities in Kosovo in 1999, and much less than most of the thousands of foreigners and Kosovans of all communities believed they were working towards between 1999 and 2005.[9]

B. Variation in Tactics and Provocations

The broader outcome can be explained by examining how the "game" between the West and local actors played out. The analysis will begin with the collapse of Yugoslavia. In terms of tactics, the following overall pattern is observed:

Preintervention, 1991–1999

1991: Albanian actors institute parallel society
1998: Albanian factions escalate violence hitting discriminate targets

---

[8] King and Mason, *Peace at Any Price: How the World Failed Kosovo* (Ithaca, NY: Cornell University Press, 2006), pp. 233–9.
[9] Ibid., p. 239.

1998–9: Serbian forces further escalate violence hitting some indiscriminate
  targets
1999: Serbian forces engage in massive and popularly supported ethnic
  cleansing
1999, spring/summer: NATO bombing campaign and beginning of UNMIK

Intervention, Internationals enter Kosovo 1999

1999, summer: A wide variety of Albanian groups engage in ethnic cleansing
Interveners institute Basic Western Intervention Game, which takes the form
  of Standards before Status (2002)
2000–2003: Many Albanians engage in low-level indiscriminate violence
2004: Albanian political actors escalate tension through a series of demonstrations and low-level provocations, eventually helping to set off the
  March 2004 riots
Interveners drop Standards before Status, institute first Standards with
  Status, followed by the Ahtisaari Plan
February 2008: Independence declared
2008: Serbian political actors employ demonstrations, some with low-level
  violence
2009: Serbs continue parallel society; violence ends

In the early 1990s, for Albanian actors, the game was about trying to bring the
West into their struggle. From 1999 to the early 2000s, the game was about
preventing returns and consolidating an Albanian state. By 2003–4, the game
was about forcing the West's hand on status and ending the Standards before
Status policy. For most Serbian actors, the game after occupation is about
preventing a decision on status, but also consolidating Serbian power north of
the Ibar and in the southern enclaves. In effect, Serbs are working to freeze the
conflict.

In most of these subgames, opponents of intervention usually win. They do
so, I will argue, through the use of emotion-based strategies. The combination
of outcomes from these smaller games explains the larger failures of the Kosovo
intervention.

II. APPLYING THE FRAMEWORK

This chapter, like all the other empirical chapters, employs the matrices developed in the theory section to explain variation within a case. The first question
regards the starting point of the analysis. This requires establishing levels of
resentment, stigma, and violence.

A. Resentment

The first analytical task is to determine whether the case is being played out
within the resentment (R) or no-resentment matrix (NR). To review, resentment

stems from the perception of one's own group being unfairly subordinated. This perception is in turn linked to visible signs and positions of political authority. Resentment is most intense after status reversals, that is, when members of a particular group experience a sharp reversal of their group's position on a status hierarchy. As outlined in the third chapter, status reversals are measured by the change in indicators of group status dominance. The most prominent of these indicators include:

(1) The language of day-to-day government
(2) The composition of the bureaucracy
(3) The composition of the police
(4) The composition of the officer corps
(5) Symbols such as street names and statues

Kosovo has seen several status reversals in its modern history, and three reversals in the last few decades.[10] Until the latter 1960s, Serbs held almost all important positions in the bureaucracy and police. Until 1966, the hard-line security chief Aleksandar Rankovic, whose fierce distaste for and distrust of Albanians was well known, made sure that Serbs were in control in Kosovo. Rankovic's removal revealed the extent of state repression of Albanians. Unconstrained by Rankovic's repressive methods, riots broke out in Kosovo in 1968. Tito's regime responded in a consistent fashion: on the one hand, the protest leaders received five-year prison sentences and the demand for republic status was unequivocally rejected; on the other hand, the regime created an independent university in Pristina and allowed the Albanian flag to be displayed alongside that of Yugoslavia. Perhaps most crucially, the regime began to promote significant numbers of Albanians into positions of political authority. Tito's repressive one-party regime again kept short-term order by combining suppression of the most obvious nationalist challenges with a quieter devolution of authority.[11]

As discussed in Chapter 7, the 1974 constitution accelerated progress toward Albanian dominance. As an entity, Kosovo gained almost all of the prerogatives of other republics (except the right to secede). At local levels, Albanians soon gained ascendancy in the police and the state bureaucracies, with

---

[10] Lazar Nikolic discusses a "pendulum of domination" and lists multiple shifts in dominance and discrimination in Kosovo: (1) The Ottoman period of 1850–1912 saw Albanian dominance. (2) The Serbs dominated and discriminated from 1912 to 1914. (3) The Albanians reestablished dominance during the First World War. (4) The Serbs again dominated in the interwar period. (5) The Albanians took control during World War II. (6) Serbs dominate in the post-Second World War era. (7) The Albanians took advantage of reform and autonomy to control political life from 1966 to the late 1980s. (8) The Serbs took power under Milosevic. (9) The Albanians dominate up to the present. See Nikolic, "Ethnic Prejudices and Discrimination," in Florian Bieber and Zhidas Daskalovski eds., *Understanding the War in Kosovo* (London: Frank Cass, 2003), pp. 57–70.

[11] In the words of Sabrina Ramet, "(T)he Kosovo case exemplifies conflict accommodation as practiced in communist Yugoslavia: jail the troublemakers but grant their nondisintegrative demands." *Nationalism and Federalism in Yugoslavia 1962–1991* (Bloomington: University of Indiana Press, 1992), p. 192.

Serbs sliding from gross overrepresentation to underrepresentation in a matter of a few years. By 1981, Albanians made up approximately two-thirds of the League of Communists in Kosovo and three-fourths of the police.[12] Serbs often complained that Albanian police discriminated against them. Whether this is true or not, as historian Noel Malcolm sums up, "No doubt there were cases where Serbs and Montenegrins came under pressure from Albanian-speaking officials and policemen, and found it a new and unpleasant experience."[13] Other scholars provide more sweeping evaluations of hierarchy. Hugh Poulton and Miranda Vickers write:

(I)n the early 1980's, the Kosovo Albanians were not suffering cultural repression. Kosovo was in effect an Albanian polity with the Albanian language in official use, Albanian television, radio and press, and an ethnic Albanian government leadership. Even the courts which were used to persecute those calling for a republic of Kosovo had ethnic Albanian judges.[14]

Serbian resentment helped drive the next status reversal. In the early Milosevic years, Serbs again took control over all visible positions of authority. In March 1989, Milosevic's forces, with the help of tanks and security forces ringing the building, took control of the Kosovo Assembly. In the spring of 1990, the Serbian Republic's Presidency announced that Kosovo's self-rule in education would be ended. Kosovo Albanians would no longer control what their children learned in school. Instead, they would be learning under a Serbian curricula developed in Belgrade. In September 1990, two hundred Albanian judges and district and public attorneys were sacked and replaced by Serbs.[15] Thousands of Serbian police poured into Kosovo, harassing Albanians without fear of repercussions. After the dissolution of the old Yugoslav state, army units moved into Kosovo from Macedonia. Kosovo was a land filled with visible signs of Serbian dominance. There is little doubt about coding a status reversal for Kosovo in 1990–91.

Kosovo is clearly a case imbued with political status competition. Accordingly, it is easy to code the case as one of mutual resentment. Obviously, Kosovo's modern history and the West's intervention must be examined through the lens of the resentment (R) matrix.

B. Stigma

Using the framework developed in Chapter 3, we can assess the level of stigma in a two-step process, with the first step involving consideration of intermarriage rates, residential segregation and ethnic flight, and racist terminology.

[12] Noel Malcolm, *Kosovo: A Short History* (New York: New York University Press, 1999), p. 326
[13] Ibid., p. 326.
[14] Hugh Poulton and Miranda Vickers, "The Kosovo Albanians: Ethnic Confrontation with the Slav State," in Hugh Poulton and Suha Taji-Farouki eds., *Muslim Identity and the Balkan State* (New York: New York University Press, 1997), pp. 152.
[15] Ibid, pp. 158–9.

Intermarriage between Serbs and Albanians in Kosovo is virtually nonexistent. Yugoslav statistics listed a 5 percent intermarriage rate for Kosovo in 1982, but that was among all nationalities.[16] The rate between Serbs and Albanians would be close to zero. In all of my travels in Kosovo, I never met anyone with a mixed Serbian–Albanian marriage or anyone who was a product of a mixed marriage.[17]

Regarding terminology, the term used by most Serbs is usually not "Albanian" but the pejorative "shiptar."[18] Albanians in Kosovo have their own pejorative term for Serbs, "shkija."

Residential segregation and flight can be considered together. By 1981, 80 percent of Kosovo's 1,445 communities were dominated by one ethnic group, many having become 100 percent Albanian. There had been a long process of separation and flight. Seventy-eight of these communities had moved from the mixed to the dominated category in the 1960s and 1970s.[19] From 1961 to 1981, 42.2 percent of Kosovo's Serbs and 63.3 percent of Kosovo's Montenegrins had exited the province.[20] Volumes have been written analyzing the exodus of Serbs from Kosovo. Even during the Communist years, the Serbian Orthodox Church was gathering figures, fearing the loss of a highly symbolic territory through Serbian flight. Some studies find that Serbs left for better economic opportunities; this interpretation is favored by many Western academics. Serbian studies, unsurprisingly, argue that Serbs were intimidated and violently pushed out.[21] By the mid-1980s, some Serbs were using the word genocide to describe the process.[22] In either case, the numbers suggest either that Serbs and Albanians did not care to live together, or that something more ominous was going on.

By the three main indicators, Kosovo clearly is a case of significant ethnic stigma. An examination of the extended set of indicators (existence of myths,

---

[16] Savezni Zavod Statistiki, 1961–88, Demografska.
[17] An Albanian working as a representative for a Western NGO told me if a child were to marry a Serb it would be like a death in the family (ZN/3/19/08). For a systematic, but problematic, statistical treatment of intermarriage in the former Yugoslavia, see Nikolai Botev, "Where East Meets West: Ethnic Intermarriage in the Former Yugoslavia, 1962 to 1989," *American Sociological Review* (June 1994) 59 (3): 461–80. As discussed later in the South Serbia case, Botev finds that Albanians in Serbia proper are 269.1 times more likely to marry other Albanians than by random mating (p. 474).
[18] For a short history of the evolution of this term, see Dejan Guzina, "Kosovo or Kosova – Could It Be Both?" in Florian Bieber and Zhidas Daskalovski eds., *Understanding the War in Kosovo* (London: Frank Cass, 2003), pp. 31–52; see in particular p. 32. As Guzina summarizes, "The Serbian version of the Albanian term for ethnic Albanians – Siptari – had acquired an openly pejorative flavour, implying cultural and racial inferiority."
[19] *Transitions* (May 1998) 5: 20–21.
[20] Zivko M. Andrijasevic and Serbo Rastoder, *The History of Montenegro* (Podgorica: Montenegro Diaspora Centre, 2006), p. 254.
[21] For example, see Marina Blagojevic, "The Migration of Serbs from Kosovo During the 1970's and 1980's," in Nebojsa Popov ed., *The Road to War in Serbia: Trauma and Catharsis* (Budapest: Central European University Press, 2000), pp. 212–43.
[22] See the discussion of the "Memorandum" later in this chapter.

evidence of a negative cultural schema, absence of political cooperation in terms of multiethnic parties and multiethnic alliances, the shunning of the group's language, and evidence of stereotyping) signifies Kosovo as a case of high ethnic stigma. Clearly, an examination of myths and cultural schemas indicates a malignant relationship between Serbs and Albanians.[23] As relations deteriorated in the 1980s, several incidents became cultural metaphors. The Martinovic case became a crusade for Serbs. In that 1985 incident, a Serbian farmer claimed that Albanians had sodomized him with a beer bottle. Serbs saw the incident as another example of Albanians violently pushing Serbs out of Kosovo, and using age-old Ottoman impalement techniques to do so. Pernicious stories arose on the Albanian side as well. In 1990, many Albanians claimed that Serbs had poisoned their children in a particular school (and devised a way to do so that would not affect Serbian children in the same schools). The fact that such stories gained so much credence indicates that something was seriously wrong with Serbian–Albanian relations. Julie Mertus, who analyzed these two incidents among others, came to the following conclusion regarding Serbian prejudice against Albanians, previously cited in the Introduction:

Kosovo was an abstraction, a set of myths in the popular imagination. Over time, the nationalism became racialized, that is, difference was framed in terms of perceived physical differences in skin, nose, ears, IQ, sexuality. In this sense, nationalism became "written on the body." Slurs against Kosovo Albanians shifted. No longer referred to as "white hats" (alluding to the hats worn by men in traditional dress), a sexualized imagery of Albanian men and women was adopted. In the mainstream Serbian and Yugoslav presses, Albanian men were declared to be rapists, although Kosovo had the lowest reported incidents of sexual violence in Yugoslavia. Albanian women were portrayed as mere baby factories, despite statistics indicating that the childbirth rates of urban Albanian women and those of other urban women in Yugoslavia were nearly identical. Accused in the past of being culturally inferior, Albanians increasingly were depicted as genetically inferior as well. This is racism of the purest sort.[24]

Politically, Yugoslavia was a one-party state up to the Milosevic era. Obviously, there was little in the way of multiethnic parties or cross-ethnic party coalitions as Milosevic's policies in Kosovo took hold.

Few Serbs learned the Albanian language; by necessity, Albanians needed to learn Serbian before 1999.[25]

Finally, a wealth of data underscore the ubiquity of stereotyping by both Serbs and Albanians. Sociologists from the former Yugoslavia and its successor state conducted seven research surveys between 1966 and 1999. These surveys attempted to measure ethnic distance, attitudes toward intermarriage,

[23] I analyzed these rumors in a presentation entitled "Balkan Rumors," given at the College de France, June 18–19, 2009.
[24] Julie Mertus, *How Myths and Truths Started a War* (Berkeley: University of California Press, 1999), p. 8
[25] Since 1999, Albanian children increasingly have not learned Serbian (personal observation).

stereotyping, interpretations of events, social tensions, and so on. Reviewing the data specific to Serbian–Albanian relations, Lazar Nikolic summarizes that "Albanians and Serbs do not live only in segmented territories, but in segmented realities and segmented time, claiming the monopoly in the victim-status.... Sociological research studied in this chapter shows that both societies, Albanian and Serbian, want ethnically pure and separate societies, and both groups claim to have suffered during the communist regime."[26] The desire for avoidance goes hand in hand with stigma; it is also a defining characteristic of the emotion of ethnic contempt.

C. Violence

The third necessary evaluation for applying the framework regards the level of violence. In the beginning years of the analysis here the coding is clearly "no violence." At the beginning of the 1990s, Albanians had little choice in the matter. Serbian force was overwhelming. Ibrahim Rugova, the uncontested Albanian leader at the time, assessed the situation and concluded, "We would have no chance of successfully resisting the army. In fact, the Serbs only wait for a pretext to attack the Albanian population and wipe it out. We believe it is better to do nothing and stay alive than to be massacred."[27] Correspondingly, Kosovo would remain, in its own repressive way, peaceful in the early post-Yugoslav years.

D. Summary

In 1991, the starting point of analysis, Kosovo was characterized by a high level of mutual ethnic stigma, Albanian resentment of Serbian political dominance, and no significant level of violence. In terms of the matrices developed in Chapter 3, the situation is box R7. Albanian political entrepreneurs thus had both the emotions of contempt and resentment at their disposal.

[26] See Lazar Nikolic, "Ethnic Prejudices and Discrimination," pp. 53–76. Nikolic brings out several noteworthy findings in this chapter. For instance, in 1990, more than 50 percent of Serbs agreed with the statement that "all Albanians are primitive and uncivilized." He also cites a 1994 survey showing that only one-third of Serbs would agree to socialize with Albanians, and more than half did not wish to live with them in the same country. Only one in ten Serbs would characterize Albanians as civilized or clean.

[27] Ibrahim Rugova, cited in Tim Judah, *Kosovo: What Everyone Needs to Know*, p. 71.

10

Waiting for the West

In December of 1989, a small group of Albanian intellectuals formed the Democratic League of Kosovo (LDK) in Pristina, which became the leading political force for Kosovo's Albanian population. The party was led by Ibrahim Rugova, a literature professor who had studied in France. To establish legitimacy for these alternative governance structures, underground elections for a Presidency (Rugova garnered 99.55 percent of the votes) and a Kosovo Parliament (the LDK won 96 of 143 seats) were held. The Kosovo Parliament declared independence in October 1991. Outside of Albania, no other country recognized Kosovo as a state. The Milosevic regime had taken control of Kosovo's political institutions and dismantled local Albanian governance. The question for the LDK and Kosovo's Albanian leadership was what to do next.

They had several choices. An incomplete list might contain the following:

They could acquiesce to Serbian rule for the time being and wait for better opportunities in the future.

They could try to reenter Serbian politics and side with anti-Milosevic parties in an effort to reform the system from within.

They could continue to boycott elections but participate in day-to-day activities relating to education, health care, and the economy.

They could not only boycott elections, but also create an entirely parallel social and political system in hopes of having it recognized as a legitimate government from the outside.

They could escalate nonviolent resistance through more direct belligerent acts of protest and civil disobedience.

They could start a series of violent provocations.

They could attempt violent rebellion.

In the end, Rugova and the LDK chose to develop a parallel society. In some ways, this choice was not the obvious one. There would be substantial costs and risks. Financing an alternative educational system required funds, which in turn required a tax system. Even with compliance, there might not be enough money to create a viable system. The same could be said for health clinics. Moreover, there was no clear payoff for such a strategy. The West, and the international community in general, did not wish to see the former Yugoslavia unravel yet further. There were no promises, or even indications, that Kosovo would ever be recognized as an independent state, despite its sacrifices. Furthermore, how long such a strategy would need to be carried out was anyone's guess. What made the Albanian leadership confident that this strategy was the way to go?

To answer this question, consider the strategic logic of box R7. The first question is whether the political actors have the ability to transform the game through the escalation of violence. As discussed above, the Albanian leadership could not seriously consider this option in the early 1990s. Almost none of the structural variables were favorable for armed resistance. Kosovo was a small state in both size and population; it was hilly, but not mountainous. Yugoslavia was not a poor state. Beyond some gross measure such as GDP, state capacity for responding to challenges in Kosovo was overwhelming, because the Milosevic regime had moved massive police and military resources into Kosovo. Furthermore, Albanians had little access to weapons. The only structural variable in Kosovo's favor was the existence of ethnic kin across the borders of neighboring states. Whether escalation of violence was a good strategy or not did not matter, it was simply off the table.

If the transformation of the game is impossible, the next question concerns mobilization of resources within R7. Chapter 6 laid out hypotheses related to this situation. Hypothesis seven predicts that escalation policies will not produce backlash from the political actors' own population. In this case, where escalation was not possible, hypothesis six is most relevant: in R7, political entrepreneurs are most likely to initiate the politics of boycott and the creation of parallel systems. The logic is that the population, desiring separation from the opposing group, will accept the costs entailed by this strategy. This logic played out in Kosovo.

Rugova and the LDK had other, less radical options than the creation of a parallel social system. They knew, however, that the powerful emotion resources of contempt and resentment would allow them to mobilize their entire population for a considerable length of time. Contempt provided the desire to separate and resentment the desire to end subordination.

The new parallel educational system illustrated how the strategy played out in practice. At first, 900 makeshift school sites sprang up before some consolidation took place. Sixty of sixty-six secondary schools continued to function in improvised makeshift classrooms, some without basics such as chairs and blackboards.[1] Textbooks in Albanian were lacking, but by 1997 more than

---

[1] Howard Clark, *Civil Resistance in Kosovo* (Sterling, VA: Pluto Press, 2000), p. 98. Chapter Five of Clark's book provides a good overview of the parallel system and its various elements.

150 new textbooks for schools and university had been produced.[2] In terms of broader figures, in 1997, 18,000 teachers were teaching 330,000 students.[3] To pay for this new system, the parallel government levied a voluntary tax collected and distributed by a municipal-level Council of Finance. Despite economic hardship, individuals, and especially small businesses, continued to contribute throughout the period.

The quality of instruction was probably not very good in many, if not most, cases. By 1997, roughly one-fourth of all students were not finishing elementary school.[4] Even Albanian commentators admit as much. However, finances and quality of education were not the principal things at stake. As Shkelzen Maliqi wrote in 1996, four years into the parallel system:

This several-years' long experience of such schooling which itself is the result of repression (children in lower grades in fact do not even know what "normal school" is) must have become a unique life school of resistance. The quality of knowledge acquired is less significant than the accelerated maturing of character that occurs as a result of the need to constantly defend personal dignity and threatened national and human values. These will not, after all, be "lost generations."[5]

Personal dignity and human values were one side of the system. Another was the fact that a parallel life meant getting away from the Serbs. Whatever the costs of the system, it would help end aspects of Serbian domination. The schools themselves were named for Albanian social and cultural figures. In the new makeshift classrooms, teachers hung portraits of Skanderbeg, the Albanian national hero. The curriculum excluded teaching of the Serbo-Croatian language.[6] The geography classes now taught the geography of Kosovo or the "Albanian lands." Certainly, history classes changed. The parallel schools provided an opportunity for Kosovo's Albanians to determine their children's educational content free from Belgrade. While Serbian tanks and police patrolled the streets, Albanians were completely free from Serbian subordination within their own schools.

The parallel system stretched outside of schools and across a wide swath of Albanian life. Rugova often described the system as one of "internal liberation." On the face of it, the strategy of building a parallel system may seem risky. Other strategies were available. Given the West's clear signals at the time that it was not prepared to recognize Kosovo in any near future, Rugova must have

---

[2] Ibid., p. 98.

[3] Ibid., p. 99.

[4] Ibid., p. 99.

[5] Ibid., p. 105. Clark is taking a passage from Shkelzen Maliqi, "Reading, Writing, and Repression," *Balkan War Report* May 1996, pp. 44–5.

[6] Denisa Kostovicova, "Shkolla Shqipe and Nationhood: Albanians in Pursuit of Education in the Native Language in Interwar (1918–1941) and Post-Autonomy (1989–98) Kosovo," in Stephanie Schwanders-Sievers and Bernd J. Fischer eds., *Albanian Identities: Myth and History* (Bloomington: Indiana University Press, 2002), pp. 157–71; see p. 167 in particular. Kostovicova points out that Albanians had also developed secret schools during the interwar period. She makes a comparison of the two periods in this work.

known that he would need to convince his followers to remain on a costly path of isolation for years. Yet, if one considers the nature of the emotion resources at his disposal, it was not such a perilous choice. Ethnic contempt, both Albanian contempt for Serbs and Serbian contempt for Albanians, provides a powerful force for separation. When combined with resentment and the desire to quickly end subordination, Albanian participation in and compliance with the new parallel system could be expected.

II. PERIOD TWO: ESCALATION OF VIOLENCE

The decision to create a parallel society led to stability in Kosovo from 1992 to 1996. Contempt's action tendency is avoidance of the opposing group. Under conditions of mutual contempt, each side found it easy to avoid the other. Albanians and Serbs had been gradually separating for many years, so the progression was not shocking. Furthermore, Milosevic had little reason to take on a new conflict in the south while fighting continued in the north. The Albanian side was still patiently waiting for the West.

Two events were to upset this equilibrium. First, the United States had brokered a deal to end the Bosnian war at Dayton with absolutely no mention of Kosovo. The West had recognized a Serbian entity within Bosnia but ignored the status of Kosovo. Moreover, the West made the deal with Milosevic as a legitimate partner in the bargaining. If the complete lack of consideration for Kosovo's plight did not discredit Rugova's nonviolent strategy, it certainly damaged it. By early 1997, 71 percent of poll respondents believed that Kosovo Albanians should radicalize their strategy.[7] The question was just how to do it.

Rugova would continue his nonprovocative parallel society strategy, even meeting with Milosevic in September 1996. Rugova and the LDK had invested much in this strategy, and a move to violence, they believed, might destroy political capital with the West. Student organizations asked what this capital had bought them and decided to engage in a series of confrontational demonstrations. On October 1, 1997, twenty thousand students clashed with police in Pristina.

The Kosovo Liberation Army (KLA) had another idea. Founded in 1993, the KLA had existed mostly as a small and shadowy group making a few sporadic attacks.[8] As late as September 1997, Rugova surmised that the KLA might actually be an invention of the Serbian intelligence services created "To make it look as if we Albanians were terrorists."[9] Events in Albania would

---

[7] BETA poll published February 17, 1997. The poll surveyed 665 Kosovo Albanians in 14 municipalities.

[8] For extensive treatments of the Kosovo Liberation Army, see Henry H. Perritt Jr., *Kosovo Liberation Army: The Inside Story of an Insurgency* (Urbana: University of Illinois Press, 2008) and Tim Judah, *Kosovo: War and Revenge* (New Haven, CT: Yale University Press, 2000), Chapters Four and Five.

[9] Rugova's statement from Main Frankfurter Rundschau, September 9, 1997.

help bring the KLA out of the shadows, however, and make it by far the most important actor in Kosovo in 1998. In the spring of 1997, the collapse of a giant pyramid scheme in Albania brought down the Albanian government and brought anarchy to the streets. During a near civil war, 2,000 civilians lost their lives.[10] Albania's bizarre tragedy was the KLA's godsend. With the collapse, the government lost control of its armories. Soon, 750,000 small arms made their way out of the armories, many ending up across the border in Kosovo.[11] Kalashnikov rifles were selling at five dollars each.[12] On top of that, Albania could now better serve as a training ground, recruitment center, and supply warehouse.[13]

For the first time, an Albanian political actor had the ability to transform the game. In terms of the framework for analysis, they could move the game from R7 to R8 by escalating violence. Although none of the "technology variables" had changed – the size and population of the state, the terrain, the level of GDP – the KLA now did possess the weapons and training to kill a significant number of Serbs. They did not, however, have the capability, on their own, to win the war that would result from initiating such killings.

For the KLA, the question could thus be framed as follows: should we escalate violence without a chance of winning the ensuing war on our own? The answer was a clear "yes." The KLA could see a clear two-step path to victory: (1) attack Serbs who are the most likely to strike back in an indiscriminate fashion; and (2) following this indiscriminate violence by Serbs, the West will have to intervene on our side. This was a risky strategy – there was no guarantee of Western intervention. In fact, the West was warning against escalation and explicitly stating that it would not intervene. The strategy would also require sacrificing Albanian civilians. Still, there is little dispute about the overall strategy of the KLA. As Henry Perritt Jr. summarizes:

By 1997 the KLA single-mindedly defined its strategy according to its perception of what would make international intervention more likely. Once it had that objective clearly in mind, the KLA adopted and refined an interrelated set of initiatives aimed at inducing the "right" kind of intervention. The KLA recognized that international fears of a bloodbath in Kosovo could be strengthened only by objective facts reifying the fears. There actually had to be some violence.[14]

Alan Kuperman's research provides a wealth of details on the KLA logic.[15] As one former commander related to Kuperman, "We knew our tactics did

[10] Chris Jarvis, "The Rise and Fall of the Pyramid Schemes in Albania," *International Monetary Fund, IMF Staff Papers* (2000) 47 (no. 1): 1–29.
[11] Shinasi Rama, "The Serb–Albanian War, and International Community's Miscalculations," *International Journal of Albanian Studies* (2002) 2 (no. 1).
[12] Judah, *Kosovo: What Everyone Needs to Know*, p. 80.
[13] Kosovo Report, p. 52.
[14] Perritt, p. 143.
[15] See Alan Kuperman's dissertation, "Tragic Challenges and the Moral Hazard of Humanitarian Intervention: How and Why Ethnic Groups Provoke Genocidal Retaliation," Ph.D. Dissertation, Massachusetts Institute of Technology, August 2002. Much of Kuperman's dissertation

not have any military value. Our goal was not to destroy the Serb military force [but to make it] become more vicious.... We thought it was essential to get international support to win the war."[16] Hashim Thaci, independent Kosovo's first prime minister and a founder of the KLA, where he served as the head of the political directorate, was explicit about the expectations of casualties: "We knew full well that any armed action we undertook would trigger a ruthless retaliation by Serbs against our people.... We knew that we were endangering civilian lives, too, a great number of lives."[17] Dugi Gorani, an Albanian negotiator at Rambouillet, stated, "Every single Albanian realized that the more civilians die, intervention comes nearer and nearer.... The more civilians were killed, the chances of international intervention became bigger and bigger, and the KLA of course realized that."[18]

Although the KLA decided that escalation of the conflict would bring about Western intervention, there was still the question of the type of escalation that would best accomplish the job. The KLA now had the capability to hit several different types of targets. These included (1) vulnerable civilian populations; (2) military installations and personnel; and (3) police. In addition to Albanian collaborators, the KLA's other main target was the police. The first public appearance of the KLA was November 28, 1997. By mid-January 1998, the KLA claimed to have killed ten Serbian police and other officials, as well as eleven Albanian collaborators.[19] *New York Times* reporter Chris Hedges described one specific assassination: "In a Jan. 23 attack whose boldness stunned the Serb authorities, rebels stepped into the road near the village of Srbica in the middle of the day and shot dead a local Serbian official, Desimir Vasic, 45, riding in his car with bullets as he lay slumped forward in the driver's seat."[20] By February, KLA members were regularly attacking policemen in Drenica; numbers killed in January and February totaled 66, as opposed to 55 in all of 1997.[21]

From an emotion-oriented viewpoint, the choice to hit Serb police would be expected. The objective was to rapidly escalate the violence. One of the chapters in a book-length autobiographical interview with KLA leader and future Kosovo Prime Minister Ramush Haradinaj is entitled, "To Win the War We Planned a Total Upheaval in Kosova."[22] As outlined in the second chapter,

---

is summarized in "Suicidal Rebellions and the Moral Hazard of Humanitarian Intervention," *Ethnopolitics* (June 2005) 4 (no. 2): 149–73.

[16] Kuperman, "Suicidal Rebellions," p. 160.

[17] Ibid., p. 160.

[18] From Kuperman, "Tragic Challenges," p. 358. Kuperman is citing A. Little, "Moral Combat: NATO at War," BBC2, March 12, 2000.

[19] Clark, *Civil Resistance in Kosovo*, p. 172.

[20] Chris Hedges, "New Balkan Tinderbox: Ethnic Albanians' Rebellion against Serbs," *New York Times*, March 2, 1998.

[21] Kuperman, "Tragic Challenges," p. 331.

[22] Bardh Hamzaj, *A Narrative about War and Freedom (Dialog with the Commander Ramush Haradinaj)* (Prishtina: Zeri, 2000); chapter heading is on p. 85.

the emotion of anger can be a most effective resource in generating overreactions and spiraling violence. Recall that anger heightens desire for punishment against a specific actor, creates a downgrading of risk, and increases prejudice and blame. Repeating from the second chapter, "Anger is a tool for creating spiraling cycles of violence that can transform an entire conflict... political entrepreneurs use anger to create a disproportionate retaliation that serves to clarify, both to one's own group and to outsiders, who is the perpetrator and who is the victim. Disproportionate reactions reveal the 'true face' of the opponent." As in the words of the KLA commander above, "Our goal was not to destroy the Serb military force [but to make it] become more vicious." One guerrilla told reporter Chris Hedges in early 1998, "The Serbs are losing control in Kosovo. They are lashing out with a fury that will only inflame the war."[23] The exact reason to imbue an opponent with anger is to "make him more vicious," to compel him to "lash out with a fury" and force him to bring about his own undoing.

It would be wrong to attribute too fine a strategic logic to the KLA's targeting in late 1997–early 1998. As an organization, the KLA was more of a decentralized movement or uprising composed of local militias than an integrated and hierarchical army. Yet those doing the targeting could not have picked a better target for generating anger and spiraling violence than Serbian police. KLA units could have hit civilians with indiscriminate violence to create fear and flight. This strategy was off the table not only because it would not have been as effective in generating violent spirals, but also because killing civilians would have diminished the Albanian cause in the eyes of the West.

KLA units could also have targeted military rather than police units. However, first, these targets would have been more difficult to hit. Second, Albanians knew that the army possessed a measure of professionalism and discipline that would limit an anger-based response. Many Albanians had served in the former Yugoslav National Army and knew its qualities. On the other hand, the police pouring into Kosovo were not such a professional group and certainly not a disciplined one; Albanians saw them as little more than criminals. Hit the police units and they could not control themselves.

In the summer of 2002, I personally witnessed the effects of the Albanian strategy. I was attending a KFOR-brokered meeting between a Serbian farmer and an Albanian farmer at a Serbian enclave in Kosovo.[24] My driver at the time was a retired Serbian police officer who had taken three bullets in the shoulder and stomach from an Albanian sniper. At one point, he had to leave the farmhouse where the meeting was held. He told me that all he could think about was killing the Albanians in the other room. This is the primary effect of anger – the burning desire to punish. In other conversations with this driver, he asked me how the United States could support a terrorist group like the Albanians. Under the influence of his anger, he was engaging in a predictably

[23] Hedges, "New Balkan Tinderbox."
[24] Field notes 8/7/02.

high level of stereotyping and blame. When I tried to explain the U.S. position, he seemed incapable of processing any level of complexity or nuance.[25] He assumed that any right-thinking people would see the Albanians as the obvious perpetrators and support action, even violent action, against them. He could not consider the broader consequences.

My driver was an example of Serbian police attitudes. Violence in Kosovo began to spin out of control. The Council for the Defence of Human Rights and Freedoms reported that Serbian forces had killed 1,934 Albanians in 1998. That number included 229 women, 213 children, and 395 elderly people. More than 40,000 houses had been burned and looted and more than 400,000 people had been displaced.[26] In February 1998, a police contingent surrounded the Adem Jashari family compound in Prekaze. After shelling the house with artillery, riflemen took out fleeing members of the clan. In all, fifty-eight lay dead. As news of the massacre spread across Kosovo, armed militias sprung up everywhere. There had to be vengeance for Adem Jashari.[27] The discriminate targeting of Serbian police had resulted in an indiscriminate response. In turn, along the lines of an anger-generated spiral, Albanians began pouring into the KLA, driven by their own anger. The violence kept spiraling. The KLA overran Orahovac; the Serbs continued to strike back. Support for Rugova and the LDK's nonviolent strategy was no longer tenable. Rugova himself joined the KLA bandwagon.

More importantly, the level of violence compelled the West to intervene. The OSCE deployed monitors at Kosovo's borders; the UN passed Resolution 1199 calling for a ceasefire and the withdrawal of Serbian forces; NATO voted on October 13 to authorize air strikes in the event of Serbian noncompliance. Soon, the OSCE was sending in a verification mission led by William Walker. Despite the presence of the West, both sides continued an armed struggle, although at a toned-down level. Serbian forces continued arresting Albanians on terrorist charges, whereas the KLA used the respite to rearm and reorganize. In his memoir, KLA commander Haradinaj described the significance of the OSCE mission: "You have to understand that due to the difficult situation that we were in, we were interested to be able to breath so to speak for a period of time. Actually, the agreement was life saving for the KLA. As far as the Dukagjini region is concerned the agreement had an important significance, and has helped us a lot for the renewal of the army."[28]

The Serbs did not take the ceasefire seriously, either, moving large numbers of forces into Kosovo in January 1999. On January 15, some of these forces killed forty-five Albanian civilians in the village of Racak. The head of

[25] The reader can go back to Figure 2.2 and trace the predicted effects of anger on preferences, information, and belief formation, all illustrated in this case.

[26] These figures are in Clark, *Civil Resistance in Kosovo*, pp. 177–8. UNHCR figures reported that in August 1998 260,000 Albanians were internally displaced and another 200,000 were refugees.

[27] Recall from the previous chapter that Jashari's figure hung over Pristina's main street at the time of independence with the saying, "Uncle, it's over." Kosovo's martyr had been avenged.

[28] Haradinaj in Bardh Hamzaj, *A Narrative about War and Freedom*, p. 115.

the OSCE verification mission, William Walker, labeled the action a massacre. The West had seen enough of Milosevic and they would not tolerate the possibility of another Srebrenica. At the end of January, the Contact Group (the United States, United Kingdom, Italy, Germany, France, and Russia) called both sides to Rambouillet, France and delivered both an ultimatum. After Milosevic refused to sign, NATO began its bombing campaign, initiating NATO's first war. As outlined in Chapter 7, the campaign went on for seventy-eight days and involved tens of thousands of bombing sorties.

Much has been written on whether the talks at Rambouillet were serious negotiations or whether Madeleine Albright and the United States had already decided to engage in bombing and presented Milosevic with a deal that no leader could accept.[29] Much speculation has also addressed Milosevic's calculations. One thing is fairly certain – the West was working from the Bosnian model of 1995. In the late summer of 1995, NATO launched Operation Deliberate Force. The three-week operation flew about 3,500 sorties against over 300 individual targets. It quickly brought the Serbs to the bargaining table and the Dayton Accord was signed in relatively short order. A U.S. interagency report stated that "Milosevic doesn't want a war he can't win. . . . After enough of a defense to sustain his honor and assuage his backers he will quickly sue for peace."[30] It was not difficult to come to such a conclusion. The combined defense budgets of NATO member states were 300 times that of Serbia, while their combined economies were 900 times greater. In the Western view, it would be near insanity for Milosevic and the Serbs to fight a war given this imbalance. In the West's thinking, there could and would be no repeat of early Bosnia, where lack of resolve and disunity permitted ethnic cleansing. This time around, galvanized by the ghost of Srebrenica, the West would threaten to bring its incredible resources to bear.

What the West could not understand was that Kosovo was not Bosnia. Beyond Kosovo's mythology, Kosovo had been part of the Serbian Republic in the former Yugoslavia. More to the point, the enemy in Kosovo was the contemptible Albanian. Whether he thought about it in such terms or not, Milosevic had a different set of emotion resources in Kosovo, ones that would help facilitate a policy of ethnic cleansing even in the face of a direct ultimatum. The West was shocked that Milosevic would begin a brutal and massive ethnic cleansing operation that would drive half of the Albanian population out of their homes. There is perhaps no better evidence of the West's overestimation of its ability to control the situation than the fact that NATO had made absolutely no plans to deal with refugees.[31] Had the West understood hatred, however, it would not have found such an act so difficult to imagine.

[29] Albright's own memoirs indicate her readiness to support the Albanians and bomb Serbia. See *Madam Secretary: A Memoir* (New York: Miramax, 2003).

[30] Quotation found in Barry Posen, "The War for Kosovo: Serbia's Political–Military Strategy," *International Security* 24 (Spring 2000) (No. 4): 39–85. Passage is found on p. 60.

[31] Independent International Commission on Kosovo, *Kosovo Report: Conflict, International Response, Lessons Learned* (Oxford: Oxford University Press, 2000), p. 86.

III. PERIOD THREE: ETHNIC CLEANSING

NATO began bombing on March 24. Additional Serbian forces moved into Kosovo, joined by various paramilitary forces. These forces committed massive human rights violations.[32] They looted and burned in more than 500 villages, destroying the bulk of more than 50 of them.[33] Some forces committed rape.[34] Based on a sampling of refugees, the American Association for the Advancement of Science (AAAS) estimated that 10,000 Kosovar Albanians were killed from March 20 to June 12, 1999.[35]

Above all, the Serbian forces were engaged in forced displacement of the Albanian population. The overall numbers speak for themselves. The UNHCR puts the figures at 848,100 refugees (driven across Kosovo's borders – 444,600 to Albania, 244,500 to Macedonia, 69,000 to Montenegro, and 91,057 to other countries). At least another half million were displaced within Kosovo. In other words, about 90 percent of Kosovo's Albanian population had been driven from their homes. At one point, six or seven trains of thirteen to twenty carriages each were carrying thousands of Albanians from Pristina to the Macedonian border.[36]

The AAAS report provides detailed information on the nature of refugee flows as well as the movement and operations of Serbian forces.[37] It also provides refugee quotations that are representative of the reasons Kosovo Albanians left their homes. Here is one of the selected quotations from Pec about the first days of massive cleansing:

The Serbs made people leave (Pec) on Thursday (April 1) at 10:00 AM. They said: "Go to Albania." They went from neighborhood to neighborhood. They burned the houses

---

[32] Annex 1 of the Independent International Commission on Kosovo summarizes data on human rights violations from several sources. Also see *War Crimes in Kosovo: A Population-Based Assessment of Human Rights Violations against Kosovar Albanians* (Boston: Physicians for Human Rights and Program on Forced Migration and Health, Center for Population and Family Health, The Joseph L. Mailman School of Public Health, and Columbia University, 1999); *Kosovo/Kosova: As Seen, As Told, An Analysis of the Human Rights Findings of the OSCE Kosovo Verification Mission October 1998 to June 1999* (Warsaw: Organization for Security and Cooperation in Europe, 1999).

[33] *Kosovo Report*, p. 309. In my interviews in 2002, I also encountered some Serbian priests who were shocked by the wanton pillaging they observed. Also see John Kifner, "How Serb Forces Purged One Million Albanians," *New York Times*, May 29, 1999.

[34] See Caroline Kennedy-Pipe and Penny Stanley, "Rape in War: Lessons of the Balkan Conflicts in the 1990's," in Ken Booth, ed. *The Kosovo Tragedy: The Human Rights Dimensions* (London: Frank Cass, 2001), pp. 67–84. Pages 78–80 provide specific information on Kosovo. As reported in the *Kosovo Report*, Human Rights Watch documented 96 cases of rape while noting the social stigmas, especially in Kosovo, that prevent victims from coming forth.

[35] American Association for the Advancement of Science (AAAS), Science and Human Rights Program (2000) "Policy or Panic? The Flight of Ethnic Albanians from Kosovo, March to May 1999."

[36] *Kosovo Report*, p. 304.

[37] The AAAS report also examines NATO bombing patterns and posits that the NATO bombing campaign did not account for refugee flows. It also establishes the irrelevance of NATO bombing in hindering Serbian actions.

as people left. There were trucks and busses waiting for us. We were treated like cows. Men and women together. They didn't allow us any baggage, clothes. Just as we were. They slapped the men around a bit. They stole everything from the houses.[38]

Another refugee from Mitrovica reported:

we left Kosovska Mitrovica four days ago (i.e. 16 April). At about 9 a.m., four or five policemen came to my house and one of them said: "Get out, go to Albania or America. You knew (that this was going to happen)." The police were wearing black camouflage uniforms, had masks, and had automatic guns. They told us we had to leave in a few minutes, otherwise we would be killed. We were told to gather by the mosque of Zhabore, where there were thousands of people. From there we went to Shipol, then to Klina, Pec, (Prizren and then to Morina). I didn't see anything happening along the road, because our tractor was covered. My son was driving the tractor, and we got stopped, and they pointed a gun at him, and demanded money. But we didn't have any money, only 25 dinars. We were lucky that they didn't kill us.[39]

Undoubtedly, many Albanians fled because of intimidation and fear. However, a consideration of the overall numbers of perpetrators and victims, the actual mechanics of the operation, and the reactions of Serbs in Serbia proper reveal that something much more than that was happening in Kosovo.

First, consider the number of Serbs involved in the operation. More than fifty thousand members of the Serbian police, military, and paramilitary contributed to the ethnic cleansing of Kosovo. Not all of these forces were organized in a tightly controlled hierarchical structure. As the quotations illustrate, various types of small units approached houses and shook down refugees on roads. There were actually plenty of opportunities to shirk directions during the operation. Refugee accounts tell of masked terrorists and outsiders, but they also mention local people and neighbors. All varieties of Serb/Yugoslav security forces were involved: the regular army, the Special Police, private paramilitary groups, armed units of the Interior Ministry, and local police and volunteers.

Second, Serbian forces could have easily killed many times more Albanians than they did. These units had complete impunity. One Serbian participant related to me some remorse about the numbers killed. He told me he wished Serbs had massively killed Albanians. He complained that the West accused Serbs of genocide, so they might as well have committed it.[40] According to UNHCR figures, the ratio of killed to total refugees and internally displaced was about 1:143 (10,000: 1,435,000).[41] Serbs showed up, made threats, watched Albanians leave, and often torched their houses.

Third, the AAAS report concludes that the refugee flows did not correlate with mass killings. As the report summarizes, "The findings of this report suggest that the refugee flows do not necessarily follow sequences of mass killings . . . there are many areas from which many refugees departed but where

---

[38] AAAS, "Policy or Panic?"
[39] Cited in AAAS, "Policy or Panic?" Interview is originally from Human Rights Watch, April 1999, Albania.
[40] Rural Kosovo, 8/7/2002.
[41] As is common in such cases, these figures are contested.

there were no massacres, and there are other areas in which mass killings were committed yet from which there were relatively few refugees."[42] Massive, indiscriminate killing is the ideal tool for generating fear and refugee flows, and certainly this is a major part of the story at this stage in Kosovo. Yet the nature of the Serbian actions and Albanian reaction shows that fear was not necessarily the driving factor in many, or even most, local cases. Serbs did not need to commit highly publicized acts of violence to generate panic and flight. Rather, what was happening seemed to be expected. In the passage quoted, the Serbian policemen say, "Get out, go to Albania or America. You knew (that this was going to happen)." In effect, an Albanian "knows" it is now time to leave.

In my conversations with Serbs and Albanians about the ethnic cleansing of March to June 1999, one aspect was particularly striking: neither perpetrator nor victim found the matter very strange. Certainly, the Bosnian war had already shown that ethnic cleansing was not a thing of the past. For Kosovars, though, ethnic cleansing was expected, it was some sort of common sense.

To expand on a point from the background chapter, the cleansing in 1999 was not the first in Kosovo.[43] In fact, the March 1999 mass expulsions were the fourth instance of ethnic cleansing in Kosovo during the twentieth century.[44] In each case, the goal was a demographic transformation of Kosovo.

The first wave of expulsion and flight came when Serbs and Montenegrins ended Ottoman control over Kosovo with the campaigns of the 1912–13 Balkan War.[45] A second wave of violence occurred in 1918–19. In 1915, during the First World War, the Serbs were forced to evacuate the region, leaving it to Austro-Hungarian control. When the Serbs returned, their entrance was even more brutal than in the Balkan Wars. They killed 800 in the Djakovica region and destroyed villages in the Rugova Gorge.[46] Italian figures put the numbers for January and February 1919 at 6,040 killed and 3,873 houses destroyed.[47] Again, Albanians fled, some to the high ground and some south to Shkoder. The reconquest of the region introduced an era of official policies aimed at transforming the ethnic numbers of Kosovo. Authorities closed schools using the Albanian language, underreported the Albanian population by 50 percent in the 1921 census, and most crucially, began programs aimed at Albanian emigration and Serbian colonization.[48] On the other side of the equation, the government ceded over 57,000 acres to 17,679 Serbian families from Montenegro, Lika, and Hercegovina in an effort to increase Serbian numbers in

[42] AAAS "Policy or Panic?" Executive Summary.

[43] The following paragraphs are largely from Petersen, *Understanding Ethnic Violence*.

[44] The 1870s would provide a fifth example, if one wished to go further back.

[45] See Chapter 7.

[46] Ivo Banac, *The National Question in Yugoslavia: Origins, History and Politics* (Ithaca, NY: Cornell University Press, 1984), p. 298.

[47] Noel Malcolm, *Kosovo: A Short History* (New York: New York University Press, 1999), p. 272.

[48] Ibid, 298–300.

the territory.[49] The Yugoslav government even enlisted international help in fostering the removal of Albanians. In 1935, Turkey agreed to take 200,000 "Turks." In 1938, the Serbs offered Turkey 15,000 dinars for each family they would take and Turkey agreed to take 40,000 families at a price of 500 Turkish pounds per family. This transfer was supposed to take place over a multiyear period stretching from 1939 to 1944, but was prevented by the outbreak of the Second World War.[50] The Serbs had a serious program to expel massive numbers of Albanians during the interwar years. The colonization program, despite the emigration of tens of thousands,[51] failed to significantly change the ethnic imbalance in Kosovo. The idea, however, persisted. Vaso Cubrilovic, a respected historian, wrote in a March 7, 1937 government memorandum entitled "The Expulsion of the Albanians," "It is impossible to repel the Albanians just by gradual colonization.... The only possibility and method is the brutal power of a well-organized state.... We have already stressed that for us the only efficient way is the mass deportation of Albanians out of their triangle."[52]

The third wave of interethnic violence occurred during the Second World War, but this time the direction of expulsion was reversed. According to German reports, forty thousand Serbs were driven out of Kosovo during Italian and German occupation of the region.[53] Serbs would remember, and inflate, these numbers in later decades.

By the beginning of the period of Communist rule, a sufficient number of similar turns had occurred in Serbian–Albanian relations to form a cultural schema. To recall from Chapter 2, the schema must contain a constant representation of the innate nature of the opposing ethnic group. The schema should provide a script specifying roles and the nature of action. The justification for action should remain the same across historical periods. Finally, the acts of violence and humiliation should possess similar, if not ritualistic, qualities. In the view of the Serbs, Albanians had consistently persecuted Serbs with the help of outside powers – the Ottomans for five centuries, the Austro-Hungarians in World War I, and the fascist powers in World War II. They were an inferior people, but one that could, through such alliances, become a threat to Serbs in Kosovo. There was no making a deal with such an enemy; Serbs would have to deal with their physical presence, possibly through cleansing or population transfer. These are the ideas that underlie the conception of hatred outlined earlier.

The introduction of a Communist state and media control sent open discussion of the Kosovo problem underground, but did not resolve or eliminate it. Dobrica Cosic, a top Communist official, was dismissed from the Central

[49] Banac, *The National Question*, pp. 299–300.
[50] For more details, see Malcolm, *Kosovo*, pp. 283–5.
[51] Malcolm, *Kosovo*, p. 286, puts the total figure at 90,000 to 150,000 from 1918 to 1941.
[52] Dusan Necak, "Historical Elements for Understanding the 'Yugoslav Question,'" in *Yugoslavia, the Former and Future: Reflections by Scholars from the Region* (Washington, DC: The Brookings Institution, 1995), p. 24.
[53] Malcolm, *Kosovo*, p. 305.

Committee for his criticisms of Kosovo. The heightened autonomy created by the 1974 Constitution brought more rumblings. Kosovo emerged as a major grievance of Serbian intellectuals in the 1980s. The form this grievance took was familiar. Dimitrije Bogdanovic's *A Book about Kosovo*, published in 1985, openly accused Kosovo Albanians of seeking a policy of Albanian ethnic purity. Similar books followed. The authors of the oft-cited and generally infamous Memorandum, a publication of the Serbian Academy of Arts and Sciences, not only broke all taboos against nationalist rhetoric, but laid out the framework of the cultural schema in explicit form:

First, there is a century-old history of national conflict in Kosovo, a series of acts of aggression and counter-aggression, of acts of violence and bloody revenge–a story of true horror. It is only human to feel sympathy "under the veil of ignorance" for the smaller Albanian people. But the little David had the upper hand most of the time because it was amply supported by overwhelming allies: the Islamic Ottoman Empire during five centuries until 1912, Austria-Hungary which occupied the entire territory during World War One; fascist Italy and Germany which did the same during World War Two; the Soviet Union and China after 1948; eventually a dominating anti-Serbian coalition in Yugoslavia itself over the last twenty years.

The Memorandum was published in 1986, well before Milosevic gained power. Milosevic did not invent these words and images, but he understood their power. On the eve of the March 1999 cleansing of Kosovo, a cultural schema was in place and current events matched the major elements of the long-held schema.[54] The Kosovo Albanians were playing their traditional role by collaborating with outside protectors, this time the West and NATO. Serbs were again persecuted, demographically overwhelmed, and driven out of their historic cradle by the actions of the newly formed KLA. The script specified action. With the removal of observers and the beginning of NATO bombing, Serbs had little to lose in carrying out their historically consistent solution: mass expulsion. Albanians, as in previous times, streamed to safety in the wake of Serbian terror. Although it is debatable whether the violence and humiliations during the expulsion had ritualistic qualities, the terror, the burning of houses, and the flight of refugees all had their precedents in previous episodes. For outside observers, the action was one of the most inhumane in Europe since

---

[54] For a more extended discussion of the relevance of Serbian national memory to the events in Kosovo, see Milica Bakic-Hayden, "National Memory as Narrative Memory: The Case of Kosovo," in Maria Todorova, ed., *Balkan Identities: Nation and Memory* (New York: New York University Press, 2004), pp. 25–40. Bakic-Hayden's treatment is much richer in analysis of symbols and narratives than the one here, but her analysis resonates in important ways with the use of schema in this work. She writes, "Therefore in Serbian self-definition of cultural, religious, and national identity, Kosovo is not a negligible thing, a mere 'myth' like any storytelling: it is a narrative that continues to interact with reality in a unique way" (p. 40). She concludes by recalling a recent anecdote she had heard in Belgrade during NATO bombing: "One reason for being a Serb is that you can fight 600-year-old battles against the Turks and their domestic collaborators, be convinced that it is happening now, and not be entirely wrong" (p. 40).

the end of the Second World War. For many Serbs, under the sway of hatred, the mass expulsions could not generate any feelings of compassion or guilt. The historical schema created an atmosphere in which the purge was something like common sense. Although it was bad, it was somehow justifiable.

In addition to helping motivate action on the ground in Kosovo, Milosevic could also presume that this cultural schema would resonate with the population in Serbia proper. There is little evidence that any sizable number of Serbs felt or feel remorse or shame at the Kosovo cleansing operation. At the time, some speculated that if Serbs knew what was being done in their name they would vigorously protest. However, given the numbers of residents in Serbia proper with family and personal connections to Kosovo Serbs, it is difficult to believe that Serbs were ignorant of what was going on in Kosovo. Milosevic has always faced opposition in Serbia. At times, it appeared that the opposition might even bring down his regime. During the bombing, however, Serbs defiantly stood on bridges with targets strapped on their backs. After Milosevic signed the peace accord that brought NATO troops into Kosovo, popular criticism focused on losing the territory rather than any crimes that may have been committed there.

During 2008, nearly ten years after the events, I sensed no remorse while residing in Belgrade for six months.[55] At the military museum, artifacts from the "War of NATO Aggression" are displayed with some pride. Serbs had defended their nation against a foe several hundred times greater than themselves.

IV. CONCLUSIONS

A. Review of Hypotheses

At the time of the collapse of Yugoslavia, Kosovo was marked by mutual ethnic contempt, a series of status reversals and accompanying resentments, and a state able to crack down on political violence. In terms of the framework developed here, the situation could be placed in box R7. In this case, where escalation is not possible, political entrepreneurs are most likely to initiate the politics of boycott and the creation of parallel systems. Leaders can anticipate that their supporters and population in general will accept the costs entailed by this strategy.

By 1997, Kosovo Albanian rebels had gained the ability to transform the conflict through the escalation of violence and move the game from box R7 to R8. Along the lines of the general logic discussed in the theoretical sections and prediction 8 and 9, they did so by using discriminate targeting to ignite anger that, in turn, set off spiraling violence. Along the lines of hypothesis 7, the KLA suffered no backlash from their population for killing Serbs. As Albin Kurti,

---

[55] During the 2008 elections, there was one marginal political figure, Cedomir Jovanovic of the LDP, who publicly stated that Serbs should admit to crimes against Albanians. His party received 5 percent of the vote.

a prominent student leader, told Chris Hedges during the time of the KLA assassinations of Serb police, "When people hear that a Serbian policeman has been killed, they are overjoyed."[56]

The spiraling violence quickly moved the game from R8 to R9. Elites did not strategically raise the level of violence. In 1998, especially after the killing at the Jashari compound, Albanians began to mobilize at local levels and form a variety of units.[57] Sections of Kosovo were in a state of civil war.

In late 1999, the situation in Kosovo was characterized by high levels of both violence and contempt. These conditions produced the underlying cognitions of the emotion of hatred. Hatred is easily ignited and heightened when a cultural schema reinforces the idea that one is dealing with an incorrigible and deficient foe. Such a schema existed in Kosovo. Under the influence of hatred, high levels of killing and cleansing are justified against an opponent who is both defective and dangerous. There is no other option but to use the harshest measures in defense. Based on this logic, Chapter 6 made the following prediction: When hatred is present, strategies of ethnic cleansing will find widespread support (prediction 11). The schema helps explain not only the popular support for ethnic cleansing and the Serbs' widespread participation in it, but also the rapid and somewhat efficient flight out of the province. In many ways, the events were just another round in a long struggle.

B. The West Is All In

The West was initially reluctant to get in. But, as discussed in Chapter 7, Kosovo was a watershed event for the West. NATO fought its first war – and redefined sovereignty in the process. The European Union, in the meantime, committed itself even more firmly to the incorporation of the Western Balkans within its structure. Although the ethnic cleansing and atrocities taking place in Kosovo were horrendous enough, Western officials also put out enhanced tales of killing during the bombings in an effort to convince their publics, and perhaps themselves, of the necessity of intervention. The first official estimates put the number killed at 44,000. Then the figures were progressively halved to 22,000 and then 11,000.[58] A UK Ministry of Defence briefing compared the events in Serbia to those that occurred in the Pol Pot regime in Cambodia.[59] I would also point out that along the lines of Chapter 5, NATO calibrated its bombing campaign to avoid backlash from their own publics. Although their

---

[56] Hedges, "New Balkan Tinderbox."
[57] See Roger Petersen, *Resistance and Rebellion: Lessons from Eastern Europe* (Cambridge: Cambridge University Press, 2001), for an analysis of similar bottom-up processes of mobilization.
[58] The UN Chief War Crimes Prosecutor, Carla Del Ponte, held a press conference in November of 1999 and admitted that the previous estimates had been much too high. As of November 10, 1999, only 2,108 bodies had been found, with Serbs killed by the KLA among that number. NATO and KLA sources had claimed that over 4,000 victims would be found in the 159 mass graves that the UN had unearthed by November 10.
[59] Posen, "The War for Kosovo," p. 68.

rhetoric was of rationality, in practice Western states also needed to consider emotions in their strategy. In any event, the West was now committed to Kosovo.

June 10, 1999, marked the end of the war and the signing of UN Resolution 1244. The resolution was filled with some convenient fictions. First of all, Kosovo legally remained a part of Serbia, although almost everyone knew that Kosovo would never be returned to Serbian jurisdiction. It was a UN mission, but the UN only controlled certain areas of Kosovo's governance system. Humanitarian affairs were led by the UNHCR. The civil administration and police were under UNMIK. The West clearly called the shots in the most important realms. For security, a Kosovo International Security Force (KFOR) would be composed of five zones, respectively administered by the United States, the United Kingdom, France, Italy, and Germany. The European Union was authorized to lead economic development. The OSCE held the reins in democratization and political institution building.

From the outset the West planned, if only in the most general terms, for an independent and Western-oriented Kosovo. By 2008, Kosovo would gain independence, but one heavily supervised by the EU. The next chapters examine the circuitous path toward that destination.

Kosovo Intervention Games, I

Chapter 4 outlined intervention games and identified a common sequencing of games. First, the intervener ends the chaos represented by the N-person assurance game. In further steps, the intervener transforms a prisoners' dilemma through manipulation of rewards and punishments and moves players to a stable era of mutual cooperation. As of June 1999, the UN, with a dominant Western influence, began playing these games in Kosovo. They did not get off to a smooth start. Then things got worse. The present chapter explains why, step by step.

I. THE N-PERSON ASSURANCE GAME AND HATRED (R9)

In the beginning stage, the incoming regime attempts to establish itself as the legitimate authority by persuading individuals to move away from nonstate self-defense groups and into compliance with the new state and state-sanctioned organizations. To review the fourth chapter, the incoming intervention government must assure individuals that it is indeed the legitimate authority and that it will be able to provide security to those who cooperate with it. If individuals perceive the incoming regime as stable, they will raise their estimates of the value of cooperation. In effect, a "tipping point" is lowered and, if individuals see other members of their reference group crossing over into cooperation with the intervener, they will also decide to move from defection to cooperation.

As the Kosovo Protection Force (KFOR) moved into Kosovo, they entered believing that they were coming to rescue endangered Kosovar Albanians. Serb forces, collaborators, and others were moving across the border into Serbia proper. The Red Cross estimated that 50,000 to 60,000 Serbian civilians left in the two weeks preceding the June 18 occupation alone.[1] The Serbs no longer posed a threat. Instead, returning Kosovar Albanians killed Serbs and other minorities and burned their homes. Crucially, they did so in the presence of

---

[1] King and Mason, *Peace at Any Price*, p. 50.

international peacekeepers, a fact that would come to haunt the mission in
future iterations of the intervention games.

As discussed earlier, the KLA and other Albanian forces systematically razed
the entire Ciganska Mahala neighborhood in south Mitrovica in the presence
of French forces. Similar incidents were taking place in other locations. In
Ferizaj/Urosevac, U.S. forces allowed Albanian groups to burn almost at will.[2]
Fleeing the violence, several thousand Serbs huddled in the center of town
as their homes were torched in surrounding neighborhoods. Local Albanians,
unhindered by U.S. troops, used the opportunity to taunt and threaten the
Serbs gathered in the open square. In Prizren, three hundred Serbian homes
were destroyed.[3]

Although tens of thousands of Serbs in the most vulnerable areas had fled,
the overall numbers of victims were still high. According to UNHCR figures
covering the first few months after the occupation, 164,000 minorities fled
Kosovo. Against those remaining, perpetrators committed 348 murders, 116
kidnappings, 1,070 lootings, and 1,105 arsons.[4] These numbers represent only
officially registered and confirmed crimes and surely do not capture the total
number of arsons and lootings. For example, in the Ferizaj/Oresevac area,
Serbs' homes totaled about 1,700, and most of them appeared to have been
burned or looted. Bernard Kouchner, present as the first full-term Special Representative of the Secretary General (SRSG), summed up the situation when he
stated, "I've been a human rights activist for thirty years, and here I am unable
to stop people from being massacred."[5]

These events have commonly been labeled "revenge killings." In the study
of emotions in the first section of this book, this explanation sees the Albanian
actions in the months after the intervention as a manifestation of anger: the
other side committed horrendous actions against our side and now they must
be severely punished. Undoubtedly, some of the killings were driven by anger
and vengeance. But if the nature of the actions is examined more closely, it
becomes clear that something more than anger was at work. Perhaps most
commonly, perpetrators targeted elderly Serbs unable to flee. These old people
had not committed crimes against Albanians. They were targeted because they

[2] GT/8/24/06. There are many stories about decapitation during these days. In Ferizaj/Urosevac,
the heads of three Serbians were reportedly placed on sticks in public view. King and Mason
(p. 50) mention decapitations in Pristina.

[3] King and Mason, *Peace at Any Price*, p. 57.

[4] These figures are from an UNHCR/OSCE report, "Overview of the Situation of Ethnic Minorities
in Kosovo," November 3, 1999. They are cited within a broader discussion of the human rights
situation in Kosovo by Jasmina Husanovic, "'Post-Conflict' Kosovo: An Anatomy Lesson in the
Ethics/Politics of Human Rights," in Ken Booth ed., *The Kosovo Tragedy: The Human Rights
Dimensions* (London: Frank Cass, 2001), pp. 263–80. There are several other reports covering
the violence in this period. See the International Crisis Group Report, "Who's Killing Whom?"
November 2, 1999; also see the Human Rights Watch report, "Federal Republic of Yugoslavia:
Abuses Against Serbs and Roma in the New Kosovo," *Human Rights Watch* (August 1999) 11
(No. 10).

[5] King and Mason, *Peace at Any Price*, p. 53.

were Serbs. Serbian homes were indiscriminately torched. Graveyards were desecrated.[6] The purpose of these actions was to eliminate the very presence of Serbs in Kosovo.

What happened in the spring and summer of 1999 in Kosovo was that both populations had been imbued with the emotion of hatred. The situation was that of box R9 in the analytical matrix. The other side both was inherently deficient and had become dangerous. Moreover, these perceptions had become locked in and confirmed by a cultural schema that provided a script and a set of roles. For the Serbs, the Albanians had performed their historical role as an underhanded people who had brought outsiders in to do their dirty work against Serbs. For the Albanians, the Serbs had just confirmed their nature as ethnic cleansers against Albanians. The overall population of Serbs had little problem with the ethnic cleansing of Albanians during the spring; the overall population of Albanians now had little problem with the cleansing of Serbs during the summer.

Even if it wanted to, the KLA was not capable of directing a centralized cleansing operation during the chaos after the arrival of KFOR. Albanians of many backgrounds carried out actions against Serbs with little regret or remorse. Under the influence of hatred, eliminating the physical presence of the dangerous and defective opponent is seen as justified, even natural. These actions required no central direction. Hatred, permeating a large percentage of the population, was enough to motivate and direct these attacks on its own. In my interviews with both Serbs and Albanians, I repeatedly heard that the ethnic cleansings that occurred during these months were unfortunate, but not unexpected.

The West does not believe in hatred. Unsurprisingly, it could not, and did not, plan to confront this force as it triumphantly entered Kosovo to do good. The first police units did not arrive until August 8, 1999. It would take three months to bring this force up to 1,400 members. After a full year, the force was not close to its fully projected strength and contained many units untrained for the task.[7] The result was not simply a loss of life and property, but a loss of legitimacy that would affect future games.

II. MANIPULATING THE PRISONERS' DILEMMA
IN THE FACE OF CONTEMPT (R8)

Eventually, a combination of ethnic flight and UNMIK security forces managed to transform the situation from box R9 to box R8, a situation of a low level of violence. Ethnic flight and the physical separation of Serbs and Albanians probably did more to change the situation than international security forces. By the fall, Serbs had lost all ability to threaten Albanians. The perception of

---

[6] Personal observations.

[7] See the section in *Kosovo Report* entitled "Slow in Showing Up: The International Police Force," pp. 110–12. After one year, the police force was only 77% of the authorized number.

danger declined and, therefore, the level of hatred could no longer be maintained. Hatred receded into contempt. Albanians were no longer driven by a desire to physically eliminate the remnant of Serbs in their presence as much as they were, along the lines of contempt, motivated to completely avoid and isolate them. The essential goal of Albanian politics, and politicians of all stripes, was to make a complete break with all things Serbian.

By the fall, the N-person assurance game was only partially solved, with significant elements not fully recognizing the new central authority as legitimate. Most significantly, the Serbs remaining in Kosovo were well on their way to developing a parallel social and political system. In north Mitrovica, Serbs established their own security and law in the form of the Bridgewatchers, the name representing the fact that one of their original purposes was to monitor the bridge spanning the Ibar River and decide who should and should not be crossing that boundary. Soon, forces in Belgrade were developing an infrastructure for sustaining the parallel system that emerged in Kosovo. Money flowed from the Serbian capital to teachers, doctors, and public sector workers, as well as to the Bridgewatchers. Members of the Serbian Interior Ministry walked the streets of north Mitrovica. Albanians were overjoyed that the West had finally arrived. The Kosovo Liberation Army, however, still existed in various forms and local remnants, and plans for its demilitarization were still in the works.[8]

A. The Intervener Strategy, 1999–2002

To address these problems, the interveners essentially set up the next stage of the Basic Intervention Game. The first steps of this process involved setting up the fundamental aspects of any game. The actors would need to be defined and spoilers excluded. The strategy set would need to be defined and limited. The payoff structure would need to be arranged so that the value of mutual reward (the R value) would outweigh the value of playing the opponent for a sucker (the T value). The hope was that this strategy would help solve Kosovo's two major problems: (1) the development of a parallel society and a Serbian ministate in the north; and (2) the lack of Serbian and other minority returns to Kosovo. The Western project in Kosovo could never be considered a complete success if the new state did not rule over all of its territories. Western leaders stated that they would not tolerate a new Cyprus or Moldova under their watch. Also, the West would not tolerate a monoethnic state. To recall the words of Michael Steiner, former SRSG, "We came to Kosovo to protect human rights and we cannot allow this country to become monoethnic."[9] The application of the Basic Game would provide rewards to Serbs to wean them away from their parallel society. It would also provide rewards to Albanians to encourage them to welcome Serbs back to Kosovo. On the whole, the strategy

---

[8] See *Institute for War and Peace Reporting*, August 3, 2002.
[9] http://www.unmikonline.org/press/2002/mon/july/lmm120702.htm#1, 12 July 2002.

would work primarily by increasing the value of cooperation (the use of a carrot) rather than threatening to punish defection (the use of the stick).

The outlines of this game are illustrated in microcosm in a report of the International Crisis Group regarding the problem in Mitrovica, the dividing line and epicenter of the conflict. On June 2, 2002, the ICG published a report titled "UNMIK's Kosovo Albatross: Tackling Division in Mitrovica." The report can be systematically broken down with reference to the elements of the Basic Game.

First, the set of appropriate actors must be defined and spoilers eliminated. The report urges the arrest of the Bridgewatchers and their elimination from any political role. Belgrade is a spoiler, but one that can be dealt with through inducements. In particular, the ICG report mentions membership in the Partnership for Peace and a Stabilization and Association Agreement with the European Union as carrots.

Second, the strategy set should be defined and limited. In Kosovo, Serbian talk of partition was off the table from the start. In Mitrovica, the ICG report urges that Serbian pursuit of a separate north Mitrovica municipality be excluded from discussion. Similarly, Kosovar Albanians cannot talk of merger with Albania or include any talk of consolidation with the Albanian-dominated regions in South Serbia or Macedonia.

The third element regards payoff structures. The centerpiece of the ICG report is the call for a "service agreement between north and south." Essentially, this is a Lockean social contract. Both parties, in this case Serbs from the Povratak Assembly and Albanian officials of the municipality, give up some control to the state and in return receive rights and benefits. The key aspect and first point is that Serbs must recognize UNMIK's administrative and policing authority and cut support for parallel structures. Correspondingly, donors would provide financial incentives for special projects to local Serbs and Belgrade if, and only if, there was evidence that Serbs were dissolving the parallel structures. Albanians would be given one year to prove that they were living up to a commitment to provide equal and integrated services to the Serbs in the north and helping to facilitate returns. If they did not, the ICG report recommended sanctions, including dissolving the Municipal Assembly.

The ICG's report on Mitrovica, as well as its overall approach, mirrored UNMIK's program for Kosovo as a whole. As in the Basic Game, UNMIK and the SRSG, Michael Steiner, were trying to transform a prisoners' dilemma into an assurance game. That is, they were trying to raise the value of rewards for cooperation above those for "suckering" the opponent. For Albanians, the carrots involved financial support for roads, schools, and hospitals. For Serbs, the carrots involved representation in the government (and in the electoral realm, a system providing for overrepresentation)[10] and help on returns for those who fled in 1999.

---

[10] Twenty seats out of 120 were automatically reserved for minorities, ten for Serbs. If Serbs voted in full force, they could have gained enough seats to become a viable coalition partner, in theory.

To Steiner's astonishment, the rewards given to Kosovo leaders could not budge them on other issues. The only piece of legislation debated in the first six months of Kosovo's Assembly concerned Kosovo's territorial integrity, a status issue that was not on the table.[11] Early in 2003, Steiner went on television to give what was often called his "sick and tired" speech.[12] Listing problems with crime, the economy, and the almost complete lack of multiethnicity, Steiner addressed the Kosovar public:

The reality is that your leaders are not in the opposition anymore. They are in power and they have real power. Your government controls 350 million euros. That's 700 million DM in the old money! It has ten ministries. It is responsible for essentials like schools, hospitals, and transport. That means your children's education. It means your health. It means your roads. These are vital responsibilities in any government. These are the issues on which elections in Europe are won and lost. Are they not worth your leaders' attention?[13]

Steiner's frustration was palpable. How was it possible that the large rewards doled out by the intervention were not having the anticipated effect on cooperation? Why were people in Kosovo not acting like western Europeans?

Steiner's effort in Mitrovica provides an example of an even bigger failure of the application of the Basic Game.[14] In an effort to bring Mitrovica's Serbs into the political process and break the hold of parallel structures, Steiner developed a plan that promised a donors conference, regular policing by Serbian members of the KPS, relocation of UN bodies to the north side of the river, and decentralization of some municipal authority so that Serbs could more directly control their own affairs, among other inducements. All the Serbs had to do was to participate in the municipal elections of October 2002. In north Mitrovica, fewer than 100 voters cast a ballot. With no Serbian representation in the Mitrovica assembly, Steiner's plans had to be scrapped. An even more discouraging result involved an UNMIK questionnaire regarding how services should be delivered. In an attempt to engage Serbs and make them feel that they were part of the larger government, UNMIK handed out 10,000 consultation sheets. Only 36 were returned.

In practice, Serbs did participate in one early election and gained eighteen seats. The Serbian coalition was named Povratak, meaning "return." and they pushed the return issue over all others. The Albanian parties ignored Povratak and Serbs lost faith in the process entirely. In this instance, Serbs did play a limited "cooperation" strategy, which went nowhere due to Albanian intransigence. Beyond intransigence, Albanians also painted a mural on the wall of the Assembly that was offensive to Serbs. I had a long conversation with one Serbian representative who detailed incidents – no translation of documents, failure to provide secure escort, etc. – that she interpreted as harassment of Serbs in their legislative capacity (QU/8/31/02).

[11] King and Mason, *Peace at Any Price*, p. 161.
[12] Ibid, 177–8.
[13] Ibid, 177–8
[14] The Mitrovica events in this paragraph are described in King and Mason, *Peace at Any Price*, pp. 150–51.

In terms of the Basic Intervention Game, these results clearly illustrate an outcome of mutual defection. The question is why the Basic Game approach did not work.

The problem is not so much that the West overestimates the value of its rewards. Rather, the West does not understand the value of defection in the wake of violent conflict, especially this particular conflict. The key to understanding the outcome lies in the emotion resources connected with box R8 in the analytical framework.

B. The Serbian Response

To understand the Serbian choice of strategy against the intervener's Basic Game, we need to consider the range of choices listed in the lower left box of Figure 1.1. The intervener instituted the Basic Game, offering political rewards to induce cooperation from the Serbian side. The Serbian opponents of the game faced severe structural constraints. Given the precarious position of their communities, the options of either escalating or deescalating violence were out of their control. In fact, none of the violent options were available. The choice boiled down to:

(1) acquiescence
(2) nonviolent engagement
(3) boycott
(4) instituting a parallel society

The intervener hoped that incentives would achieve acquiescence to its game; at the very least, the intervener hoped the incentives would prevent the strategy of parallel society, which would "freeze" the conflict.

Serbian opponents did, as indicated, choose to maintain parallel structures, albeit ones that might engage UNMIK on some issue areas. This choice was not a difficult one if the available emotion resources of R8 are were taken into account. Here, the political entrepreneur could employ anger, resentment, and contempt. Although the use of anger to create spiraling violence could not be considered, resentment, and especially contempt, served as powerful resources. Most importantly, Serbian contempt for Albanians meant that the preference ordering of the Serbs in Kosovo was not that of the prisoners' dilemma.

Game theory does not usually make an effort to incorporate the role of emotion into its games, but the Kosovo case brings the importance of the emotion of contempt to the fore. How should we reassess the preference orderings? The Basic Game starts with the assumption of a prisoners' dilemma ($T > R > P > S$) and works to transpose the T and R values to create an assurance game. With a high level of contempt, though, the low value of P must be reconsidered. Under the influence of contempt, players will fail to conform to Western assumptions in at least two ways. First, they will positively value avoidance of the other group. Second, they will absolutely loathe being played for suckers by the contemptible other group. That is, S will have an extremely low value. The first effect will raise the value of defection; the second will lower the value of cooperation.

In sum, contempt raises the value of defection (P and T in game terms). Under the influence of contempt, a player's preference ordering can be presented as T > P > R > S. I will call this the "contempt" preference ordering. With this ordering, the dominant strategy is defection. Knowing that their population holds these preferences, the Serb leadership across most of Kosovo and in Belgrade could be confident that their population would support the development of a parallel society. Moreover, the population could be counted on to sanction local Kosovar Serb political leaders who might choose cooperation rather than defection within UNMIK's game.[15]

B. The Albanian Strategy

Of all possible positions to occupy, the opponents of intervention strategy are best able to affect intervener policy if the situation resembles box R8. In that position, the political entrepreneur can utilize a variety of emotion resources and, if structural variables allow, transform the game in both directions by changing the level of violence.

After the intervention in Kosovo, Albanian political entrepreneurs could consider an array of resources. On the structural side, the presence of KFOR prevented escalation to a high level of violence (such an option would not have been desirable even if the possibility existed). However, the presence of remnants of the KLA provided some ability to employ violence if desired. As for emotion resources, because the interveners drove out the Serbian government, resentment was no longer directly relevant or useful, at least not in the short run (after a few years, resentment against UNMIK would apply). However, contempt and anger were still available. Given these features of the situation, Albanian political entrepreneurs possessed a fairly wide range of feasible strategies.

Playing within box R8, possible strategies included:

(1) Hitting the Serbs with discriminate violence to try to provoke them into a counterproductive retaliation (use of anger)
(2) Orchestrating or "greenlighting" low-level indiscriminate violence versus Serbs in order to prevent returns and encourage flight (use of fear)
(3) Promoting separation and lack of engagement with Serbs (use of contempt)
(4) Acquiescence to the intervener's game (involving concessions to Serbs, especially on the crucial issue of returns), without efforts to completely eliminate the potential for low-level violence

---

[15] There are several examples of such incidents, the most prominent involving Oliver Ivanovic in Gracanica.

There was also the choice of trying to deescalate violence entirely. Playing the game in box R7,

(5) In an effort to exhibit unwavering support for the intervention regime, Albanian political actors could have attempted to thoroughly demobilize all remnants of the KLA, demilitarize the society as a whole, and publicly chastise and shame any community member who committed violence against minorities.

(6) Albanian political entrepreneurs could have deescalated violence but pursued remaining grievances through engagement in the form of demonstrations and other nonviolent protests.

Of course, UNMIK hoped that its set of rewards would encourage the choice of strategy 5 or 6. It certainly believed that the offered rewards and threatened penalties would outweigh the value of avoiding and isolating the opponent (strategy 3). There seems little evidence that UNMIK was at all prepared for strategies 1 and 2.

The Basic Game is structured to persuade players that cooperation is desirable and violence is no longer even an option. Albanian political entrepreneurs had other ideas. They chose to use a combination of strategies 2 and 3 – avoidance and low-level violence. Strategy 1 would clearly have been counterproductive. The intervener had drawn a "red line" against open violence and such actions would have destroyed important goodwill that was emanating from the West. Strategy 2 would not destroy this political capital as long as it was not blatant. Strategies 4, 5, and 6 might have allowed Serbs to return and develop a significant political and social presence, so they went against the essence of Kosovar Albanian political goals and psychology. A combination of strategies 2 and 3 remained a viable avenue for consolidating the Kosovar Albanians' hard-won victories. By no means could Kosovo be anything other than an Albanian state, free of Serbs and Serbian oppression.

The first part of the strategy, avoidance, is readily explained. The majority of Albanians held the "contempt" preference ordering, as did Serbs. If both players hold these preferences, the fact that the other side is not trying to cooperate is not important; mutual defection, and thus mutual avoidance, is a perfectly acceptable outcome. As discussed in the previous section, Steiner's appeals went unheeded. The value of avoiding Serbs outweighed the carrots offered to induce cooperation and tolerance.

The game analysis provides another important insight. The mutual defection (P, P) outcome would be predicted even if only one player held the "contempt" preference ordering ($T > P > R > S$). Whichever player holds those preferences will have a dominant strategy of defecting. The other player, realizing that the opponent has a dominant strategy of defecting, can then only choose between the sucker payoff (S) and the mutual defection penalty payoff (P). In either the prisoners' dilemma payoff *or* the assurance game payoff, mutual defection will be the optimal choice. For the Kosovo case, this suggests that if the Serbian side was driven by contempt, the Albanian side would still defect.

The second aspect of the strategy, low-level violence against Serbs, is more controversial. Few dispute that Albanians committed a significant number of violent actions against Serbs, even after the end of the emergency period (late June to September 1999). The numbers were not large; after all, a process of flight had almost completely separated the populations by the fall. Still, a steady drumbeat of incidents produced and maintained a significant level of fear in Kosovo's Serb population and in the Serbian displaced persons camps across the border. Furthermore, members of the international community charged with returning IDPs to a viable and safe setting had to take these events into account when considering promoting or allowing returns.

Most incidents were unclaimed and mysterious – a bomb set here and a grenade thrown there. Some were clearly organized. The most important event was the bombing of the Nis express bus convoy in February 2001.[16] The convoy consisted of five buses carrying 250 Serbs protected by seven armored personnel carriers. A remote-controlled bomb detonated 200 pounds of TNT, killing eleven and injuring eighteen.[17] As one Serb told me, if a person can be killed even in a protected convoy, where can one feel safe, and why would anyone consider returning?[18]

Beyond the numbers of victims of violent action, there was a sense of impunity for the perpetrators. Although Serbs lived mainly in protected enclaves, the UN documented the murders of 273 Serbs between 1999 and mid-2003 through various forms of violence – burnings, shootings, bombings, and grenade attacks. Moreover, there was not a single conviction for any of these killings. An arrest was made in the Nis bombing incident, but the prisoner mysteriously escaped from the heavily fortified U.S. Camp Bondsteel. The escape was seen throughout the Serbian community as an example of the complicity of the United States in the ethnic cleansing of Serbs from Kosovo. The image of Madeleine Albright kissing Hashim Thaci in July 1999 reinforced such theories in the minds of Serbs.

It is not at all clear to what extent these attacks were organizationally directed, although the Nis bombing was seemingly a sophisticated operation. Members of international organizations disagree on the direct involvement of the KLA. The OSCE issued the following statement: "It would appear that there is an orchestrated campaign, or campaigns organized by, as yet, unidentified elements whose aim was to terrorize minority populations, destabilize the province and prevent democratization and peaceful co-existence."[19] Human Rights Watch goes further, asserting that the antiminority violence was aimed at the "removal from Kosovo of nonethnic Albanians in order to better justify

---

[16] The Nis bus bombing and the killing of fourteen farmers in Gracko in their fields in July of 1999 were the most commonly cited fear-evoking events appearing in my conversations with Kosovo Serbs.

[17] King and Mason, *Peace at Any Price*, p. 98.

[18] GT/8/24/06.

[19] OSCE, Third Assessment, Executive Summary, p. 1.

an independent state."[20] Even the International Crisis Group summarized that "There seems to be little doubt that certain elements of the KLA appear to be building pressure to chase out Serbs, Roma, Gorani and anyone else who does not fully support the demand for an independent Kosovo."[21]

The mistake here is to believe that "orchestration" was necessary for these attacks. In my view, the vast majority of Albanians supported the elimination of Serbs from Kosovo. One must also keep in mind that, at this point in Kosovo, the lines between political, military, and criminal organizations were not so clear. Thaci and Haradinaj were leaders in the KLA who became party leaders. Agim Ceku fought against the Serbs as far back as the war in Croatia. The followers of these emerging leaders had connections going back to violent organizations. In the absence of clear signals to the contrary, many such men believed they had a "green light" to continue violence against Serbs in the present. It was also easy for them to commit low-level violence against Serbs in vulnerable communities. In sum, a strategy of low-level violence needed little organization or planning; it just needed a go-ahead signal.[22]

In my view, these signals were provided. First of all, President Rugova and the LDK Party remained silent on the question of returns. Rugova was considered the quintessential "nonspoiler" in Kosovo, a leader who had emulated Gandhi only a few years previously. Yet not even Rugova consistently condemned the acts of violence against minorities. One of the only prominent leaders who did so, publisher Veton Surroi, suffered death threats and was attacked as a traitor with a "Slav stink."[23]

In the summer of 2002, I saw the poster shown in Figure 11.1 displayed on walls in public areas. The caption reads, "Do not allow criminals to come back in Kosova!" The picture shows a man in military uniform pulling back the head of a young Albanian boy in order to slit his throat. The picture is accompanied by information describing the perpetrator, which reads, "The Serb criminal Gorolub Paunovich (1969), ex-PTT employee in Vushtrria, while slaying an unidentified Albanian boy. Witness say that this criminal took part in the crime on the family of Hamdi Uglari (1999)." I wish to emphasize two points about the poster. First, it provides no new information. Everyone knows that the Serbs committed atrocities. Rather, the poster is a direct attempt at evoking emotion. The image presents a specific scenario: Serbs committed terrible crimes. But they are going to return and they will do so while laughing in the face of Albanians.

Second, and more to the present point, this poster was simultaneously pasted in several locations in Kosovo. Printing and displaying this image took some level of coordination and organization. Some political actor was attempting to play on Albanian emotions that would encourage strong action against Serbian

---

[20] Human Rights Watch, *Under Orders: War Crimes in Kosovo. Abuses after June 12, 1999*, p. 2 (New York: Human Rights Watch, 2001).
[21] International Crisis Group, November 1999 report.
[22] I owe these insights largely to KC/7/5/08.
[23] King and Mason, *Peace at Any Price*, p. 83.

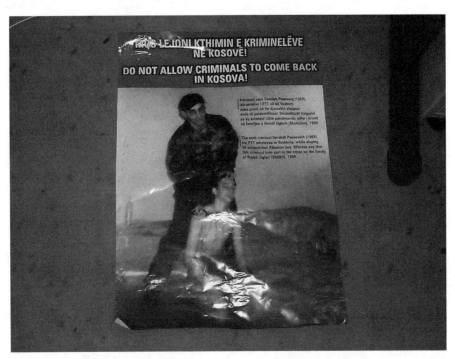

FIGURE 11.1. Publicly Displayed Poster in Kosovo, Summer 2002.

returns. Without condemnations from their leaders, without the deterrent of arrest and convictions, and with the messages provided by such posters, potential perpetrators understood that their actions against Serbs could go on with impunity. Given the nearly universal desire among all segments of Kosovo's Albanian population to see a new state free of Serbs, it was not hard to signal a "green light" on violence. A population filled with contempt is ready and able to see such a signal.

Regardless of the level of coordination involved, the violence in 2000–2002 was effective in creating fear throughout the Serb population. Every Kosovar Serb I talked with during my four trips to Kosovo claimed to have been a victim or to know a victim of violence or intimidation during this period. As of 2008, few believed that it was generally safe for Serbs to return to their homes.[24] Many believed that the emergency period from June to September 1999 should not be distinguished from later periods – it was just one long period of harassment and intimidation. The numbers would indicate that such fears should have declined. In fact, by November 2000 the weekly murder rate was only at four. But the emotion of fear does not calculate numbers in such a straightforward manner. After the killings that occurred during the first year of intervention, Serbs withdrew into their own world. Imbued with fear,

[24] Over half of the Serbs working for UNMIK's Provisional Institutions of Self Government left within six months, often citing various forms of harassment. See King and Mason, *Peace at Any Price*, pp. 158–9.

Player 2

Cooperate   Defect

Cooperate	R1, R2	S1, T2
Defect	T1, S2	P1, P2

Player 1

FIGURE 11.2. 2 × 2 Game (Figure 4.1 Repeated).

they heard every new attack with heightened sensitivity. Reports of danger were given increased weight, whereas reports of increasing safety were readily dismissed. If low-level violence was a strategy, it was a highly successful one. Serbs never have returned in any significant number.

III. STANDARDS BEFORE STATUS

A. The Change in the Intervener Game

By 2002, the Basic Intervention Game had failed to move Albanian and Serbian players off the mutual defection equilibrium. The intervention regime seemingly realized that its rewards were unlikely to move the Serbs from defection. However, there was one giant stick that might be wielded against the Albanians. The policy of Standards before Status was designed to break the mutual defection stalemate by threatening to withhold the one big prize that Albanians truly cared about – independent status. Although discussion of final status was not on the table in the early years, it was always the elephant lurking in the room. Now, the internationals would put this reward on view, but only to threaten never to provide it. In terms of the game, UNMIK was threatening to assign the highest negative penalty for continued defection (P). The P value would thus sink below the S value, transforming the Albanian preference function to $R > S > T > P$. In that case, the Albanians would have a dominant strategy of cooperation even if the Serbs were sure to defect. In the intervener's calculations, it would be in the Albanian side's long-term interest to be played for the short-term sucker.

In terms of the 2 × 2 game (with Serbs as player 1 and Albanians as player 2), the strategy was to move the game from the bottom right cell of mutual defection (P, P) to the bottom left cell (T, S). Then, over time, the Serbs would come to value offered rewards more than obstinacy; the game would then end up at mutual cooperation (R, R) (see Figure 11.2).

UNMIK originally planned a different route to mutual cooperation, but if one player was completely intransigent, then perhaps it could force the other player toward cooperation and then eventually bring the intransigent player along.

B. The Albanian Response

Although the Serbs continued to play boycott and build a parallel society, the Albanians grew tired of the new policy. They saw it as hypocritical. Many European countries would not meet the eight standards specified by Steiner. Moreover, with no mention of status at all, the incentive to rigorously pursue those standards was lacking. More than anything, why should Albanians put up with condescending threats from UNMIK?

On top of that, UNMIK's threats were not credible. Albanian actors had their own "stick" to use against the interveners. Because of UNMIK's failure to solve the security situation completely in the first stages of the intervention, Albanians had retained a capacity to mobilize for violence. Given their recent experience as victims of violence and the reserve of anger it had produced, Albanian political actors could unleash retaliatory violence against specified targets, including internationals. In fact, they had learned this lesson early on.

The cognitive antecedent of anger is that a specific actor has committed a blameworthy action. The individual imbued with anger then becomes an "intuitive prosecutor" and zealously tries to punish that actor. In February 2001, an Albanian youth was killed in north Mitrovica. As in the poster (Figure 11.1), Serbs had committed a crime against an innocent Albanian. Someone had to be punished. Violence began. As King and Mason summarize, "As before, a minor provocation from one side was more than reciprocated by the other, and the spiral escalated dangerously."[25] The perpetrator Serbs, ensconced in the north, could not easily be attacked. However, the international forces, seen by Albanians as covering for the Serbs, soon became the target. Angry mobs set KFOR vehicles aflame, threatened UN headquarters, and torched the French military headquarters. Rioting went on for two days, resulting in dozens of military and, perhaps, 100 civilian casualties.

The key point about this 2001 case is the reaction of the SRSG at the time. In response to the riot, Hans Haekkerup promised the Albanians that he would disband the Bridgewatchers, rotate French forces out of Mitrovica, and extend the zone of confidence farther into the Serbian part of town. Basically, he promised everything he could to end the riot, even though he did not have the authority to fulfill some of these pledges. The lesson was clear to the opponents of intervention: the international community cannot prevent mob violence and will probably appease it.

By late 2003, Albanians were growing weary of the stagnant Standards before Status policy. They began to threaten to use their stick. All around

---

[25] King and Mason, *Peace at Any Price*, pp. 95–96.

Kosovo, Albanian leaders were implying that if the status issue remained unaddressed, they may not be able to control their frustrated populations. Who knows what might happen? Kosovo could "explode." In order to make this ambiguous threat more plausible, Albanian leaders organized increasingly provocative demonstrations. In terms of Figure 1.1, the change in strategy involved nonviolent engagement, but with a twist. Albanian leaders wished to show that Kosovo was on a slippery slope. If a policy change did not occur, low-level violence, most likely in the form of riots, was right around the corner.

B. The Incident at Hotel #1

By late 2003, Albanian leaders were willing to push things farther down the slippery slope. As an International Crisis Group report wrote:

The last quarter of 2003 saw Kosovo Albanian politicians increasingly deploying the extremist bogeyman as leverage in their negotiation with the international community. Prime Minister Rexhepi noted of the 14 October 2003 Pristina demonstration: "We don't like to see those protests on those placards, but if UNMIK continues to ignore our needs, if it refuses to transfer more power to us, then the internationals here will face big demonstrations and everyone will be crying 'UNMIK go home.'" In late September, President Rugova warned that if the independence of Kosovo was not recognized, sooner rather than later extremists could be expected to form a unified Albanian state.[26]

Prime Minister Rexepi would not just wait for demonstrations to happen. On December 6, 2003 he provoked an incident designed to bring the status issue to a head in the presence of a key international body.[27] A World Bank delegation came to Mitrovica to meet with Kosovo representatives and Rexhepi, who essentially served as host. Rexhepi had been a resident of north Mitrovica before the separation of populations.[28] He still visited his property there occasionally, using a small temporary bridge in order to avoid provoking a reaction from the Bridgewatchers. But the time for avoiding provocations was now over. With the World Bank delegation in tow, Rexhepi would cross the main bridge. After all, he was the Prime Minister of Kosovo and should be able to go anywhere in the country.

When it was time for lunch, Rexhepi led the delegation to the bridge in order to cross over and have lunch at Hotel #1, a hotel with a restaurant that served as an informal meeting place for Serb leaders on the north side. The party

---

[26] International Crisis Group Europe Report No. 155, "Collapse in Kosovo," April 22, 2004, p. 10.

[27] This section is based on conversations with a number of Serbs and Albanians in Mitrovica as well as with UNMIK officials (BY/6/30/08, EM/7/1/08, ZT/7/4/08, KC/7/5/08, TT/8/8/06, RO/8/11/06, HM/7/3/08). Several were eyewitnesses or participants in the event. Also see the ICG report, "Collapse in Kosovo," pp. 12–13, for a description of the incident.

[28] As noted in Chapter 8, Rexhepi would become mayor of south Mitrovica after serving as Prime Minister.

consisted of Rexhepi, the World Bank delegation, armed Albanian bodyguards, and television and newspaper reporters.[29] Television would capture Rexhepi with a coterie of armed Albanians crossing the bridge into Serbian territory. Albanian television would do an interview with Rexhepi from the north side of the Ibar.

Before crossing the bridge, Serbian members of the Kosovo representatives (Ivanovic and Bogdanovic) left. They most certainly knew that violence was likely to occur soon. Even if violence did not occur, by staying with the delegation party they would be seen as legitimizing Albanians crossing the river. Rexhepi did not inform the owner of Hotel #1 that the delegation was coming. The owner would have immediately closed the restaurant if Rexhepi had provided notice.

As the delegation crossed over, Rexhepi made a point of showing himself publicly, stopping at a local shop to buy some bananas. Word about what was taking place at Hotel #1 soon spread over north Mitrovica. As the World Bank delegation sat down in the restaurant, a mob gathered outside, pelting the building with stones. While Rexhepi went out the back door, the shocked World Bank delegation fled onto their bus. The driver, undoubtedly shaken by the situation, made a wrong turn and ended up at the hospital. In a panic, he crashed through a gate. Delegation members escaped through the hospital. Meanwhile, the Serbian mob, estimated at 50 at Hotel #1 but perhaps 1,000 at the hospital, trashed the World Bank's bus and KPS police cars.

Rexhepi used the cover of the World Bank visit to north Mitrovica. One of two things could have happened. The meetings could have occurred without violence. In that case, Rexhepi, as Prime Minister, could claim a small reestablishment of sovereignty over the north; he could claim to have laid down the principle that the north was not a separate political entity and diminish the aura of Serb leaders there. This outcome was not likely. As it happened, the excursion set off a wave of violence in full view of an important international delegation. They could see how volatile Kosovo's present system, under Standards before Status, actually was. They could see that Serbs were unreasonable and violent – they would not let the Prime Minister cross the river and have lunch.

Most Serbs see the incident at Hotel #1 as linked to the riots that occurred a few months later in March 2004. Albanian political actors were choosing to create provocations and demonstrations that illustrated the precarious nature of Kosovo under present policies. Kosovo was ready to explode. In March 2004, it actually did.

B. March 2004

By early 2004, anti-UNMIK demonstrations had become commonplace. Every year in March, Kosovo organizations commemorated the beginning of the

---

[29] Rexhepi claims that the media just happened to run into the party.

NATO bombing campaign that led to Kosovo's break from the Serbs. On March 16, an estimated 18,000 Albanians took to the streets in cities across Kosovo to protest the arrest of KLA members for war crimes.[30] Reporting on these demonstrations, the newspaper *Epoka e Re* reproduced the slogan, "UNMIK watch your step, the KLA has gunpowder for you too!"[31] At the same time, hundreds of Serbs from Caglavica and Gracanica were blocking the main highway to Pristina and pulling motorists from their vehicles. Albanians wondered why Serbs were allowed to get away with such things. With a well of anger aimed at both Serbs and UNMIK, an event occurred in the late afternoon of March 16 that would set off massive riots.

In the evening, Kosovo television reported that Serbs had chased Albanian children into the Ibar River, with three drowning. Similar to the February 2001 incident described earlier, as in the poster, Serbs were again killing Albanian children. Media outlets, especially television, began what an OSCE report termed "a clear case of incitement."[32] The OSCE report further summarized:

What the organizers of extremist anti-UNMIK demonstrations had failed to achieve in the past, the news concerning the drowning of the three children succeeded in doing. It offered a perfect emotional motive for popular outrage and a good tool for sentimental manipulation by extremist individuals and groups longing for escalation.[33]

With the Albanian population already primed for action, another round of demonstrations on March 17 would take a dramatic turn.[34] Two different groups of Albanian protestors met outside UNMIK headquarters in South Mitrovica – schoolchildren organized by their teachers and health-care workers who had planned to demonstrate against UNMIK's privatization plan. Security forces turned back a march toward the Main Bridge. After a pause, a second wave of protestors, now much larger, brushed by the KFOR troops, onto the bridge, and over to the Serbian side. In a matter of minutes, hundreds of Serbs gathered in defense. No international forces arrived for twenty minutes. Small battles then took place at several locations across North Mitrovica, with four Albanians shot dead and many more wounded. At UNMIK headquarters, defenders used water cannons and gas canisters against would-be assailants.

Although international security forces took control in North Mitrovica, news of the fighting soon reached Pristina. Within a short time, thousands of Albanians, including many students from the University, were marching toward Caglavica. They were met by security forces. As an ICG report states, "KFOR

---

[30] Miklos Haraszti, "The Role of the Media in the March 2004 Events in Kosovo," Organization for Security and Co-operation in Europe (OSCE), Vienna 2004.
[31] ICG report, "Collapse in Kosovo," p. 14.
[32] Haraszti, "The Role of the Media in the March 2004 Events in Kosovo," p. 12.
[33] Ibid., p. 4.
[34] The following paragraphs are from eyewitness accounts (BY/6/30/08, YJ/7/1/08, ZT/7/4/08, KC/7/5/08, TT/8/8/06, EM/7/1/08, RO/8/11/06) supported by ICG, "Collapse in Kosovo," especially the Appendix, which provides a detailed account of the order of events.

sources described the first day at Caglavica as a 'medieval battle' – hand-to-hand fighting from early afternoon to the late evening. Caglavica became a battle of wills between mob and security forces."[35]

By the afternoon of March 17, riots spread across Kosovo. In some areas, organization was more apparent than in others. In Prizren, a crowd of 200 faced off against fifteen German police officers. Crowds blocking the road from both sides prevented the arrival of reinforcements. Children were placed in the front of the crowd and delivered messages during negotiations with the Germans. In the end, it was agreed that the Serbs could leave but that the Albanians would be allowed to destroy property, including a centuries-old church. As in Svinjare, a village south of Mitrovica where all 130 houses were destroyed in the March riots, KFOR troops decided to defend lives (by removing them) rather than property. Gjilani/Gnjilane witnessed less violence overall; however, in the city itself, seventy Serbs huddled in fear at the Serbian Orthodox Church.[36] Three U.S. KFOR officers arrived to tell them that there were no resources available to protect them and they would have to leave. In other areas, the United States, operating with less stringent rules of engagement, effectively prevented violence. One woman living in Gracanica at the time told me that she generally hated Americans, but when she heard U.S. forces were coming from Camp Bondsteel to help pacify the situation in central Kosovo, she was overjoyed.[37] KFOR had not been able to prevent rioters from burning houses in surrounding villages and were fighting hard at Caglavica. The residents of Gracanica, the most populous Serbian town south of the Ibar, feared for their lives. In Peja/Pec, the riots only subsided when Ramush Haradinaj, through U.S. influence, intervened.

In all, UNMIK estimated that riots had broken out in thirty-three different locations involving 51,000 participants.[38] No less than 700 Serbian homes had been destroyed; rioters had damaged 36 Serbian Orthodox Churches, some severely; the pogrom had generated 4,000 new refugees and left 19 dead and 1,000 injured.[39]

When the riots began, several Albanian political leaders added fuel to the fire. UN spokesperson Dave Chappell believed that local leaders were directing the attacks, citing clear targets in each locality.[40] One member of Parliament from the PDK stated on the first day of the riots, "The barbaric act of the killing of the children . . . has provoked a legitimate revolt by the Albanian population. This should be a lesson for the international community."

In the aftermath, no major party leader condemned the riots. Rugova stated that they were the result of understandable frustrations. Haradinaj's party,

[35] ICG, "Collapse in Kosovo," p. 46.
[36] DB/6/3/08.
[37] KX/6/4/08.
[38] ICG, "Collapse in Kosovo," p. 15.
[39] King and Mason, *Peace at Any Price*, p. 5.
[40] Jeta Xharra and Alex Anderson, *Institute for War and Peace Reporting*, March 18, 2004.

the AAK, claimed that Serbian parallel structures were responsible for the riots.[41] The PDK issued a statement that "Serbs are misusing the good will of Albanians to create an equal society for all. They don't want to integrate into Kosova society. Even five years after the war, their will remains the same – the will for violence against Albanians. This can no longer be tolerated."[42] Even the moderate Veton Surroi wrote an editorial in *Koha Ditore* that excused Albanian behavior.[43]

For most Albanians, the riots had been a legitimate political tool, one necessary to show that the threat to withhold status indefinitely was not going to be tolerated. As summed up in the International Crisis Group's report on the March events:

Until 17–18 March, the contest for dominance appeared to be an unresolved three-way affair, with Albanian anxiety growing that they were being compelled to submit to what they considered the arrogance and assertiveness of both UNMIK/KFOR and the Serbs. KFOR was being seen less a partner, more a quasi-occupier. UNMIK's condescending tutelage was not leading anywhere. By mounting roadblocks and beating Albanian motorists, Kosovo Serbs were still behaving like they owned the place. Kosovo Albanians perceive they have now reversed these relationships. UNMIK's confidence is punctured, its staff concerned for their security.[44]

Two former UNMIK employees, Iain King and Whit Mason, provide a similar summary through the words of Western officials in Kosovo:

More then a year after the riots, the security situation remained uncertain. One Western diplomat, speaking in August 2004, said, "They could very easily do it again – they're just biding their time. But if independence is delayed, or if it's denied them, expect something much worse. And again, we probably wouldn't be able to stop it." Another international official described the tacit threat of another outburst of violence, worse than that of March 2004, as "the big Albanian veto" – to be used against any status options they don't like. In reality, this "veto" had hung in the air from the beginning and continually deterred UNMIK and KFOR from imposing the international community's will.[45]

UNMIK believed that in the Basic Game, they could wield a stick against the Albanians. It turned out that the Albanians wielded a bigger stick against the interveners. It is important to consider the nature of this stick. Albanian political entrepreneurs did not control any type of "riot system" with which to churn out a riot.[46] Western political scientists look for manipulative evil leaders and extremists behind violent events, as they did with the March 2004 riots. These

---

[41] Tanja Matic, *Institute for War and Peace Reporting*, March 18, 2004.
[42] Ibid.
[43] A reprint of Surroi's article was posted on *Transitions on Line* on March 24, 2004.
[44] ICG report, "Collapse in Kosovo," p. 22.
[45] King and Mason, *Peace at Any Price*, pp. 196–7.
[46] For a discussion of riot systems, see various works of Paul Brass.

riots, as the ICG report argues, were more spontaneous than organized.[47] In many of the thirty-three riot locations, local leaders may have promoted and directed the violence, but the fact is that more than 50,000 Albanians, of a population of less than two million, were involved in a major violent escalation within a day.[48]

The key explanatory factor both in the low-level violence and in the February 2001 and March 2004 riots was the emotions inherent in the situation represented by box R8. In the cases represented by R8, a wealth of emotion resources was available. If the Serbs committed violence against Albanians, as in the cases of the dead children in Mitrovica or the incidents in which Albanians were being pulled out of cars in Caglavica, Albanian political actors knew that their population would burn with anger and that tens of thousands would be ready to participate in punishment immediately. As was true with low-level violence, all that was necessary was a "green light."

In the case of low-level violence, I argue that the Albanian political leadership, connected remnants of the KLA and other violent groups, and the general population all understood that the return of Serbs would be highly negative for the consolidation of Albanian rule in Kosovo. Given the lack of security provided by the international community (recall the lack of a single conviction for any murder of a Serb over several years), the strategy of low-level violence was effective in creating fears that effectively cleared Serbs out of every urban area south of the Ibar.

In the case of the March riots, anger and contempt for Serbs mixed with resentment against UNMIK and the international intervention. Political leaders had been organizing demonstrations and provocations, such as the one at Hotel #1, against the interveners for months. As in the quoted passages, they wanted to exercise the "big Albanian veto" over the policy of Status before Standards. The drowning of the children in the Ibar focused all the anger and resentment of the Albanian population. All that was needed was another green light. It was provided through statements by political leadership legitimizing the riots and a media willing to provide incitement. Igniting anger was not at all difficult. It was actually harder to stop it. Without the action of Rexhepi in Caglavica and Haradinaj at Pec, the riots would have escalated further.

Although international intervention could prevent sustained high-level violence, the emotional resources of cell R8 provided a way to escalate to high violence for two days. It was a stick large enough to change the intervention game yet again.

---

[47] See the section in the ICG report "Collapse in Kosovo" entitled "Spontaneous or Organized Violence," pp. 15–18.

[48] In proportional terms, the equivalent number in the United States would be eight million people.

Kosovo Intervention Games, II

After the March 2004 riots, Western leaders reassessed their strategy in Kosovo. Analysts and diplomats in the United States saw the riots as a wake-up call to push for final status. Europeans were more inclined to claim that violence should not be rewarded.[1] Most importantly, Westerners knew that they could not credibly threaten to put off the status question indefinitely. To do so might bring on "another March 2004."

I. ANOTHER CHANGE IN THE INTERVENER GAME: STANDARDS WITH STATUS

The interveners had come to accept that they needed to take Albanian threats into account and they had resigned themselves to the fact that Serbs were likely to defect for the foreseeable future. In terms of the 2×2 game, the broad contours of intervention strategy remained the same as with Standards before Status. The task was first to move the Albanian side to unilateral cooperation (T, S) and then eventually to get the Serbs on board to move the equilibrium to mutual reward (R, R). Although the broad strategy was similar, the tactics had changed. With the new policy, Standards with Status, the West did not threaten to withhold status, but rather promised to grant an independent status. Instead of being sequenced, the issues would be dealt with simultaneously.

The new policy was entirely a Western one. The idea was to weave the "carrot" of European integration into the standards-setting process. Kai Eide,

---

[1] For an example of the U.S. position, see the Radio Free Europe/Radio Liberty reports written by Patrick Moore in the wake of the riots (RFE/RL reports Volume 8, issue 13 and 15). Moore's reports refuse to lay any specific blame on Albanians. Many Europeans did not hesitate to do so. For example, a former United Nations special envoy to the Balkans, Carl Bildt, in "Why Kosovo Must Not Submit to Violence" (*Financial Times*, March 22, 2004), wrote that "There can be no question that this was a deliberate attempt to drive away as many Serbs as possible, to inflict maximum damage on the UN and to test how far Nato could be driven into accepting the new realities."

a NATO ambassador, wrote two reports outlining the new policy. The first addressed the March 2004 riots and concluded that Standards before Status was unworkable. The second enunciated the new Status with Standards policy and recommended the start of future status negotiations. Not only was the taboo on discussing independence lifted, but independence became the basis of policy. The latter report did not develop any comprehensive plan; it was assumed that the details would work themselves out. The Contact Group pushed UNMIK, now led by Soeren Jessen-Petersen, to drop two-thirds of the standards. Only the standards most relevant to solving the status issue were to be pursued.

The logic of the new version of the game was to offer Albanians the ultimate "carrot" – independence and guaranteed freedom from Serbs forever. In terms of the 2 × 2 game matrix, the West was raising the value of cooperation for the Albanian player to the highest level that it could. In effect, the West, by offering independence and integration into Europe, was again trying to change the preference ordering for Albanians to R > S > T > P. Albanians would accept being "suckered" in return for their ultimate prize. They would agree to make concessions to the Serbian side. The full logic of this effort would come into play with the follow-on to Standards with Status – the Ahtisaari plan.

A. The Albanian Strategy

When the new game was introduced, the situation was still at box R8. Here, Albanian political actors had many resources and, therefore, many feasible strategies. If they maintained low-level violence, remaining in R8, the following tactics could be employed:

(1) They still had the ability to threaten and green-light low-level violence
(2) They could try to use anger to incite riots
(3) They could play on resentment against the internationals in the form of continued demonstrations
(4) They could pursue policies to isolate Serbs, building on contempt

Alternatively, they could deescalate the conflict and move the situation to box R7 and a situation of no violence. In R7, political entrepreneurs still had powerful emotion resources sufficient for the following strategies:

(5) They could still use normal politics of resentment against the intervener
(6) They could still try to isolate Serbs, drawing from a reservoir of contempt

Albanian political actors decided to deescalate violence, move the game to R7, and play both options 5 and 6. There was no longer any reason to green-light low-level violence. A violence-based strategy was employed to prevent Serbian returns and a significant Serbian presence. After March 2004, those goals had been accomplished. The violence had displaced 4,000 additional Serbs; more Serbs were now leaving Kosovo than trying to enter. No city south of the Ibar could expect any significant return, because of both the deterrent effect produced by the March riots and simply the passage of time. Five years after

1999, many Serbs had established lives in Serbia proper and were never going back. Violent strategies create fear and anger, but those emotion resources had lost their usefulness.

There was also little reason to incite riots. At this point, Albanians had won the game – independence was coming. There was no need to risk a backlash from the West when the West was promising to integrate Kosovo into Europe. Even without violence, there would be a range of resources available to pressure the West in the new stage of the game.

As this strategy played out, violence levels continued to decrease. There were occasional violent incidents, such as the sniper attacks and market bombings in Strpce in November 2005. On the whole, however, interethnic violence decreased.[2] Although the effects of fear still lingered, more and more Serbs felt safe in traveling out of their immediate areas. Most notably, there were no more significant riots or clearly organized incidents such as the bombing of the Nis bus convoy.

B. The Serbian Strategy

Serbs had little ability to transform the game through violence. They would have to decide among options in box R7. They could:

(1) Acquiesce in the new intervener game and begin cooperation with Albanians
(2) Continue a policy of building a parallel society and using boycotts
(3) Launch a series of provocative demonstrations

Option #1 was a nonstarter. The third option presented difficulties because it was not clear what to demonstrate against. During this period of status negotiations, both the policy and the exact nature of the final outcome were still ambiguous. The Serb leadership thus chose the second option. With continued financial support from Belgrade, Serbs continued to live in their separate political and social world.

II. INDEPENDENCE AND THE AHTISAARI PLAN

The Ahtisaari plan was the anticipated follow-on to Status with Standards. It was designed to offer both the Serbs and the Albanians the things they had always wanted. The Albanians would receive independence. Along the lines of the logic discussed in Section I, the Ahtisaari plan was designed to encourage the Albanian side to accept the sucker payoff and grant considerable concessions, at least on paper, to the Serbs.

---

[2] UNMIK police reported that interethnic crimes were down to 15–25 actual cases (versus reported cases) a month in 2005, with a decreasing trend over time (ICG Report, "Kosovo: the Challenge of Transition," p. 8).

After several years of involvement in Kosovo, the West had essentially accepted the desire of Kosovo's people to live separately and abandoned the more ambitious goal of broader reconciliation. My own reading of the Ahtisaari plan is that it is an excellent deal for the Serbs, at least from the viewpoint of an outsider. Almost a quarter of Kosovo's territory could come under Serbian autonomy; Serbs could sustain a special relationship with Belgrade and could receive funding from Belgrade as long as the transfer was transparent and for public use; minority rights would be protected through the Bandinter "double majority" principle; Serbs would retain their automatic seats in the parliament; north Mitrovica would become a separate municipality with autonomous secondary education and health care systems; block grants would be used instead of earmarks to enhance autonomy; religious and cultural sites would receive generous protection areas. The Albanian side gave a lot away – but by signing on they received independence in return. The West was granting a side payment large enough to dramatically increase the value of the sucker payoff in the game with the Serbs. In effect, with the acceptance of the plan and the granting of independence, the game was moved to the lower left cell.

A. Western Substrategies for the Post-2008 Period

For the equilibrium of mutual cooperation to be reached, however, Serbs would have to be induced to cooperate eventually. For the European mission taking over from the UN, the key word here was "eventually." In the view of the EU officials that I talked with in 2008, the Serbs have no choice but to begin cooperation; they cannot stay out of the European integration process.[3] Furthermore, there is nothing for the Serbs to concretely attack; they will have no target under the technocratic reforms to be instituted in Kosovo. The EU is nothing more than a set of political and economic practices and norms enveloping the region. No one can shoot or bomb a set of practices. I was told that fighting the EU is like fighting the spread of the English language.

Given the view that integration of the Western Balkans was inevitable, the EU's project would be best advanced by avoiding confrontation to the greatest extent possible. The Serbs, in the view of EU officials, were holed up in the "dark ages" on the north side of the Ibar; they would see the wonderful lives of the Albanians, progressing under democracy and capitalism, and they would join out of envy, if not for the sake of their pocketbooks.[4] Under these assumptions, the EU would like to pull back the international police presence to avoid any appearance of being an occupier.

If the conflict was ever to be "unfrozen," Serbs would need to dissolve their parallel society and move to cooperation with the Albanians under one common government. In addition to a belief in the spread of democracy and the rule of law, Western officials also show great faith in the power of the market

---

[3] YO/3/19/08; JR/319/08.
[4] YO/7/3/08.

to dissolve parallel structures. For example, the OSCE published something of a "how to" to dissolving parallel structures for 2006–7.[5] The guide stated that "Simply closing down parallel structures dealing with health care and education is not an acceptable solution. The final aim should be comprehensive inclusion of the existing parallel public services into a unified system." The report goes on to make recommendations in three categories:

The first category aims at *reducing the demand* for parallel structures, i.e., improving the services offered by UNMIK and the PISG and thus gaining public confidence.

The second category aims at reducing the supply of parallel services by negotiating with parallel service providers to ensure a *reduction of service*.

The third category aims at *enforcing certain policies/measures* that can be applied by the relevant actors to integrate parallel services providers into Kosovo's governmental structures.

In effect, the OSCE recommends a market solution to the frozen conflict and parallel system. As service provision in independent Kosovo improves, more Serbs will leave their parallel system to obtain the superior services of the Kosovo state. As the parallel Serbian system begins to erode, some Serbs will see their future in the new state system and begin negotiating a transfer. Remaining Serbs will be brought along through enforcement of laws.[6]

Corresponding with the strategy of nonconfrontation, the EU hopes to implement the general lines of the OSCE strategy in a slow and ad hoc fashion. Some Serbian localities will be more vulnerable or less hostile than others. Their local leaders, for the good of their communities, will begin cooperating with the central Kosovo government, first informally, and then formally. The EU will claim no triumph. If the Ahtisaari plan is being implemented in a certain locality or region, the EU will not publicly play up that fact, so that there would be no appearance of Serbs "losing" some sort of contest.[7] Eventually, there will be a tipping point at which Serbs begin folding their parallel structures into those in Pristina.

This process was sometimes discussed in Kosovo in 2008 as the "southern strategy." Of the 130,000 Serbs living in Kosovo, 75,000 live south of the Ibar.

[5] Organization for Security and Cooperation in Europe, Mission in Kosovo, Department of Human Rights, Decentralization and Communities (2007), "Parallel Structures in Kosovo, 2006–2007."

[6] All of the interviewees in 2008 agreed that the scenario envisioned in the OSCE document is unlikely to play out over all of Kosovo's territory and, in some ways, is already dated. Above all, Serbs have strongly consolidated control in the region north of the Ibar River. With the financial support of Belgrade, health care and educational systems are robust. Birth rates are substantial; unlike the southern enclaves, north Mitrovica does not face drastic demographic decline. As several violent incidents in the wake of Kosovo's independence illustrated, the Serbs in the north can also generate a strong and even violent response to perceived threats.

[7] JR/7/3/08.

Although a few of the enclaves are relatively stable, such as the one in Strpce/Shterpca, others consist of aging populations badly in need of state services. In the southern strategy, the Serb-controlled north is essentially quarantined and the focus turns to the vulnerable southern enclaves. In these communities, Serbs will tie into the OSCE scenario and begin cooperating with the Kosovo state structures out of necessity. Certain communities with a history of interethnic tolerance, such as those in the Gjilan/Gnjilane area, might serve as showcases to illustrate the benefits of tying into the Kosovo state system. Some Serb leaders, such as Rada Trajkovic, were willing to move in this direction relatively soon after the intervention. In the optimistic versions of this scenario, along the lines of the "dark ages" idea mentioned previously, even the Serbs in Mitrovica and the north will sense they are being left behind and, in a few years, will begin to slowly integrate their parallel system into the state system.[8]

Some Albanians spoke privately about a "northern strategy." The idea here is based on the perception that the north is run more or less as a criminal enterprise. If the heads of this enterprise were to be cut off, in essence a decapitation strategy, the Serbs in the north would become more willing to begin integrating their parallel structures with Kosovo state structures. Most of the versions of the scenario, as I was hearing in 2008, emphasized the key role of Marko Jaksic as the "godfather" of the north. Some supporters of the northern strategy hoped to see him arrested; others suggested that he simply be pushed out of Kosovo and into retirement in Serbia proper. If the solid structure of the north were to crack, the south would certainly follow. Given the EU's confidence in its long-run abilities, this northern strategy is unlikely to be implemented.[9]

B. The Albanian Strategy

At the time of this writing, Albanians were still living in the glow of independence. They had won; it was no longer time to fight. Some Albanians, however, still chafe under the terms of conditional independence. They believe that the

---

[8] In the final stages of completion of this book, some U.S. State Department documents relating to Western strategy in Kosovo were leaked (Wikileaks). In one particularly revealing document, U.S. Ambassador Christopher Dell, in a briefing written to Philip Gordon, Assistant Secretary of State for Europe, essentially outlined U.S. strategy as it stood in January 2010. The terminology differs from what I heard in my discussions, as Dell outlines as a "northern strategy" what I usually heard termed a "southern strategy." In both, the logic is the same: success in inducing cooperation in the more vulnerable southern Serbian population should be used to push the Serbs in the north into cooperation. Ambassador Dell saw the glimmerings of a successful first stage in this plan when significant numbers of Serbs participated in Kosovo municipal elections for the first time in 2009. Dell also wrote that this strategy depends on the EU threatening to block Serbia's progression into the EU. The leaked document was published by the *Guardian*, "US Embassy Cables: Partition of Kosovo Hardening, Warns US Ambassador," December 9, 2010 (http://www.guardian.co.uk/world/us-embassy-cables-documents/246223/).

[9] In the leaked U.S. State Department briefing, Ambassador Dell emphasized that the U.S. strategy avoided direct confrontation and had elements of a "soft approach." It would not seem supportive of the type of "northern strategy" discussed in this paragraph.

Ahtisaari plan, if the Serbs were ever to take advantage of it, gives away far too much.[10] In the summer of 2008, Albin Kurti's Vetevendosje movement was protesting against the lack of sovereignty actually enjoyed under conditional independence. However, for the foreseeable future, Albanians will acquiesce in the Western game.

C. The Serbian Strategy

In my conversations in 2008, most Serbs hoped for eventual partition at the Ibar River. Eventually, in a common Serbian view, all the actors may come to see partition as the best outcome to the "frozen conflict." One Serbian official told me that the strategy is to "talk and talk and talk" to drag out the frozen conflict in Kosovo until an appropriate time for partition talks arrives, probably ten years in the future.[11] Few Serbs believe that their fellow Serbs south of the Ibar have a future.

In 2008, Serbs chose to consolidate their parallel structures, employing a series of provocations in the days after independence was declared. In the immediate postindependence period, three different major events helped to freeze Kosovo's conflict to an even further degree.

On February 17, 2008, the Kosovo parliament declared independence. Two days later, several hundred Serbs attacked the border posts north of Mitrovica. Many wore ski masks; some drove bulldozers. The control booths were both torched. The actions were supported, if not outright directed, by Belgrade. Slobodan Samardzic, head of the Ministry for Kosovo and Metohija in Belgrade, announced that "the attacks were in accordance with general government policies" and that "Belgrade has the intention to take over the customs in northern Kosovo." He said the customs points had been intended to become part of Kosovo's state border, "and we are not going to let that happen."[12]

On March 14, 300 Serbs, mostly former judicial workers from the pre-1999 period, broke into the courthouse in north Mitrovica and began an occupation of the building. A resulting standoff became the center of a power struggle between some elements of UNMIK and the Serbs over control of the north. On March 17, the UNMIK police entered the building at 5:30 A.M. and made about fifty arrests. However, there were not enough transports to transfer those arrested for processing. While dozens of Serbs sat handcuffed in open view of the town, hundreds of Serbs poured out of their homes and began attacking the international security forces. The protestors threw fragmentation grenades, tossed Molotov cocktails, and fired live ammunition. One Ukrainian UNMIK police officer bled to death because the battle was so intense that rescue

---

[10] YM/3/20/08.

[11] JK/5/28/08. The secession of Republika Srpska from Bosnia is also included in many scenarios.

[12] Dan Bilefsky, *New York Times*, "Angry Serbs Burn Border Posts in Kosovo," February 20, 2008.

vehicles could not approach for two and one-half hours.[13] At least 42 other UNMIK police officers were injured, many seriously, and approximately 70 Serbs were injured, 15 seriously. Samardzic again made statements supportive of the Serbian response. Remarking on the riot, the British UN Ambassador stated, "What we saw yesterday showed the lengths to which some people . . . in the Kosovo Serb community are prepared to go."[14] For Serbs, that was exactly the point. Most Serbs saw the UNMIK operation as a purposeful humiliation of Serbs – the action took place on March 17, the anniversary of the riots against them four years earlier; Serbs were visibly displayed in handcuffs. Given this perception, the vehemence of the response could have been expected.

On May 11, 2008, Belgrade organized both parliamentary and local elections for Kosovar Serbs. It was the first time since 1999 that they had voted in both elections. As these elections were a clear affront to Kosovo's sovereignty, UNMIK's head repeatedly called the elections illegitimate. The incoming EU bodies would refuse to even have informal contact with the Serbian assembly.[15]

In the weeks immediately following Kosovo's declaration of independence, Serbs, with direct help from Belgrade, had challenged Kosovo's borders, its attempt to establish its legal system and laws north of the Ibar, and its electoral institutions. It was all part of the "functional separation" policy enunciated by the Serbian Ministry for Kosovo and Metohija. In 2008, at least, there was a clear and strong policy of building a parallel society. What the future would bring, especially under pro-Western Serbian governments, could be another story.

III. CONCLUSIONS

The international community, one dominated by Western ideas and interests in this case, made four different attempts to create a unified and multiethnic Kosovo. The Basic Game evolved into Standards before Status, which led to Standards with Status, and finally to the Ahtisaari plan. The progression was characterized by increasingly less ambitious aspirations. In the first stage, policy centered on positive inducements to both sides; in the second round, the intervener relied on the stick; the third round amounted to appeasement; the fourth basically offered a bribe.

By the last round, the West simply accepted that Serbs and Albanians were not really willing to live with each other, at least in the short to medium term. The most likely outcome was a "frozen conflict" at the Ibar. The Ahtisaari plan, with its heavy element of decentralization and separation, applied in the south. Perhaps the forces of European integration and the passage of time would change the relationships between the two groups, but the faith in an

[13] UNMIK Press Briefing, March 18, 2008.
[14] UNMIK Press Briefing, March 19, 2008.
[15] YO/7/3/08.

ability to engineer a solution centered on manipulating a narrow set of "sticks and carrots" had been lost.

The major problem was the dominant heritage of stigma and violence. When Pieter Feith took over as EU Special Representative and head of the transition team in Kosovo in March 2008, he stated that "No healthy society lives in the past." But was it possible for people in Kosovo who have lived through horrendous violence, suffered under ethnic stigma, and inherited the legacy of numerous cycles of domination simply to shed the past?

13

Kosovo Conclusions

In the summer of 2001, I was staying at a hilltop farmhouse in a NATO-protected Serbian enclave in rural Kosovo. Two years earlier, Serbian forces drove hundreds of thousands of Kosovar Albanians out of their homes, burning and killing along the way. Approximately fifty KFOR soldiers were protecting about twenty-five mostly elderly Serbs from possible violence from the surrounding Albanian population. The soldiers' local headquarters was located across from my hosts' farmyard. Chickens pecked the ground around armored vehicles and jeeps, barely noticing a short column of armed soldiers passing through on their way to a nearby lookout point. Young soldiers casually came and went from the kitchen of my hosts, whom I will call Dragan and Mira.[1] The elderly couple's two adult sons, whom I will call Nikola and Dusan, now living across the line in Serbia with no future in Kosovo, sat at a picnic table and conversed and joked in the shade of a large tree.

Neither the mood nor the topic of conversation was representative of recent local history. The nearest significant city, Podujevo, had been the scene of fierce fighting and cleansing two years earlier. The hostility had pervaded the countryside as well. This enclave was the last pocket of Serbs in the region. Down the road, all other nearby Serbian populations had been driven out, many of their houses destroyed, and their graves desecrated.

In the midst of this destructiveness, the farmyard would serve as the site of what was both a normal and remarkable meeting after the sun set. After complete dark descended, a lone figure drove up the hillside lane in a small truck loaded with some watermelons. This was Hydayet,[2] a young Albanian man who had worked for Dragan since he was a boy. Dragan told me that he considered Hydayet as a "son." The reason for the late night delivery was clear. If other local Albanians saw Hydayet helping these Serbs, he would suffer

---

[1] To protect confidentiality, I do not use real names.
[2] Also a pseudonym.

strong social sanctions. Hydayet was risking much to bring a few watermelons to Dragan.

Dragan, his two sons, and his Albanian "son" sat at the picnic table and discussed the state of their families and the activities of their children. It was a very normal conversation. For me, an outsider, the meeting was also remarkable because I knew that these three "brothers" had played starkly different roles in the recent conflict. The eldest son, Nikola, had "been involved" in Serbian actions in Kosovo. I did not want to know all the details, but he did show me his machine gun and RPG launcher, stashed in his home across the border in Serbia, and indicated his willingness to fight again. The younger son, Dusan, had fulfilled his duty by serving in the reserve police, but tried to avoid any actions that would prevent him from having a clear conscience. The Albanian "son" would tell me the next day that he and his family fled Serbian cleansing in 1999.

Hydayet told me that he could give me a ride to Pristina in a few days. He could not pick me up at the farmstead in the daytime, but if I descended the hillside through the woods, he would be waiting for me on the road. I got into the car a little after sunrise and he told me that he would be picking up his young son, who wanted to see an American. As the six- or seven-year-old jumped into the back seat, his face was absolutely beaming. As an American, I was something of a marvel and hero to this boy. Then I said a few words in Serbian to Hydayet. The boy's face immediately clouded over and he began to wail. Hydayet said something to the boy and then to answer my puzzlement he told me that his son asked him why we were speaking that awful language. It was my first lesson that many people love Americans, until we do something they dislike. Hydayet told him that it was all right, that I was connected with Dragan.

Such is the complexity of personal relations in an ethnic conflict zone. An old Serbian man and his wife live under siege and cannot wander more than a hundred yards from their house; a young Albanian man who two years before needed to flee ugly Serbian forces now risks his position in the local community to bring the old Serbian man a simple luxury such as a watermelon; one Serbian son is "involved" on the side against Albanians, one of whom he has known as a "brother"; another Serbian son wishes to support his nation but tries to do so in a way that he can live with a clear conscience. And they all sit and talk and laugh at the same picnic table one night two years after the most gut-wrenching violence witnessed in Europe in over fifty years.

The United States and Western Europe, collectively known as the West in this book, increasingly step into such situations. The West does so, I will argue, with a certain mentality. They assume that "people are people" everywhere, mainly concerned with the safety and economic welfare of themselves and their families. For the Western intervener, individuals everywhere are basically straightforwardly rational. Once manipulative leaders are cleared away, all that is needed is to establish a clear and fair set of rules for all citizens and a solution will follow. If people of different ethnic groups can sit around a common picnic table, why can't they become common citizens of a larger community?

This book provides a particular answer to that question. Individuals clearly do interact and easily mix in daily interactions. But they also live through powerful experiences connected to their group memberships. They experience prejudice and stigma; they are victims and perpetrators of violence; they live through periods of being dominated by others. Despite his friendship with Dragan, Hydayet would not wish to go back to a situation of being dominated by Serbs. Despite his relationship with Hydayet, Nikola would never accept Serbs being second-class citizens in Kosovo. It is hard to believe that either had forgotten about the violence that had wrought havoc on both of their families, although neither would openly talk about it at the picnic table. Despite their cordial personal interactions, both men were embedded within larger historical and social processes that defined the meaning of being Serb and Albanian.

When the West intervened in Kosovo, it defined success in terms of recreating a multiethnic state. To accomplish its goals, interveners invested enormous sums of money and numbers of soldiers. Despite this Herculean (or perhaps Sisyphean) effort, Kosovo's cities have effectively become monoethnic. Thirty thousand Serbs lived in Pristina before the intervention. By 2008, the number was down to a couple of hundred, or about one percent of the previous number. Another major city, Podujevo, became Serb-free a few years after intervention; the final two residents, elderly Serbian women, were jeered by crowds as internationals escorted them out. The north of Kosovo remains de facto Serbia. The Ibar River serves as the demarcation line in one of the world's most intractable "frozen conflicts." South of the Ibar, Serbs live in isolated and impoverished rural communities.

I. ASSESSING THE METHOD AND ITS HYPOTHESES

How should social scientists explain this outcome? As opposed to more common current political science approaches, the method here begins by considering the lived experiences of the broader populations in conflict. It concentrates on ethnic stigma, changes in political status dominance/subordination, and the legacy of violence. An analytical framework addressing these factors placed the starting point for the explanation of Kosovo's recent history in the bottom left box (also referred to as box R7 for shorthand) in Figure 3.2 (repeated as Figure 13.1).

In Kosovo, Serbs and Albanians did not intermarry, they lived in increasingly segregated communities, they believed pernicious myths about one another, and they held basic prejudices against one another. Furthermore, Kosovo had witnessed a series of political status reversals, with the most recent coming with Milosevic's sacking of Albanians from positions of authority in the late 1980s.

The analytical framework developed in the first section of the book generated hypotheses about what to expect starting in this box, R7. The insight that the

Violence

	No Violence	Low Violence	High Violence
Low	**Resentment-** R1	**Anger** **Resentment-** R2	**Fear** R3
Medium	**Resentment** R4	**Anger** **Resentment** R5	**Fear** R6
High	**Contempt** **Resentment+** R7	**Anger** **Contempt** **Resentment+** R8	**Hatred** R9

(Stigma: Low / Medium / High on vertical axis)

FIGURE 13.1. Distribution of Emotional Resources with Resentment (Figure 3.2 Reprinted).

emotion of contempt allows political elites wide leeway to pursue policies of separation yielded the following prediction:

> *Prediction 6*: In R7, political entrepreneurs are most likely to initiate the politics of boycott and the creation of parallel systems.

Correspondingly, Albanian political leaders were able to institute and sustain a robust parallel society for many years.

If violence is or becomes a viable option, other hypotheses stated:

> *Prediction 8*: In R7, we are likely to observe periodic and perhaps frequent initiations of targeted violence.
> *Prediction 9*: We are more likely to see escalation of violence in R7 than in NR7.

These predictions played out, but in a form beyond what the hypotheses would predict. Albanians did gain sufficient weapons to consider violent strategies by 1998. As predicted, Albanian groups began discriminate attacks on Serbian targets, specifically against Serbian police. In this case, these attacks led to high levels of violence very quickly. Rather than periodic attacks, the situation escalated to civil war.

A fourth prediction stated:

> *Prediction 7*: Under conditions of contempt, players who initiate violence will suffer little backlash from their own population.

In Kosovo, there was no backlash for killing Serbian policemen. In fact, there was little backlash for instituting any form of violence, even attacks that were almost certain to bring retaliatory violence against the Albanian population.

The situation quickly escalated to high violence, or the bottom right box, shorthanded as R9. The theory section predicted that this situation was most likely to generate the emotion of hatred, especially if a cultural schema supporting the cognitive foundations of that emotion was present. In Kosovo, I argued that such a schema was activated and that hypotheses related to hatred should apply. The basic prediction here is:

> *Prediction 11*: In a situation of hatred, strategies of ethnic cleansing will find widespread support.

For many Serbs in the spring of 1999, ethnic cleansing of Albanians from Kosovo was justified, even somewhat natural. Likewise, as Albanians returned in the summer of 1999, violent cleansing actions against Serbs and collaborating minorities were accepted as natural.

In 1999, Kosovo was occupied by international forces, with Western political forces dominant. As the situation moved back to one of low-level violence, the situation fit the middle box, R8. Few specific hypotheses can be made here. There is one general prediction:

> *Prediction 12*: Political entrepreneurs, especially if they retain the ability to use violence, will have a wide variety of tactics available to them. They are likely to have considerable leverage over the intervener.

In Kosovo, Albanian political entrepreneurs, I argue, green-lighted low-level violence in an effort to consolidate Kosovo as an Albanian state. They also instigated demonstrations and provocations that threatened violence and eventually led to the massive March 2004 riots, which fundamentally changed intervention policy in Kosovo. In box R8, the opponents of intervention may very well have bigger "sticks" than the intervener.

By 2005, the situation in Kosovo returned to its starting point – the lower left box, R7. This time it was the Serbs who engaged in the predicted policy of parallel society and boycott. To avoid the political status dominance of Albanians and simply to live in their own society, Serbs have developed a parallel system throughout Kosovo and live in de facto Serbia north of the Ibar River. Time will tell if international policies will erode this situation.

II. WHAT IS THE VALUE-ADDED OF THIS APPROACH?

A. The Specific Dependent Variable

In the Introduction, I briefly outlined some of the contributions I hoped this method might make to the study of ethnic conflict. My first claim was that by including emotion resources in the analysis of intervention I can explain variation in the implementation of opponent tactics better than other approaches can. These tactics are the specific dependent variable of the project.

In particular, the approach outlined helps explain variation in the timing and nature of violent escalation during intervention. Most political scientists develop theories based on structural variables alone. Consider how a "technology" approach would examine Kosovo. In such a method, the primary variables are the size of the country, the power of the state to control violent actors, and mountainous terrain. Kosovo possessed none of these. In fact, the Serbian state, the primary variable in this approach, had a massive presence in Kosovo. No structural theory would have predicted an escalation of violence, and certainly not one that would lead to an independent state for the rebels.

The approach here makes far different assumptions about the agency of political entrepreneurs in places like Kosovo. They are not automatically deterred when the structural forces align against them. Instead, they look for a wider set of resources. They also consider the emotions of their own people and the opponents. In Kosovo, when Albanian political actors gained a minimum level of force, they hit on a strategy to provoke Serbs into a retaliatory spiral that might bring in the West. These political actors had a theory about anger, and it how it might be used to get around their lack of "technology." They also had a theory about the way that the international system worked and what was necessary to make that system work in their direction. In short, these actors possessed a level of creativity and agency that technology-based approaches deny them.

By including emotions, the approach here not only explains escalation in the absence of technology, but also helps explain the specific choice of target. Employing a strategy aimed at provoking anger, the KLA hit the undisciplined Serbian police rather than civilian targets or the military. On the other hand, during the first years of intervention, the strategy designed to create fear involved hitting indiscriminate civilian targets. Political entrepreneurs consider how to use anger and fear; their strategies change accordingly.

The approach here helps explain not only the choice of violent strategies, but also choices among a range of nonviolent strategies. Choosing to create a parallel society is a radical policy. Yet both Albanian and Serbian political actors believed they could pull it off. Their beliefs and strategy are based again on a consideration of emotion resources, in this case contempt.

The approach here provides an explanation for the rare cases of popular support for ethnic cleansing. This emotions-based approach forces us past easy explanations based on evil and manipulative leaders.

B. The General Dependent Variable

The broader dependent variable is success or failure in intervention outcomes. The ultimate success or failure of an intervention is determined by a broad set of factors, including the overall will, the resources of the intervention force, and broader changes in the international system. No one variable or set of variables will provide a succinct explanation for this outcome.

Yet it is safe to say that in terms of creating a multiethnic state, Kosovo is a failure. Given the enormous resources expended here, the West hoped for better than an addition to the list of "frozen conflicts."

Western failure can be seen in another form: despite having resources that dwarfed those of any actors in this impoverished region, the West was usually not in control of the progression of the game. First and foremost, the West was brought in through the escalation of the KLA. Once in, the West threatened Milosevic with massive bombing. Not only did Milosevic not immediately capitulate, he began an ethnic cleansing campaign that the West was powerless to stop. When Western and international troops entered Kosovo, they were powerless to stop Albanians from committing ethnic cleansing of Serbs. Once established, the West instituted no less than four attempts to reconcile the opposing groups. In the end, the West appeased the violence of the March 2004 riots and ended up with a plan that essentially allows separate societies. These outcomes came about despite its spending billions of dollars and deploying tens of thousands of troops over a decade in a country the size of Connecticut.

How should this outcome be explained? Above all, the West's confidence in its own ability to impose its own type of "rationality" on Serbs and Albanians was far off the mark. Westerners did not understand the depth of the psychological need of Albanians to completely free themselves from even the most minimal Serbian influence. Accordingly, they could not understand why their "carrots" seemed so devalued and why intransigence was so valued. As shown by their embarrassing and unprepared response to the March 2004 riots, the West could not guess how quickly anger could mobilize a population for violence. The Serbian contempt that drives the maintenance of the postindependence parallel society is still a mystery to the EU officials who took the reins in Kosovo.

As a related point, given their broader view of their own agency, the opponents of intervention could employ a wider range of resources than the intervener. They possessed a flexibility that the West did not, a flexibility that allowed them to stay one step ahead in the game. Furthermore, Western inability or unwillingness to stop violence in the early stages of intervention created a lack of confidence and respect, and left violent options on the table.

Despite the myriad failures of Western policy, the West is likely to eventually integrate the entire Western Balkans region into Europe, including Kosovo and Serbia. For the side of the Western Balkan peoples and leaders, there is simply no other option than to conform to Western economic and political norms.

On February 21, 2008, I attended a massive rally in Belgrade protesting Kosovar independence. Thousands of people, many bussed in from surrounding regions, entered the area in front of the Parliament Building. The Radical Party leader Nikolic and other political figures spoke, as well as tennis star Novak Djokovic (via satellite), basketball great Bodiroga, and film director Emir Kusturica. The leader of the DS, Kostunica, made a fiery speech saying that Kosovo is Serbia's first name. At the end of the demonstration, much of the crowd filtered through the parks and small streets before gathering into a vast stream on Kralj Milan Avenue to head to the Serbian church Sveti Sava for a special mass. At Slavija Circle, I stopped to survey the scene. Nearby, youths were destroying a McDonald's restaurant, the foremost symbol of the United States in this region. A car exploded in flames. I heard that the U.S. Embassy in another part of town was also being torched.

The events seemed a last cathartic release for Serbs on Kosovo. A few weeks later, Serbs would vote in elections that would allow Boris Tadic, already the Serbian president, to form a pro-European government. The new government would of course not accept the independence of Kosovo, and would proclaim that they would never accept it, and it would continue to support Serbian parallel institutions. But Kosovo would not be allowed to interfere with Serbia's progress toward Europe. Serbia would unofficially be a "good neighbor" and would cooperate, if only unofficially, on a host of technical issues in Kosovo.[3] Tellingly, Tadic arranged a trip to Romania on February 21 so that he could be out of the country during the demonstration.

For the West, Kosovo's independence would finally put the problems emanating from the collapse of Yugoslavia to rest. As the President of the International Crisis Group, Gareth Evans described the situation a day after independence:

> It certainly smoothes things a little to have in Serbia now a President like Tadic who is really a committed European and, I'm sure deep down inside whatever he says publicly, who is rather relieved that history has moved on and that Serbia, in fact, can put the Kosovo thing behind it and move to a genuinely full blown European commitment. It's going to be a messy business with Serbia, it's going to be a messy business internationally, for some time, because the emotion will linger on, the sentiment will linger on and the political imperative to complain about Kosovo independence will still be there. But this is really the best course for everyone. This is the last twitch of the Yugoslav dinosaur.[4]

Milosevic had used the emotionally charged Kosovo issue to begin his ascent to power in Serbia during the late 1980s. Kosovo was the primary case at the beginning of the collapse of Yugoslavia. Kosovo was also the dominant case at the end of the long and bloody conflict. Had Westerners understood that anything involved in Kosovo was always going to be "messy," that emotions and sentiments were always going to be dominant factors there, then the conflict might have been shorter and less bloody.

III. INTRODUCTION TO THE NON-KOSOVO CASES

The following four chapters are designed to accomplish several goals. Above all, they are a test of the methods and findings from the Kosovo chapters. The same

---

[3] RK/7/18/08.
[4] International Crisis Group, February 18, 2008.

method is applied to South Serbia, Macedonia, Bosnia, and Montenegro. Each case begins with background on demographics and other significant structural factors and a review of the coding of violence, resentment, and stigma that establishes the game's starting point. The chapters then follow the movement, or lack of movement, across cells within the matrix.

All of the cases involve significant Western intervention, including the Dayton Accord, the Ohrid Accord, and several less-known Western-brokered agreements. At crucial junctures, I identify a choice set and then determine why a given political actor made a specific choice within that set. I also assess whether the hypotheses developed in Chapter 6 can explain this variation in choices. Finally, I comment on the West's success or failure in achieving its stated goals.

In combination with Kosovo, the South Serbian, Macedonian, and Montenegrin cases cover the entire territory of what I have termed the *Southern Subsystem*. As already covered in the background material, at the end of World War I, the Ottoman Empire collapsed and borders were drawn across the new system of nation-states. A significant number of Albanians were left outside the boundaries of the new state of Albania. Following World War II, these Albanians found themselves in sizable and compact populations within four federal units of Yugoslavia: Kosovo, Serbia, Macedonia, and Montenegro.[5] Nearly 100 years after the Ottomans left the region, the West stepped in to help resolve the festering issues connected to this Albanian diaspora. It is important to consider all the cases of this region in order to tell a coherent narrative of its recent history. The cases are clearly not independent of one another. Above all, the events in Kosovo in 1999 had a direct effect on what happened in all of the other cases. Following the precedent set in Kosovo, political actors in South Serbia escalated violence in 2000; following the events in both Kosovo and South Serbia, the National Liberation Army in Macedonia escalated violence in 2001. Moreover, some Albanian rebels were actors in multiple cases.

These four cases form the basis of two paired comparisons. The first pair is South Serbia and Macedonia. Because both are within the Southern Subsystem, they share many features of history and culture. In both cases, the main axis of contention is between Albanians and a Slavic group.[6] In both, Albanian rebels employ violence to transform the game. The two cases differ, I will argue, in the level of stigma. South Serbia resembles Kosovo as a case of high mutual ethnic stigma with contempt as a resource. The progression of the game in South Serbia is R7–R8–R7. On the other hand, Macedonia is a case of medium ethnic contempt. The progression of the game in Macedonia is R4–R5–R4.

---

[5] There is also a sizable Albanian population in Greece. Originally, I wished to include that case in this study, but space considerations prevented it.

[6] I learned the hard way that many Macedonians consider the designation of Macedonians as Slavs to be offensive. Macedonians trace their history to a period that includes Alexander the Great. Slavs did not enter the Balkans until about the seventh century A.D., hundreds of years after Alexander's reign. Thus, the Slavic designation denies this lineage. My designation of Macedonians as Slavs follows common categorizations by linguists and is not intended to offend.

Although the decision to escalate is very similar in both cases, the postescalation politics of the two cases differs. The comparison of these two cases allows an examination of the differing resentment-based politics of cell R7 and cell R4. In R4, as the Macedonian case will show, political actors have space for political maneuvering and the creation of new political narratives.

The second comparison sets off Bosnia versus Montenegro. Both cases begin the era of Yugoslavia's collapse in a benign starting position. In fact, I will argue that both are not only cases of low ethnic stigma between key groups, but also of low resentment. The starting point for each is designated as NR1 (low resentment, low stigma, no violence). Despite this starting point, the Bosnian case quickly proceeds to high violence. Bosnia's progression is NR1–R1–R2–R3–R1. In contrast, Montenegro, with the same starting point, goes on to eventually split from Serbia without any violence at all. Although there are many reasons for these two very different outcomes, I will argue that a crucial factor is the emotion of resentment. The comparison highlights the connection among the historical foundations of identity, the speed of resentment formation, and the ability to mobilize for violence.

14

South Serbia

The main highway between Belgrade and Athens runs through the Presevo Valley in South Serbia. The road cuts through three municipalities, akin to counties in the U.S. system – Presevo, Bujanovac, and Medvedja – which administratively and politically define the term "South Serbia."[1] The thickly wooded high hills, or low mountains, that define the valley's western side separate Serbia from Kosovo. In 1947, the Yugoslav government drew this boundary line, which would come to influence political events in the region decades later.

The three municipalities form a small area – 1,249 square kilometers, or a little less than half the land area of Rhode Island. The defining feature of the region is demographic variation across districts (see Table 14.1). According to the 2002 census, Albanians dominated the southernmost Presevo district, composing 89 percent of the population, and Serbs dominated the Medvedja district, composing 67 percent of residents, whereas Bujanovac was split among Albanians (55 percent but clustered in rural areas), Serbs (34 percent, more concentrated in the city of Bujanovac), and Roma (9 percent, also in the city).[2]

One other demographic feature would come to play a huge role in the modern political history of the region. As part of the deal ending NATO's bombing in June 1999, the Serbian government and NATO signed an agreement to create a 5-kilometer demilitarized zone to separate Serbian and NATO forces in order to prevent incidents and accidents. Only lightly armed Serbian police forces could enter this zone, usually termed the Ground Safety Zone (GSZ); the agreement strictly prohibited the entrance of military units. In the two southern municipalities of Presevo and Bujanovac, the GSZ covered an area

---

[1] All three districts lie in the Presevo Valley, which must be distinguished from the Presevo municipality.

[2] Figures taken from International Crisis Group, "Southern Serbia: In Kosovo's Shadow," Europe Briefing No. 43, Belgrade/Pristina/Brussels, 27 June, 2006, p. 3.

TABLE 14.1. *Population Distribution in South Serbia*

	Serbs	Albanians	Roma
Presevo	2,984 (8.55%)	31,098 (89.09%)	322 (0.92%)
Bujanovac	14,782 (34.14%)	23,681 (54.69%)	3,867 (8.93%)
Medvedja	7,163 (66.57%)	2,816 (26.17%)	109 (1.0%)

with 20 Serbs and 22,000 Albanians (see Figure 14.1).[3] This small, ethnically homogenous pocket would serve as a safe haven for rebels who would escalate the conflict in the period following the occupation of Kosovo.

There are two other aspects of the Presevo Valley that are essential to understanding its politics. The first is its economic and electoral marginality. Although it is difficult to make sense of unemployment statistics, because so many citizens of the valley work abroad, either legally or illegally, there is no denying that the economic situation is bleak. In a 2006 report, the International Crisis Group estimated 70 percent unemployment;[4] other reports list similar figures.[5] Moreover, there is little hope of any near-term economic revival. For example, all ten of the state-owned properties in Presevo were unprofitable in 2006.[6] International funding had decreased and there was little hope of significant foreign investment. In my discussions with local officials I asked what advice they would give to their children about a future in the valley. They replied that they would have to advise them to leave because they could not foresee many future opportunities for young people in the Presevo Valley.

Politically, the valley's seventy thousand Albanian residents have little electoral clout. Serbia has a population of about eight million. At best, Albanian parties could expect to elect two representatives to the Serbian parliament, and more likely, they can count on just one. Even regionally, Presevo and Bujanovac are just two municipalities in the broader seven-municipality district of Pcinja. Serbian political forces and parties have always dominated at the district level.

Second, Albanians in the valley have always and almost universally wished to have their territory attached to Kosovo. They made this desire known long before the Kosovo war of 1999. In 1992, local Albanian parties organized an unofficial referendum backing full autonomy and the right to unite with Kosovo.[7] Of the 47,000 Albanian residents participating in the referendum (essentially the entire adult population of Albanians in the region), 95 percent

---

[3] International Crisis Group, "Peace in Presevo: Quick Fix or Long Term Solution?" ICG Balkans Report No. 116, Pristina/Belgrade/Brussels, 10 August, 2001, p. 2. Many residents trace this imbalance back to 1912. As many residents relate, as Serbian forces entered the region, Albanians fled to the hills, where their families have remained ever since.

[4] International Crisis Group, "Southern Serbia," p. 1.

[5] Beata Huszka, "The Presevo Valley of Southern Serbia alongside Kosovo: The Case for Decentralisation and Minority Protection," CEPS Policy Briefs, issue 1–12, 2007. Huszka cites figures of 60% unemployment in Bujanovac and 70% in Presevo.

[6] ICG, "Southern Serbia," p. 7.

[7] DY 6/9/08. DY was involved in creating the 1992 referendum.

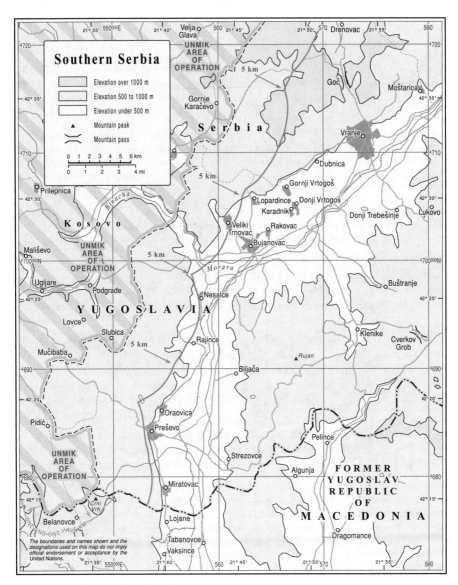

FIGURE 14.1. Map of South Serbia

favored the secession option.[8] Following the Kosovo war, many of the region's Albanian politicians still cite the 1992 referendum as a legitimate indicator of popular will. Local residents often refer to their region as eastern Kosovo.

[8] See Belgzim Kamberi, International War and Peace Reporting, "Presevo Albanians Eye Autonomy," Balkan Crisis Report, 14 February, 2002.

I. STIGMA, RESENTMENT, AND VIOLENCE: ESTABLISHING THE STARTING POINT OF ANALYSIS (LATE 1990S)

During the 1990s, the situation in the Presevo Valley placed it in box R7: high stigma, significant resentment, and no violence.

Stigma: The situation of Albanians and Serbs in the Presevo Valley is not much different from the situation on the other side of the border. Examining the three primary measures of stigma demonstrates this similarity. Intermarriage rates were close to zero. Nikolai Botev, in a definitive study of intermarriage rates in the former Yugoslavia, found that Albanians in Serbia proper, who are most likely to encounter Serbs in their daily lives, were 269.1 times more likely to marry other Albanians than would be estimated for random mating. In contrast, the figure for Serbs in Serbia proper was 3.56.[9] The Serbian figure reflects the fact that Serbs often marry members of other minorities, such as Hungarians in Voyvodina, but rarely marry Albanians. Second, there was residential segregation and ethnic flight of Serbs, although not as severe as in Kosovo. Although the Bujanovac municipality had balanced numbers of Serbs and Albanians in the early 1990s, neighborhoods there were segregated. In accord with informal rules, Serbian and Albanian children did not go to school together. Third, the same ethnic terminology and slurs existed as in Kosovo.

A consideration of the second tier of stigma indicators confirms that South Serbia should be designated as a case of high stigma. An entire set of myths and cultural schemas reinforce this judgment. The Belgrade media commonly refer to the valley's Albanian population as "terrorists." Albanian complaints are often dismissed as those of a whining group of disloyal troublemakers.[10] Each side tells stories about the other side's conspiracies and violence. Because the region is small and politically marginal, it is difficult to find survey data on stereotyping, but there is little evidence that these phenomena are qualitatively different from the situation in Kosovo. Serbs rarely bother to learn the Albanian language.

On the highway running along the eastern edge of Presevo, a sign listed the mileage to Decani, the Pec Patriarchy, and Gracanica – all sacred sites for Serbian Orthodoxy lying across the border in Kosovo. There was no mileage sign for Pristina or any other predominately Albanian location in Kosovo. Local Albanians regarded this as an indication of Serbia's disregard of all things Albanian.

---

[9] See Nikolai Botev, "Where East Meets West: Ethnic Intermarriage in the Former Yugoslavia, 1962 to 1989," *American Sociological Review* (June 1994) 59 (No. 3): 461–80. See the table on p. 473 and the discussion on p. 474. Botev finds that Serbs outmarried more than any other group (see discussion on p. 475).

[10] I make this statement based on numerous personal conversations. My own conversations reflect the summary statement made by James Lyon of the International Crisis Group: "Albanians feel peace has not ended tensions with Serb security forces and wish to join the (Presevo) valley with Kosovo, while Serbs feel the Albanians are a disloyal, irredentist minority." Lyon is quoted in "Serbia's South Watches Kosovo," *Balkan Insight*, November 6, 2007.

Resentment: To review, the indicators for resentment are (1) the language of day-to-day government; (2) the composition of the bureaucracy; (3) the composition of the police; (4) the composition of the officer corps; and (5) symbols such as street names and statues. In the 1990s, by all observable measures, Albanians were a strongly subordinated group; on every indicator, Serbs dominated South Serbia. All official business was conducted in the Serbian language. The local police were completely dominated by Serbs, as were the courts, the state bureaucracy, and socially owned enterprises.[11] Unlike the situation in Kosovo, Albanians had never been on top of the ethnic hierarchy in South Serbia, so there had been no reversals. However, Albanians did hold powerful grievances over their subordinate political status in the region.

Violence: The pervasive military and police presence in the region in the 1990s was effective in preventing violence. Furthermore, as the Albanians of South Serbia were less than 1 percent of Serbia's total population, they were a particularly vulnerable group, especially in the Milosevic era. At the beginning point for analysis, South Serbia presented a case of no violence.

II. ESCALATION: MOVEMENT FROM R7 TO R8

During the 1990s, the Albanian population and political actors had little choice but to sit tight, pass unofficial referenda, and hope that the events in Kosovo might create opportunities in the Presevo Valley. The overpowering Serbian military presence constrained Albanian leaders' ability to move the game to box R8. As in Kosovo, the only realistic use of violence was as a trigger to bring in the support of the West.

In contrast, if such a strategy of escalation did present itself, there would be little constraint on using it. Above all, there were low opportunity costs for violence. The Albanians of Presevo Valley were a stigmatized, subordinated, impoverished population. Furthermore, given the mutual stigma with Serbs, they could expect that they would not suffer backlash from their own population if violence was used against Serbs. In sum, there was little to lose through escalation.

The conclusion of the Kosovo war did indeed provide an opportunity to escalate. NATO and Serbian forces signed the Military-Technical Agreement, better known as the Kumanovo Agreement, on June 9, 1999. Plank 4A of the agreement read:

To establish a durable cessation of hostilities, under no circumstances shall any Forces of the FRY and the Republic of Serbia enter into, reenter, or remain within the territory of Kosovo or the Ground Safety Zone (GSZ) and the Air Safety Zone (ASZ) described in paragraph 3. Article I without the prior express consent of the international security force ("KFOR") commander. Local police will be allowed to remain in the GSZ.

---

[11] With the exception of the police force, the numbers were still greatly skewed in 2006 in many state and socially owned enterprises. See Huszka, "The Presevo Valley of Southern Serbia alongside Kosovo," p. 3.

Here was the structural shift that allowed Albanian political entrepreneurs the opportunity to escalate violence and move the game to R8. For some Albanian political actors, especially those with experience from Kosovo, the ethnically homogenous areas of the GSZ provided a possible base of operations, a launching pad for regionwide escalation. In their calculations, the West could not possibly allow such escalation to happen. Kosovo had already provided a script. Rebels would initiate a spiral and the West would be ready to take the side of Albanians against Serbs. In the perception of many Albanians in the Presevo Valley, all the Albanians had to do was provide a reason for Western interveners to come to the aid of friends.

There were still choices to be made in the specific nature of escalation – in particular, a decision on targets. Unsurprisingly, the emerging "Liberation Army of Presevo, Medvedja, and Bujanovac (UCPMB)" repeated the anger-based strategy of the Kosovo Liberation Army.[12] As the ICG summed up, "The UCPMB apparently expected the Yugoslav authorities to react harshly, sparking a flood of refugees into Kosovo and forcing NATO to intervene."[13] In this case, the choice of targets was overdetermined. The best choice for generating anger is usually the least professional armed force – that is, the police. The terms of the Kumanovo Agreement allowed only the police to operate within the GSZ, and forbade the presence of the Serbian military. Rebels could have hit civilians, but clearly any strategy aimed at justifying Western intervention could not use civilians as the main targets. Moreover, few Serbian civilians lived within the GSZ.

Beginning in the winter of 2000, the UCPMB initiated attacks concentrated on the Serbian police. Serbian figures listed 967 attacks on police, 155 on civilians, and 38 on military personnel and property.[14] Although these Serbian government figures must be examined with much skepticism, the ratio of attacks on police versus civilians and military probably does indicate the nature of the fighting. The ICG provides casualty numbers for the entire conflict of approximately 100 dead with 12,500 Albanian refugees.[15] Nebojsa Covic, the moderate Serb who would come to lead the Coordinating Body for South Serbia, listed figures for the beginning and middle stages of the conflict: 296 attacks, 11 dead, 38 injured, and 2 kidnappings from June 1999 to November 21, 2000.[16] The conflict then became more intense. On November 22, four more Serbian policemen were killed. In February 2001, Serbs attributed an

---

[12] For an eyewitness description of the UCPMB, see the opening section of John Phillips' *Macedonia: Warlords and Rebels in the Balkans* (New Haven, CT: Yale University Press, 2004). One matter of common speculation is the relationship of this guerrilla force with the United States. On that issue, see Bob Churcher, "Kosovo Lindore/Preshevo 1999–2002 and the FYROM Conflict," Conflict Studies Research Centre, Ministry of Defence, UK, March 2002.

[13] Ibid, p. 3.

[14] Bujanovac Press Center, "Terrorist Attacks and Provocations in the Ground Safety Zone," January 8, 2002. The report is based on figures from the Serbian Ministry of Internal Affairs.

[15] International Crisis Group, "Southern Serbia: In Kosovo's Shadow," p. 2.

[16] International Crisis Group, "Peace in Presevo," p. 3.

attack on a bus convoy across the border near Podujevo, which killed ten civilians, to forces originating from the GSZ. At the same time, three more police were killed by a mine in the GSZ.

In summary, the UCPMB's strategy tried to inculcate anger in Serb forces and generate a disproportionate response that might require, or at least justify, Western intervention. This strategy both failed and succeeded. On the one hand, it failed to generate a grossly disproportionate response from Serb forces. There would not be the equivalent of a Racak massacre in South Serbia.[17] From their peripheral location in the hills on the Kosovo border, Albanian rebels did not realize how much the political context for their revolt had changed. Since the Kosovo bombings, the Serbs had deposed Milosevic after a fraudulent election (October 2000). Zoran Djindjic and Voyislav Kostunica, Milosevic's successors, promised a new and more moderate path. Djindjic backed up his words by packing Milosevic off to the Hague for trial. The West was hopeful about the change and signaled a desire to cooperate with the new regime. Correspondingly, the new Serbian leadership also looked for ways to signal its moderation to the West. Most conveniently, the moderate forces that had replaced Milosevic in Belgrade could communicate their new moderation by putting the brakes on violence in South Serbia. In an effort to prove that the new democratic forces in Serbia could be trusted partners, Covic and other moderate Serbs actually sought to engage NATO in this case.

In contrast, the escalation did successfully raise international fears of another refugee crisis in the Balkans. The UNHCR believed that up to 60,000 people could possibly be displaced by the conflict and that spiraling violence could spill into Kosovo.[18] Most importantly, the escalation succeeded in bringing about its primary goal: Western intervention. This intervention, though, was not what the UCPMB rebels had hoped for. Unlike the situation in Kosovo, the West would not charge in with overwhelming military force and take control away from the Serbs. Contrary to the wishful thinking of some Albanian actors, Western powers were not going to go to war for the sake of 70,000 Albanians in the Presevo Valley. Already uneasy about the changes in sovereignty norms produced by the Kosovo conflict, Western powers would not rush into another potentially border-abolishing military action. To the contrary, Western interests clearly lay in bolstering the prodemocracy forces that had taken power from Milosevic in October 2000.

Although Kosovo was the first time that NATO fought a war, South Serbia was the first conflict where NATO acted as a peace broker, forging what came to be known as the Konculj Agreement.[19] Negotiated by US KFOR advisor

[17] If the conflict had gone on longer, there might have been one. Following the bus attack, some Serbian officials made ominous comments. See International Crisis Group, "Peace in Presevo," p. 3.
[18] International Crisis Group, "Peace in Presevo," p. 6.
[19] The name refers to the village where Shawn Sullivan (NATO Head of Office) and Shefqet Musliu UCPMB signed a demilitarization agreement on May 20, 2001.

Shawn Sullivan in March 2001, the agreement allowed Serbian military forces to reoccupy the GSZ in return for the implementation of a plan to address Albanian grievances.

III. THE INTRODUCTION OF THE BASIC GAME IN SOUTH SERBIA: STAGE ONE, ESTABLISHING SECURITY (R8 TO R7)

The intervention in South Serbia was a classic example of the Basic Game. To recall, the first stage of the game addresses security issues. In South Serbia, actors reestablished the control of a single sovereign through a careful and phased introduction of Serbian military units into the GSZ. A ceasefire was signed on March 12. On March 14, Serbian military forces (carrying only light weapons) took control over Sector C (the strategic section of the GSZ on the Macedonian border), thus preventing the flow of weapons and the chance of a cross-border escalation. Military forces were only allowed to enter Sector B, the stronghold of the UCPMB, on May 24. Serb forces took control over the remaining areas of the GSZ on May 31, over two months after the beginning of the operation.

The reoccupation of the GSZ can be examined in terms of the N-person assurance game. In effect, the gradual consolidation of the zone assured increasing percentages of Albanians that they could safely transfer their political allegiance from the Albanian rebels back to the Serbian state, at least in formal terms. Late in the process, a UCPMB commander did try to reverse the process by taking over the village of Oravica and threatening further actions.[20] By that time, however, the reoccupation had progressed to a stage that neither local Albanians nor Albanians in Kosovo (pressured by the United States and Europe) would support rebel actions.[21] Essentially, the process had passed the tipping point.

The Serbian government temporarily moved 15,000 soldiers and police into the Presevo Valley, or about one soldier for every five Albanians. These numbers would soon decline, but significant forces remained.[22] Moreover, NATO monitored the area and the OSCE set up an office in Bujanovac in November 2001. Escalation became very difficult.

IV. THE SECOND STAGE OF THE BASIC GAME AND THE POLITICS OF BOX R7

After May 2001, the game in South Serbia would be played within Box R7: high mutual stigma, significant resentment, but very low levels of violence.

---

[20] UCPMB Commander Shpetim (which means Savior), along with over 100 units, took control of the village of Oravica. The Serbian military defused the situation.

[21] Rugova, Thaci, and Haradinaj all came out with statements that the conflict must find a political solution.

[22] In 2003, there may have been approximately 5,000 units. See International Crisis Group, "Southern Serbia's Fragile Peace," December 9, 2003, p. 13.

The Western-supported Covic Plan directly addressed the two overarching issues in South Serbia – the secessionist politics of the Albanians and the exclusionary politics of the Serbs. Both would be addressed through a series of interactions or, in other words, an iterated game. The Covic Plan, also known officially as "The Program for the Solution of the Crisis in the Pcinja District," envisioned the following set of steps:

(1) The Albanian rebels would give up all pursuit of autonomy or border change and agree to demilitarization.
(2) In return, Serbs would grant amnesty to the rebels.
(3) Under OSCE supervision and training, Serbia would immediately institute a plan to create a multiethnic police force in the valley.
(4) Serbia would hold new municipal elections (in July 2002) to correct past imbalances in local government.
(5) Albanians were expected to participate in these elections rather than boycotting them.
(6) Further steps would create a multiethnic judiciary, reform the school system, provide multiethnic media, and correct imbalances in the social enterprise sector.

Along the lines of the Basic Game, the process aimed to raise the value of cooperation through political and material payoffs. As the game progressed, the intervener strategy concentrated on financial carrots and confidence-building measures. The latter would include the investigations of alleged human rights abuses, the withdrawal of the Serbian military from population centers, and devolution of some government powers to the local level. A formal institution, the Coordination Body for South Serbia, would oversee progress according to a three-year timeline. This Serbian body would be further monitored by the OSCE, NATO, and the U.S. Embassy in Belgrade. A plethora of Western NGOs, Western states, and international organizations awarded financial payoffs to both sides. The United Nations Development Program (UNDP) established an office and the Cooperative Housing Foundation played a major role. No less than thirteen sources of foreign funds poured into the small region. As the International Crisis Group summed up, "In short, the international community has been the oil that greases the wheels of the peace process" in South Serbia.[23] The Covic Plan basically called for the implementation of the second stage of the Basic Game. With the trust and communication developed during this stage, and with the continued help of the international community, both players could hopefully eventually reach the third stage and move to the superior stable equilibrium of repeated mutual cooperation.

V. HOW THE GAME PLAYED OUT IN SOUTH SERBIA

Of all of the cases examined in this book, South Serbia may have had the most going for it. Almost every structural and international variable favored

[23] International Crisis Group, "Southern Serbia: In Kosovo's Shadow," p. 4.

the success of intervention and the Basic Game in South Serbia. Structurally, the conflict involved a very small minority – the Albanians of South Serbia compose less than one percent of the population of Serbia proper. This impoverished minority had few resources and was dependent on outside aid. The Western interveners possessed significant carrots to provide this aid. No less than thirteen states and NGOs donated funds to "grease the wheels of the peace process" in this small territory. South Serbia covers a territory half the size of Rhode Island. When NATO permitted Serbian military and police to reenter this small region, there was one Serbian solider for every five civilians during the crucial stage when state authority was reestablished. In comparison, President Obama's 2009 decision to "surge" in Afghanistan would end in a total of about one U.S. troop for every 283 Afghan civilians.

Almost as crucial as these force ratios, the West could constrain the actions of local Albanians through politicians in Kosovo proper. The political leaders of Kosovo – Rugova, Thaci, and Haradinaj – all knew that the West took a dim view of any type of "Greater Albanian" politics. Kosovo's Albanian leadership made sure to publicly state that the Albanians in South Serbia would have to make their own way within Serbia and that they should cooperate fully with the intervention. The political leaders in Belgrade were also ready to comply. After the end of Milosevic, the new regime in Belgrade was anxious to appear rational and "Western." Covic essentially partnered with the West in creating and implementing the plan that bore his name.

On the whole, the South Serbia case proceeded according to the theory and goals of the Basic Game in some ways and diverged in others. To understand this mixed course of events, it is first necessary to understand the meaning of the most fundamental elements of the game in practice. Above all, what did cooperation and defection mean in this case? For the Albanians, cooperation meant participation in elections and other political institutions of the Serbian state. Defection could come about in a number of ways: boycotting elections and other political institutions, raising the issue of secession, committing or supporting violence. On the Serbian side, cooperation meant accepting Albanians into political and economic institutions, sharing funds, and participating in Presevo Valley's political life.

Certain players did cooperate in the early rounds of the game. Following the Covic Plan, the Serbian regime did implement some dramatic improvements in the position of Albanians in the police force. Albanians had deeply resented the pervasive daily presence of Serbian armed forces, and strongly desired a change in the composition of the police force. Albanian police took positions quickly and progress was maintained over a period of years. By 2006, more than half the police force was composed of Albanians (277/437).[24] However, as late as 2008, Albanians complained about an overly heavy presence of military and

---

[24] International Crisis Group, "Southern Serbia: In Kosovo's Shadow," p. 6.

special force units (gendarmerie), and many Albanians still claimed that the "real" power in the police is still held by Serbs.[25]

On language, federal level laws addressed imbalances in South Serbia. According to a federal law on minority language use passed in 2002, Albanian became an official language, alongside Serbian, in Presevo and Bujanovac.

Moreover, both Albanian and Serbian leaders cooperated in the reduction of violence. Despite a significant presence of military and police, there were incidents that threatened to spiral out of control.[26] On February 4, 2003, an ethnic Albanian member of a state security organ was killed in Bujanovac. Serbian police then raided two villages. Albanians responded with demonstrations. Then an antitank mine destroyed a vehicle carrying gendarmerie, killing one and wounding two others. The violence continued into March with an attempted bombing and the killing of two Albanians. Another series of violent incidents occurred in August 2003, when a group calling itself the Albanian National Army claimed credit for firing mortars on a military facility in Dobrosin and shooting at a police checkpoint near Konculj. Soon after, a hand grenade was thrown at the main mosque in Presevo and an explosive device went off near Presevo's cultural center.[27] In both series of violent events, local leaders were quick to disassociate themselves from the violence and deescalate the situation.[28] By 2008, the Presevo Valley was basically peaceful, even as Kosovo declared independence.[29]

Despite cooperation at higher levels on each side, there were also plays of defection in the game. From the Albanian side, these defections came mainly in the form of boycotts. Albanians boycotted or threatened to boycott almost every national election. There was a boycott of the December 2000 elections and then the October 2002 national election (but not the local election).[30] There was also a boycott of the May 11, 2008 election by major Albanian parties.[31] Furthermore, Albanians would not create a national council, the

[25] Interview DY/6/9/08 and VP/6/10/08. Also see Huszka, p. 5. As Huszka notes, "The presence of Gendarmerie is very intimidating for local Albanians, as they drive around in the villages brandishing their machine guns in a demonstration of force" (p. 5).

[26] See International Crisis Group, "Southern Serbia's Fragile Peace," pp. 4–10.

[27] Skender Latifi, "Alarm Bells in South Serbia," Institute for War and Peace Reporting, September 4, 2003.

[28] Many Serbs, including Covic, believed that the February violence was the responsibility of Shefket Misliu, former commander of the UCPMB, although Misliu explicitly denied the charges. See Shaban Buza, "Ex-Rebel Chief Denies South Serbia Presevo Attack," Reuters, February 28, 2003.

[29] Here, "basically peaceful" refers to the lack of interethnic violence. There is significant criminal violence in the Presevo Valley.

[30] One Institute for War and Peace Reporting report chose to include the following paragraph: "Sulejman Hiseni, an ethnic Albanian from Bujanovac, told IWPR, that the boycott of Serbian presidential elections made perfect sense for the local population. 'I don't see what Belgrade can expect from Albanians here because they will never accept Serbia as their country,' he said, reflecting the views of many in the area." See Institute for War and Peace Reporting, "Presevo Albanians Snub Belgrade Again," written by several contributors, November 11, 2002.

[31] The Party of Democratic Action, led by Riza Halimi, did participate.

typical body in Serbian government for addressing minority issues. Albanians also boycotted the Coordination Body for South Serbia in August 2007. From the Serbian side, defection came in declining support for equal funding and hiring practices at local levels.

Because of the major demographic differences within the three municipalities of South Serbia, success and failure of the Basic Game can best be observed by breaking South Serbia down into three cases.

A. Presevo Municipality

In the June 2004 local elections, the moderate Party of Democratic Action led by Riza Halimi failed to gain a majority. Instead, Ragmi Mustafa, leader of the Democratic Party of Albanians (PDSH) and closely linked to the UCPMB, took power. Mustafa was an explicit proponent of a "Greater Kosovo." In fact, he was perhaps the most vocal elected political leader on this subject in the entire Balkans. In February 2009, Mustafa, then head of Presevo's parliament, stated, "The strongest wish of the Albanians from the Presevo valley is to be part of the independent state of Kosovo."[32] Mustafa brought up the 1992 referendum, supporting the legitimacy of partition – a clear act of defection from the intervention game. Despite clear exhortations from major Albanian politicians outside his municipality not to break the taboo on partition, Mustafa was winning a local election, perhaps because of it.

The Covic Plan called for the government to place more Albanians in state positions of authority. Beyond the police, the judiciary is the most important institution of authority and political status in South Serbia. Years after the Konculj agreement was penned, Albanians in Presevo, which was nearly 90 percent Albanian in 2001, held only five out of ten positions in the prosecutor's office and were only eleven out of forty total employees in the municipal court.[33] The distribution of funds was even more skewed. The Serbian government allocated 2,710 dinars (31 Euros) per capita in Presevo compared with 15,364 dinars (178 Euros) in primarily Serbian Medvedja.[34]

Most significantly, there are practically no Serbs left in the Presevo municipality.[35] Serbs do not perceive a future in Presevo, and they can often receive good prices for their property from Albanians returning from abroad. As one Balkan Insight report wrote in the concluding sentence of an article on Presevo: "No one in the town now expects the quiet process of ethnic separation to stop. On the contrary, it appears to be reaching its natural conclusion."[36] The goal of maintaining a multiethnic society in the Presevo municipality is essentially out of reach because it is no longer a multiethnic municipality.

[32] "South Serbia Albanians Look to Kosovo," *Balkan Insight*, February 16, 2009.
[33] Huszka, p.3.
[34] International Crisis Group, "Southern Serbia," p. 5.
[35] Ivica Stepanovic, "Serbs Sell Up in Presevo," Balkan Investigative Reporting Network, November 17, 2005.
[36] Ibid.

Serbian individuals and families decided neither to play cooperation nor defection. They simply left the game altogether.

B. Bujanovac

Because of its balanced demographic distribution, Bujanovac had been a contested municipality. However, after the 2002 elections, the contest was largely over. Albanian political parties came to control the government in the Bujanovac municipality. By the end of the decade, Albanians had replaced Serbs in almost all municipal posts.[37] Serbs reacted negatively after this status reversal. In fact, in a clear defection from the intervention "rules," some local leaders attempted local separation. In 2006, local Serbs called for a referendum to divide the municipality in two. Trajko Trajkovic, a local leader, stated, "Ever since Albanians came to power in 2002, Serbs in Bujanovac have been second class citizens, without the means in the local assembly, as a minority, to defend their interests."[38] The Serbian government did not support the effort, as it would lead to similar demands by Albanians in Presevo and elsewhere, thus leaving the minority Serbs to fend for themselves.[39]

Despite the change in local control, federally appointed positions still favored Serbs. With an Albanian:Serbian population ratio of 55:34, Albanians still only were one of eight in the prosecutor's office and only four out of forty-four employees of the municipal court in Bujanovac in 2007.[40] On the funding issue, the Serbian government allocated 3,771 dinars (43 Euros) to the Bujanovac municipality per capita, less than one-fourth of Medvedja's figure.[41]

C. Medvedja

Like that of Presevo, the politics of Medvedja has become simpler due to demographic changes. After the violent conflict, most Albanian residents left the municipality and have not returned. The number of Serbs in Medvedja had also been bolstered by the Kosovo War. In July and August 2001, I met several former Serbian residents of Kosovo who found themselves on the other side of the border in Medvedja.[42] In 1999, many believed that they would be

---

[37] Tim Judah, "Serbia's Southern Borderland Remains Stuck in Limbo," *Balkan Insight*, April 14, 2010.

[38] Nikola Lazic, "Partition Demand Fuels South Serbia Tensions," *Balkan Insight*, February 16, 2006.

[39] Western embassies were involved with trying to create a multiethnic local government from 2008 until 2010, but with no success. See Judah, "Serbia's Southern Borderland Remains Stuck in Limbo."

[40] Huszka, p. 3.

[41] It is worth keeping in mind that Presevo and Bujanovac are municipalities embedded within broader administrative structures. At the seven-municipality district (okrug)-level government based in Vranje, Serbs are completely dominant, despite Albanians making up 25% of the district's population.

[42] Interviews M1, M2, M3, M4 on 7/29/2001 and QD 8/7/2001. I also spoke with displaced Serbs in Krsumlija (a town further to the north), who composed perhaps thirty percent of the town's population.

returning to their homes in Kosovo within a short period of time. By 2001, they had consolidated a life in Medvedja. They also helped consolidate Serbian dominance in Medvedja.

In conversations with Serbs, Medvedja is generally no longer considered part of the South Serbia "problem," and correspondingly, no longer really part of South Serbia. As mentioned in Section A, Medvedja was receiving about five to six times the amount of state funding that Presevo receives. Serbs dominate the municipal government.

VI. SUMMARY AND EVALUATION

Western intervention, with its view of rationality, concentrates on arranging sticks and carrots. In the Presevo Valley, it focused on doling out rewards to an impoverished region (in other words, raising the value of R in the prisoners' dilemma). To a lesser degree, the intervention aimed to punish those who engaged in boycott, exclusion, and separation (in other words, lowering the value of the T payoff).

As a first cut at a summary, we can evaluate hypotheses regarding patterns of provocation, that is, the specific dependent variable. The game in South Serbia was being played in R7. As in Kosovo, local political entrepreneurs could play on contempt and resentment to block cooperation. With contempt as a resource, political actors can raise the specter of "being suckered" to powerful effect in order to try to counter the value of the intervener's sticks and carrots. Likewise in R7, the emotion of resentment can also be a formidable resource. Imbued with resentment, individuals focus on status inequalities and will respond strongly to appeals and complaints about unjust subordination. Consideration of these emotion resources led to the following hypotheses.

> *Prediction 6*: In NR7 (only contempt) and R7 (contempt and resentment), political entrepreneurs are most likely to initiate the politics of boycott and the creation of parallel systems.

In South Serbia, this hypothesis was confirmed, especially at local levels. Albanians in South Serbia boycotted all Serbian national elections for fifteen years from the early 1990s until 2007.[43] Albanians also did not participate in the national council system of minority representation in Serbia and sometimes boycotted the Coordination Body of South Serbia. Serbian politicians in Bujanovac attempted local partition after a status reversal in 2002. Albanian politicians won elections while breaking speech taboos on the secession issue.

> *Prediction 7*: Under conditions of contempt, players who initiate violence will suffer little backlash from their own populations.

[43] Huszka, p. 6.

This hypothesis also found support. There is little evidence of any local Albanian backlash from the escalation of 2000. In fact, former UCPMB commanders became respected political leaders. Albanian leaders from around the region, however, did not appear to support violent politics after the spring of 2001, which leads into the next hypothesis.

Prediction 8: In R7, we are likely to observe periodic and perhaps frequent initiations of targeted violence.

There were minor escalations for about two years after the signing of the Konculj agreement, but on the whole, ethnic violence was low. This hypothesis is clearly not supported, although at least partly for reasons discussed next.

Prediction 9: We are more likely to see escalation of violence in R7 (contempt and resentment) than in NR7 (contempt).

There was violent escalation in South Serbia when structural conditions allowed it. After 2001, there was never another sustained violent engagement between an armed Albanian group and Serbian forces.[44] This finding is hardly surprising, given structural and political factors. During the crucial stages of reestablishing Serbian state control, the military/police:civilian ratio was an astounding 1:5 in a territory that was half the size of Rhode Island. All major Kosovar Albanian elites urged the end of violence. Although we might have seen targeted killings in South Serbia, as suggested by prediction 8, another major escalation would have been difficult to imagine.

Prediction 10: With contempt, nonviolent provocations such as speeches and posters will highlight the perceived inherent negative qualities of the other side. With resentment, these provocations will emphasize current changes in status relations. In situations of both contempt and resentment, both types of provocations should be observed.

In R7, both contempt and resentment are available resources. From the Serbian side, images associated with contempt seemed to prevail. Presevo Valley's Albanian population was often portrayed negatively as disloyal and "terrorist." From the Albanian side, resentment appeared to be a more powerful force. Albanian politics concentrated on status inequality and the continued political dominance of Serbs.

For the Albanians, it was also important to maintain distance from Serbs and the Serbian government, as would be expected in the presence of ethnic contempt. As the ICG summarized in 2006:

Since the 2005 reorganization, the Serbian government has acted in good faith to improve its operation but has been undermined by Albanian politicians, who see advantage in a more confrontational stance toward Belgrade. Under pressure from the more nationalist elements among their constituents, particularly those sympathetic to the

---

[44] International Crisis Group, "Southern Serbia's Fragile Peace," p. 5

UCPMB commanders, many wish to avoid the appearance of cooperating too closely. This has led to gamesmanship in which many Albanian politicians jockey to avoid being branded as collaborationist.[45]

This statement illustrates the difficulty of transforming the political situation of R7 in the presence of contempt. Although the intervener provides high payoffs for cooperation, the very act of cooperation with a stigmatized opponent produces a negative cost that outweighs material and political inducements. Even the appearance of collaboration, or iterated cooperation, with the stigmatized and dominating opponent produces penalties that can maintain strategies of defection. As in Kosovo, the value of mutual defection (P) could sometimes be driven higher than that of mutual reward (R).

Looking at these hypotheses as a whole tells a certain story. The Western intervener's sticks and carrots were sufficient to deter violence and initiate top-down changes in laws and hiring practices, but were insufficient to prevent local boycotts and municipal-level segregation, or to convince individuals and families to remain in an ethnically mixed setting. The emotions of contempt and resentment often served as valuable and effective resources for many local politicians.

Did the West accomplish the goals of its intervention in South Serbia? Given the results on the specific dependent variable, the outcome on the general dependent variable is hardly surprising. To be sure, there were some clear successes on primary Western goals: ethnic violence in the Presevo Valley diminished to very low levels; few talked openly of border change and few viewed the chances of border change in the near run as realistic; the ranks of the police were diversified. There were also some clear failures. Many years after the Konculj agreement, the Serbian government still distributed funds unequally across the three municipalities of South Serbia. Albanians still sensed unjust subordination at many political levels. Most importantly, and clearly against one of the West's highest priorities, no one could credibly argue that South Serbia had become a well-functioning multiethnic system. In fact, two of the three municipalities – Presevo in the south and Medvedja in the north – are now more easily characterized as monoethnic than as multiethnic. The intervention could not stop individuals or families from exiting the game. If individuals believe that their side has lost the game in a situation of R7, they are likely to leave if they are able. Many, if not most, Albanians in Medvedja and Serbs in Presevo have chosen this option, leaving any question of cooperation at the local level meaningless. In sum, depending on how one looks at the region, Western intervention has been either a qualified success or a qualified failure.[46]

---

[45] International Crisis Group, "Southern Serbia," p. 5.
[46] Perhaps most Westerners would rate the case of South Serbia as a success. In its reports the ICG praises the Serbs at several junctures for their "rationality" and "maturity" in pursuing a nonviolent, internationally monitored program in the Presevo Valley. ICG, "Southern Serbia," p. 6, discussed Belgrade's "new maturity" in a response to a shooting; ICG, "Peace in Presevo," p. 6, in reference to the Covic Plan, discussed the international "sense of relief that Belgrade

As Tim Judah summed up in the opening line of a 2010 summary article, "Its ultimate fate still uncertain, South Serbia appears condemned to permanent decline, accentuated by emigration, ethnic deadlock and lack of investment."[47]

FINAL COMMENTS

In all of my travels in the Balkans, South Serbia was the most depressing place to visit outside of refugee camps. The feeling derived from more than just the teeming masses of unemployed youth on the streets or the completely dilapidated train stations. The Albanians I met in Presevo and Bujanovac had no identification with Serbia and would not in the foreseeable future. They led diminished lives as second-class citizens. A waiter I talked to in Bujanovac plans to go to Tirana to study; he would never consider going to Belgrade. Few local youths believed they had a future in Serbia. My experience is matched by many other reports. Valon, a pupil in Presevo High School, stated, "I would never go to study there because I would not be physically safe and I fear discrimination at the hands of Serbian students." "I want to study law so I'll try to enter the faculty in Pristina. I know competition is fierce. If I don't succeed, I will be forced to try at some other university because there is no higher education in Presevo."[48]

The Albanians' plight is stoked by their belief that they could lead heightened and more fulfilling lives if only their little strip of land could be joined to Kosovo.

Many, especially those with a background in the UCPMB, hope for the chance to fight again, but they understand that the international community will not reward violence unless it happens in the context of larger regional events.[49] They know that their only realistic chance is if the Serbs in northern Kosovo break away from Kosovo. Only then might the international community sanction a trade of territory between Serbia and Kosovo.

Albanians in the Presevo Valley feel a deep reliance on the West, but they believe that they only receive attention if there is violence. An Albanian administrator provided me with the table of international investments reproduced as Table 14.2.[50] In the period immediately following the violence, from 2001 to 2003, investment was relatively heavy. When violence dropped to very low levels, he pointed out, the level of funding dropped precipitously. The obvious

had finally proven itself capable of developing a rational, violence-free proposal to improve ethnic Serb-Albanian relations." Also see the UNDP report by Tom Thorogood, "The South Serbia Programme: Lessons in Conflict Prevention and Recovery," Issue Title: Conflict and Development, Issue Number: 06/2007.

[47] Judah, "Serbia's Southern Borderland Remains Stuck in Limbo."

[48] Driton Salihu and Jasmina Arsic, "Brain Drain Sucks Life from Southern Serbia," *Balkan Insight*, March 5, 2009.

[49] S interview 6/10/08. Former fighter. Also, DY 6/9/08.

[50] He appeared to have these figures ready for any visitor.

TABLE 14.2. *International Investment in the Presevo Valley*

PASQYRA TABELARE E INVESTIMEVE ME DONATORËT E JASHTËM VITI 2001, 2002, 2003, 2004, 2005

NR.	DONATORËT	2001	2002	2003	2004	2005	GJITHËSEJT
1	USAID-OTI	32.237.831.00	14.519.733.00	–	–	–	46.757.564.00
2	CHF	26.254.568.00	19.780.272.37	140.343.062.91	48.009.740.01	42.635.832.57	277.023.475.86
3	QEVERIA NORVEGJEZE	14.407.177.00	4.601.611.00	31.797.293.72	12.912.027.75	6.479.612.00	70.197.921.47
4	ITALIA	8.430.000.00	–	10.729.322.40	–	–	19.159.322.40
5	GJERMANIA	14.722.830.00	DY KOMP JUTERA PENTIUM-3	–	–	–	14.722.830.00
6	SUEDIA	600.000.00	1.503.060.00	–	–	–	2.103.060.00
7	EAR	20.975.480.00	4.144.500.00	–	–	–	25.119.980.00
8	AUSTRIA-HILVERK	1.170.000.00	–	4.200.000.00	–	–	5.370.000.00
9	SDC	–	30.300.000.00	8.353.118.00	–	–	38.653.118.00
10	TEAR-FUND	2.605.939.10	–	–	–	–	2.605.939.10
11	UNDP-REP	–	41.206.918.46	25.000.000.00	–	–	66.206.918.46
12	UNDP-SSMIRP	–	1.552.500.00	4.386.250.00	–	–	5.938.750.00
13	KRYQI I KUQ NDERKOMBETAR	–	–	688.580.00	–	–	688.580.00
	GJITHËSEJT:	121.403.825.10	117.608.594.83	225.497.627.03	60.921.767.76	49.115.644.57	574.547.459.29

lesson to be learned is that violence is the best way to get the West's attention,[51] and that it may be necessary again in the Presevo Valley.

One final field experience serves as a metaphor for the Presevo Valley. One afternoon, my Albanian translator and I decided to lunch in Bujanovac. We went downtown and found two restaurants on opposite sides of the main street. Entering one, we quickly realized that it was Albanian by the U.S. flags adorning the room. That restaurant was completely empty and no one came for five minutes. We left and entered the restaurant across the street. It was filled with perhaps fifteen elderly Serbs intently watching a movie featuring Serbian resistance fighters in the Second World War. The metaphor is the following: the Albanians had checked out of the Presevo Valley, whereas the remaining Serbs were only living in the past. Neither group, the locally ascendant but still nationally stigmatized Albanians, nor the declining Serbs, would have much of a future here.

Presevo Valley is often considered a Western success. Perhaps it is. Maybe this is all we can expect from the situations represented by R7.

[51] DY 6/9/08.

15

Macedonia

One night in the summer of 2006, I took a flight from Belgrade to Skopje, leaving at 9:30 P.M. After an hour's delay and a taxi ride into the center of the city, I reached my hotel after midnight. The night clerk asked me my business and when I mentioned that I was a political science professor, he directed me to the couch in the lobby. He proceeded to lecture me on the unique contributions of the Macedonian people and land for three hours. He produced a litany of events starting with Alexander the Great and leading through Cyril and Methodius and up through revolts against the Ottomans. He railed against those who would turn Macedonians into "nothing," some nondescript group of Slavs with no independent history or contributions of their own. The situation had been made worse, he continued, by Albanians. The international community had sided with Albanian "terrorists" and kicked the Macedonians from the second row of the bus to the third. Macedonians had always been second-class citizens in the world, he complained, but now, even in their own country, they were behind Albanians.

The history and political lesson went on until 3 A.M. I listened partly out of curiosity about how long it could go on, but more out of sympathy for some of his views. I knew enough about regional history to know that surrounding peoples had seen Macedonians as "nothing," or at least Macedonia as something less than a full-blown nation. The Greeks deny their name; the Serbs deny that they have their own church; the Bulgarians say they do not have their own language. As this chapter will show, Western powers have indeed worked to improve the position of Albanians in Macedonia.

Until 1991, no Macedonian state had existed to represent and protect a Macedonian nation. The collapse of Yugoslavia finally allowed Macedonians to fulfill this historical longing. The Preamble of the first constitution emphatically proclaimed the new state as "the national state of the Macedonian people, which guarantees the full civic equality and permanent co-existence of the Macedonian people with the Albanians, Turks, Vlachs, Roma, and other nationalities." The state was a national state of ethnic Macedonians; notably,

Albanians were just one group among other minorities. Perhaps unsurprisingly, Albanians boycotted the referendum that led to Macedonian independence.

As this chapter illustrates, Macedonia's post-Communist political evolution followed many of the same contours as that of Kosovo and South Serbia. Albanian rebels escalated violence as a means to bring in the West, and the West responded by intervening and bringing in a form of the Basic Game. Again, the nature of nonviolent politics rotated around a bitter conflict over issues of status and resentment. In the Macedonian case, though, the outcome differed. Despite ethnic Macedonians' historical longing for a nation-state for their own group, by the mid-2000s Macedonia had for all practical purposes become a binational state, with Macedonians and Albanians sharing the state and its power. How ethnic Macedonians have come to grip with this reality is a major focus of this chapter.

I. ESTABLISHING THE STARTING POINT (R4)

The Macedonian case must be analyzed with the resentment matrix. Perceptions of status inequality and an obsession with political status characterized the Macedonian state from the start. At the inception of the state, Albanians strongly perceived a sense of second-class citizenship. Numbers backed up their grievance. Although composing more than 20 percent of Macedonia's two million population,[1] up until 2001 Albanians held only 3.1 per cent of positions in the police and military.[2] Albanians only made up 10 percent of all public servants.[3] The Albanian language was not an official language of the central government. In short, on matters of day-to-day visible authority, Macedonia was a state run by ethnic Macedonians. In stark contrast to neighboring Kosovo, Macedonia's Albanian population enjoyed all fundamental legal rights, yet Albanians still did not see themselves as equal in the new state. In a UNDP study conducted in 2000, more than 94 percent of Albanians claimed they did not possess enough rights.[4]

On the other side, many ethnic Macedonians sensed a threat to their status not only from their history and geographic position, but also from demographics.[5] In the 1961 census, Macedonians composed 71.2 percent to

---

[1] Albanians believed they comprised much higher numbers, maybe even 40 percent. This perception of course only led to a greater sense of status inequality when they contemplated the figures in positions of authority.

[2] John Phillips, *Macedonia: Warlords and Rebels in the Balkans* (New Haven, CT: Yale University Press, 2004), p. 65.

[3] Ulf Brunnbauer, "The Implementation of the Ohrid Accord: Ethnic Macedonian Resentments," *Journal on Ethnopolitics and Minority Issues in Europe* (2002) (Issue 1): 13.

[4] United Nations Development Program study conducted in 2000.

[5] For historical background on Macedonian nationalism, see Ivo Banac, *The National Question in Yugoslavia: Origin, History, Politics* (Ithaca, NY: Cornell University Press, 1984), pp. 307–28. Macedonia's problem of identity and development has been severe enough historically to be labeled a "syndrome." See for example Myron Weiner, "The Macedonian Syndrome: A

the Albanians' 13.0 percent, a ratio of about 5.5 to 1. Thirty years later, the 1991 census produced the following numbers: 65.3 percent Macedonians, 21.7 percent Albanians, 3.8 percent Turks, 2.3 percent Roma, 1.9 percent Serbs, 0.4 percent Vlachs, 2.0 percent other. The ethnic Macedonian-to-Albanian ratio had fallen to 3 to 1 and seemed destined to drop further. Macedonian perception of the threat from the change in overall numbers was exacerbated by more specific demographic features. The Albanian population of Macedonia is concentrated along the borders with Kosovo and South Serbia; Albanian families and political parties have tight connections across these lines, which had little significance during Yugoslav rule. Given these factors, the Albanian population could conceivably secede and remove part of the Macedonian state's rightful territory.

Contentious and sometimes violent political events reinforced the obsession with status issues that predominated in Macedonia's ethnic politics. Given their cultural and political proximity and cross-border connections, Albanian political actors in Macedonia often mirrored the actions of those in Kosovo and South Serbia. In Macedonia, as in the other cases, Albanians held a clandestine referendum on independence in January 1992, with more than 90 percent voting for independence. Moreover, Macedonia's Albanian population boycotted the census. In March 1992, 40,000 Albanians demonstrated in Skopje for higher autonomy. In November, riots in Skopje left four dead and destroyed fifty shops.

The conflict might have worsened in those early years had not the United Nations intervened. In 1992, the UN established the United Nations Preventive Deployment Force Mission (UNPREDEP[6]) with an initial deployment of 700 soldiers and about 100 observers, staff, and interpreters.[7] It was the first time the UN had ever established a preventive deployment of force. In June 1993, the United States contributed an additional 300 troops. The force, created on the request of Macedonian President Kiro Gligorov, served in Macedonia from 1992 to 1999. The mission ended when China vetoed its renewal, almost certainly in response to Macedonia's recognition of Taiwan.

Despite the presence of the UN force, the period bore witness to several political incidents involving issues of Albanian political status. Albanians created an Albanian-language university in Tetovo, but the Macedonian state refused to recognize it. In 1995, police clashed with 1,500 demonstrators at this site of contention, leaving one dead. In 1997, the Albanian mayors of two major cities illegally hoisted Albanian flags over public buildings. The Macedonian government's response resulted in three dead, 312 arrested, and a declaration

---

Historical Model of International Relations and Political Development," *World Politics* (July 1971) 23: 665–83.

[6] The force was originally called UNPROFOR and was authorized by the UN Security Council by Resolution S/RES/795.

[7] See Zoran Ilievski, "Country Specific Reports on Conflict Settlements, Country Report on Macedonia," p.15.

of martial law in the city of Gostivar. In 1998, several police stations suffered bombings.[8] In short, status struggles permeated Macedonian politics, which necessitates that the case must be analyzed with the resentment matrix.

At the starting point, there was little violence. In looking at the overall level of ethnocommunal violence in this period, the total number killed could be counted on one's fingers. Macedonia was tense, but political actors did not regularly engage in violent acts that caused significant casualties.

Ethnic stigma is not so straightforward in this case. An examination of the first-tier indicators shows that Macedonia was undoubtedly characterized by a significant level of ethnic stigma. First, ethnic intermarriage was essentially zero. In fact, in this country of more than two million people, a grand total of 16 interethnic marriages took place between Albanians and ethnic Macedonians in the entire country in 1999.[9] Second, neighborhoods are segregated and Albanians in many rural areas rarely intermingle with Macedonians.[10] A 2001 report of the "Ethnobarometer" concluded that "(T)he almost total absence of dialogue and social interaction between ethnic Macedonians and ethnic Albanians in everyday life is rather striking."[11] On the other hand, ethnic communities were not clearly engaged in ethnic flight. Unlike the Kosovo case of the same years, neither ethnic Macedonians nor Albanians claimed to be intimidated and harassed out of their homes. On the third key indicator, derogatory terminology, Macedonians did use the pejorative term "Shiptari" but also commonly used "Albanci."

Without question, the Macedonian case was not one of low stigma. The question is whether the case should be categorized as medium stigma or high stigma. In other words, should the Macedonia case be placed in the same category as Kosovo and South Serbia? The second tier indicators of stigma are mixed. First, stereotypes pervade the speech of ethnic Macedonians and Albanians. There are also sets of ideas and images that approach myth, if not the sophistication of a cultural schema. My own experience in the field matched that described by Robert Hislope, a specialist on Macedonian politics:

A cultural racism permeates Macedonian society, particularly among ethnic Macedonians. During a visit in November and December of 2000, I witnessed this in countless

---

[8] These bombings occurred in the Albanian-dominated northwest and were generally thought to be related to the escalation across the border in Kosovo.

[9] Brunnbauer, "The Implementation of the Ohrid Accord," p. 15.

[10] In a study conducted by the Norwegian University of Science and Technology on political and social values among ethnic groups in Macedonia and Bosnia, Macedonian Albanians had significantly stronger negative attitudes on ethnic intermarriage and also the most negative response to the statement, "I have friends among the other nationalities and I want to improve my personal relations with them." See Kristen Ringdal, Albert Simkus, and Ola Listhaug, "Values in Southeastern Europe: A Comparison of Bosnia-Herzegovina and Macedonia," paper prepared for the Tenth International Seminar "Democracy and Human Rights in Multiethnic Societies," Konjic, Bosnia-Herzegovina, July 9–13, 2007.

[11] Ethnobarometer, *Crisis in Macedonia: Progress Report* (Rome: 2001). Quoted in Brunnbauer, "The Implementation of the Ohrid Accord," p. 14.

instances. It showed up in the endlessly cruel jokes about *"Shiptari"* (derogatory term for Albanians), in the waiter who mercilessly cursed the Albanians he saw on television, in the shop clerk who responded to my browsing for a Muslim-style scarf that "this is not Albania," in the security guard who informed me that the main problem with Macedonia is that is has "too many Muslims," Essentially, Macedonians express a cultural hierarchy that portrays themselves as "advanced" and Albanians as "backwards." In many respects, the situation is analogous to race relations in the USA in the 1950s. Albanians who are more modernized and open to friendship with Macedonians are typically referred to as *"Albanci."* In this case, the term *"Shiptari"* is reserved for migrants from Kosovo, villagers, and criminals. Albanians draw similar distinctions. Macedonians who are accepted by Albanians are said to be "like an Albanian."[12]

On several occasions, I heard Macedonians describe the Albanian community in terms of an ant colony: a group informally coordinated to work toward a certain project, in this case the furtherance of Albanian political goals.

On the other hand, elements of Albanian–Macedonian relations distinguish them from Kosovo, South Serbia, and other cases of high stigma. Although stereotypes pervaded Macedonian culture, their nature was not as pernicious as in other cases and lacked the sexual and violent nature of the myths and rumors often heard in Kosovo. Furthermore, as indicated in the passage by Hislope, ethnic Macedonians did not necessarily use the term "siptar" toward all Albanians. Rather than lumping all Albanians into one inherently deficient cultural group, as in cases of high stigma, ethnic Macedonians reserved the pejorative term for Albanians perceived as lower class.

By far the most positive property of Albanian–Macedonian relations can be found by considering indicators of political cooperation. Strikingly, every ruling coalition in Macedonia since 1992 included ethnic Albanian political parties. Clearly, a strong norm of elite inclusion has existed throughout independent Macedonia's short political life. This norm did not develop over time, but was present even at the inception of the state. These coalitions placed Albanians into heads of ministries, the vice presidencies, and high-level management positions in public administration. Although ethnic Macedonians dominated the day-to-day positions of authority and force, Albanians did occupy both high-level and visibly symbolic positions in the coalition governments.

To summarize: Given the muted features of ethnic flight, the somewhat nuanced and limited use of derogatory terminology and stereotyping, and the impressive record of political cooperation among elites, the level of ethnic stigma in Macedonia appears to be significantly lower than in the Kosovo and South Serbia cases. That is not saying a whole lot; relations are poor among ethnic Macedonians and Albanians. Yet they merit designation as an intermediate level of stigma rather than the highest level.

---

[12] Robert Hislope, "Between a Bad Peace and a Good War: Insights and Lessons from the Almost-War in Macedonia," unpublished draft, p. 9. A published version can be found in *Ethnic and Racial Studies*, (2003) 26 (Issue 1): 129–51.

As it stood in the mid-1990s, the Macedonian case exhibited little open violence, pervasive status concerns, and a medium to high level of stigma. Accordingly, I place it in box R4 – with resentment but not contempt as emotion resources – for the starting point of analysis.

II. MUTUAL COOPERATION DURING THE 1990S (R4)

In the era from Macedonian independence until the late 1990s, both ethnic Macedonians and Albanians generally played cooperation. In game terms, both sides held assurance game preference functions (R > T > P > S). According to the logic of the game, there are two equilibria: mutual cooperation (R) and mutual defection (P). If the opponent cooperates, it is best to cooperate; if the opponent defects, it is likewise best to defect. Despite ethnic Albanian status grievances, mutual cooperation suited both ethnic Albanian and ethnic Macedonian political actors – neither wished to default from the political balance despite its deficiencies.

In the 1990s, Albanians clearly held status-based grievances. They protested over the absence of an Albanian language university, the lack of official status for the Albanian language, the nature of the Preamble, the law against flying flags, and other matters. Yet despite their resentments, Albanian political actors played "cooperation." Their choice had much to do with the lack of alternatives. In the 1990s, the choice set for ethnic Albanians theoretically consisted of the following options:

(1) Escalate violence and move the game to box R5
(2) Play defection in the form of a parallel society, as was occurring at the same time in Kosovo
(3) Play defection in the form of boycotts
(4) Continue cooperation, even from a position of subordinate status

The first option could not even be considered during most of the 1990s. Even given the weakness of Macedonian state security structures, ethnic Albanians could not effectively defend themselves from retaliation. Just as importantly, potential Albanian rebels could not hope that violent escalation would find any Western support. To the contrary, it would be condemned. The second option, although possible, was also a nonstarter. Unlike Kosovo, there was no popular secessionist scenario among Albanians. In this situation of medium ethnic stigma (box R4, with a lack of contempt as an emotion resource), there was simply not enough support for a costly parallel society strategy with dubious future payoffs. The third choice, defection through boycott, also did not seem to promise any sure rewards. If Albanian political actors chose "defection," their ethnic Macedonian counterparts, along the logic of the assurance game, would also move to defection. Ethnic Macedonians could choose to exclude Albanian political parties from positions in ruling coalitions and the division of spoils. Boycotts and other blocking strategies would only succeed if the cost of mutual defection was high enough to force the ethnic Macedonians to reconsider Albanian political grievances. In the 1990s, the costs for mutual defection were much higher for the Albanians than for the Macedonians. Ethnic Macedonians dominated employment in the state sector; they could conduct the state's basic functions without participation by Albanians. Ethnic Macedonians could continue business as usual. Accordingly, option three was unlikely to create leverage for Albanian political demands. "Cooperation" for Albanians meant the continuation of a deeply unsatisfying status quo, an equilibrium where resentment would inevitably produce periodic protests over symbols and language. But it was the best, and perhaps the only realistic, strategy during the 1990s.

III. THE DECISION TO ESCALATE (MOVING THE GAME TO R5)

The game had drastically changed by 2000. Two forces operated to reorder Albanian preferences. First, regional developments modified the balance of force in Macedonia. At the conclusion of the violence in South Serbia, some members of the KLA and UCPMB wandered south to join with locals in the National Liberation Army (NLA) of Macedonia. The armed conflicts in Kosovo and South Serbia provided weapons and experience that evened up the force abilities between rebels and government. Given the weakness and incompetence of the Macedonian armed forces, equalizing this balance was not particularly difficult.

Beyond the structural factors, Albanian political actors could now count on a norm of Western involvement. Albanian political actors had escalated violence in Kosovo in 1998 and in South Serbia in 2000. In both instances, the West had intervened. By this time, a pattern had been established: rebels would target police and armed forces of the state in an effort to generate anger; state forces would overreact, creating a crisis that would produce potential refugee flows; the West would intervene and address the grievances of the rebels. As one of the commanders of the National Liberation Army in Macedonia, Arban Aliu, succinctly stated, "Kosovo inspired us a great deal. We can do the same thing here."[13]

In the 1990s, the Albanian preference ordering was R > T > P > S, an assurance game. With the changing balance of force and the promise of Western intervention into an escalated conflict, the status quo no longer held its relative value. The new ordering became P > T > R > S. It may seem odd that mutual defection would become the most preferred outcome, valued even over the capitulation ("suckering") of ethnic Macedonians.[14] However, ethnic Albanians, following the script as it played out in Kosovo and South Serbia, wished above all to again bring in the West as a semipermanent arbiter

---

[13] Hislope, "Between a Bad Peace and a Good War," p. 18.
[14] Given the changes in regional politics, the relative position of ethnic Macedonians was weaker and the chance for concessions probably much greater than in the 1990s.

between the two sides. Unlike the case of ethnic Macedonian capitulation (with the T value), the outcome of mutual defection (with the P payoff), and especially mutual violence, would most likely accomplish this goal. The continuation of the status quo (mutual cooperation and the R payoff) would neither bring in the West nor force concessions (thus both P and T were preferred over R).[15]

To return to the choice set for this game, the best strategy now became the first option – violent escalation and the transformation of the game to R5. By escalating violence, Albanians would likely produce anger in their Macedonian opponents. Accordingly, Macedonian anger would change (at least in the short run) the ethnic Macedonian preference function from R > T > P > S to T > P > R > S (anger raising the relative value of defection and the T and P payoffs). Under the influence of anger, ethnic Macedonians could not help but wish to strike back against an ethnic Albanian escalation. The ethnic Macedonian population could not tolerate being played as suckers and would avoid that payoff if at all possible. Under the emotion of anger, the ethnic Macedonian population felt the need punish its opponent (and accept the P value of mutual defection that would result) rather than to forgive and try to return to the old status quo (R). Given the changing preference orderings for both players, the game easily moved to mutual defection (defection being a dominant strategy for both players), resulting in the miniwar of 2001.

The escalation began in earnest with a gun battle on February 26, 2001 in the village of Tanusevci in the hills above Tetovo. On March 4, Macedonian forces suffered their first deaths. By March 22, Albanian forces were openly contesting control of Tetovo, Macedonia's second largest city, in broad daylight. The Macedonian military responded by sending in "antiquated Bulgarian T-72 tanks and rumbling Mi-24 helicopter gunships flown by Ukrainian mercenary pilots."[16] By March 23, UNHCR estimated that approximately 20,000 people had fled the fighting area. Low-level fighting continued through the spring and into the summer.

Western officials knew the game that was being played. In May, NATO Secretary General Lord Robertson labeled the NLA as "a bunch of murderous thugs whose objective is to destroy a democratic Macedonia and who are using civilians as human shields" in a cynical bid to provoke "another Balkan bloodbath."[17] A top U.S. official in Macedonia, Christopher Hill, stated, "It's very disappointing that people who were so helped by NATO actions should now become the problem. . . . Some of them believe that they can somehow sucker the international community into being left with no choice but to support them. I believe . . . they have done great harm to the cause that they believe

---

[15] It can be noted that even if the Albanian preference ordering at the time had been T > P > R > S, defection would have been the dominant play.

[16] Phillips, *Macedonia*, p. 86.

[17] Quotation taken from Illievski, "Country Specific Reports on Conflict Settlements, Country Report on Macedonia," p. 7; originally from BBC News, May 7, 2001.

they're supporting."[18] Contrary to Hill's prediction, as the rest of this chapter will show, the leaders of the NLA would force the signing of the Ohrid framework, which would garner enormous benefits for Albanians. Albanian rebels would gain amnesty, create a new political party that would later become part of a ruling coalition, and even push for state pensions as compensation for their fighting, all the while supported by the United States.

Given its new and strong commitment to the region, it was not surprising that the West would come in at some point if the conflict dragged on. The only question regarded the terms of a settlement. If the Macedonian government had managed to regain control over its territory and create a semblance of peace, the eventual outcome might have been more favorable to ethnic Macedonians. If a stalemate had ensued, the Albanians would have had to be granted more concessions.

When Macedonian forces gained control around Tetovo, Albanians moved their operations toward Kumanovo and took control of several villages. Macedonian armed units responded with heavy artillery, helicopter rockets, and tank fire.[19] As one former defense official told me, Macedonian tactics were sometimes indiscriminate, but they lacked the ability to do anything more sophisticated or controlled.[20] Neither side inflicted many casualties. Total numbers killed are generally estimated at about 200, including 60 Macedonian police and military.[21] Neither the armed forces nor the population seemed to possess the will to engage in violence at anywhere near the level seen in Kosovo. Importantly, the conflict did generate significant numbers of refugees and internally displaced, with figures numbering in the tens of thousands.[22]

Low-level violence continued through the spring and into the summer. The conflict reached a new level when Albanian forces took control of Aracinovo on June 9, 2001, a hamlet only ten kilometers from Skopje. From this location, the NLA could threaten to bomb the capital. Whether the NLA had capabilities of launching shells against civilian targets was unclear, but the effect was to bring the war out of the hills and into the streets of the capital city.

At this point, the West decided to step in forcefully. After Macedonian forces began a campaign of heightened shelling of Aracinovo, the EU brokered a deal that sent in U.S. troops to evacuate the NLA with its weapons. The town's residents were left under the protection of foreign organizations, including the OSCE. The episode clearly diminished Macedonia's sovereignty. Macedonian nationalists, believing that the political leadership had betrayed the nation and forfeited a potential military victory against Albanians, surrounded the

---

[18] Quoted passage in Phillips, *Macedonia*, p. 98.

[19] Ibid, p. 103.

[20] YO 3/5/08.

[21] See for example, Brunnbauer, "The Implementation of the Ohrid Accord," p. 2.

[22] ICG Balkans Report No. 113, "Macedonia: Last Chance for Peace," June 20, 2001, provides a figure of 42,700 Albanian refugees fleeing to Kosovo and about 50,000 internally displaced of all nationalities (p. 1).

presidential palace and demanded the resignation of President Trajkovski. Mobs attacked Western embassies and foreign businesses.

Western political forces stepped up their engagement. The United States diplomat, Robert Frowick, had already worked to unify the leading Albanian political parties and the NLA in Kosovo in May. By August, a U.S. special envoy, along with a special representative of the EU, brought the leading Macedonian political parties and Albanian parties together to sign the Ohrid Framework Agreement (OFA).[23] The Albanian rebels' decision to escalate had again brought in the West and yet another round of the Basic Game.

IV. INTRODUCTION OF THE BASIC GAME

The first step of the basic game is to create universal compliance with the state. This task usually involves demobilizing and disarming armed units that possess the ability to challenge the state. In Macedonia, this first stage went according to the script. A British-led force of 4,000 NATO troops deployed almost immediately after the signing of the peace agreement. Operation Essential Harvest collected thousands of weapons from NLA forces. The action was more important symbolically than in terms of actual weapons collection. Few believed that rebels could not gain access to weapons again; many believed they had retained their most essential weapons. Rather, the operation signaled that a new era, one where Western forces were now inextricably involved for the medium if not long term, had begun in Macedonia. John Phillips summarizes the meaning of NATO's entry:

The arrival of NATO troops was also a remarkable success story for a rebel force that only a few weeks previously was being derided in the West as a group of terrorists and thugs. The overriding aims of the NLA had been to get foreign countries involved in its fight with the Skopje Government and to earn international respect.

The transformation of the guerrillas' image had been achieved in less than six months. When the NLA started firing from the hills above Tetovo, Lord Robertson denounced them and indicated that NATO would help to stifle the violence. When Macedonians responded with artillery fire aimed at Albanian hill villages, NATO said that the Skopje Government was retaliating with reasonable restraint. The NLA's strategy followed classic phases. The initial gunfire had been aimed to attract a disproportionate response from the Government. Once that was achieved, the aim was to provoke the sympathy of foreign powers and to force western envoys to arrange a peace deal that met their demands.[24]

---

[23] I am leaving out a discussion of the negotiation process, which was both complicated and fascinating. Most relevant here, some hardliners used violent provocations to try to influence or derail the process in its end stages. For descriptions of that process, see Phillips, *Macedonia*, pp. 128–36.

[24] Phillips, *Macedonia*, p. 147.

With security established, the game no longer involved a consideration of violent escalation. Political actors would not transform the game by moving it into R_5. Rather, the game was now going to be played within cell R_4 – it would be nonviolent and played in a situation of medium stigma. In cell R_4, the only emotion resource available for political entrepreneurs is resentment. The way political actors did or did not use this emotion became a dominant feature of Macedonian politics in the years after the OFA was signed.

The emergence of the OFA and its subsequent operation can again be analyzed through the 2×2 game. As the West entered, both players were still primed for defection. The actual signing of the accord illustrated the bitterness between the parties. The Macedonian leader Georgievski's comments were loaded with sarcasm; Albanian leader Xhaferi made his comments only in Albanian, making the Macedonian representatives seethe. Over the next months, low-level violent provocations rattled Macedonia.[25] In response, the West attempted to use its resources to create incentives to increase the value of mutual cooperation (the R payoff), in effect substantially changing the contours of the game.

In light of the OFA, the benefits of mutual reward were obvious for the Albanians. The Ohrid Framework Accord consisted of six major planks:

(1) Amendment to the Constitution: The Preamble would be changed to include Albanians as a second constituent people of Macedonia, instead of just another minority.
(2) Language: Albanian would become an official language in all municipalities with more than 20 percent Albanian speakers.
(3) The university issue: The Government would provide for an Albanian-language university.
(4) Positions of state authority: There would be "positive discrimination" to attain equitable distributions in the police and other state positions. Five hundred minority police were to be added annually.
(5) Decentralization: Power would be devolved to local levels. This change meant that Albanians, rather than the Macedonian-dominated central government, would control more power in Albanian-dominated municipalities.
(6) Introduction of Badinter voting mechanisms, essentially providing a minority veto over laws of special concern to minority communities.

Several issues were left undecided: Albanian as an official language for the entire country (versus local use); the requirement for an ethnic Albanian vice president; decentralization of the state police; specification of which laws came under the Badinter mechanism. These issues would return to become the focus of Macedonian politics.

---

[25] See International Crisis Group, "No Room for Complacency," October 23, 2003, for a list of violent provocations in the wake of Ohrid.

As is evident, the OFA met nearly every Albanian demand. There is no question about the value of mutual cooperation for the Albanian side in this newly structured game. Mutual cooperation (receiving the R value) would bring valuable rewards and was the surest and smoothest way to get those rewards (thus R was valued over T).[26]

The bigger question is why the Macedonian side also played cooperation. Certain provisions clearly hurt the economic, as well as the political position of the ethnic Macedonian community. Consider the changes in state employment (positive discrimination) required by the OFA. Albanians, living in traditional communities bolstered by remittances from family members living abroad, did not rely on the state for employment. On the other hand, Macedonians depended heavily on state employment. Furthermore, the change of the Preamble was a symbolic humiliation for many ethnic Macedonians. In fact, the changes on almost every issue worked to erode the status dominance of ethnic Macedonians.

Given the lack of reward for Macedonians to cooperate, why did they not defect from the implementation of the OFA? Why did the emotion of resentment, or spite, not drive the Macedonians toward the defection option? Clearly, the Macedonian nationalist party played on such resentments and did call for defection. In fact, the leader of VMRO, Georgievski, at one point called for building an Israeli-like wall in Macedonia in order to preserve Macedonian dominance over a majority of the territory. As of 2003, the majority of Macedonians did not support the agreement and three-quarters said they would protest against its implementation.[27] Yet the ruling Macedonian political leaders continued cooperation.

The overriding answer to this puzzle is that they had little choice. Comprising 1.5 million members and lacking regional allies, ethnic Macedonians are dependent on the international community. They could not defeat the Albanian insurgents militarily, they could not have their name internationally recognized without the support of the United States and Western powers, they could not hope to improve their economic situation without Western help. Above all, many Macedonians saw no hope of a better future without eventual membership in the EU. For the Macedonians, the carrot of potential EU membership was an overwhelmingly powerful incentive, one that they were not willing to risk losing through defection on the OFA. In the immediate post-Ohrid years, Macedonian political actors could have received the temptation payoff (that is, defecting while the Albanians cooperated). Early on, they might have scored political points with a significant number, and possibly a majority, of ethnic Macedonians. However, the obvious long-term dependence on the West precluded this choice.

---

[26] It would be better to receive these rewards with the cooperation of ethnic Macedonians than to receive them with the complications and frictions involved with ethnic Macedonian defection and the "sucker/temptation" payoffs.

[27] ICG, "No Room for Complacency," October 23, 2003, p. 21.

V. THE POLITICS OF MITIGATING RESENTMENT

There is more to the story than the power of EU conditionality. Ethnic Macedonians came to grips with their situation relatively quickly and began to accept a binational state. To understand how this happened, it is necessary to consider the nature of politics based on resentment. As discussed in the theory chapter, emotions based on situations or events – anger, fear, resentment – fade over time. The intensity of emotion declines. Chapter 2 depicted various functions of decay ranging from exponential to inverse exponential rates (see the figures in Chapter 2). What psychologists and social scientists do not understand very well is the rate of decline in intensity.

It is likely that these rates are determined less by the physiology of the brain and more by politics. Political leaders can change the cognitive antecedents that create emotions. The cognitive antecedents of resentment are that one's group is located in an unwarranted subordinate position on a status hierarchy. If political entrepreneurs can shape perceptions of the nature of the status hierarchy, they can then affect the rate of decline of the emotion. In terms of the graphs, perhaps they can change the rate of decline from inverse exponential to exponential.

I suggest that such a phenomenon occurred in Macedonia. Given the power of international constraints on defection from the Basic Game, Macedonian political leaders framed events in a way that took the sting out of the Macedonian decline in status. Foremost among these framers was President Boris Trajkovski, who repeatedly insisted that "There is no need for any party to view the framework agreement as a defeat. Time has given proof to our expectations of a truly European agreement – one that would end possibilities for territorial solutions to ethnic questions."[28] To be equal with Albanians was a blow for many ethnic Macedonians, but if both sides were to be incorporated into a new European political structure, the zero-sum nature of the status competition within Macedonia would be muted.

As the evidence suggests, this new narrative took hold. Perhaps most telling are the poll number confidence ratings of NATO and the EU.[29] Respondents were asked if they held a favorable view of the EU and NATO (see Table 15.1). In September 2001, NATO helped broker the Ohrid Accords. To an amazing extent, both the Macedonian and Albanian populations saw the event as a Western intervention to aid the Albanian side. Accordingly, in September 2001, 99.5 percent of Albanians had a favorable view of NATO, compared to 6.3 percent of Macedonians. However, three years later, a majority of Macedonians held a favorable view of NATO.

[28] Ana Petruseva, "Ohrid Two Years On," Institute for War and Peace Reporting, August 19, 2003.
[29] See "The Process of Decentralization in Macedonia: Prospects for Ethnic Conflict Mitigation, Enhanced Representation, Institutional Efficiency and Accountability," supported by Freedom House-Europe and the United States Agency for International Development, Sofia–Skopje, 2006.

TABLE 15.1. *Percentages Holding Favorable Views of Western Institutions*

	Macedonians		Albanians	
	EU	NATO	EU	NATO
2001 January	17	6	80	90
2001 July	18.7	6	80.1	95
2001 September	14.8	6.3	98.9	99.5
2002 February	14.4	6.9	91.5	95.8
2002 March	26.1	12.3	81.9	87.2
2003 January	30	25	82	83
2003 December	50.7	40	85.7	78
2004 May	68	49.4	82	76.1
2004 September	70	55	84	80

By that time, NATO membership had been redefined as a precursor to EU accession. Favorable impressions of the EU during the same time period had risen even more dramatically among Macedonians, from 14.8 percent in September 2001 to 70 percent in September 2004.

As numerous members of both sides told me, the desirability of EU membership was about the only thing they could agree on. A survey in November 2005 showed that 94 percent of the total population supported EU membership.[30] As EU politics muted the domestic competition, at least some citizens from both groups also began to create a narrative about the 2001 violence. They would state that it was in no way a civil war but a creation of a few political actors.[31] Macedonians toned down their rhetoric about needing an ethnically defined Macedonian state for the Macedonia nation. Instead, they began describing the Macedonians' remarkable ability to adapt and survive, and saying that Macedonians, by their unenviable geographic position, are "condemned to tolerance."[32]

It is unlikely that such a redefinition of conflict and group status could have occurred in Kosovo, South Serbia, or other regions of intense ethnic stigma. The emotion of contempt is based on the perceived inherent nature of an opposing group. Emotions based on such perceptions do not fade as quickly, nor are they as susceptible to the framing efforts of political actors. I will come back to this point in a later section.

VI. CHALLENGES TO THE BASIC GAME

The game between Macedonians and Albanians may have been muted, but it was still played, bitterly at times. As predicted by box R4, the issues and

[30] Institute of Democracy "Societas Civilis" (IDSCS), "Public Opinion in Macedonia about the EU Integration Processes," Skopje, November 2005.
[31] XF and ZD 3/3/08.
[32] EK 3/4/08.

provocations rotated around status issues. I will discuss only two major challenges, one from each side, to generate illustrations of more general problems.

A. Decentralization

More than any other single reform, the implementation of the decentralization planks of the OFA had the potential to wreck the entire process. As a response to the problems inherent in the Dayton Accords in Bosnia, Western interveners included decentralization as part of the Macedonian game. In Bosnia, a bifurcated federal state structure allowed ethnic political entrepreneurs to control large territories that could be used as bases for separatist politics. In order to prevent the same phenomenon from occurring in Macedonia, the Ohrid Framework aimed to produce power both at the center and at the local level, but not at a regional level. Undoubtedly there would be conflict between Albanians and Macedonians, but it could be channeled and confined to multiple localities, where it could be more easily contained.

In carrying out the reform, the OFA required a revision of municipal boundaries, as well as a reduction of the total number of municipalities from 120 to 84.[33] These changes would put Albanians in the majority in a few municipalities, most notably Struga and Kicevo. Furthermore, the plan would raise Albanian numbers above the 20 percent threshold necessary to trigger language rights and changes of symbols in other municipalities, most notably in Skopje itself. Many Macedonians saw the implementation of this plank of the OFA as simply a way to gerrymander Albanian dominance or unfairly reduce Macedonian status. To sabotage the reform, Macedonian groups held 41 local referenda on decentralization, asking whether the reorganization should be implemented. Unsurprisingly, all 41 referenda registered opposition to the reform. In July 2004, 20,000 people gathered in Skopje to protest the proposed law.[34] The World Macedonian Congress collected 150,000 signatures against it.[35] These efforts led to a national referendum on municipal boundaries on November 7, 2004.

The referendum would fail if turnout did not reach 50 percent. Stating that Euro-integration depended on implementation, the governing coalition urged voters to defeat the referendum through a boycott. All Western actors backed the boycott of the referendum. The U.S. Undersecretary of State, Marc Grossman, had warned that the referendum presented "a choice between the past and the future." The United States also pledged nearly 10 million dollars to defray the costs of the decentralization plan.[36] In a remarkably blatant intervention, the United States abandoned its practice of staying out of the

[33] In 1992, at the time of independence, there were 34 units. The number was increased to 123 in 1996.
[34] For an overview, see Policy Brief No. 1, Center for Research and Policy Making, "Macedonian Ethnic Politics Post Ohrid Agreement: The Issue of the New Law on Local Government Boundaries," Skopje, August 9, 2005.
[35] Ilievski, "Country Report," p. 9.
[36] Policy Brief No. 1, Center for Research and Policy Making, Skopje, August 9, 2005, p. 13.

Macedonia–Greece name dispute and officially recognized Macedonia under its constitutional name only a few days before the election. Many Macedonians responded by backing the Government/U.S. position and boycotted the poll. Although 94 percent of voters opposed the new boundaries, only 27 percent of the electorate participated – far below the necessary threshold. The boycott succeeded; decentralization went forward as planned.

B. Brinkmanship

Albanian leaders continued to draw on the ongoing status concerns of their group as a political resource for several years post-Ohrid. This tactic was hardly surprising, given the background of the NLA and the political party that emerged from it. Consider the following statement released by the NLA during the fighting on its war aims:

Macedonia's ignorant view and hypocritical disrespect of the demands and patience of Albanians has surpassed all limits. Our people have for decades been insulted, discriminated against and banned from all civilization traditions in Macedonia.... Therefore, we decided not to allow further humiliation and trampling on our dignity.[37]

After the fighting stopped, leaders of the NLA formed a new political party, the Democratic Union for Integration (DUI). The leader of DUI, the former NLA commander Ali Ahmeti, gave his inaugural speech under a huge Albanian flag in Tetovo. The party did not, or could not, turn off the rhetoric about ethnic Macedonian disrespect for Albanians. Many Albanians believed that they were still being shut out of power, despite the implementation of the Ohrid Framework.[38] There was a feeling among many Albanians that the Macedonians perceived that they were paternalistically "giving" rights to Albanians. As one Albanian asked me, "Who are *they* to give rights to *us*?"[39]

DUI played on this well of resentment to become the largest Albanian party in Macedonia. When DUI was shut out of the ruling coalition, despite gaining a majority of Albanian seats in the 2006 elections, they initiated a boycott of Parliament and demanded resolution of several status issues left unresolved by the OFA. These issues included specification on which laws should be subject to Badinter principles and enhanced recognition of Albanian as an official language. Provocatively, DUI asked for a rule requiring that the largest Albanian party be included in any ruling coalition. Such a rule would essentially establish a formal binational consociational system with little regard for ideological incompatibility or programmatic coherence in the ruling coalition. More provocatively, DUI asked that the Albanian insurgents (NLA members) of the 2001 conflict basically be recognized as the equivalent of Macedonian government soldiers and be awarded equivalent pensions and benefits. Most

[37] Quotation in Phillips, *Macedonia*, p. 87.
[38] I base this statement on several conversations held in Tetovo, Kumanovo, and rural Macedonia in the summer of 2006.
[39] CU.

provocatively, Ahmeti stated that if the Macedonian parties did not uphold their end of any agreement, he "won't go home" after the next boycott – the former guerrilla leader clearly implying that he might take up arms.[40] Albanians would not be "given" anything; as equals to anybody, they would "take" it as their right.

With some exceptions, the parties in Macedonia that took the most radical positions on status issues often tended to prevail. Even partners in the same ruling coalition often put out conflicting nationalist statements on the same policy issue. For example, after the two leading nationalist parties (VMRO on the Macedonian side and DUI on the Albanian side) formed a ruling coalition in the summer of 2008, they gave conflicting statements about proposed laws on flying the Albanian flag and police reform. As one analyst described the coalition, "This is a marriage of interest and necessity so the rules of the game are not precise. The two are trying to show their own electorates that they have not kneeled down before the other party."[41] The Western promise of EU membership and the use of conditionality limited the range of play and sometimes affected the outcomes, but the nature of the game, and its use of ethnic resentment, usually remained the same. It was often still a matter of who was perceived as kneeling down to whom.

VII. EVALUATION OF HYPOTHESES

As discussed earlier, a comparison of the Serbia and Macedonia cases can illuminate differences in the politics of cell R4, with a medium level of ethnic stigma, and R7, with a high level of ethnic stigma. The key difference is that the emotion of contempt is not a ready resource in R4. Chapter 6 listed several hypotheses that relate to the presence/absence of contempt. These predictions can be rephrased to fit this more precise comparison of box R4 and R7.

> *Rephrased Prediction 6*: Political entrepreneurs are more likely to initiate the politics of boycott and the creation of parallel systems in R7 than in R4.

When the opposing group is an object of contempt, the politics of separation can form a "common sense." The logic is that "we can never live with those people, so we need to separate." This logic is less likely to apply in situations of medium stigma without the force of contempt. Taken as a whole, the Macedonian case supports this hypothesis. When two major party leaders did call for partition (the ethnic Macedonian Georgievski and the Albanian Arben Xhaferi), they met strong opposition and were even marginalized to an extent.

---

[40] For an overview and discussion of these events and the "Skopje Agreement" that resulted, see Ilievski, "Country Report," 27–30.

[41] Commentary of Biljana Vankovska, professor of law at Skopje University, quoted in Sinisa-Jakov Marusic, "Macedonia's New Government Faces Ethnic Challenge," *Balkan Insight*, July 10, 2008.

The boycott of the referendum on decentralization was used to continue cooperation rather than hinder it. The result indicated that a majority of citizens wished to continue cooperation. Unlike Kosovo, no area of the state operates independent of the central government. In Macedonia, political actors threaten boycotts far more often than they carry them out. Still, threats of boycotts remained a part of Macedonian political life.

To recall from South Serbia, Albanians boycotted all Serbian national elections for fifteen years, from the early 1990s until 2007, did not participate in the national council system of minority representation in Serbia, and sometimes boycotted the Coordination Body of South Serbia. Serbian politicians in Bujanovac attempted local partition after a status reversal in 2002. Albanian politicians won elections while breaking speech taboos on the secession issue. In short, for this hypothesis, the predicted difference appears to hold. South Serbia, in R7, has seen a higher prevalence of boycotts and a continued politics of separation.

> *Rephrased Prediction 7*: Actors who initiate violence are more likely to suffer backlash from their own population in R4 than in R7.

In South Serbia, there was little or no evidence of any backlash from the 2000 escalation. Former rebel commanders became respected political leaders, although they did not support violent politics after the spring of 2001. In Macedonia, the Albanian political actors who escalated violence in 2001 were also richly rewarded in political terms. National Liberation Army leaders came to lead political parties that garnered majorities of Albanian votes. When these leaders were indicted for crimes related to the war they initiated, massive numbers of their in-group members came out to protest. The same leaders offer vague threats of violence when things do not go their way. On the whole, there were few differences between these R4 and R7 cases. In both, rebels who escalated violence not only suffered no backlash but also became popular political leaders. In both, none of the former rebels dared violently challenge a political landscape that had been transformed by Western intervention. The absence of violence might be partly the result of anticipation of a backlash; it is most surely a result of the diminished utility of violence in the postintervention period.

> *Rephrased Prediction 8*: In both R4 and R7, we are likely to observe periodic and perhaps frequent initiations of *targeted* violence.

In both cases, rebels escalated violence and transformed the game through targeted violence. In the postintervention period, neither case saw rounds of significant targeted violence.

> *Rephrased Prediction 10*: In R4, with resentment but not contempt, nonviolent provocations will emphasize current changes in status relations. In R7, with both contempt and resentment, nonviolent provocations

such as speeches and posters may highlight the perceived inherent negative qualities of the other side and/or status politics.

This hypothesis receives strong support. The issues and imagery in Macedonia were permeated by status concerns. There was little open rhetoric about the other side's inherently problematic nature. In the South Serbia case, to review, we saw Serbs portraying Presevo Valley's Albanian population as disloyal and often "terrorist." Albanians emphasized status inequality and the continued political dominance of Serbs, but also stressed maintaining distance from Serbs and the Serbian government, as expected when ethnic contempt is present.

The General Dependent Variable

Macedonia has been a target of international intervention almost since its founding. The United Nations conducted its first preventive mission, UNPREDEP, in Macedonia in 1992, almost immediately after the state's inception. When internationals pulled out, Macedonia lapsed into its miniwar. When internationals came back in, violent conflict abated. At its most basic level – as a mission to prevent violence – intervention has succeeded in Macedonia.

On other levels, outcomes have also been positive. The Basic Game went according to plan. The first phase conducted demobilization and disarmament, even if much of it was symbolic. The central state gained control over its territory. The Ohrid Framework Accord established an iterated game and moved both players up to mutual cooperation, at least much of the time. Although it cannot be said that the game was played smoothly, given the constant threats and nationalist demands, at least it was played.

Western interveners can claim success, but as in South Serbia, conditions for success were favorable. In particular, the weak hand of ethnic Macedonians essentially dictated the general outcome from the start. Ethnic Macedonians could not hope to survive outside of the EU. The EU's conditionality card provides the ultimate leverage. Although the process could have been either smoother or rougher than it was, it is difficult to see divergence from the path of EU accession. The real choices lie with the Albanian side. Albanian nationalists could pursue a range of pan-Albanian politics from outright secession (conceivable if the EU path becomes blocked) to forms of a de facto "Greater Albania," where the Albanian populations of Kosovo, Macedonia, South Serbia, and Albania proper draw closer together in cultural (which seems inevitable in any case), economic, and political ties.

VIII. MITIGATING RESENTMENT

As the previous section has shown, cases of R4 can be expected to differ from cases of R7 in predictable ways. The comparison of South Serbia and Macedonia supports some of these predictions, although not all of them. The difference between the two categories of cases might be seen better in a less formal way – in the types of creative politics used to mitigate resentment. Cases fitting into R4 should provide more opportunity for political elites to pursue more tolerant politics than in R7. In R7, the presence of contempt acts as both a resource for and a constraint on political entrepreneurs. As a resource, ethnic contempt provides incentives to play the politics of separation and boycott. As a constraint, widespread ethnic contempt operates to block or impede a range of reconciliatory strategies that would run into opposition from a contempt-driven political base. In R4, on the other hand, political actors are freed from the constraints of ethnic contempt and not tempted by its promise as a resource. They must still deal with the constraints and opportunities of the emotion of resentment, but they have more leeway in doing so.

The Macedonian case shows how resentment alone may not create the nearly impassable obstacles to political cooperation that contempt does. Consider the cognitive frameworks of both emotions. Contempt is simply about the inherent negative qualities of the opposing group. In effect, an individual believes that "there is something wrong with members of group Y." As defined and measured here, a high level of stigma is necessary to create the emotion of contempt. The emotion involves a deep cultural set of negative attitudes embedded in the language (derogatory terminology), social practices (strictures against intermarriage and the learning of the out-group's language), and even common sense about where one lives (segregation practices). These cognitions are not subject to ready decay. When they become part of a cultural schema, the cognitions – and the emotion – may come to the surface at any time. In a period of conflict, the political entrepreneur has few tools to address this deeply held cognitive framework. The political actor cannot easily argue that the contemptible out-group, especially after a period of violence and struggle, may not be that bad after all. Contempt creates a "common sense" idea of avoidance, and common sense is difficult to assail.

The emotion of resentment, in contrast, has a more complex cognitive framework, more amenable to change by the political entrepreneur. For resentment, an individual perceives that "I am a member of group X and group X is unjustly subordinated to group Y." There are three elements here. First, there are ideas about Y, the unjustly dominant group; second, there are notions about X, that is, about who "we" are; third, there is a story about the relationship between X and Y, or, how the groups came to be in their respective positions. With contempt, only the nature of Y is at issue. With resentment, self-definition and narrative history are also at play.

Consider what happened in Macedonia. Ethnic Macedonian political actors did not spend a lot of effort extolling the virtues of the Albanians, but they did redefine themselves. Instead of being a weak people who were losing their dominant status in a Macedonian nation-state, they became a clever people who were finding a way to preserve their nation in the face of hostile neighbors. The struggle with Albanians should be seen in light of a broader history in which Macedonian patriots fought against the Turks, Communists, Bulgarians (a bit problematic for members of VMRO), and others to preserve their vulnerable nation. They also redefined the nature of the present situation. Instead of ethnic Macedonians being unjustly equal to the minority Albanian population, both ethnic Macedonians and Albanians would be two parts of the vast collection of European ethnic and national groups. Cooperation with Albanians, in this view, should not be seen as defeat, but rather as one necessary step of the praiseworthy path of the Macedonian nation.

As discussed in the theory chapter, if the cognitions about a situation or relationship change, the resentment is predicted to fade. As argued here, this phenomenon seemed to occur in Macedonia in the mid-2000s. The Ohrid Framework Accords changed status relations and created a high level of resentment among ethnic Macedonians, but the reframing of the national narrative did seem to increase the rate of decay of the emotion and reduce its intensity. Refer again to figures in the second chapter. In Macedonia, the decline in the intensity of the emotion could be characterized as changing from an inverse exponential rate to the exponential rate. Such an interpretation would correspond to the numbers in Table 15.1.

Surely, resentment still pervades Macedonian politics. Recall the experience with the hotel clerk that began this chapter. The point is that the emotion of resentment, in the absence of ethnic contempt (as seen in cases with the highest levels of ethnic stigma), did not on its own destroy the possibilities for further cooperation between the groups in conflict. Politicians are more free to practice politics as an art in cell R4 than in R7.

The comparative question here is whether this same change in narrative could have taken place in Kosovo or South Serbia, cases with both resentment and contempt as indicated by cell R7. For reasons mentioned, I think not. There is no realistic way for the Serbs in Kosovo not to see themselves as "losers" to the Albanians. No reconstruction of narrative can reduce the sting of losing to an inferior people. No redefinitions of the situation will readily change long-held cultural schemas. For over ten years after the Kosovo bombing, the chosen option of Serbs, unsurprisingly, was for separation in one form or another. It is good to keep in mind that their Albanian counterparts had chosen the same strategy in the early 1990s. Change in Kosovo is likely to take decades rather than years.

16

Bosnia

I. QUESTIONS

The Bosnian case presents several puzzles. First, why was this conflict so bloody during the war? The most reliable source, Mirsad Tokaca's "Human Losses in Bosnia-Herzegovina 1991–1995," better known as "The Bosnian Book of the Dead," documents at least 97,000 deaths,[1] with hundreds of thousands displaced. Much of the violence was indiscriminate and targeted against civilians. Tokaca's figures indicate that 40 percent of the victims were civilians and that 83 percent of civilian victims were Bosniaks,[2] compared to 10 percent Serbs and 5 percent Croats.

Second, why has more progress not been made toward the creation of a functioning, centralized state fifteen years after the signing of the Dayton Accord? What accounts for progress on some issues but not others?[3] As outlined in the seventh chapter, the Western-brokered Dayton Accord ended the war and set up a bifurcated consociational political system. Fifteen years after the Dayton Accord was signed, Bosnia (BiH)[4] limps along as a functioning state, but one, by all accounts, with many dysfunctional elements. By definition, states need to accomplish basic missions – establish a monopoly over violence, regulate taxation, control borders, establish property rights, field an army, maintain a judicial system. By 2010, Bosnia had managed to accomplish only some of these fundamental missions. The nature of progress toward a functional state raises some puzzles. For instance, why was Bosnia able to eventually field an

---

[1] Mirsad Tokaca, "Human Losses in Bosnia-Herzegovina 1991–1995." Tokaca's database sorts the victims by name, place, and circumstances of death. The Research and Documentation Center in Sarajevo released this data base in June 2007.

[2] For an explanation on the name Bosniak, versus Muslim, see Appendix 1.

[3] Andrew Radin attempts to answer this very question for Bosnia and other cases, in his dissertation, "Politics as War by Other Means: The Limits of Third-Party State- building after Civil Wars," Massachusetts Institute of Technology, in progress as of 2010.

[4] See Appendix A for an explanation of terms.

army, but not to effectively centralize the police force? Why did the EU carrot not lead to more progress? As the High Representative to Bosnia, Valentin Inzko, stated in a speech to the European Parliament in January 2010, "In the last four years Bosnia has been in a political stalemate...not a single reform has been adopted that would give the state increased competences needed for active participation in the EU accession process."[5]

A third question, perhaps less puzzling given the violence of the war, regards the complete lack of nation building in Bosnia. Very few individuals consider "Bosnia" as their national homeland. In fact, in Banja Luka, the capitol of Republika Srpska, it is difficult to encounter teenagers who have ever been to Sarajevo, or even wish to travel there.[6] The main reason Bosnia survives is simply the lack of alternatives. As a 2009 International Crisis Group report aptly summarizes, "BiH's legitimacy and stability do not rest on a foundation of patriotism or common identity but instead on a community of interest, reinforced by the absence of viable alternatives and a common fear of violent disintegration. RS's Serbs may resent the state, but BiH's long-term stagnation would eventually damage their fortunes too."[7]

As Chapter 7 summarized, the West was a key player in Bosnia before, during, and after the war. The case is central for all scholars of Western intervention. This chapter aims to specify key reasons that the Western program has not always accomplished what it set out to do.

II. ADDRESSING QUESTIONS

As this chapter will show, three emotions – resentment, fear, and anger – and their sequencing and interactions provide key answers to the three puzzles of Section I. As in the other cases, the analysis will follow the evolution of the case across cells in the matrices.[8] In the Bosnian case, the progression runs as follows:

$$NR_1 – R_1 – R_2 – R_3 – R_1$$

As late as the 1980s, Bosnia was characterized by neither high stigma nor significant resentment. The collapse of Yugoslavia, along with the drive to create an independent Bosnia, brought status politics to the fore, moving the case to R_1. As militias formed, the situation moved rapidly into significant levels of violence (R_2). At that point, Serbian forces initiated a strategy of

---

[5] "Inzko Calls on EU to Maintain Focus on Bosnia," *Balkan Insight*, January 27, 2010.

[6] Of graduating high school seniors in Banja Luka, 80 percent had never been to Sarajevo. For this figure and others regarding ethnic "unmixing" in Bosnia, see Gordon Bardos, "The New Political Dynamics of Southeastern Europe," *Southeast Europe and Black Sea Studies* (September 2008) 8: 171–88. See especially p. 182.

[7] International Crisis Group Europe Briefing No. 57, "Bosnia's Dual Crisis," November 12, 2009, p. 16.

[8] Recall the discussion of cases and their use in comparative analysis at the end of Chapter 6.

high indiscriminate violence, moving the case into R3. The Dayton Accords introduced a version of the Basic Game that moved the game back to R1.

This progression cannot be fully understood without comprehending the role of emotions as resources. Emotions played a crucial role at several stages in the progression of the case. Serb resentment versus Bosniaks was most fundamental. Most Serbs do not wish to live in a political entity where Bosniaks are the plurality, let alone a majority. This was true at the collapse of Yugoslavia and continues to be true years after Dayton. In his war crimes trial at the Hague, Radovan Karadzic, outlining his views of the origins of the war, stated that Serbs "wanted to live with Muslims, but not under Muslims."[9] Although Karadzic said many things, this statement captures the perceptions and thinking of many Bosnian Serbs, especially those who participated in the violence. In 2003, a UNDP survey asked Bosnian residents if they supported "a state of citizens," meaning a "one person, one vote" system. For Serbs, a "state of citizens" means that the political will of the Bosnian plurality could be imposed on the Serbian minority. Unsurprisingly, 52 percent of Bosniak citizens supported such a system; only 9 percent of Serbs did so (17 percent for Croats). In late 2009, Florian Bieber wrote that "Bosnian institutions will for the foreseeable future need to have a system that allows one of the entities or constituent peoples to block decisions."[10] In sum, for twenty years, Serbs have worked hard to prevent possible subordination to Bosniaks.

The situation for Croats has been different. Most Croats live in the Bosniak–Croat Federation. Although Croats fight to retain autonomy within the Federation, significant numbers have left for Croatia, even though many who left retain property and official residence in Bosnia. Although the Western view is that Orthodox Serbs, Catholic Croats, and Muslim Bosniaks are just three ethnic groups that should be able to get along, there is a problem in that both Serbs and Croats resent having to live in a situation in which they perceive possible domination by Bosniaks. For many Serbs, the solution was first to fight and then, after Dayton, to block political evolution toward a centralized Bosnian state. For many Croats, the solution is to exit. Members of both groups do not seem to feel comfortable in a state where Bosniaks are the largest group.[11]

Resentment has not been the only emotion at play within the progression of the case; fear and anger have also played key roles. Serbian forces employed indiscriminate violence to create fear, which was central to their project of

[9] Taken from Arthur Max, "Karadzic Asserts He Guarded Serbs from Islamic Militants," *Boston Globe*, March 2, 2010.
[10] Florian Bieber, "Dayton Bosnia May Be Over – But What Next?" *Balkan Insight*, 10 December 2009.
[11] Perhaps this should not be so surprising given the fact that the majority (57.5 percent) of Swiss voters, in a 2009 referendum, voted to pass a constitutional amendment banning the construction of new minarets and U.S. citizens in New York rail against the construction of an Islamic center in the vicinity of the World Trade Center location. In Bosnia, the West seems mystified that ethnic groups with a Christian heritage might have some resistance to living in a state with a Muslim plurality/majority.

ethnic cleansing. The path to violence in this low-stigma case involved a sequencing of resentment and fear. Finally, the stalemate over the progression of Dayton is not only the result of Serbian resentment. It is also partially due to Bosniak anger at Serbian genocide,[12] best seen in the compromise-denying politics of certain Bosniak political leaders.

III. ESTABLISHING THE STARTING POINT

Resentment: In the period immediately following the Second World War, Serbs occupied a disproportionate number of visible positions of authority in the Bosnian governance structures. By the 1960s, a generational change had occurred and the numbers evened out. By the 1980s, the political–ethnic status hierarchy was not a major issue for most of the population. As all groups spoke the same language (Serbo-Croatian was considered a single language at the time in Bosnia), there was no contest about whose language would be used in schools or public bureaucracies. In short, prewar Bosnia was not consumed by political resentments. Accordingly, the NR matrix should be used at the starting point of analysis.

Stigma: For many academics, Bosnia was an exemplar for multiethnic relations. Observers often cite high rates of intermarriage as proof. Chip Gagnon cites a variety of surveys and statistics.[13] For instance, in a 1990 survey, 80 percent of Serbs, 77 percent of Muslims, and 66 percent of Croats answered that ethnicity should not be taken into account in considering marriage partners.[14] Gagnon notes that the 1981 census indicates that 15.8 percent of all Bosnian children were the offspring of mixed nationality parents and that 16.8 percent of all Bosnian marriages in 1981 involved different nationalities.[15] Donia and Fine state that 40 percent of all Bosnian urban marriages were ethnically mixed.[16]

Nikolai Botev's statistical study challenges the conventional wisdom on Bosnian intermarriage.[17] Botev found regional variations in intermarriage rates

---

[12] Without getting into the debate over whether Serb actions constituted genocide, the Bosnian view is unequivocally that Serbs did commit genocide. Recent court rulings have established that genocide was committed, but that Belgrade was not responsible. There are many important debates over these terms.

[13] V. P. Gagnon, *The Myth of Ethnic War: Serbia and Croatia in the 1990's* (Ithaca, NY: Cornell University Press, 2004); see pp. 40–42 in particular.

[14] Ibid, p. 40. The figures are from Ibrahim Bakic and Ratko Dunderovic, Institute for the Study of National Relations in Bosnia-Hercegovina, "Gradani Bosne I Hercegovine o medunaciconalnim odnosima," *Oslobodenje*, March 22, 1990.

[15] Ibid., p. 42.

[16] Robert J. Donia and John V. A. Fine, *Bosnia and Hercegovina: A Tradition Betrayed* (New York: Columbia University Press, 1994), p. 186.

[17] See Nikolai Botev, "Where East Meets West: Ethnic Intermarriage in the Former Yugoslavia, 1962 to 1989," *American Sociological Review* (June 1994) 59: 461–80. Also see the exchanges between Gagnon and Botev on intermarriage in V. P. Gagnon, "Reaction to the Special Issue of AEER War among the Yugoslavs," *Anthropology of East Europe Review* (Spring 1994) 12: 50–51.

and also found that intermarriage rates, contrary to popular wisdom, were not rising in the years before the war. Moreover, intermarriage rates between the two Christian groups, Eastern Orthodox and Catholics, were significantly higher than those between Christians and Muslims.[18] Overall, intermarriage rates in Bosnia were close to the Yugoslav average (11.9 percent versus 13.0 percent).[19]

Other sources contribute to a more complex picture. Tone Bringa's well-known anthropological work *Being Muslim the Bosnian Way* devotes several pages to a discussion of intermarriage practices. In her fieldwork in a small community in central Bosnia, she found that intermarriage was relatively rare and usually discouraged.[20] As Bringa points out, norms can significantly vary between rural and urban Bosnia.

There is little evidence of residential segregation, although many villages and small communities retained ethnic divisions. Unlike Kosovo and other areas to the south, there is no evidence of residential flight taking place in the period before the war. Muslims, Croats, and Serbs commonly lived and mixed in many neighborhoods and cities without trouble. Derogatory terminology and labels were not common in the population's vocabulary.

In the period preceding the collapse of Yugoslavia, taken as a whole, these three measures code Bosnia as a case of low ethnic stigma. In sum, the starting point for the Bosnian case (as it stood in the late 1980s) is one of low resentment, low ethnic stigma, and no violence (NR1).

At least two complicating factors need to be addressed before heading into the progression of the case. First, a distinction should be made between Muslims[21] as individuals and Muslims as a nation. Along the lines of low stigma, Serbs and Croats may not see anything deficient about Muslims as individuals. However, few Serbs and Croats, I would argue, would see the Muslim nation as equivalent to the Serbian or Croatian nation. These beliefs simply followed the contours of the practices of the Yugoslav state. The Yugoslav government did not recognize "Muslims" as a nation, as opposed to a religious group, until 1968. As one former high-ranking Bosnian Serb official told me, nations have a language, a literary history, and common sense of history, and, he asserted, the Muslims met none of those criteria.[22] In all my discussions with Bosnian Serbs, few, if any, believed that Muslims could legitimately be defined as a nation before the war. Interestingly, most believe that the war had transformed them into a legitimate nation, although one too influenced by the Islamic religion and at odds with the Serbian nation.

---

[18] Botev, "Where East Meets West," p. 475.
[19] Botev, "Where East Meets West," p. 469. The rate in Voyvodina, by contrast, was 28.4 percent.
[20] Tone Bringa, *Being Muslim the Bosnian Way: Identity and Community in a Central Bosnian Village* (Princeton, NJ: Princeton University Press, 1995). See pp. 79–80 and pp. 149–54 in particular.
[21] I am using the term "Muslim" here, as that was the official as well as common usage in the late 1980s, that is, at the starting point of analysis that is under discussion here.
[22] LM 4/3/08.

Second, it is essential to understand the differences between urban and rural Bosnia. The above points about intermarriage and residential integration need some qualification. To cite Tone Bringa again:

While in the village people of different ethnoreligious backgrounds would live side by side and often have close friendships, they would rarely intermarry. In some neighborhoods they would not even live side by side and would know little about each other. And while some families would have a long tradition of friendship across ethnoreligious communities others would not.[23]

Donia and Fine similarly write:

While urbanization moved Bosnian cities and towns in the direction of becoming melting pots, peasants and village dwellers retained much of their previous character, despite the universal availability of many modern amenities and greater participation in the market economy. Thus the historical distinctions between peasants and urbanites remained and, in some ways, were reinforced during the socialist era, even as the number and relative demographic strength of urban dwellers increased vastly. Most villages remained ethnically segregated, and mixed marriages were much less common in rural areas than in cities. . . . The continued dichotomy between rural and urban attitudes contributed to the spread of the Bosnian conflict in 1992 and 1993, for peasants were drawn to the ethnic militias more readily than long-term urbanites. Many urban dwellers of all national allegiances perceive the conflict as one in which primitive peasants are seeking to destroy urban civilization in Bosnia.[24]

Sabrina Petra Ramet holds that social memory in the countryside differed from its urban counterpart.[25] Rural Serbs and Croats were more likely to see Muslims as the heirs of Ottoman occupation – a system in which non-Muslims seldom owned land and lived as second-class citizens. In the more traditional rural areas, survivors of the atrocities of the Second World War and their descendants maintained both networks and active memories.[26] Ramet concludes:

But there is a world of difference between a national movement founded on urban mobilization (even if it manipulates the symbols and mythologies of the countryside, in its own distorted mirror) and a national movement based, to a great extent, on rural mobilization. From the standpoint of the potential for chauvinist excesses, for the suspension of any notions of tolerance and for excesses of violence, the latter, rural mobilization, is, as Eugen Weber has noted, the more dangerous.[27]

Understanding the urban/rural differences in Bosnia is crucial to understanding the mobilization for war. One essential point is that Bosnia cannot be equated

[23] Bringa, *Being Muslim the Bosnian Way*, p. 4.
[24] Donia and Fine, *Bosnia and Hercegovina*, pp. 186–7.
[25] Sabrina Ramet, "Nationalism and the 'Idiocy of the Countryside': The Case of Serbia," *Ethnic and Racial Studies* (1996) 19: 70–87.
[26] On the transmission of the memory of the Second World War in Serbian refugee families, see Mila Dragojevic, "The Politics of Refugee Identity: Newcomers in Serbia from Bosnia and Herzegovina and Croatia, 1991–2009," unpublished dissertation, Brown University.
[27] Ramet, "Nationalism and the 'Idiocy of the Countryside,'" p. 85.

with common slogans about a "multiethnic paradise" based on experiences in Sarajevo. In much of Bosnia, especially rural Bosnia, there was a strong perception of group and a sense of group history. As one Serb told me about the countryside, "people were ready to take sides" there.[28] Although resentment and stigma may have been absent at the starting point of analysis, in Bosnia there were cleavages imbued with political meaning that were ripe for mobilization.

IV. RESENTMENT RISES: MOVEMENT FROM NRI TO RI

Slovenia had successfully left Yugoslavia in the summer of 1991. During the fall, the war in Croatia was raging.[29] In Bosnia, many actors began to consider the possibility and meaning of an independent Bosnia with a Muslim plurality. The issue was whether Serbs and Croats would become second-class citizens in a new Bosnia.

Bosnia's Serbian and Croatian residents had realistic reasons to anticipate status reduction in the new state. Although the Yugoslav Republic of Bosnia-Hercegovina had developed power-sharing formulas for maintaining balance among the three constituent nations, there was no guarantee that this would continue. In fact, Izetbegovic had explicitly ruled out group power-sharing in favor of "one person, one vote" political institutions sure to favor the Muslim plurality. Izetbegovic was, in effect, promising to overturn the consociational nature of Yugoslavian rule.

There were other problematic aspects of Izetbegovic's politics and background. In 1970, Izetbegovic wrote *The Islamic Declaration: A Programme of the Islamisation of Muslims and Muslim Peoples*. This work stated that the "attainment of the Islamic order is a sacrosanct goal which cannot be overridden by any vote."[30] In 1990, Izetbegovic's political party – the Party of Democratic Action (SDA) – became the first openly Islamic party in post–Second World War Yugoslavia.[31] Although the SDA did not openly seek a program of dominance, some of its statements regarding the takeover of power appeared to embrace such a position. As Xavier Bougarel has summarized:

(T)he political project of the SDA has always revolved around three main goals: the sovereignty of the Bosnian Muslim nation, the independence and territorial integrity of Bosnia-Hercegovina and the territorial autonomy of Sandjak. Together, these three objectives comprise what could be called the <<greater Muslim>> project of the SDA:

---

[28] KU 4/12/08.
[29] See Chapter 7 for a review of these events.
[30] Aleksandar Pavkovic, "Anticipating the Disintegration: Nationalisms in the Former Yugoslavia, 1980–1990," *Nationalities Papers* (1997) 25: 427–40. Quotation is from p. 435.
[31] For an overview of Bosnian Islam in the 1990s, see Xavier Bougarel, "Cultural Identity or Political Ideology? Bosnian Islam since 1990," paper presented for the Annual Convention of the Association for the Study of Nationalities, Columbia University, New York, April 15–17, 1999.

a state composed of Bosnia-Hercegovina and Sandjak, in which the Muslims would be the majority, and the Serbs and Croats would be reduced to national minorities.[32]

In its effort to establish a Muslim majority status, the SDA urged Muslim participation in the 1991 census with the slogan, "On our numbers depend our rights." With the historical baggage of the Ottoman Empire and the political victory of an Islamically defined and oriented political party, many Serbs and Croats foresaw the unpleasant possibility of political subordination to an ethnic group that was not even recognized as a nation until 1968.[33]

Not many people recognize that Serbs and Croats were already work-ing for autonomy before war broke out. Between September 12 and 20 in 1991, months before the outbreak of war, Serbian political actors created Serbian autonomous oblasts (SAOs) across the country (the Eastern and Old Hercegovina SAO, the Bosanska Krajina SAO, the Romanija SAO, the North-east Bosnia SAO).[34] Serbs also formed a Serbian National Council and, in October, an Assembly of the Serb Nation of Bosnia-Hercegovina. In Novem-ber, Bosnian Serbs held a referendum in which almost all Serbs expressed a desire to remain in a rump Yugoslavia. Croats followed the Serbs' lead and established their own autonomous oblasts. By the spring of 1992, Serbian and Croatian nationalists had put down claims over most of Bosnia's territory.

Given the continuing crisis and erosion of state authority, militias developed among all three groups. The rise of Serbian militias is well known. Croats deve-loped a Croatian Defense Force. Muslims organized the Bosnian Muslim Green Beret force, which totaled up to 40,000 members at the outbreak of hostili-ties, as well as the Patriotic League, with more than 100,000 members.[35] The Bosnian Interior Minister estimated that 250,000 to 300,000 Bosnian citizens were armed by the first months of 1992.[36]

Facing these potentially destructive political and military forces, the Muslim political leadership had several choices:

(1) They could choose to remain in a rump Yugoslavia and dispel any chance of war
(2) They could work toward a cantonal arrangement that might satisfy Serbian and Croatian desires for autonomy
(3) They could continue to push for an independent, unified, and fully sovereign Bosnia

[32] Ibid., p. 12.
[33] Pavkovic, "Anticipating the Disintegration: Nationalisms in the Former Yugoslavia, 1980–1990," summarizes, "In this context, the affirmation of an Islamic religiously-defined identity in politics was viewed, by many Serbs and Croats, as a drive towards renewed political and economic dominance of the Muslims over the other nations in Bosnia-Hercegovina," from p. 436.
[34] Steven L. Burg and Paul S. Shoup, *The War in Bosnia and Hercegovina: Ethnic Conflict and International Intervention* (Armonk, NY: M. E. Sharpe, 1999), p. 73.
[35] Ibid., pp. 74–5.
[36] Ibid., p. 75.

As discussed in Chapter 7, Izetbegovic and his allies chose the third option. The choice was driven by two calculations. Neither the first nor the second choice would produce and guarantee the status position for Muslims sought by Izetbegovic and others. They would rather take chances on an outbreak of violence than be under the Serbs. Second, the strategy assumed a good chance of Western help or intervention.[37] Both Izetbegovic and Haris Silajdzic quite explicitly stated that they based their choice on expectations that the West would support an independent Bosnia. As Silajdzic states, "My main priority in the whole strategy was to get Western governments and especially the United States to get involved, because (Serbs) had the whole army."[38]

For reasons tied to resentment, the strategy was bound to fail. Many Serbs were not going to accept the possibility of becoming a people subordinate to the Muslims. Perhaps war could have been averted if a federal, consociational system had been created to assuage Serbian resentments, but most Serbs were unlikely to willingly accept a Muslim plurality. As Nikola Koljevic, one of two Serbian members of the State Presidency and a moderate, summed up as the issue of independence was coming to a head:

I can understand the Muslim need or fear, if you wish, of Serbian and Croatian domination, and I can see that quite clearly. But you cannot make up for that by placing Serbs in the position of a minority. I say to them that is must be decided whether it will be a unified Bosnia that will not be absolutely sovereign, or a sovereign Bosnia that will not be absolutely unified, meaning a Muslim Bosnia. Let a Muslim Bosnia be sovereign. Can Bosnia be both sovereign and unified, integral, at the same time? Hardly.[39]

As cantonal and confederal solutions became unlikely, the prevailing perception that one side would dominate the other became pervasive. Many Serbs asked themselves why Serbs, as a "real nation," should ever be dominated by Muslims, especially when Serbs had control of superior force. But neither did the Muslims wish to be dominated. Led by Izetbegovic, the Muslims chose option three from the list, hoping that the West would deter the outbreak of violence, or intervene if violence occurred.

V. RI TO R2: FROM RESENTMENT TO VIOLENCE

The rapid path to high levels of violence surprised almost everyone. Few realized how quickly lines between sides were drawn. Bosnia was no longer a resentment-free place; impending status questions had transformed the situation from NR1 to R1. The next movement would be toward violence.

---

[37] Alan Kuperman, "Suicidal Rebellions and the Moral Hazard of Humanitarian Intervention," *Ethnopolitics* (June 2005) 4: 149–73. See especially the series of statements of top Bosniak leaders on p. 158.

[38] Ibid., p. 158.

[39] This passage comes from Burg and Shoup, *The War in Bosnia and Hercegovina*, pp. 126–7. Burg and Shoup also provide a counter passage from Izetbegovic that reveals the diametrically opposed thinking between the two leaders.

On February 29/March 1, Bosnia held a referendum on independence, with nearly all Muslims and Croats voting yes and nearly all Serbs boycotting. The next day, barricades went up in Sarajevo. On March 3, Izetbegovic announced Bosnia's independence. Soon after, law and order began to break down across Bosnian localities. Local police forces began to split along ethnic lines.[40] The first battles usually took place between Serbs and Croats, groups that had already been fighting in Croatia. Fighting broke out in Bosanski Brod in early March, in the Doboj region during the second week of March, and then in Derventa in the third week. By the end of the month, Goradze and other localities had been sucked into the spreading violence.[41]

The situation had clearly passed into box R2. The question became whether it would pass into R3.

VI. R2 TO R3: LOW VIOLENCE TO HIGH VIOLENCE

Because they held the superior military position in the conflict, the initiative turned to the Serbs. They had at least four strategic choices:

(1) Attempt to deescalate violence and return the contest to R1
(2) Do nothing with the game, possibly remaining at an equilibrium of low-level, localized violence
(3) Attempt to escalate to R3 through discriminate, targeted violence
(4) Escalate to R3 using indiscriminate violence

The Serbs chose the last option. In early April, the first massacre occurred when Arkan's paramilitary forces came in to support local units in Bijeljina. A month and a half later, in the midst of escalation across Bosnia, General Ratko Mladic took over command of the Bosnian Serb Republic's newly formed army. In the next few months, indiscriminate violence against civilians occurred in many of

---

[40] One high-ranking police official told me that police forces had a strong ethnic component dating back to the Second World War. In his narrative, he stressed that many Serbian Partisan families in Bosnia had suffered large losses during the war. In the decade following the war, the Communist Party placed many members of these Serbian families, some of whom had been orphaned during the war, in the Bosnian police force. The Communists believed that their experience and sense of victimization would make them especially loyal police officers. These police officers held a sharp sense of their ethnicity due to the ethnically based fighting in Bosnia during the Second World War and their sense of family victimhood. The respondent believed that members of the police in Bosnia had always held a heightened sense of ethnicity and history and that they were often the basis of the first local mobilizations for violence. QE 4/14/08.

[41] See Burg and Shoup, *The War in Bosnia and Hercegovina,* for a detailed discussion in their chapter "Descent into War." Stathis Kalyvas and Nicholas Sambanis provide an overview of the Bosnian Civil War in a case study used to assess the work of Collier and Hoeffler. See "Bosnia's Civil War: Origins and Violence Dynamics," in Paul Collier and Nicholas Sambanis eds., *Understanding Civil War: Evidence and Analysis,* Volume 2 (Washington, DC: World Bank Publications, 2005), pp. 191–229. The authors describe the Bosnian Civil War as a symmetric nonconventional war, "a type characterized by a mix of regular and irregular forces fighting in territory defined by clear frontlines and a political context shaped by state collapse. These wars tend to generate high levels of violence" (p. 212).

Bosnia's 109 municipalities. Similar methods were used in most cases. Serbian militias, often helped by locals, would gain control of a locality. Sometimes the action was preceded by bombardment from regular forces, aimed to soften up resistance. After the regular force took control of the locality, non-Serbs were indiscriminately killed, deported, or sent to internment camps. Often, the violence was laced with acts of humiliation and also the destruction of religious symbols, such as mosques.

The variation in violence across time and across municipalities is revealing. Almost half of all victims died during the first three months of the war;[42] violence was highest in ethnically polarized municipalities, that is, where two groups faced each other in roughly equal numbers;[43] violence was high in areas bordering Serbia and along the line between what became Republika Srpska and the Federation.[44] This pattern of violence illustrates the political program behind it. Serbian actions seem clearly aimed at quickly clearing areas that were strategically crucial to constructing a viable Serbian entity. The violence was aimed at "cleansing" the most contested areas (those where Muslims and Croats could maintain majorities and control of local governments) and "cleansing" the crucial areas along the borders that would define the new entity. This strategy had its counterpart in Croatia, where Serbian forces had gained control of key swaths of territory and then the UN had come in to freeze those gains. As Burg and Shoup summarize, "(D)evelopments in Croatia encouraged Belgrade to engage in a quick and bitter campaign of ethnic cleansing once Bosnia declared its independence, and then present the world community with a *fait accompli*, hoping the UN would then step in to ratify this change."[45]

The strategic choice of indiscriminate violence was shaped by a few key factors. The Serbian side did not have overwhelming numbers of soldiers. Furthermore, the balance over time would not be in the Serbs' favor. As Chip Gagnon and others have pointed out, the Milosevic regime had tremendous difficulty enlisting soldiers from Serbia proper.[46] For example, General Kadijevic had hoped to raise five brigades for the campaign in Croatia, but the JNA could not raise even two. On the other hand, Bosnian Serbs joined up in far greater numbers.[47] Significant numbers of locals participated in the

[42] See Tokaca's data from the Research and Documentation Center.
[43] See Stefano Costalli and Francesco Moro, "A Local-Level Analysis of Violence and Intervention in Bosnia's Civil War," unpublished manuscript.
[44] Ibid.
[45] Burg and Shoup, *The War in Bosnia and Hercegovina*, p. 126.
[46] See Gagnon, *The Myth of Ethnic War*, p. 2.
[47] Burg and Shoup, p, 83. The fact that Bosnian Serbs joined up whereas Serbs from Serbia proper did not support the argument that resentment drove behavior in Bosnia. Only Serbs in Bosnia would be affected by perceived status changes in Bosnia. Serbs in Belgrade, Novi Sad, and other cities in Serbia proper would never personally experience those political changes. A theory based on the emotion of resentment stands opposite theories that rely on some form of reference to a vague nationalist dogma. A theory based on resentment is linked to actual lived experience. I wrote extensively on resentment-driven rural Bosnian Serbs in *Understanding Ethnic Violence:*

violence. There was also no shortage of paramilitary forces. The strategic choice would need to fit the nature of these personnel.

Crucially, the strategy required rapid population change. The strategy did not depend on killing enemy fighters as much as driving the entire population out of contested and strategically important regions. The goal was to quickly create "facts on the ground," particularly facts showing that key areas were indisputably controlled and populated by Serbs.

The choice of indiscriminate violence avoided the manpower constraints and fit the goals of the Serbian side. The strategy did not require an advantage in terms of disciplined and professional soldiers. Militias could easily fit into the operation to provide a role in attacking and terrorizing the population; locals could provide much of the needed information and manpower.

More importantly, indiscriminate violence is a relatively low cost way to create fear. To recall from the second chapter, political entrepreneurs generate fear in order to trigger the action tendency of flight. By employing indiscriminate violence, Serbian forces could produce a situation where no Bosniak or Croat could be sure that he would not be caught up in sweeps or arbitrarily killed by a Serbian paramilitary unit. The only sure way to be safe, and to ensure the safety of one's family, was to pick up a few valuables and immediately flee. Given the hundreds of thousands of refugees and displaced persons in Bosnia, the desired effect was undoubtedly achieved. Furthermore, the boundaries created through indiscriminate violence, ethnic flight, and demographic homogenization became the basis of the Dayton Accords.

Despite a benign starting position, emerging resentments helped move the game from NR1 to R1; the use of indiscriminate violence and fear drove the game to R3.[48] The West then intervened to change the game back into a nonviolent form. In effect, they hoped to structure a game within R1, to use a set of sticks and carrots to create a functioning and sovereign Bosnian state.

Fear, Hatred, and Resentment in Twentieth Century Eastern Europe (Cambridge: Cambridge University Press, 2002), pp. 231–42.

[48] The Bosnian war was of course an extremely complex conflict. The fighting differed from region to region, as did alliances and cooperation among the warring groups. In the finishing stages of this book, an investigator had recently found 18 notebooks of General Mladic's wartime diaries and piles of documents and computer memory sticks. Most relevant to the analysis here are some of the uncovered conversations between high-level Serbian and Croatian commanders. As a *New York Times* article summarizes, "These include what prosecutors describe as details of secret deals between Serbs and Croats to divide Bosnia and drive the Muslims out of many areas. General Mladic recorded a meeting on Feb. 3, 1994, also including Mr. Karadzic, in which the Bosnian Croat leader Jadranko Prlic is quoted as saying: 'We need to agree on 2–3 things today. Muslims are the common enemy. There are 2–3 ways to keep them down (first, militarily, by breaking their backbone).' At another planning session, General Mladic notes that Slobodan Praljak, a Croatian now on trial for war crimes, says: 'If you kill 50,000 Muslims more, you will not achieve anything. Their population will quickly recover. The population should be exchanged.'" See Marlise Simons, "Data on Balkan Wars Found in Home of Suspect," *New York Times*, July 10, 2010. I examine Serb–Croat collaboration in more detail in *Understanding Ethnic Violence*.

The game did not go quite according to plan. The next sections work to explain the second and third puzzles from the chapter's first section – why we see only inconsistent progress after fifteen years of Western intervention.

VII. MOVEMENT BACK TO R1 AND THE INTRODUCTION OF THE BASIC GAME

A. Basic Game: First Stage

The first stage in the Basic Game is to end the anarchic features of an *N*-person assurance game that characterize social breakdown during civil war. The Bosnian case, in contrast to many other civil wars, did not exhibit these anarchic features. At the end of the war, Serbian forces faced off against the forces of a Bosnian–Croatian alliance across demarcated lines that would become the border between Republika Srspska (RS) and the Federation. The Dayton Accord (see Chapter 7 for background and a summary) ratified already existing spheres of control rather than working to establish control in the first place. Ethnic cleansing had homogenized much of Bosnia's territory and reduced the number of contestable, and potentially violent, hot spots. The war reduced the non-Serb population living in Republika Srpska from 46 percent to 3 percent.[49] Likewise, the Serbian population in the territory of the Federation fell from 17 percent to 3 percent.[50]

To ensure that the proposed lines of authority were peacefully maintained, a NATO-led Implementation Force (IFOR) composed of 60,000 multinational troops took over from UNPROFOR on December 20.[51] Their mission was to carry out disarmament and demobilization and to oversee basic tasks of occupation. By January 1996, IFOR had established a 4-kilometer-wide buffer zone between opposing armies, demobilized 300,000 fighters, and collected heavy weapons.[52] Establishing peace was not a major problem, especially given the deterrent effect of such a large peacekeeping force. Before yielding to an EU force in 2004, NATO troops would serve as peacekeepers in Bosnia for nine years without a single service-related fatality.[53]

Moreover, the Dayton Accord contained a Bosnian constitution in the form of Annex 4. Bosnia-Hercegovina was an internationally recognized state with a written set of rules (however problematic) from its inception. The fighting was over, but a new political struggle commenced.

[49] Elizabeth Pond, *Endgame in the Balkans: Regime Change, European Style* (Washington, DC: Brookings Institution, 2006), p. 151.
[50] On demographic homogenization and the reduction of chances for war, see Chaim Kaufmann, "Intervention in Ethnic and Ideological Civil Wars: Why One Can be Done and the Other Can't," *Security Studies* (1996): 62–100.
[51] With a population of 4.5 million, that comes down to one peacekeeper for every 75 citizens.
[52] Roland Paris, *At War's End: Building Peace after Civil Conflict* (Cambridge: Cambridge University Press, 2004), p. 100.
[53] Pond, *Endgame in the Balkans*, p. 161.

B. Basic Game: Second Stage

In practice, the construction of Bosnia was a Western project from the beginning. Everyone understood that the High Representative would be a European, that at least one German and one American would serve as chief deputies to the High Representative, and that the head of the OSCE mission would be an American.[54] Given this reality, I will use the terms "the West" and "the intervener" interchangeably.

To achieve peace, the West had to make a deal with nationalist leaders Slobodan Milosevic and Franjo Tudjman. The Dayton Accord needed to give these players much of what they wanted to draw them into the game. In effect, the Dayton Accord created two countries (with the Federation further broken into ten cantons) within the boundaries of Bosnia. However, the West believed it had the power to shape the game and push players toward the creation of a single, more unified state.

As in other Balkan cases, this contest could be viewed as a simple iterated PD between two players. In this case, the most important players were the Bosnian Serbs of Republika Srpska and the Bosniaks of the Federation (the Croats of the Federation playing an increasingly secondary role). Although the playing of the game would become incredibly complex, its essence was simple: the West would use sticks and carrots to gradually create a functioning Bosnian state through centralization of governance. On issue after issue, the West would attempt to change the payoff structures of the actors from those of the PD to those of the assurance game by raising the value of mutual cooperation above that of all other outcomes. Then the task simply becomes one of coordination and formal institution-building. Various governance issues would be taken up sequentially. A centralized functioning state would emerge after several rounds of play. That was the theory.[55]

C. The Specifics of the Game

Given the West's overarching goals, cooperation in this game meant agreeing to proposals to centralize powers on an issue-to-issue basis. Defection meant rejecting and obstructing moves to develop a centralized government. Defection could be accomplished in several ways. The Dayton Accord provided actors with two formal ways to block a proposal. Each of the three constituent peoples could use a "vital national interest veto." Also, under the Dayton constitution's "entity voting" provision, two-thirds of the representatives of any entity can block any legislation.

---

[54] Elizabeth M. Cousens, "From Missed Opportunities to Overcompensation: Implementing the Dayton Agreement on Bosnia," in Stephen John Stedman, Donald Rothchild, and Elizabeth M. Cousens eds., *Ending Civil Wars: The Implementation of Peace Agreements* (Boulder, CO: Lynne Rienner Publishers, 2002), pp. 531–66. See p. 544 on Western dominance.

[55] For a broad study of the success and failure of various reforms in Bosnia, see Andrew Radin, "Shh . . . The Locals Can Hear Us Arguing: International Reform Efforts in Post-Dayton Bosnia," unpublished manuscript.

A more procedural, but commonly used method of defection is "strategic absenteeism." As many governmental bodies have complex rules on quorums, groups can block action simply by failing to show up. Serbs often used this tactic in the Council of Ministers. Some instances of absenteeism in Bosnia were quite striking. For instance, after being elected the Serbian member of Bosnia's collective presidency, Momcilo Krajisnik chose not to show up at his own inauguration ceremony.[56] Another form of defection involved the blatant breaking of taboos. The West drew three lines in the sand, one for each of Bosnia's groups: (1) Croats could not raise the issue of a third entity (to make them equal to the RS); (2) Serbs could not raise the issue of secession; (3) Bosniaks could not develop a procedure enabling them to outvote the other groups. Players who wished to wreck the progress of ongoing legislation could do so by threatening these actions, thereby throwing the whole system into temporary turmoil. Finally, entities could simply choose not to implement laws passed at the state level.

Western interveners clearly believed that they had the resources to prevent defection and induce cooperation. This confidence rested on a few basic assumptions. First, the West believed that a new set of actors favorable to cooperation would quickly emerge to play the game. In the West's view, "bad guys" started and sustained the civil war, but postwar democracy would eliminate them. Freed from their wartime blinders, citizens empowered with democratic rights would place their pocketbooks and children's future ahead of the counterproductive agendas of the nationalist parties and their war criminal leaders and vote them out of office. Moderates, through electoral competition, would replace ultranationalists. Second, the war had so ravaged Bosnia that economic "carrots" would be a powerful tool in transforming the game. In game terms, the offer of economic incentives should easily raise the value of mutual cooperation (R) above that of nationalist competition (seeking the T value) or continuation of the status quo and stagnation (P). Third, the "carrot" of economic integration with the European Union would act as a powerful enticement.

The game did not work out as planned, at least not on all rounds of the game. To understand how the game did play out, it is necessary to consider the nature of emotion resources in the situation represented by box R1. In this cell, the emotion of resentment is present,[57] but not the emotion of contempt. In this situation, members of different groups do not wish to avoid all contact with opposing groups, as in the case with contempt, but there is a visceral reaction to issues of political subordination. Actors driven by status concerns and the emotion of resentment will most vigorously oppose changes and legislation that would allow the opposing group to gain visible, day-to-day authority over their own group. Accordingly, a resentment-based view would make differing predictions on different issues of cooperation: resentment-driven actors should try to block police and judicial reforms that would allow members of the

[56] Cousens, "From Missed Opportunities to Overcompensation," p. 552.
[57] Hypothesized to be at a lower level than in R4 and especially R7.

opposing group to directly impose authority on the in-group's territory. In the Bosnian case, the resentment-driven Serbs would be expected to vehemently oppose any changes or legislation that would allow Bosniaks to enter the RS in positions of authority, such as police and judges. Note that the territorial division of Bosnia, with its creation of the RS entity in the Dayton Accord, substantially differentiates the Bosnian case from Macedonia. In Bosnia, there has been a clear "red line" at which one group can be seen crossing over into the other group's jurisdiction. Furthermore, the Serbs in Bosnia, operating from a position of relative strength and with Serbia next door, were not inclined to try to mitigate resentment, as was the case with Macedonian ethnic actors.

On other issues on which political status and the possibility of political domination are not in play, political elites will have a more difficult time mobilizing opposition or finding support for political provocation. Accordingly, on issues without clear status implications, political entrepreneurs, unable to count on resentment as a sure resource, would be more likely to play cooperation.

These points can be translated into game terms. The PD assumes that the preference ordering for both players is $T > R > P > S$. However, most Serbs liked the Dayton Accord status quo, which effectively produced Serbian self-rule and precluded Bosniak political dominance. When the intervener brought changes to Dayton that could possibly change ethnic status relations, many Serbs preferred any outcome of defection (T or P) to cooperation. Accordingly, on some key issues the Serbian preference ordering was $T > P > R > S$.[58] On other issues, the Serbian preference order was that of the PD ($T > R > P > S$). With the latter ordering, intervener sticks and carrots would be better able to raise the value of R above T to transform the situation to an assurance game along the lines of the Basic Game.

Although the Bosniaks did arguably possess a general PD ordering, the situation was probably more complex for Bosniaks than this simple representation can capture. Serbs killed tens of thousands of Bosniak civilians. In the Bosniak view, and that of many others, the Serbs committed the worst act of genocide in post–World War II history with the mass killings in Srebrenica. The Serbs indiscriminately shelled Sarajevo. Not surprisingly, the Bosniaks were filled with anger.

To recall, anger heightens desire for punishment against a specific actor. Under the influence of anger, individuals need to specify a perpetrator and seek retribution. Anger distorts information in predictable ways, producing attention funneling; under the influence of anger, individuals "perceive new events and objects in ways that are consistent with the original cognitive-appraisal dimensions of the emotion."[59] That is, the emotion of anger justifies the desire for punishment and pushes the individual to seek information that will further justify vengeance. Anger can create an obsession with retaliation.

---

[58] This ordering is the same as a contempt preference ordering.

[59] J.S. Lerner and D. Keltner, "Beyond Valence: Toward a Model of Emotion-Specific Influences on Judgment and Choice," *Cognition and Emotion* (2000) 14.

Although anger fades over time, Bosniaks have been continuously confronted with vivid images and events that kept the cognitive antecedents of anger alive. Many Serbian war criminals remained at large for years, Karadzic until 2008 and Mladic still in 2010. Moreover, the very existence of the RS, an entity founded on genocide in the eyes of Bosniaks, was a reminder of the victimhood and humiliation of Bosniaks.

The West may have assumed that economic incentives would be enough to sway Bosniaks to cooperation. However, the case demonstrates that economic carrots cannot always push the R value above the T value. After all, from the Bosniak perspective, was a movement toward "mutual cooperation" (R) really just? Why should the perpetrator get the same deal as the victim? A just solution would not preserve the group privileges of genocidal actors in the way that the Dayton Accord did. Rather, justice should require the perpetrator to make sacrifices. Justice should require the international community to force the Serbs to give up their ill-gotten entity. Justice should require the Serbs to accept the S value and accept a "state of citizens," even if that produced political power for the Bosniak plurality.

In addition to problems involved with these preference functions, the West's strategic choices were limited by the nature of the Dayton Accord. Because the constitution itself formed a plank of the Dayton Accord (Annex 4), the West (obligated to uphold and implement the Accord) could not unilaterally change any element of Bosnia's constitution.[60] They could only encourage local actors to make such changes themselves. In game terms, this fact constrained the West from imposing certain "sucker" payoffs for recalcitrant actors. For instance, the intervention regime could not unilaterally change the structure of the legislature.

VIII. THE PROGRESSION OF THE BASIC GAME

The Western goal was to erode entity powers in favor of centralized ones by taking on governance issues sequentially. The history of this effort can be broken down into four general periods.

A. 1995–8: Beginning Years

The intervention regime first took on freedom of movement (which required a new system of automobile license plates that did not give away one's area of residence), currency, telecommunications, and other reforms that helped improve daily life across all of Bosnia. On these issues, there were some successes. The interveners also took on the issue of returns, although with little success.

---

[60] For a discussion of these limits, see Zoran Pajic, "Bosnia and Hercegovina: A Statehood Crossroads," in Stefano Bianchini, Joesph Marko, and Milica Uvalic eds., *Regional Cooperation, Peace Enforcement, and the Role of the Treaties in the Balkans* (Bologna: Longo Editore Ravenna, 2007), pp. 79–91.

During this period, the West employed very basic economic and political incentives. For example, in 1997 the Open Cities Initiative offered increased donor funds to municipalities that were receptive to minority returns.[61] The interveners also tried to reward "friends" who were viewed as more likely to cooperate. Roland Paris summarizes an important 1996 case where the more moderate Biljana Plavsic (later convicted of crimes at the Hague) faced off against hard-line Karadzic supporters: "International peacebuilding agencies and Western governments encouraged Plavsic to defy Karadzic and his supporters by providing millions of dollars in financial assistance to Plavsic loyalists and by funding aid projects in parts of Republika Srpska where Plavsic had the strongest support, while denying similar funding to areas controlled by Karadzic."[62]

B. 1998–2003: Recognition of Fundamental Problems and the Introduction of the Bonn Powers

It did not take long, however, to see that this incremental and fine-tuned sticks-and-carrots strategy would only go so far. Despite assumptions about elections elevating moderate leaders, nationalists won almost every election in the immediate years after Dayton. More shockingly yet, voters elected some leaders who were clearly set against the Western project. The election of Nikola Poplasen to the RS Presidency over Plavsic in September 1998 jolted the West. A collection of passages from the *New York Times* article on the election captures the West's reaction:[63]

If Poplasen has won, it means the Bosnian Serbs are telling the West, "We don't care about you or your money or your quaint ideas about reconciliation with Muslims or Croats," said a European diplomat, who termed the unofficial results "staggering."

"The West offered an implicit deal to the Bosnian Serb people," said a senior European diplomat. "The deal was: Life will get much better for you. You won't be an isolated, hated gang on the edge of Europe. You can keep this thing called the Serb republic if that makes you feel better, even though it is the bankrupt half of a poor country. But in return you have to start thinking like modern Europeans. It looks as if they have rejected that deal, and things are going to get bad for them and for us."

A European official in the Bosnian Serb republic said he expected most European countries to scale back or end projects there. "How can we possibly justify doing otherwise if a man like Poplasen is in charge?" he said. "Let them have a year or two of suffering to see if they change their minds."

Hard-line actors remained, but more disturbingly, voters, under free elections, did not seem to value the promised payoffs for mutual cooperation more than the present reality of continued mutual defection.

---

[61] Cousens, "From Missed Opportunities to Overcompensation," p. 549.
[62] Paris, *At War's End*, 103.
[63] Mike O'Connor, "Serbs in Bosnia Appear to Shun Favorite of U.S." *New York Times*, September 17, 1998.

If carrots were not working, then the West would have to use a bigger stick. In December 1997, the so-called Bonn powers were instituted. Although unable to change the constitution, the West could use these newly enunciated powers to remove individuals from office without appeal, even those democratically elected, and to pass some laws by decree. In October 1999, the Bonn powers were invoked to remove Poplasen from power. After nationalists made gains in the 2002 elections, High Representative Paddy Ashdown increasingly employed Bonn powers. In 2004, Ashdown dismissed sixty officials from the RS in one swoop, including the speaker of the Bosnian Serb National Assembly. The West had decided to create democracy through clearly nondemocratic means. Bosnia increasingly became a Western protectorate.

C. The Promise of EU Membership: 2003

Along with the bigger stick came a different kind of carrot. In 2003, the EU made incorporation of Bosnia an official policy. The reality of possible EU membership for Bosnia sank in. All sides could agree on the desirability of accession; being connected to Europe would bring clear benefits. For most Serbs in the RS, it was better to be connected to Brussels than to Sarajevo. With the EU officially taking over from the UN, the West could play the accession card with increasingly powerful effect.

The combination of stick and carrot did move the game. By 2006, the Bosnian state developed eight state ministries in the following areas: communications and transport, civilian affairs, human rights and refugees, justice, defense, foreign affairs, foreign trade, and finances. In practice, only three critical areas functioned in a centralized manner as of 2008 – defense,[64] indirect taxation (VAT), and the high judiciary.[65] However, progress was being made on several issues that did not directly involve a change in local ethnic group status relations. The next question is why that progress stalled in the second half of the decade.

D. Stalemate

Richard Holbrooke and Paddy Ashdown, perhaps the two foreign diplomats most influential in Bosnia's birth and political evolution, wrote in late 2008 that "the country is in real danger of collapse."[66] In their article they saw the Bosnian Serbs and Bosniaks as engaging in mutually reinforcing and counterproductive actions. In the authors' view, Milorad Dodik, as a the representative

---

[64] Although a national army was created, integration was not by individual but by ethnic unit, thus avoiding subordination issues.

[65] This statement is based on two interviews with high-ranking foreign diplomats. KH 4/17/08 and FL 4/18/08.

[66] Paddy Ashdown and Richard Holbrooke, "A Bosnian Powder Keg," *The Guardian*, October 22, 2008.

of Bosnian Serbs, had "in two years, reversed much of the real progress in Bosnia over the past 13, crucially weakened the institutions of the Bosnian state, and all but stopped the country's evolution into a functioning (and EU-compatible) state." As Holbrooke and Ashdown point out, Dodik was able to prevent centralization and maintain the Dayton status quo by being able to employ the secession card. As was mentioned, the progression of the game could be halted, at least temporarily, by simply raising this taboo issue. On the other hand, the authors note that Dodik's intransigence is complemented by that of his Bosniak counterpart, Haris Silajdzic. The latter "has stressed the need to abolish the two entities that make up Bosnia, to create one non-federal country." Taking the two together, Holbrooke and Ashdown summarize: "Dodik professes to respect Dayton and Silajdzic wishes to revise it, but both men are violating its basic principle: a federal system within a single state. This toxic interaction is at the heart of today's Bosnian crisis."

Although Holbrooke and Ashdown's argument is accurate, their focus is not broad enough to explain the strategic choices of Dodik and Silajdzic fully. To understand these choices, one needs to examine the emotional resources at play.

The change in issues at play goes far in explaining Serbian actions. In earlier rounds, the issues involved license plates and border control. In 2005, the EU brought up the issue of police reform.[67] To meet EU standards necessary for concluding a Stabilization and Association Agreement, Bosnia would have to meet three criteria: (1) the state, rather than the entity, would control the budget and laws on police matters; (2) policing would need to be free of politics in hiring, etc.; (3) police districts would be drawn on technical grounds. In effect, the West required the abolishment of entity police forces and the creation of larger, more centralized police districts that would cut across entity boundaries.

For many Serbs, the war had been fought to prevent Muslims from being in positions of authority over Serbs. Although earlier reforms did not bring this possibility to the fore, police reform certainly did. The RS police were the foundation of Bosnian Serb autonomy. Serbs would police other Serbs. The proposed police reform, especially in its plans for redistricting, would allow Bosniak police to operate on RS territory. When the issue first came up in 2005, the Republika Srpska Parliament voted against the bill 56–10, issuing a statement that "Any model of (new) organization of police in Bosnia, whose police districts would cross the interentity border line is unacceptable."[68] At this point, and especially on this issue, Serbian politicians could rely on resentment as a powerful resource.

The West believed it was only a matter of time, accompanied by the proper penalties, before the Serbs would cave in. The statement of the British ambassador to Bosnia was typical: "So police reform will happen. The question is whether it happens quickly, and leads to benefits. Or slowly. The slower it

---

[67] For summaries of the attempts at police reform, see International Crisis Group Europe Report No. 164, "Bosnia's Stalled Police Reform: No Progress, No EU," September 6, 2005.

[68] Cited in EUBusiness, September 14, 2005.

goes, the more negative measures there will be against those who do not fulfill their obligations to implement Dayton and make progress down the road to Europe."[69]

In 2007, the High Representative Miroslav Lajcak believed he could counter Serbian resistance through the use of Bonn powers and threats to withdraw the EU carrot. In October, Lajcak went on the offensive. He announced that "it has become quite certain that BiH politicians have chosen isolation instead of integration, and that they have rejected (the) European perspective of the country. That is a devastating fact for this state."[70] Lajcak then initiated a "shock and awe" campaign with a series of edicts meant to bring the weight of the High Representative down on reform opponents.[71] The first edict aimed to eliminate the possibility of defecting from the game through strategic absenteeism in the Council of Ministers. Either the members of the body would change their own rules or they would face the imposition of Bonn powers. Milorad Dodik, then in control in the RS, did not back down, and threatened a boycott. As the crisis continued, Dodik made barely veiled threats to call for a referendum on RS secession. Although Lajcak did not back down, his superiors did. Javier Solana, the EU's Common Foreign and Security Policy head, decided to defuse the situation. Members of Bosnia's governing coalition signed a declaration that made some relatively minor reforms while leaving the entity police forces essentially intact. In a face-saving measure, the EU declared the reforms sufficient for the signing of the Stabilization and Association Agreement. The EU failed to carry out the threat of withdrawing the EU carrot.

The Serbian side played defection and got away with it. Despite the High Representative's threats, Serbs maintained control over the core institution of RS autonomy and did not forfeit the EU carrot. Dodik could play such a bold game and win, I would argue, because he could rely on Serbian resentment to block this particular reform. He would receive little pressure to cave in from other Serbian political leaders or the general population and his electoral base. He could not have relied so heavily on this resource in opposition to other reforms. The problem for the West was that the Basic Game had reached a stage where the most sensitive issue areas were bound to come up. The West's system of sticks and carrots, even with the EU carrot as part of the mix, would have to find a way around the powerful sway of the emotion of resentment if the game were to progress all the way to a centralized EU-ready state.

The Bosniak side also contributed to the politics of stalemate in the period 2006–10. As Holbrooke and Ashdown point out, Silajdzic's calls for the abolishment of the RS are a political nonstarter. It is not only the Serbs who would reject that change out of hand, but the West as well. An ICG report sums up the

---

[69] Statement of Matthew Rycroft, British Ambassador to Bosnia-Hercegovina, September 22, 2005.

[70] International Crisis Group Europe Report No. 198, "Bosnia's Incomplete Transition: Between Dayton and Europe," March 9, 2009, p. 11. The report is citing Lajcak's speech in Banja Luka of October 18, 2007.

[71] ICG, "Bosnia's Incomplete Transition," p. 11. See pp. 12–14 for a more complete summary of Lajcak's series of edicts.

role of Silajdzic, and his Party for Bosnia and Hercegovina (SBiH), in helping to create and perpetuate political stalemate:

> The SBiH seems untroubled by the lack of Serbian support for its major positions and uninterested in seeking common ground. Though Serb votes are required for constitutional or institutional reform, this is not the party's primary concern. A sympathetic observer believes Silajdzic is holding out until the international community, led by the Obama administration, realizes Bosnia is in crisis and intervenes to replace the Dayton order with a new constitution without entities. . . . It is no small irony that a party staking its hopes on international intervention attracts broad condemnation from foreign officials. Indeed, a seasoned diplomat commented that Silajdzic's party "was living in a make-believe world."[72]

Silajdzic and other SBiH members have held out hopes that the International Court of Justice would make rulings, especially on genocide conventions, that would delegitimate the RS and help lead to its abolishment.

Silajdzic's fury over the very existence of the RS as a state based on genocide helped scuttle possible solutions on police reform. At one point Dodik explored the possibility of a version of reform that would enhance state control of the RS police and approached Haris Silajdzic with a deal. Silajdzic rejected the offer on the grounds that it would allow the RS police to retain their name, which, in turn, would require Bosniaks to recognize the RS as a permanent part of Bosnia, rather than a temporary one. This demonstrates the force of anger. Having to deal with a "genocidal entity" (the RS), some Bosniak political leaders have decided to act more as prosecutors than politicians, foregoing possible deals to pursue punishment.

E. Resentment and Anger in Combination

The interplay of resentment and anger in Bosnia goes far to explain the halting nature of progress in Bosnian state-building and the almost total absence of progress in building any kind of new common Bosnian identity.

Consider the case of the Ferhadija Mosque in Banja Luka, an internationally recognized cultural heritage site built during the sixteenth century. During the war, Serbian militias destroyed the mosque on May 7, 1993 (May 7 is the Serbian Orthodox holiday of St. George). Sixteen mosques dotted Banja Luka before the war, and all of them were leveled during the conflict. Eight years after the destruction of the Ferhadija Mosque, internationals and buses carrying about 1,000 former Muslim residents came to Banja Luka for a ceremony to mark plans to rebuild the Mosque and lay a cornnerstone. When they arrived, more than a thousand Serbian protestors met them.[73] The Bosnian Serbs chanted, "This is Serbia," and "We don't want a mosque," as well as invoking the name of Radovan Karadzic. As the event turned violent, the delegation (which included Jacques Klein, the head of the United Nations in

---

[72] ICG, "Bosnia's Incomplete Transition," p. 7.

[73] For details, see the *New York Times* article from May 8, 2001, "Bosnian Serb Crowd Beats Muslims at Mosque Rebuilding."

Bosnia) rushed to find protection in the nearby Islamic Center. After some beatings and burning of prayer rugs, several Serbs chased a pig onto the site where the mosque had stood.

Despite the ugliness of the event, even the most moderate Serbs I talked to in Banja Luka had a difficult time finding remorse. A Bosnian Serb who often worked closely with Bosniaks in Sarajevo in the cultural field related to me that the Bosniaks had entered Banja Luka "euphoristically." She blamed the international community for allowing Bosniaks to come into Banja Luka by the busload.[74]

While in Brcko, Bosnia, I asked people why the international community's rebuilding of mosques in Brcko went by without incident whereas in Banja Luka the Ferandija Mosque ceremony led to violence. One Serbian couple told me that the answer was simple: Banja Luka is a symbol of Serbdom. As they explained, Banja Luka is "ours" whereas Sarajevo is "theirs." Although Serbs admit that Sarajevo is "theirs," Bosniaks will not admit that Banja Luka is "ours," so they wish to challenge Serbs by bringing in busloads of Muslims under international cover. Brcko, on the other hand, possessed no such symbolic meaning. Brcko was a mixed town both before and after the war. In Brcko, religious sites possessed no powerful national meaning and could not be used effectively for provocations.[75]

The couple's views of "ours" and "theirs" matched Bosnian demographic realities. By 2006, the Sarajevo canton was estimated to be 80 percent Bosniak, 11 percent Serb, and 6 percent Croat, as compared to 49 percent/29 percent/7 percent numbers in the 1991 census.[76] Although recent census data did not exist, Bosniaks seemed nonexistent in Banja Luka. By the mid-2000s, demographics and politics had combined to form common-sense notions of "ours" and "theirs" that left little room for "Bosnia."

Events such as the Ferandija Mosque incident only served to harden the boundaries. Serb resentment over Bosniak intrusion led to attacks and sustained Bosniak anger. Although the emotion of anger fades, these incidents create the cognitive antecedents to perpetuation of anger. The Serbs are seen again as unrepentant perpetrators of genocidal acts. As one international told me, only half in jest, when Serbs encounter Bosniaks in the halls of government in Sarajevo, they are met with the greeting, "Good morning, you committed genocide against us."[77] Such is not the foundation for a common Bosnian nation.

IX. CONCLUSION: A FEW NOTES ON BRCKO AND THE FUTURE OF BOSNIA

For a political scientist interested in violence and reconstruction, Brcko is an extremely interesting place. As the municipality is the sole land corridor

---

[74] JU 4/16/08.

[75] Q and N 4/20/08.

[76] Nidzara Ahmetasevic, "Bosnian Returnees Quietly Quit Regained Homes," Institute for War and Peace Reporting, August 31, 2006.

[77] FL 4/18/08.

connecting the eastern and western halves of the RS, Brcko sits at the most important strategic location in all of Bosnia. Hence, during the war, Brcko was the site of continuous military contestation, accompanied by killing and displacement. Neither side could drive the other out of the municipality. A Bosniak–Croat alliance held the southern two-thirds of the district while the Serbs, bolstered by Serbian displaced persons flowing in from Jajce and other towns, came to compose more than 97 percent of the city proper's population.[78] No less than nineteen detention camps dotted the small area. Half of Brcko's homes were destroyed during the war.[79]

Not surprisingly, the postwar status of Brcko became the single most contentious issue at the end of the negotiations at Dayton. The Serbs wanted to connect the two halves of their entity, whereas the Bosniaks and Croats wished to absorb the municipality into the Federation as a means of preventing the RS from mobilizing for continued conflict.[80] In order to prevent the collapse of the negotiations, the parties agreed to turn the matter over to binding arbitration under UN arbitration rules. After three rounds of "awards" announced from 1997 to 1999, the Arbitral Tribunal created a territorial condominium under strict international supervision. The territory would be shared by both entities, but neither entity would possess administrative authority.

In reality, Brcko became something of a United States protectorate. Until 2004, the American administrator simply bypassed elections and appointed the mayor and all members of the assembly. Unlike the rest of Bosnia, constituent nations were granted no veto powers. Local neighborhood councils were abolished.[81] The United States also poured money into the district. Whereas in other areas of Bosnia the interveners forcibly evicted refugees from houses that they had occupied (a conflict-producing policy), in Brcko, the administration simply built new houses. While reconstructing a destroyed mosque, the administration also built a new Serbian Orthodox church, even though one had not been destroyed during the war. Most importantly, the U.S. interveners increased salaries far above any other area in Bosnia.[82]

[78] International Crisis Group Balkans Report No. 144, "Bosnia's Brcko: Getting In, Getting On, and Getting Out,", June 2, 2003, pp. 2–3. For an earlier ICG report, see International Crisis Group Bosnia Project Report No. 31, "Brcko: What Bosnia Could Be," February 10, 1998.

[79] Melissa Sinclair, "Brcko: International Incubation," in *Solutions for Northern Kosovo: Lessons Learned in Mostar, Eastern Slavonia, and Brcko* (Defense and Technology Paper 4), Hans Binnendijk, Charles Barry, Gina Cordero, Laura Peterson Nussbaum, and Melissa Sinclair, eds. (Washington, DC: National Defense University Center for Technology and National Security Policy, August 2006), pp. 41–9. See p. 41 on destruction of homes.

[80] The prewar population of Brcko was only 21 percent Serbian, according to the 1991 census (45 percent Bosniak and 25 percent Croat), figures providing support for the Federation position.

[81] Carl Dahlman and Gearoid O' Tuathail, "Bosnia's Third Space? Nationalist Separatism and International Supervision in Bosnia's Brcko District," *Geopolitics* (2006) 11: 651–75. See p. 669 on neighborhood councils.

[82] Funding was four times that of state institutions. See Dahlman and O' Tuathail, "Bosnia's Third Space?" p. 670.

Through this combination of protectorate powers and financial largess, Brcko became the most celebrated Western success story in all of the Balkans. As the ICG states:

Once seen as the most likely flashpoint for any renewed warfare in BiH, Brcko has since prospered to such an extent that it is regularly and rightly invoked as the shining example of international stewardship in BiH and as a model for emulation for the rest of the country.[83]

The ICG summary echoes what High Representative Ashdown stated in March 2003: "This city, once known as a 'black hole,' is steadily becoming a model for the whole of BiH. When the rest of the country accomplishes what has been accomplished here, BiH will be a much more developed country."[84]

Although Brcko contains only 2 percent of Bosnia's territory, an enormous amount has been written about it, often in comparison with the perceived "failed" case of special municipal government in Mostar.[85] I went to Brcko in the spring of 2008, partly for obvious professional reasons and partly for personal reasons. Brcko is my wife's grandmother's home town. Before she passed away in the mid-1990s, Baba Kata, as I knew her, would make me endless cups of Turkish coffee at my wife's family home near Chicago. Born around 1905, she told tales of her youth.[86] Baba Kata related a story about a young man who was so smitten by her beauty that he broke a bottle, cut his hand with the glass, dripped the blood on a handkerchief, and gave it to Baba Kata to demonstrate his passion for her. As I walked down Brcko's main boulevard, I imagined this scene playing out in one of the town's older buildings. I also knew something of the town's mixed ethnic heritage. Baba Kata's first name was Katica, recognizable to anyone from the region as a Catholic name. In fact, Baba Kata considered herself a Catholic Serb, a combination seen as a contradiction in terms today, but more possible back in the time when she was born, an era of Austrian political control. It was through Baba Kata's stories that I first learned about Brcko's ethnic diversity and rich history.

What I found in Brcko was a success story, but not one as straightforward as is often portrayed. First, it was difficult to separate out the positive institutional effects from the effects of higher salaries and funding. As one police officer told me, police salaries were high enough to deter anyone from making any trouble.[87] Everyone I talked with noted the pacifying effects of high

[83] International Crisis Group, "Bosnia's Brcko"; see the Executive Summary.
[84] Ibid, p. 1.
[85] See, among others, Florian Bieber, "Local Institutional Engineering: A Tale of Two Cities, Mostar and Brcko," in *International Peacekeepers* (Autumn 2005) 12 (No. 3): 420–33; Carl Dahlman and Gearoid O' Tuathail, "Bosnia's Third Space? Solutions for Northern Kosovo." Also see Michael W. Doyle and Nicholas Sambanis, *Making War and Building Peace: United Nations Peace Operations* (Princeton, NJ: Princeton University Press, 2006), pp. 231–43.
[86] The exact date of birth is unknown because documents were destroyed, and because Baba Kata was illiterate, she had no letters or diaries.
[87] 4/20/08.

salaries. Many residents had been displaced persons from other areas who found refuge in Brcko; others had suffered during the war. Few wanted to create any provocation that would interfere with their currently secure life.

More striking was the compartmentalization of life. Residents of Brcko had developed a set of norms to prevent possibilities of conflict. As I sat on the terrace of the Posavina Hotel, itself a reported site of massacres fifteen years earlier, people would point toward the main square and identify the cafes that Serbs frequented and the places where Bosniaks hung out. Informal "rules of engagement" governed many social interactions. At work, it was understood that no one should talk about ethnicity. Leaving work, most entered back into monoethnic personal worlds. In schools, the rules were more formalized. Students of all nationalities went to the same schools, but were segregated for activities that could cause friction.

Despite its relative success, Brcko is not a shining example of ethnic reconciliation. After the violence of the war, such reconciliation would be too much to expect. In light of emotion theory, though, compartmentalization of life could be seen as a very positive outcome, especially if the emotions of resentment and anger are the major sources of conflict. As opposed to contempt, both resentment and anger are predicted to fade over time. If interveners can create the opportunity for groups to develop their own "rules of engagement" to prevent conflict in the short or medium term, then the dissipation of these emotions might allow for a fuller form of reconciliation to occur in the not too distant future.

There is one problem in the logic, however. What if the level and nature of violence that took place in Bosnia created the cognitions that underlie ethnic stigmas? What if Bosniaks have come to see Serbs or Serbian culture as inherently genocidal? Then the game is no longer being played in Box R1. Then the forces of contempt, an emotion that does not predictably fade over time, come into play. The transformation of anger and resentment into contempt and hatred is not something we understand very well. The continued evolution of Bosnia provides a test.

17

Montenegro

Montenegro is a tiny country. Yet it provides some key methodological insights for this study. The Montenegrin case clearly differs from the rest of the former Yugoslavia in terms of violence and provocations. This small multiethnic entity did not experience protracted war (as in Croatia, Bosnia, and Kosovo) or violent escalation (as in South Serbia and Macedonia) or even a short secessionist war (as in Slovenia). Even as Montenegro seceded from its confederation with Serbia, politics remained remarkably civil. For the first time, part of the former Yugoslavia split off without bloodshed. The contrast with Bosnia could not be starker.

During the 1990s, political actors inside Montenegro looked to the West for signals to help guide their strategies. After the Kosovo intervention and the subsequent deepening of commitment to the region, the West brokered two major agreements: (1) the Belgrade Agreement of March 2002, which created the State Union of Serbia and Montenegro, a temporary political arrangement aimed to ease the possible separation of Montenegro from Serbia with minimum disruption to regional politics; (2) the 2001 Ulcinj Agreement, which, similarly to the Ohrid and Konculj agreement, aimed to address the status concerns of Montenegro's Albanian population. The implementation of both of these accords went according to plan. In terms of the more general dependent variable, the West accomplished its goals. In terms of the specific dependent variable, political actors did not meet Western intervention with violent tactics or even engage in significant nonviolent provocations.

There are some obvious reasons for these benign outcomes. First, Montenegro is a very small place, dependent on tourism for much of its income. Second, given the small size of the Albanian minority (5 percent), ethnic Albanian political entrepreneurs were not likely to mobilize violence in the way seen in Kosovo, Macedonia, and South Serbia (although the numbers in South Serbia were also small). Third, the interventions came after the West had firmly established a strong commitment to the region. Fourth, Milosevic was deposed in October 2000. Following his removal to the Hague, all sides, including the new leaders in Belgrade, were anxious to have good relations with Western powers.

Yet there is something more interesting going on with this case, especially in comparison with previous cases. The method of this work identifies lived experiences – status reversals, prejudice, violence – that leave residues in the form of emotions, which, in turn, can become political resources. These experiences are based on perceptions of group relationships: group X committed violence against my group; group Y has negative characteristics; group Z is unjustly dominant over my group. For much of Eastern Europe in modern history, perceptions of groups and group hierarchies have been relatively clear. Along the lines identified in the work of Ernest Gellner, the functions of modern state-building required language and education policies that served to separate and elevate some groups over others. The ethnofederal politics of the socialist regimes in the USSR, Yugoslavia, and Czechoslovakia acted to reinforce common sense notions of ethnic group identity. In the cases covered thus far, I have found perception of group and group hierarchy relatively unproblematic. I argued that perception of group was robust even in Bosnia, especially in rural Bosnia. But Montenegro is different. The question of "who is X and who is Y" played out differently there. The fluidity in identity among members of the dominant Slavic/Orthodox population – sometimes calling themselves Serbs, sometimes Montenegrins, and occasionally Yugoslavs – has been the most important factor preventing mobilization for violence. This fluidity has helped to create a wider set of political options conducive to smoother ethnic relations in the country overall.

I. WHO IS A SERB? WHO IS A MONTENEGRIN?

A. Background

In many ways, Montenegro is similar to the other cases in the Southern Subsystem. Its small population (620,145)[1] is a mix of Slavic/Orthodox, Muslim/Bosniak, and Albanian citizens. Like other areas, Montenegro is relatively poor, especially in the inland region, and known for its corruption.[2] On the other hand, Montenegro is also endowed with some unique features. The land and its leaders played a complicated game with the Ottomans over centuries that garnered and sustained an unusual measure of autonomy. Despite its small size, Montenegro carried republic-level status during the years of socialist rule

---

[1] 2003 Census figures.

[2] Montenegro garners significant pages in Misha Glenny's *McMafia: A Journey Through the Global Criminal World Underworld* (New York: Alfred A. Knopf, 2008). See pp. 21–6. As Glenny summarizes, "Throughout most of the 1990's, Djukanovic's country, Montenegro, with a population of just 650,000 (regarded by the rest of the Balkans as a legendarily indolent people), was the focal point of a multibillion-dollar criminal industry that generated income from America through the Middle East, central Asia, the Maghreb, the Balkans, and western Europe (p. 23)."

TABLE 17.1. *Demographics in Montenegro, 1948–2003*

	1948 %	1953 %	1961 %	1971 %	1981 %	1991 %	2003 % A	B
Montenegrins	90.7	86.6	81.4	67.1	68.5	61.9	40.64	43.16
Serbs	1.8	3.3	3.0	7.5	3.3	9.3	30.01	31.99
Muslims	0.1	1.5	6.5	13.3	13.4	14.6	4.27	3.97
Bosniaks	0	0	0	0	0	0	9.41	7.77
Croats	1.8	2.3	2.3	1.7	1.2	0.9	1.05	1.1
Albanians	5.2	5.6	5.5	6.7	6.5	6.7	7.09	5.03
Yugoslavs	0	0	0.3	2.1	5.6	3.3	0	0
Other	0.4	0.7	1.0	1.6	1.5	3.3	1.57	1.67

Note: Table Created by the author from census statistics. The 2003 census was adjusted – the B column presenting figures that exclude family members living abroad.

(unlike Kosovo). It was the only republic not to break away from Serbia after the collapse of Communism.

The unique feature most relevant to the present purposes concerns the fluidity of identity. One look at the Montenegrin census figures and their changes over time is all that is needed to see that ethnic dynamics in Montenegro differs substantially from that in other areas of former Yugoslavia. As Table 17.1 illustrates, within the population of Orthodox/Slavic (Serbian) speakers,[3] the percentage identifying themselves as Serbs increased from 3.3 percent in 1981 to almost 32 percent in 2003. Correspondingly, those identifying as Montenegrin dropped from 68.5 percent to 43.16 percent. Those identifying as Muslim more than doubled between the 1961 and 1971 censuses. By the 2003 census, a new Bosniak identity superseded, but did not eclipse, the number identifying as Muslim. The figure for those exercising their right to call themselves "Yugoslavs" waxed and waned. Through it all, the figures for the Albanian category remained remarkably steady.

About 70 percent of Montenegro's citizens speak Serbian and identify Orthodoxy as their religion. By any status or power measure, the politics within this population has largely determined Montenegro's fate. As the census figures indicate, the numbers fluctuate between those identifying as Montenegrin and those as Serbian. In fact, while traveling in Montenegro, one will often encounter families in which one sibling identifies as a Montenegrin and another as a Serb. In one prominent example, at the inception of an independent Montenegrin state in 2006, the Montenegrin Foreign Minister, Miodrag Vlahovic, declared himself a Montenegrin whereas his brother declared himself a Serb.[4] As part of my fieldwork in Montenegro in 2006, I began asking everyone I encountered about how siblings can differ in this identification. The answers

---

[3] In postindependence Montenegro, there has been effort to establish a Montenegrin language as separate from the Serbian language. I will use the term Slavic here.

[4] See ICG Europe Briefing no. 42, "Montenegro's Referendum," Podgorica/Belgrade, May 30, 2006. See footnote 7.

varied in both length and substance. One taxi driver, after first explaining how he was both an atheist and Orthodox, described how he came to identify as Montenegrin whereas his brother identified as a Serb.[5] The major difference, he explained, was that his brother was more connected with history and monasteries whereas he was more oriented toward the future. As an older brother, he was more able to see the "whole political picture" than his younger sibling. Most explanations, similar to this one, tied some family dynamic to a broader view of the historical and political relationship between Serbia and Montenegro.

The question of whether Montenegrins are a separate ethnic group or only another form of Serbs (and to those hailing from the region, a higher form of Serbs) goes back hundreds of years. Before the nineteenth century, Montenegro's small mountain-based population was centered on a number of tribes and clans.[6] Two potentially contradictory elements helped define the nature of these tribes. First, they were fiercely independent. The Ottomans found it more worthwhile to coopt them than to try to subdue them. As Banac summarizes, "So strong was this code of tribal solidarity, based on social ownership and internal hierarchy of valor, that the Montenegrins were able to hold their own against the Turks in centuries of mutual ravage."[7] The Ottomans essentially granted de facto independence in 1718 in the Peace of Pozarevac. Second, many of these tribes had ties to Serbia and the imagined community of "Serbia." In fact, many of Serbia's revolutionary leaders would descend from these tribes.[8] Moreover, a rich folklore tied together the fate of Montenegro and Serbia in the popular imagination. As Banac further describes:

[T]he Serb tradition percolated down to the consciousness of most ordinary herdsmen by a system of mnemonic devices by which the church continually admonished the Montenegrins to remember the glories of the Nemanjic state. Time and again, Montenegrin rulers took the lead in attempting to restore the medieval Serbian empire.[9]

These two conflicting desires – to retain the dignity of independence and to be a type of Serb – formed a fundamental and recurring dilemma for the Slavic/Orthodox of Montenegro.

B. Serb and/or Montenegrin: Round 1, Statehood and Loss of Statehood

In 1878, the Congress of Berlin recognized Montenegro as a separate state. In the fall of 1912, Montenegro joined with Serbia and other Balkan states to

---

[5] Field notes 7/1/06. Also interviews with BD and YO.

[6] In 1921, Montenegro's population numbered less than 200,000. For a brief review of Montenegrin history, especially covering the unification of Montenegro with the Kingdom of Serbs, Croats, and Slovenes, see Ivo Banac, *The National Question in Yugoslavia: Origins, History, Politics* (Ithaca, NY: Cornell University Press, 1984), pp. 270–91.

[7] Banac, *The National Question in Yugoslavia*, p. 272.

[8] The Karadjordje dynasty descended from one of the Vasojevic clans, for example.

[9] Banac, *The National Question in Yugoslavia*, p. 274.

permanently push the Turks out of the region. In 1914, Montenegro gave its unconditional support to Serbia during the July crisis that precipitated the First World War and, as the fighting began, placed its army under Serbian leadership. The war itself set off a series of Machiavellian machinations befitting Balkan stereotypes. Suffice it to say that as the war concluded, Serbian forces moved into Montenegro and began steps to unify the two states. One step included an election of deputies to a Great National Assembly that would vote on the future status of Montenegro. The list of candidates favoring unconditional unification was printed on white paper whereas the list of opponents was printed on green paper; thus a competition of "Whites" versus "Greens" ensued, with the former based in the towns and the latter in the countryside.[10] The "Whites" won a majority, deposed King Nikola by a 163–0 vote, and formed a five-man executive committee to implement unification. Some of the "Greens," on the other hand, took up guns in January of 1919.[11] As in the escalations that would occur 70 years later, the Greens' rebellion aimed at precipitating Allied intervention. Bolstered by their interpretation of Wilson's Fourteen Points, and statements by the British Prime Minister and the French Government, the Greens put their hopes in intercession and adjudication.[12] However, no intervention was forthcoming. Instead, the Whites and the army sought retribution. War ravaged Montenegro for months and violence simmered for several more years.

It is important to keep in mind what the war was about. The Greens were not adamantly opposed to any reconciliation with Serbia – they were opposed to unconditional and unilateral unification. In the eyes of the Greens, the Serbs simply did not show any respect for Montenegro and its history. At the time, even outside observers readily diagnosed the fundamental problem. As a member of a joint American–British mission, the British diplomat Earl John de Salis wrote a detailed report. The Earl stated that no one denied that Montenegro might need to be unified with Serbia and the budding Yugoslav state. However, the issue was "to be able to join it as Montenegro, and not as a prefecture of Serbia, as free Montenegrins, in line with the tradition and the past of their country, and not as yes-men of Belgrade, to join it on equal footing as the Slovenes, the Croats and the very Serbs."[13] This obsession with equality with Serbia would wind its way through Montenegrin politics over many decades.

[10] Banac, pp. 285–6.
[11] Known as the Christmas Rebellion as Christmas on the Orthodox calendar falls on January 7.
[12] See Serbo Rastoder's discussion on pp. 161–9 in Zivko M. Andrijasevic and Serbo Rastoder, *The History of Montenegro* (Podgorica: Montenegro Diaspora Centre, 2006).
[13] See Andrijasevic and Rastoder, *The History of Montenegro*, pp. 170–71. Banac provides a similar interpretation: "the allegiance to the ex-king was not the principal source of the Green movement. Most Greens respected the king, but their first loyalty was to Montenegro's dignity. Most of them, in fact, were not opposed to a unification with Serbia, 'but only befittingly,' that is, on conditions of equality and the preservation of Montenegrin identity. Above all, the *zelenasi* were motivated by wounded patriotism." *The National Question in Yugoslavia*, p. 288.

TABLE 17.2. *Ethnic Composition of the Yugoslav Officer Corps (1970s)*

	Officers	Percent of Expected	Generals	Percent of Expected
Serbs	60.5	152	46.0	115
Croats	14.0	63	19.0	86
Montenegrins	8.0	320	19.0	760
Macedonians	6.0	103	5.0	86
Muslims	3.5	41	4.0	48
Slovenes	5.0	61	6.0	73
Albanians	2.0	31	0.5	8
Hungarians	0.5	22	0.5	22

Note: From Petersen, "The Organization of the Military in Multiethnic States," unpublished manuscript (1988). The figures for percent of expected are a ratio of officer corps numbers divided by the population of the group in Yugoslavia as a whole.

C. Serb and/or Montenegrin: Round 2, Communist Yugoslavia and Montenegro

As the Second World War played out in Yugoslavia, Montenegrins were able to gain not only equality but also overrepresentation in the emerging Communist state. Above all, the ethnofederal nature of the new state would pacify the fundamental status concerns of many Montenegrins. The new system granted five ethnic groups – the Slovenes, the Croats, the Serbs, the Macedonians, and the Montenegrins – their own Yugoslav republics, the highest form of official status.[14] Notably, Montenegrins gained republic status despite composing only 2 percent of Yugoslavia's population. Montenegro's republic status would become a sore point for Kosovo's Albanians, who totaled more than double the number of Montenegrins but would never achieve the same republic status. For the Communists, the promise of federal status had been an important wartime recruiting tool because the designation would go a long way toward addressing the Montenegrins' post–First World War grievance. In effect, with republic status, Montenegrins and Montenegro achieved official equality with Serbs and the Serbian Republic.

Furthermore, based on their outsized numbers in the Partisans, Montenegrins were vastly overrepresented in the postwar state's military and bureaucracy. In the late stages of the war, Montenegrins commanded eight of the eighteen Partisan corps and numbered eight out of twenty-three in the Partisan Supreme Command.[15] As the figures from the 1970s in Table 17.2 illustrate, Montenegrin overrepresentation in the military persisted across generations.

Even when Montenegro separated from Serbia in 2006, many of the most visible political figures in the federal government in Belgrade were Montenegrin

---

[14] The sixth Republic, Bosnia, was highly multiethnic; Muslims were not officially recognized as a "nation" until much later.

[15] Andrijasevic and Rastoder, *The History of Montenegro*, p. 227.

in family background, including the President of the state (Boris Tadic), the Interior Minister (Dragan Jocic), the Chief of the Security-Intelligence Agency (Rade Bulatovic), and several key advisors to Prime Minister Kostunica.[16] In Serbia and much of the rest of former Yugoslavia, people often derided Montenegrin overrepresentation in government positions.[17]

In 1948, only 1.8 percent of the citizens in Montenegro declared themselves as Serbs. The numbers for Serbs in the 1953 and 1961 censuses increased only slightly (to 3.3 percent and 3.0 percent, respectively). After a blip to 7.5 percent in 1971 during a period of nationalist agitation across Yugoslavia, the figure again fell to 3.3 percent in 1981. Given Montenegro's position in the state system and bureaucracy, the historical and ethnic issues underlying Serb/Montenegrin identity were largely dormant. An "umbrella" political identity of "Montenegrin" covered almost all the Slavic/Orthodox without much controversy. Only years after the collapse of Yugoslavia would the fundamental dilemma – both to retain the dignity of independence and to be a form of Serb – again come to the fore.

D. Establishing the Starting Point for Analysis at the Collapse of Communism (1991)

As Yugoslavia collapsed, individual republics declared independence and seceded from the federation. From the end of Yugoslavia in 1991 until 2006, the fundamental question in Montenegro also concerned secession. In turn, this question was tied to the nature of relations between Serbs and Montenegrins.

As far as the indicators of resentment go, those identifying as Montenegrins (61.9 percent of the Republic's population in 1991) could not complain about undeserved subordinate status either within Yugoslavia or within the Republic of Montenegro. As will be discussed below, Albanians (and to a lesser degree Muslims) were clearly beneath Montenegrins/Serbs. Among Montenegrins and Serbs in 1991, who was "on top" or "underneath" was not clear and perhaps did not even make sense as a question. The concept and emotion of resentment depend on a firm perception of group hierarchy, which further entails a firm perception of groups and where they are placed on a hierarchy. In the Serb–Montenegrin case, there was no resentment, because the fundamental comparison processes that underlie the emotion were not a pervasive or prominent part of social and political life.

Likewise, ethnic stigma was not a factor in the Montenegrin–Serb relationship. Intermarriage was common. Individuals shifted back and forth between Montenegrin and Serb identities, and both identities commonly existed within a single family. The core measures of stigma – intermarriage, residential segregation and flight, and derogatory language – do not have the same applicability.

[16] ICG Europe Briefing no. 42, "Montenegro's Referendum," Podgorica/Belgrade, May 30, 2006, p. 8.
[17] I make this comment based on personal experience.

Serbs often told jokes about Montenegrins' aversion to labor, but these were often told in good humor.

In short, the case of Montenegrins and Serbs is one of no resentment and no ethnic stigma. The case as it stood at the time of the collapse of Yugoslavia can be placed in box NR1. Following the hypotheses generated in Chapter 6, we should not expect policies of boycott or parallel society, the use of violence, or the use of provocations in general. If a political actor were to employ violence, we should expect a significant backlash from in-group members.

E. Serb and/or Montenegrin: Round 3, A New Federation and the Development of Resentment (R1)

As described earlier, by the mid-1980s, Yugoslavia had evolved into a system where each republic (Slovenia, Croatia, Bosnia, Serbia, Macedonia, and Montenegro), as well as each of the two provinces within the Serbian Republic (Voyvodina and Kosovo), had one vote on the eight-member Presidium. In effect, control over four units could create a veto over Yugoslavia-wide policy. Milosevic gained this objective through the "anti-bureaucratic revolution" that put his followers in control of Serbia, Kosovo, Voyvodina, and Montenegro by means of mass rallies and intimidation. In Montenegro, Milosevic's followers included Momir Bulatovic, President of Montenegro from 1990 to 1998, and Milo Djukanovic, Prime Minister of Montenegro from 1991 to 1998. Djukanovic would become the defining figure of Montenegro's politics for a generation.

On March 1, 1992, both Bosnia and Montenegro held referenda on independence.[18] The wording in the Montenegrin poll read, "Are you in favour of the option that Montenegro, as a sovereign Republic, continues to live in the joint state – Yugoslavia, truly equal with other republics that wish the same?"[19] Despite all the issues of legitimacy connected with such a referendum under the pro-Milosevic leadership, the level of participation and results are indicative of the nature of ethnic relations in Montenegro at the time. Of all registered voters, 66.04 percent participated, meaning that nearly 34 percent boycotted or did not show up at the poll. Of those voting, 95.94 percent cast a preference to stay connected with Serbia. Clearly, the majority of Albanians and Muslims boycotted, not surprising given the relationship of their coethnics in Kosovo and Bosnia with the Milosevic regime. Just as clearly, an overwhelming majority of the population registered as Serb and Montenegrin in the 1991 census (71.2 percent of the total population) voted to remain with Serbia.[20] Even if Montenegrin political elites had wanted to sever their republic from Serbia, there was no emotion resource available for doing so.

---

[18] All republic-level units in Yugoslavia possessed the constitutional right of secession.

[19] Andrijasevic and Rastoder, *The History of Montenegro*, p. 261

[20] For further summary of these points, see Srdjan Darmanovic, "Montenegro: Miracle in the Balkans?" *Journal of Democracy* (April 2007) 18 (no.2): 153.

After all other Yugoslav republics had voted to secede, Serbia and Montenegro were left to patch together a new Yugoslavia. By late April of 1992, a new constitution gave form to a new federation: the six-republic Socialist Federal Republic of Yugoslavia (SFRY) was reduced to the two-republic Federal Republic of Yugoslavia (FRY). If ever there was a federation geared to produce status discrepancies and resentments, this was it. In this dyadic federation, one member had 6.4 times the territory, 15.9 times the population, and 17.9 times the GDP.[21] Although Montenegrins voted for a sovereign and equal Montenegro, they were unlikely to get one, with this type of power imbalance, especially with Milosevic at the helm of the partner republic.

Almost immediately, Montenegro was forced to confront some unpleasant realities because of its connection to Serbia and Milosevic. The United Nations embargo severely punished the new federation. Also, the Yugoslav National Army conscripted Montenegrin reservists for fighting in Hercegovina, where 165 died and an additional 236 were disabled.[22] Despite the absence of significant public protests of the war, the costs of political alliance with Serbia were apparent and severe.

The consequences of the Milosevic regime and the war were also apparent to many citizens of Serbia proper. In the winter of 1996–7, demonstrators protested in mass on Belgrade's streets. In Montenegro, during the same period, Prime Minister Milo Djukanovic broke ranks with Milosevic, stating that Milosevic should not "remain in any place in the political life of Yugoslavia."[23] Correspondingly, in 1997, the major political party in Montenegro, the Democratic Party of Socialists, who were tied to Milosevic, split into two factions. Djukanovic led an anti-Milosevic faction that retained the name Democratic Party of Socialists (DPS), whereas the other faction called itself the Socialist Peoples Party (SNP). In October 1997, Djukanovic ran for President of Montenegro and won a narrow victory. At first, Djukanovic's DPS did not pursue an independence agenda. For example, Djukanovic's postinaugural "vision statement" discussed only a reform agenda for the entire FRY and stated that the country was not threatened by Montenegrin separatism but only by economic and social neglect. Yet despite official statements, the possibility of separation now entered the political realm.

Belgrade politicians made moves to establish dominance, and the reactions of Montenegrin counterparts set off a status and power competition that widened the gulf between the sides. After Djukanovic became president of the Montenegro Republic, Belgrade raised Djukanovic's rival within Montenegro, Momir Bulatovic, to Federal Prime Minister. The Montenegrin government retaliated by rejecting Bulatovic's appointment and ignoring him. In another instance, the federal government refused to recognize Montenegro's newly appointed

[21] Andrijasevic and Rastoder, *The History of Montenegro*, p. 262.

[22] Ibid, p. 263.

[23] Stojan Cerovic, "Serbia and Montenegro: Reintegration, Divorce, or Something Else?" Special Report, U.S. Institute for Peace, 2001, p. 3.

representatives. In return, Montenegro prevented the federal government from implementing policies on Montenegrin territory.[24] Gradually, in battles over sovereignty, the Republic of Montenegro seized one jurisdiction after another from the federal government, in the process ignoring the FRY constitution.

When the Kosovo war broke out, Montenegro declared neutrality. After the war, the Montenegrin government adopted a dual currency system, using the German mark as a second currency (the mark was adopted as the only currency in November 2000 and replaced with the euro in 2002). Belgrade responded with a trade blockade. Perhaps most critically, in July 2000, Milosevic worked to change the FRY constitution to unify the state. He did so without a consultation with Montenegrin politicians or state officials. With a federation so unequal in territory, population, and wealth, the changes meant the end of any pretense of equality between the two federal republics. As the historian Serbo Rastoder sums up:

Instead of an equal republic – Montenegro became just one of the electoral units of the newly regulated state. This unambiguously showed that there could be no joint state with Serbia in which Montenegro could be more than just "the twenty-seventh electoral unit."[25]

As late as February 1999, only 21 percent of survey respondents in Montenegro supported independence.[26] The events surrounding the Kosovo war and its aftermath changed the circumstances. By October 2000, shortly after the Milosevic ouster, the numbers were more even. The situation had come to mirror the post–First World War scenario eighty years earlier. As with the "Whites" in the previous era, one faction would accept nearly unconditional unification with Serbia. As with the "Greens" in the previous era, one faction sought independence if equality was not an option.

Federation with Serbia had changed basic aspects of life in Montenegro. Montenegrin citizens had suffered under an embargo; Montenegrin young men had been sent off to fight, and some to die, in Bosnia; Montenegrins had witnessed political moves that challenged their conceptions of equality. These lived experiences brought about beliefs that Montenegrins were unjustly coming under Serbian power. The case does not neatly fit the definition of resentment used in this work. Montenegrins did not experience everyday domination by ethnic "others" in the police or bureaucracy. Yet the sense of status reversal, that the autonomy of Montenegro was being replaced by the dominance of Serbia, became a powerful force. In important ways, the conflict

---

[24] ICG Balkans Report No. 101, "Current Legal Status of the Federal Republic of Yugoslavia and of Serbia and Montenegro," Brussels/Podgorica, 2000.

[25] Andrijasevic and Rastoder, *The History of Montenegro*, p. 269.

[26] Zoran Radulovic, "Montenegrin Public Opinion at a Turning Point," Podgorica, AIM, September 24, 1999. The Kosovo war was apparently a turning point. According to Srdjan Darmanovic, all surveys from the second half of 1999 to 2006 showed a slight majority for independence ("Montenegro: A Miracle in the Balkans?," p. 154).

could be viewed as moving from the NR1 box to the R1 cell. Accordingly, we would expect actions and rhetoric to become fully imbued with the language of resentment.

F. Western Intervention: The Belgrade Agreement, and "Solania"

In its battle with the Federal state, the Republic of Montenegro had gained control over most government functions by the early 2000s. Djukanovic then decided to steer toward full legal independence. At this point, after the Kosovo War, the West had fully committed to intervention in the region. Worried about the effect and precedent of Montenegrin secession on Kosovo and Bosnia, the EU and the United States put the brakes on Djukanovic. Led by the efforts of Javier Solana, EU High Representative for the Common Foreign and Security Policy, the EU brokered a deal between Serbia and Montenegro known as the Belgrade Agreement. The accord, signed on March 14, 2002, ended the ill-fated Federal Republic of Yugoslavia's short-lived existence. The State Union of Serbia and Montenegro took its place. By creating a weak parliament and central government, the Belgrade Agreement essentially codified Montenegro's de facto independent powers. To many in the region, the political institutions of this new union seemed so weak and so artificial that they referred to the new entity as "Solania," in reference to its EU creator and its artificial nature. Above all, it was a caretaker institutional solution. A clause written into the agreement allowed either of the two constituent members to call for a referendum on independence after a period of three years. In effect, the Belgrade Agreement gave Montenegrins an "opt-out" clause.

To get the parties to agree to the Belgrade Agreement, the EU held out promise of an accelerated EU accession as a "carrot." A few short years earlier, Djukanovic had aligned with Milosevic. By the time "Solania" was in place, Djukanovic and the separatists were playing up the promise of European inclusion to their constituents. In the elections of 2002, Djukanovic led a coalition of parties under the banner "Democratic List for a European Montenegro."

From 1997 to 1999, Montenegro had witnessed the politics of gradual dissociation. The fall of Milosevic provided a more clear and peaceful path toward independence. As politics evolved, so did the identities of Orthodox Slavs in Montenegro. In 1981, only 3.3 percent of the population declared itself "Serbian." At the time of the collapse of Yugoslavia ten years later, the numbers had increased to 9.3 percent. As the politics of separation manifested themselves, approximately another 20 percent of citizens switched their self-identification from "Montenegrin" to "Serbian" to create a total of about 30 percent. In 1948, over 90 percent of the population self-identified as Montenegrin; by 2003, only 40 percent did so. By the mid-2000s, Montenegro was a truly multiethnic state with no group able to claim a majority.

As the three-year wait period approached its end in February 2006, it was clear that the ruling coalition in Montenegro would pursue the opt-out option.

Again, the EU acted as the referee between the two sides.[27] Two Serbian-speaking Slovaks would supervise the referendum on separation. Miroslav Lajcak served as EU special representative and Frantisek Lipka was later tapped to preside over the Republic Referendum Commission. Having been through the "velvet divorce" that ended Czechoslovakia, the two Slovak diplomats seemed exceptionally appropriate for the task.

The rules of the referendum contained some wrinkles. In order to get both the unionists and separatists to participate, the threshold for separation needed to be set at a level where both sides could imagine victory. The agreed-on threshold was 55 percent. In other words, a 45 percent negative vote would be enough to block independence.

With all relevant parties, including the Serbian government, agreeing to bind themselves to the outcome, unionists and the independence bloc conducted campaigns to sway voters. The strategies of each side went predictably. For the independence bloc to garner 55 percent, they would need to bolster the turnout of minority voters. Accordingly, their billboards were written in the Latin script, rather than Cyrillic, and even occasionally in Albanian. The independence bloc emphasized that Montenegro was a civic state and not an ethnic state. They played heavily on the theme of joining Europe and rapid EU integration under their leadership. They repeatedly emphasized that continued union with Serbia would slow down, or even prevent, movement into Europe. They painted the unionists as remnants of the past.

The unionists appealed to those who worried about changes in pensions and job opportunities if cut off from Serbia. They also appealed to those with a deep cultural affinity with Serbia. The more strident unionists were likely to see the referendum in ethnic and historical terms. Those who were identifying more and more with Serbs, and the political parties representing that constituency, steered their political rhetoric to match Serbian cultural schemas. The daily newspapers aligned with Serbian political parties (*Glas Crnogoraca* and *Dan*) wrote of Albanian secessionist plots. They characterized Montenegro as a site of historical struggles where Slavic/Orthodox peoples could again fall victim to the machinations of Albanians and Croatians.[28] Representatives of the pro-Serbian parties (the Serbian People's Party, the People's Party, and the Socialists People's Party) often suggested that any referendum decided by minority votes would lack legitimacy.[29] The unionists also made personal attacks on Djukanovic, stating that an independent Montenegro would be little more than a mafia state with Djukanovic as godfather. The unionists, however,

---

[27] Several European organizations were involved, with the Council of Europe Commission for Democracy through Law especially influential on important technical issues, such as electoral thresholds.

[28] For a more extended discussion, see Florian Bieber, "The Instrumentalization of Minorities in the Montenegrin Dispute over Independence," European Centre for Minority Issues, Policy Brief #8, March 2002.

[29] Ibid, p. 4. Bieber in turn cites a report from the Helsinki Committee for Human Rights in Serbia, *Albanians in Montenegro*, April 2001.

did not use derogatory stereotypes about Montenegrins. Although the unionist core was composed of the 30 percent of the population identifying as "Serbs," the vast majority of those Serbs had listed themselves as "Montenegrins" in previous censuses. Given the split nature of many Slavic/Orthodox families, any ethnicity-based derogatory campaign rhetoric could logically be directed only against minorities, especially Albanians. Unsurprisingly, there was no violence or even much fear of it during the campaign. A series of televised debates proceeded in a civil manner.

The referendum was held on May 21, 2006 with 86.49 percent of the electorate participating. With a 55 percent threshold needed to affirm independence, 55.53 percent voted for independence. Although Boris Tadic, the President of Serbia, called to congratulate Montenegro two days after the referendum, many unionists in Montenegro did not readily accept the outcome. They filed 241 objections to the election commission, most of them rejected by Lajcak. Unionists complained that the referendum was stolen by Albanians and Muslims/Bosniaks. In fact, a majority of Slavic/Orthodox voters undoubtedly voted for maintaining the union. The question is why they did not do more to affect or challenge the outcome.

By the 2003 census, more than 30 percent of the country identified as Serbian and formed the core of unionist opposition. The referendum on independence passed by a razor-thin margin, and only due to minority votes. There were at least two strategic options that unionists could consider to alter the aftermath of this outcome. First, the use of violence was theoretically possible. Only weeks after the referendum, a prominent Montenegrin Serb laid out the following to me.[30] Twenty minutes after the polls closed, supporters of independence took to the streets to declare victory and celebrate – the results could not have been known at this time. According to him, had unionists also taken to the streets in the thousands and declared victory, a clash, and likely a violent one, would have occurred. The result would have polarized the population and could have delegitimized the election or overwhelmed the outcome, which, in the opinion of the speaker, had been rigged anyway.[31] In his opinion, the unionists were too cowardly to make this move.

Following the strategies of many other political actors seen in previous cases, a second option would have been to attempt to use the politics of separation in the form of boycotts, parallel societies, and territorial division. Yet it seems that none of these separatist tactics were ever seriously considered.

[30] YM/6/21/06.

[31] Despite, or perhaps because of, the presence and verification procedures employed in the referendum, most people I talked to in 2006 did, in fact, believe that the election had been rigged. As one highly educated Albanian in Macedonia explained, the West wanted an independent Montenegro and they would not have allowed the referendum unless they were sure of the outcome. These comments are typical of a broader Balkan tendency to engage in conspiracy theories. In this case, the razor-thin outcome seemed too convenient to many, exacerbating existing beliefs in rigged political processes.

G. Analysis

Under Western supervision in the form of the Belgrade Agreement, Montenegro separated from Serbia. It did so without violent escalation, riots, boycotts, attempts at territorial or internal political separation, or even very much ethnically derogatory language. Obviously, the ouster of Milosevic was essential for paving such a smooth path. FRY politics had entered a new phase. Clearly, the EU deserves much credit. The two Slovak diplomats, Lajcak and Lipka, were the ideal choices for supervising a "velvet divorce." Although initially opposed to Montenegrin secession, the EU showed flexibility in guiding a secessionist process. The EU played the "carrot" of EU accession well. However, it should be noted that it is not clear what would have happened had the vote been 54.9 percent for independence (instead of 55.5 percent). The continuation of the Serbia and Montenegro Union, with over half the citizens of Montenegro voting against it, would have been problematic, to say the least. It is not clear that the EU had a contingency plan if the referendum failed.[32]

Perhaps the biggest reason for the smooth transition was that members of the Slavic/Orthodox citizens of Montenegro had little stomach for seriously confronting each other. They were Montenegrins, Serbs, Montenegrin Serbs, Montenegrin Montenegrins, people who called themselves Serbs in one census and Montenegrins in the next and vice versa, families where the father identified more as a Serb than a Montenegrin and the mother more as a Montenegrin than a Serb and whose children took after one parent more than the other. As the fluctuating census figures illustrate, the decades following the post–First World War violence had served to make the cultural boundary continually more fluid. Milovan Djilas, the author of *The New Class* and *Land without Justice*, was undoubtedly the most famous modern writer and intellectual to hail from Montenegro. He described his home region as "one land with two souls."[33] Other modern social scientists describe the situation as a dilemma of "national homo duplex" or "double or divided national consciousness."[34] Whatever terms are used, the types of provocation seen in other regional conflicts were unlikely to be seen here. As in the example in Section F, some politicians could theorize about provocations on the day of the referendum, but the reality was that the actual voting procedure went off without a hint of a serious incident.[35] One should not underestimate the level of residual bitterness or downplay the fact that the Serbian identity has found institutional form in new political parties. But these issues should not be exaggerated either.

[32] As Darmanovic summarizes, "Thus it seems hard to believe that the EU will use the Montenegrin case as a model, even if things worked out in the end." See "Montenegro: Miracle in the Balkans?" p. 156.
[33] Can Karpat, "Serbia and Montenegro: Unhappy Couple on the Way of Divorce?" AIA Balkan section, January 16, 2006.
[34] Terms used by Srdjan Darmanovic, a well-known social scientist in Podgorica.
[35] Florian Bieber, "Voting Day: Looking Each Other in the Eye," *Transitions on Line*, May 23, 2006.

II. ASSESSING HYPOTHESES

Following hypothesis 1, political actors are predicted to forego polices of boy-cott or parallel society in a case of low stigma. This hypothesis is difficult to assess for Montenegro. On one hand, political actors had several opportunities to pursue the politics of separation but chose not to. In 1992, when every other Yugoslav republic opted for secession, Montenegrins voted overwhelmingly not to separate.[36] The politics of secession emerged most openly only after a struggle for dominance took place between the Republic of Montenegro and the Federal Government in Belgrade (helping move the game from NR1 to R1). In the 2006 referendum, a majority of Slavic/Orthodox citizens voted against separation. Despite that fact, Serbian politicians and parties did not pursue the politics of boycott or separation after the referendum. On the other hand, the prediction clearly fails. Under Western supervision, political actors did pursue an independent state and succeeded in obtaining one. If there can be a politics of separation, secession obviously fits the definition.

Following hypothesis 2, political actors who employ indiscriminate killing of civilians can expect a backlash in cases where contempt is absent. In Montene-gro, violence was nonexistent. Although some politicians may have thought about options and strategies, none of them chose to put them into play.[37] Hypothesis 4 states that "we are more likely to see the use of violence in cases of resentment than cases without resentment." Although the situation arguably evolved into one involving resentments, violence did not occur between Serbs and Montenegrins. Most commentators do not believe that violence was a real possibility. As Srdjan Darmanovic writes, "Unionists who might have been prone to violent imaginings could find no powerful sponsors."[38]

Hypotheses 5 and 10 address the style of nonviolent politics. Hypothesis 5 predicts that with a move from NR1 to R1 we should see a correspond-ing emphasis in public demonstrations on group status issues. Prediction 10 reads, "With contempt, nonviolent provocations such as speeches and posters will highlight the perceived inherent negative qualities of the other side. With resentment, these provocations will emphasize current changes in status rela-tions. In situations of both contempt and resentment, both types of provoca-tions should be observed." In the referendum of 2006, the independent bloc did not use much of either form of rhetoric. The unionist bloc conformed to the prediction: they did employ derogatory terminology toward stigmatized minorities such as Albanians, but employed more status-based rhetoric when addressing Serb–Montenegrin relations.

The following anecdote sums up and illustrates the situation between Serbs and Montenegrins. Right after the May 21 referendum, a Serbian friend of mine

---

[36] To recall prediction 4A, "the case of NR1 should see the highest chance of acquiescence."

[37] This observation only leads back to the question of why no powerful sponsor for a violent option, or even a very provocative option, ever emerged.

[38] Darmaonvic, "Montenegro: Miracle in the Balkans?" p. 156.

in Belgrade announced that he was sick and tired of Montenegrins and wished them good riddance. I asked him, whether he would also wish to bar the new Montenegrin "foreigners" from Belgrade's universities and health facilities as retaliation. He seemed put off by my question, saying that Montenegrins would just go to Zagreb and he would rather have them in Belgrade. I then asked him what actions he would take against the Montenegrin secessionists. He replied that he would now go to Greece on vacation instead of the Montenegrin coast. With some bitterness he said that the Montenegrins, left to their own corruption and indolence, would probably let the coast go to rot anyway.

Six weeks after the referendum, I was in Bar, on the Montenegrin coast. I received a phone call from the same Belgrade friend. He was a few kilometers up the road in Petrovac-na-Moru and invited me to come up and join his group. I asked him about his previous pledge to boycott the Montenegrin coast. He explained that his friends had some beautiful property there, so why not enjoy it?[39]

III. ALBANIANS IN MONTENEGRO

Of the approximately 40,000 Albanian residents of Montenegro (6.7 percent of the population in the 1991 census), close to half live in the southern tip of the country in an area adjoining Albania. Most of the remainder live near the capital city of Podgorica in the suburb of Tuzi (in a broader district named Malesia), with a significant number also found in Bar.

Coming from fieldwork in Kosovo and Macedonia, I naturally asked people about the "Albanian question" in Montenegro. The issue seemed obviously relevant. Albanian groups had launched violent escalations in every neighboring region – Kosovo, South Serbia, and Macedonia. Many commentators, including the ICG,[40] felt the need to address the "Greater Albania" question, and a "Greater Albania" certainly included Ulcinj, if not Malesia. It was not clear why the politics of neighboring regions should not spill over into Montenegro. Yet many people were puzzled, even annoyed, by the question. They simply did not see much of an issue.[41]

There are some obvious reasons for the absence of an "Albanian problem" in Montenegro. The Albanian population is relatively small and concentrated in one corner of the country. Unlike Kosovo, there is no historic pattern of violence. There are also some less obvious answers. Some academic sources point to a common historical and cultural background among Albanians and Montenegrins. As Sistek and Dimitrovova write, "The Albanian population which fell under Montenegrin dominance resembled Montenegrins in many

---

[39] I doubt that my experience was unique. See for example the interview in "Serbs Greet Independence Vote with Shrugs," Nikola Jovanovic and Dragana Nikolic Solomon, *Institute for War and Peace Reporting*, May 22, 2006.
[40] International Crisis Group, "Pan-Albanianism: How Big a Threat to Balkan Stability?" Europe Report No. 25, February 2004.
[41] Interviews with YO and QT in particular.

aspects of tribal structure, moral code, and patriarchal values which were almost identical in the case of Montenegrin and north Albanian tribes."[42] In my discussions with Slavs, I often heard that one of the reasons for good relations was that many Albanians in Montenegro are Catholic (which is especially true for the population in Tuzi) and that these Christian Albanians had served to create what political scientists usually term cross-cutting cleavages. The point here is that many Slavic Montenegrins could tell me some version of a historical narrative that explained the lack of friction between Montenegrins and Albanians.[43]

A. Establishing the Starting Point of Analysis: R4

As late as 2002, Albanians in Montenegro (6 percent of the population) held only 0.03–0.05 percent of positions in state structures; they were underrepresented in all positions of day-to-day authority, including the police and the judicial system.[44] The situation was no better at the time of the Yugoslav collapse in 1991. In fact, in 1992, Albanian political representatives had put forth a Memorandum on the Special Status of Albanians.[45] There is no question that this case must be seen in terms of resentment.

The first-tier criteria of ethnic stigma (intermarriage, residential segregation, common derogatory terminology) indicate significant prejudice toward Albanians. Intermarriage was very rare. In Montenegro, Albanians are 59.9 times more likely to marry another Albanian than would be expected randomly (as opposed to a figure of 269.1 in Serbia proper).[46] As discussed, residential patterns are concentrated. Some newspapers used only the term "siptar" in reference to Albanians.[47] This is not a case of low ethnic stigma. Unlike the case of Serbs/Montenegrins, or even the Muslims/Bosniaks, the census figures show the remarkable lack of fluidity of the Albanian identity in Montenegro.

The second tier of criteria (existence of myths, evidence of a negative cultural schema, absence of political cooperation, the shunning of a group's language, and evidence of stereotyping) depicts a more nuanced situation. As discussed, many Montenegrins held beliefs in common history or cross-cutting cleavages rather than negative schemas. Moreover, when Montenegro moved into

---

[42] Frantisek Sistek and Bohdana Dimitrovova, "National Minorities in Montenegro after the Break-Up of Yugoslavia," in Florian Bieber ed., *Montenegro in Transition: Problems of Identity and Statehood* (Baden-Baden, Germany: Nomos Verlagsgesellschaft, 2003), p. 169.

[43] For a more extended treatment of this point, see Jovan Nikolaidis, "Multiculturalism in Montenegro and the City of Ulcinj," in Nenad Dimitrijevic ed., *Managing Multiethnic Local Communities in the Countries of the Former Yugoslavia* (Budapest: Open Society Institute, 2000), pp. 447–57. See especially 449–52.

[44] Sistek and Dimitrovova, pp. 172–3.

[45] Sistek and Dimitrovova, p. 173.

[46] See Nikolai Botev, in "Where East Meets West: Ethnic Intermarriage in the Former Yugoslavia, 1962 to 1989," *American Sociological Review* (June 1994) 59 (No. 3): 461–80; see p. 474 for the numbers on Montenegro.

[47] See Bieber, "Instrumentalization," p. 6.

highly competitive electoral politics, two-thirds of Albanian voters preferred to vote for multiethnic coalitions rather than an ethnic Albanian party. Furthermore, several mainly Montenegrin political parties had prominent Albanian members.[48]

Given this mixed set of indicators, as in Macedonia, I place the starting cell for analysis as R4 – significant political resentment, and a medium level of stigma.

B. The Flow of Events

With the Kosovo war, the West committed to transforming the Western Balkans. However, events in the wake of the Kosovo occupation had not gone smoothly. Albanian forces in South Serbia began a violent escalation in 2000; Albanian forces began another violent escalation in Macedonia in March 2001. On the other hand, Montenegro would prove to be a different case.

As the possibility of Montenegrin independence emerged, separatist political actors considered the hard reality that they might not be able to reach majority support among the Slavic/Orthodox population alone. Success would depend on the support of ethnic minorities. In other words, the emerging independence forces had strategic incentives to support minority positions.

In Montenegro, everything lined up for a successfully brokered agreement between Albanians and the Montenegrin government in the early 2000s. The West was committed and wanted to head off any chance of another escalation. The key political bloc within Montenegro, the pro-independence forces aligned with Djukanovic, needed Albanian votes. Moreover, cultural schemas promoted, rather than prevented, cooperation between a small nonthreatening Albanian minority and the government.

In 2001, the West helped broker what is known as the "Ulcinj Agreement." The agreement was created with the help of a series of roundtables mediated by the Project on Ethnic Relations, a group with members from the OSCE, the U.S. Embassy, U.S. academics, and members of NGOs, as well as key leaders from Montenegro and the FRY government.[49] The document covered six key issues of concern to the Albanian minority:

(1) A maternity hospital in Ulcinj
(2) Restoring municipal status to Tuzi
(3) Establishing an Albanian language faculty at the University of Montenegro
(4) Official recognition of diplomas gained in Tirana and Pristina
(5) Additional border crossings into Albania
(6) Appointment of ethnic Albanians as Chief Judge and Chief of Police in Ulcinj

---

[48] Sistek and Dimitrovova, "National Minorities in Montenegro," p. 171.
[49] See the Project on Ethnic Relations (PER) report, "Interethnic Relations in Montenegro," Third PER Roundtable: Albanians in Montenegro, July 5, 2002.

All of these goals were achieved by 2005. The West was further engaged by advising on a new set of minority laws.

Few people outside of Montenegro, or even inside Montenegro, have heard about or care about this agreement and its implementation. By Balkan standards, this politics was dull. There was no violent escalation, and little evidence of any thought of violence. There were no Albanian referenda on territorial autonomy or secession. There were no Albanian boycotts of republican elections (outside of an informal boycott of the 1992 antisecessionist referendum). In Montenegro, Albanian politics has been the "normal" politics of box R4, motivated by resentment against what is perceived as unjust subordination. Politics has been a matter of gaining positions of authority and changing the municipal status in areas of Albanian demographic preponderance.

There were obvious structural reasons for this outcome. Certainly, demographics and geography helped to preclude violence. International political factors also worked against any effort to move the situation to box R5. Undoubtedly, Montenegro has not solved all of the outstanding issues with its Albanian minority, nor have Albanians been without grievances.[50] But the comparative absence of an "Albanian question" seems to go beyond these structural factors. Consider that an ICG report states, "Montenegro is praised by Kosovo Albanians and the Albanian government for its treatment of its Albanian minority."[51]

IV. LESSONS FROM THE MONTENEGRIN CASE AS A WHOLE AND A COMPARISON WITH BOSNIA

In his well-known article, which essentially denies the existence of *ethnic* violence, John Mueller writes:

Thus it is entirely possible to imagine Bosnian-like chaos in prosperous Quebec or Northern Ireland if the Canadian or British authorities had attempted to deal with cultural conflicts by encouraging murderous rampage rather than through patient policing and political accommodation.[52]

In contrast, the work here suggests that "Bosnian-like chaos" was unlikely to occur even in Montenegro, let alone Quebec. In fact, I doubt that it would have occurred in Montenegro, even if Milosevic had remained in power for another decade. When political actors contemplate the use of violence, they must take into account costs, or the lack of costs, related to ethnic stigma. In the Montenegrin case, there was not only a lack of stigma, but even a lack of clear group distinctions at the time of Yugoslavia's collapse. It was one thing to launch violence against Croats and Muslims; it would have been quite another for Milosevic to launch mass murder against Montenegrins. Had he done so in the late 1990s, his regime would have been so delegitimized that

---

[50] See ICG Europe Report No. 153, "Pan-Albanianism: How Big a Threat to Balkan Stability?" February 25, 2004. See Section VI in particular for a discussion of serious grievances.

[51] International Crisis Group, "Montenegro's Referendum," p. 9.

[52] John Mueller, "The Banality of 'Ethnic War,'" *International Security* (2000) 25 (1): 42–70. Passage is from p. 68.

the throngs who brought him down in October 2000 might have done so a few years earlier. If Djukanovic actually believed that Milosevic could just send a few "thugs" into Montenegro to create another "Bosnian chaos" it is doubtful that Djukanovic would have stated that Milosevic should not "remain in any place in the political life of Yugoslavia" in 1997 or that he would have so freely started an anti-Milosevic political party with secessionist overtones.

In Montenegro, cultural/historical factors also entered into the Montenegrin–Albanian relationship to mitigate conflict. Everyone could tell a narrative about cross-cutting cleavages, common cultural practices, and a history of nonviolence. This narrative enabled political cooperation and alliance formation in the years leading up to the 2006 referendum on independence. Political scientists sometimes try to create reliable measures of "cultural distance" to use as a variable to explain chances of conflict and violence. These methods often employ measures of linguistic proximity. This chapter supports the motivation behind such efforts – cultural issues do matter in explaining variation in conflict and cooperation. The Montenegrin–Albanian relationship suggests, however, that idiosyncratic historical and cultural relationships are likely to outweigh factors such as linguistic proximity.

Students of conflict and violence need to better understand the potential for mobilization of cleavages. In Montenegro, it took almost a decade of embargoes and institutional struggle before a latent cleavage between ethnic Montenegrins and Serbs fully evolved. In contrast, local Serbian and Croatian political actors in Bosnia developed claims for autonomy over three-fourths of Bosnia's territory by March 1992, well before actual fighting broke out. In Montenegro, the progression from NR1 to R1 took almost a decade. In Bosnia, the game moved swiftly from NR1 to R1 once a Bosnian state with a Muslim plurality became a distinct possibility. In effect, the politics of resentment mobilized the Serbian and Croatian populations in Bosnia. Although the rapid movement to R2 and especially R3 was a largely a matter of decisions in Belgrade and Zagreb, the calculus behind those decisions might have been different if groups within Bosnia had not already mobilized.

One could ask the following counterfactual in addressing the nature of culture, mobilization, and war: what if Muslims had composed nearly half the population of Montenegro in 1992 as they did that of Bosnia? Recall that on March 1, 1992, both Bosnia and Montenegro held referenda on independence. The wording in the Montenegrin poll read, "Are you in favour of the option that Montenegro, as a sovereign Republic, continues to live in the joint state – Yugoslavia, truly equal with other republics that wish the same?" Almost certainly, the Muslims would have voted negatively as they did in Bosnia, preparing the grounds for secession. Almost as certainly, the Serbs/Montenegrins would have perceived a strong possibility of status reversal. They would have likely coalesced under a common identity. Not wanting to live "under the Muslims," they would have likely mobilized for autonomy and war. Almost certainly, the Milosevic regime would have provided support. The progression would have been as in Bosnia, a rapid progression from NR1 to R1 to R3.

Having group labels is one thing, but their content is another. Social scientists need to develop a better understanding of the psychology of resentment. If members of groups perceive that they are likely to unjustly "live under" another group, the possibility of rapid mobilization is high. Rapid mobilization can lead to violent incidents, to anger and a desire for retaliation. This sequence prepares the way for political actors with more malign intentions. Much is written about manipulative leaders. We understand far less about the interplay of emotions, which is just as essential a part of the process.

18

Conclusion

I began this book with Figure 1.1, repeated here as Figure 18.1. The first chapters were designed to flesh out the component parts of this framework: the second chapter developed the concept of emotions as resources; the third chapter addressed the strategic use of those resources; the fourth chapter outlined the nature of intervener games; the fifth deepened the analysis of the opponent strategies; the sixth formulated hypotheses based on the work of the previous chapters. In the next eleven chapters, I applied this framework to intervention in the Western Balkans. Starting from the upper left of the diagram, the empirical chapters examined intervention "games" in Kosovo (standards before status, status with standards, Ahtisaari Plan), South Serbia (Konculj Agreement), Macedonia (Ohrid Accord), Bosnia (Dayton Accord), and Montenegro (Belgrade Agreement, Ulcinj Agreement),

In each case I identified the presence or absence of widely shared experiences relating to intervention and conflict – status reversal, prejudice and stigma, violence and victimization. The residues of these experiences were treated in their specific forms as the emotions of resentment, contempt, anger, fear, and hatred. I then considered the role of these "emotion resources" in conjunction with more standard structural variables. Within the case studies, I identified dozens of key junctures and strategic decision points for testing the hypotheses. Although the results of these tests were often nuanced, the role of emotions was often clear and powerful.

Instead of simply summarizing results, I wish to use this concluding chapter to address several broader issues: the future of the Balkans; the future of Western intervention more generally; policy-related implications of this study; and methodology-related issues.

I. THE "END OF HISTORY" IN THE BALKANS

On July 20, 2002, I traveled to Ohrid with another U.S. political scientist to interview Kiro Gligorov, the former Macedonian President. After many years

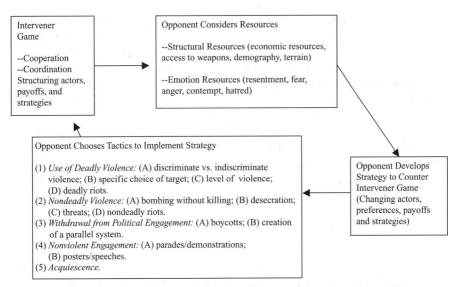

FIGURE 18.1. Western Intervention and the Nature of Its Opposition (Figure 1.1 Reprinted).

as President, and a near-fatal assassination attempt, he had retired to a villa on the hill above the town. As I wandered the streets of Ohrid the night before our interview, I spotted what appeared to be a concert going on at the end of the main street.

As it turned out, the "concert" was actually a political rally. And it was no ordinary one at that. The multimedia show was put on by the Minister of the Interior, Ljube Boskovski, who went by the moniker "brat Ljube" (meaning "brother Ljube") because he liked to call everyone he met "brother" or "sister." I arrived during a singing performance. The singers were followed by videos projected on a large screen showing present-day Macedonian heroes in a unit called the Lions. The Lions were a 1,400-strong special police force created by Boskovski and named after both his hotel in Croatia and his "Lion" brand of red wine. In the video, members of the Lions were kissing their wives and children goodbye before going out on a night operation against terrorists, whom I took to be Albanians. In other parts of the video brother Ljube is wearing some sort of samurai-looking outfit, ascending a mountain. I must admit that I did not fully understand the meaning of that segment of the program. I believe the background music lyrics posed the question, "Who is your friend?" A poet followed the video with a dramatic reading. Eventually, brat Ljube himself emerged on the stage for a fiery speech.

It was odd to see this type of event in a town like Ohrid, a developed tourist resort city. A few blocks away, kitschy tourist shops sold trinkets and ice cream vendors doled out cones to children. The brother Ljube show seemed a bit dramatic for the relaxed surroundings. Brat Ljube, however, was always known for his theatrics. He had fought in Croatia in the early 1990s before returning to Macedonia. Entertainers and social figures would gather at his Skopje home to drink wine and listen to his fiery rhetoric.[1] In May 2002, he personally demonstrated the use of a rocket launcher, during which flying shrapnel hit three people, including a journalist. In another incident, Boskovski's units killed an Indian and six Pakistani "terrorists" (reported as "mujahadin"), who were simply illegal immigrants. Brat Ljube was convicted of war crimes for the burning and killings at Ljuboten in August 2001.

In 2001, Boskovski had railed against the West, stating, "Macedonia is a sovereign state and we cannot have the attitude of a protectorate."[2] In 2009, Boskovski returned to Macedonia after spending four years in prison at the Hague. A repentant Boskovski ironically described his epiphany while criticizing current Macedonian politicians and parties for nationalism:

Of course, there was a time when romantic nationalism was often expressed. That's the same spirit that has now infected the ruling VRMO-DPMNE.... I'm talking of the period of the early Nineties. We haven't abandoned that concept but in real politics you have to be aware that the time of romantic nationalism is past. Our Prime Minister is now trying to show that he is awakening our national consciousness, which for me is very funny.... I think that trying to impose theories, opening up historical themes, defying the international community, and actually defying ourselves, is unproductive for Macedonia.[3]

Brat Ljube had embraced modern European thinking. Four years in prison at the Hague had no doubt cleared his mind. Yet, taking a broader view, brat Ljube never had a chance in the long term. Once the West began its absorption project in the Balkans, the brat Ljubes of the region would eventually either have to change their stripes or fade away.

As one European diplomat told me, "Being European means renouncing history."[4] For Western Europeans, history primarily means the horrors and enmities of the Second World War. Being European means renouncing the nationalism that led to the worst excesses of that period. To an increasing extent, being European also means embracing technocracy and consumerism.

This has been a difficult task for many residents of the Western Balkans. After all, the creation and evolution of a firm national identity in Macedonia barely had time to coalesce in the first place. Despite the political costs, many ethnic Macedonians were happy recently to see the airport in Skopje given the title "Alexander the Great Airport." The nation-building project in Macedonia was never quite completed. Likewise, in Bosnia the recent violence was instrumental in solidifying Bosniak group identity. For better or worse, Srebrenica is a large

---

[1] See Ana Petruseva, "Rise and Fall of Macedonia's Nationalist Showman," Institute for War and Peace Reporting, March 17, 2005, for more details on Boskovski.

[2] In the *New York Times*, from Reuters, "Macedonia Peace Process Lurches into Crisis," November 11, 2001.

[3] Darko Duridanski, "Old-Style Nationalism Has No Future in Macedonia," *Balkan Insight*, June 18, 2009.

[4] ZU 12/12/09.

part of Bosniak national identity, and it is difficult for them to renounce its meaning so soon after that tragedy.

Other groups, perhaps Serbs in particular, are proud of their identities. Serbs talk of Serbia being a "Great Little Nation" and can easily bring up a litany of Serbia's outsized role in major events: the Battle of Kosovo, the 1804 Uprising versus the Ottomans, the rejection of Austria-Hungary's ultimatum in 1914 and the tremendous contribution of Serbs to the allied cause, the Serbian role as "big brother" in the foundation of the first Yugoslavia, the resistance to Hitler and suffering at the hands of neighboring nations in the Second World War, and their defiance of Stalin in 1948–53.[5] In the view of many Serbs, why should Serbs be expected to renounce this proud history and embrace the mantle of war crime perpetrators as if they were Nazi Germans?

Becoming European by renouncing history is not an easy task to ask of Balkan peoples. If there was any region of the world where the emotions of the past were interacting with an imposition of "rationality" in the present, it may have been the Balkans from 1987 to 2008. Yet the Balkan peoples really have no other option than to embrace the path set out by the West. In Serbia in October 2008, even the Serbian Radical Party's leader, Tomislav Nikolic, embraced the road toward Europe by deciding to form a new and more Western-oriented party. His move fractured the last serious anti-Western political force in the region. There was no alternative to technocracy and capitalism. History has ended in the Western Balkans.

Many Balkan citizens, especially those of the younger generation who have less connection to the past, are more than willing to accept this outcome. Now that they have lived through turmoil, poverty, and confining visa restrictions, only the West and its imposition of the rule of law can provide an antidote to the chronic corruption and poverty of their nations.

In short, politics is becoming "normal" in the Balkans. As the war and violence recede into the past, the emotions of fear and anger will fade. With populations homogenized through ethnic cleansing, issues of ethnic status are still problematic in some regions, but have become manageable. The number of areas where the emotion of resentment will be a ready and relevant resource is declining. There is now no doubt which group is dominant in Croatia, Serbia, Kosovo, or Republika Srpska. Serbs and Montenegrins will continue their constructivist dance in Montenegro, but that is likely to be a tame affair. The future in Bosnia as a whole and in the Federation in particular still presents a situation of unresolved status ordering. But, because of ethnic homogenization, the conditions for war no longer exist. In Macedonia, Albanians and ethnic Macedonians will contest political status for the foreseeable future, but the promise of Europe is effectively tamping down problems. Without high levels of violence, the emotion of hatred will not rear its head.

[5] Svetozar Stojanovic, from a series of articles in *Politika* published January 23 to February 2, 2008.

Ethnic stigmas will persist, as will the emotion of contempt. This emotion will help sustain segregation across several areas in the region. However, that is the case over much of the world. In short, the political entrepreneurs of the Western Balkans will lack many of the emotion resources of the near past. They will lack the resources for the politics of provocation. After twenty years of turmoil, they will have to participate in something like "normal" politics, at least as normal as that seen in Belgium.[6]

II. THE FUTURE OF WESTERN INTERVENTION

As addressed briefly in the Introduction, I would speculate that we will likely see continued Western intervention in the coming decades, even if it is dressed up in some form of "international" guise. The combination of the erosion of sovereignty norms, the continual expansion of the understanding of "threat," and the plethora of new NGO and military capabilities and organizational inertia will likely push the West toward continual intervention.

On the U.S. side, the intervention in Iraq, despite all its political fallout, is more and more coded as "victory" rather than disaster. Barack Obama campaigned on finding a solution to the "necessary war" in Afghanistan, later justifying troop increases, and getting them with little resistance, during his Nobel Peace Prize speech.

On the other side of the Atlantic, the European Security Strategy Statement of December 2003 can be read as a justification for foreign intervention. As it explicitly states, "In an era of globalization, distant threats may be as much a concern as those near at hand."[7] Statements from the report read as if they have been directly lifted out of a text outlining the liberal peace theory:

The best protection for our security is a world of well-governed democratic states. Spreading good governance, supporting social and political reform, dealing with corruption and abuse of power, establishing the rule of law and protecting human rights are the best means of strengthening the international order.[8]

Given this reasoning, it is unsurprising that the EU statement concludes that:

Active policies are needed to counter dynamic threats. We need to develop a strategic culture that fosters early, rapid, and when necessary, robust intervention.[9]

The West has been playing a global game of sticks and carrots for quite some time. The International Monetary Fund and its policies of structural adjustment serve as a prime example; the United States and its Millennium

---

[6] For a more negative view, see Gordon Bardos, "The New Political Dynamics of Southeastern Europe," *Southeast European and Black Seas Studies* (September 2008) 8 (No. 3): 171–88.

[7] Brussels, "A Secure Europe in a Better World: European Security Strategy," December 12, 2003, p. 6.

[8] Ibid., p. 10.

[9] Ibid., p. 11.

Challenge Account provide another.[10] The United States continues to maintain and expand military potential capable of controlling all common space over the globe.[11] In 2006, the U.S. Department of Defense issued a directive that prioritized stability operations as a core mission.[12]

The West will be intervening. The only question is whether this intervention will be indirect or direct, and how often it will involve military interventions and/or outright occupation. This work has produced insights that illustrate what the West can expect when it does directly intervene.

III. POLICY-RELATED IMPLICATIONS

I will simply list eleven policy-related implications here:

(1) If the contest is being played in R7 – a situation of high ethnic stigma where the emotion of contempt is a ready political resource – interveners should dramatically lower their expectations about what can be accomplished. The West should recognize that not all peoples want to live together. It is not the moral duty of the West to impose its own vision of multiculturalism in every country around the world.

In situations such as R7, no confidence-building sequencing of issues is likely to induce long-term cooperation. Rather, de facto partition should be seen as a realistic, and acceptable, outcome. De facto partition can prevent violence while putting off final status issues until a more fortuitous time. De jure partition can create finality, which in some cases may be desired, but it can also create a legal precedent, which may not be desired.

In the meantime, interveners should promote "good neighbor policies" – informal expectations about cooperation – to solve practical issues. It is possible that the situation will improve in the long run. If not, some more formal separation or partition may be necessary.

Note that unlike some other theorists, I am not advocating separation after all violent conflicts. I am arguing that interveners should be able to distinguish the level of ethnic stigma between groups in conflict and calibrate their expectations accordingly. Situations such as R1 (Bosnia) and R4 (Macedonia) should not be lumped together with those such as R7 (post-2001 Kosovo). The current outcome in Kosovo could have been reached more quickly and with less suffering, less death, and less expense if interveners had proper expectations going in.

---

[10] On this and related issues, see John Tirman, "The New Humanitarianism: How Military Intervention Became the Norm," *Boston Review* (December 2003/January 2004).

[11] See Barry Posen, "Command of the Commons: The Military Foundation of U.S. Hegemony," *International Security* (Summer 2003) 28 (No. 1): 5–46.

[12] For a more extended discussion of expanded missions, see James Dobbins, "Preparing for Nation-Building," *Survival* (October 2006) 48: 3, 27–40.

(2) Situations characterized by R4 – moderate level of ethnic stigma but with significant resentment – call for heavy doses of decentralization to *local* levels. In R7, the emotion of contempt both creates popular desires for separation and provides a ready resource for political actors to create policies and provocations based on that resource. In R4, the lower level of ethnic stigma allows more creative policies. When contesting groups are consumed only by status issues, politicians cannot so easily push buttons for policies of separation. By decentralizing authority to the local level, especially in police and judicial matters, the intervention regime can take the sting out of political resentment. With a lower level of ethnic stigma and a lack of strong contempt, political actors can work together from the center while allowing individuals to deal mainly with co-ethnics at the local level. With all the problems remaining in Macedonia, the situation and the policy were better matched than in other Balkan cases.

(3) If the game is being played in R8 (and maybe R5) – a situation of high contempt, high resentment, and significant violence – the intervener should try to make any possible alliances with local and regional groups. In this situation, where all emotion resources are available, the game is stacked against the intervener. The best the intervener can probably do is to make deals to encourage political groups to deescalate to R7.

(4) The intervener may have the power to prevent escalation to high levels of violence but not have the power to eliminate lower levels of violence (a possible scenario in cells 2, 5, and 8). If the situation is R8, with high levels of contempt, the intervener should expect continued ethnic cleansing by low-level means. With high contempt, a group's members need little formal direction in committing acts, or at least supporting acts, that drive the opposing side out.

(5) Although ethnic stigma and contempt are critical to understanding many intervention outcomes, they need not be present in all cases of high violence. In fact, political actors finding themselves in R2 may believe that escalation through indiscriminate violence is their best strategy. Without high levels of contempt, the emotion of fear is the best resource for separating peoples and consolidating political and territorial gains.

(6) In cases of low ethnic stigma, the progression toward violence will likely be facilitated by a sequence of emotions. Resentments can solidify boundaries; targeted violence at local levels can create anger and revenge fueled cycles of low-level violence; state actors and organized militias may then employ indiscriminate violence. The Bosnian war provides an example.

(7) Interveners should assume no long-term friends. The swirl of emotions involved with status reversals, violence, and stigma, often combined with the stench of corruption, is likely to change the game over any period of years. Early "friends" will find themselves compelled to work against the intervener and early "enemies" will become erstwhile allies. Related,

identifying types of "spoilers" will be a difficult enterprise. Even non-spoilers are likely to use emotion resources when available. The nature of resources is often more crucial than the nature of "spoilers."

(8) Status reversals are powerful forces. The political problem that the West often sees is lack of group rights. In practice, the problem is often loss of what is seen as natural dominance or imposition of unnatural subordination. The West did not understand either the Sunnis in Iraq nor rural Bosnian Serbs in this regard.

(9) Smaller groups seen as collaborators of some sort in the preintervention period will be especially vulnerable to attacks during the power vacuum when the intervention regime is taking over. These groups will require special protection.

(10) If the primary goal is to prevent violence, the best strategy would be to side with the most powerful groups and exchange recognition for policies enshrining and ensuring minority rights. If the West had allowed Serbia and Croatia to divide up Bosnia, there probably would not have been a war, or 100,000 dead, or billions in aid. Nor would there likely have been a Kosovo war. Albanians in Kosovo might not have engaged in a strategy of separation if they had not believed in the possibility of Western support. Obviously, political and moral issues are at play here. Civil wars and intervention are often a matter of political and moral choices. The West should have some clear logic in making those choices.

(11) Interventions are messy affairs. Potential interveners should think hard before doing them.

IV. METHODOLOGICAL ISSUES

Appendix B takes up methodological issues in some depth. In this section, I make some general comments. My methodological goal in this work has been ambitious. To understand the asymmetric competition between Western interveners and their opponents, I needed to understand the nature of the resources at play in that competition. A basic observation from the field was that opponents of Western intervention, lacking material resources, employ an alternative set of resources based on local experiences. Following this line, I needed to develop an analytically valid and manageable way to address the role of what I have called the "residue of experience," especially those experiences related to the upheaval of violent conflict and Western intervention. I borrowed from the theory and conceptualization of emotion for this goal.

Perhaps the major methodological innovation in this work has been the inclusion of "emotion resources" in a study of the strategic interaction between interveners and opponents. In this method, emotions are treated as resources in much the same way that traditional structural resources such as weapons and money are. In other ways, the work is rather straightforward social science. I examined the role of these emotion resources within basic strategic action frameworks. I developed hypotheses able to predict variation in types of opponent tactics. Emotions are not included in many works of social science, especially political science, but there is no reason that they cannot be included, outside of methodological inertia.

I examined and tested these hypotheses across nearly every intervention in the Balkans over a twenty-year period. In the course of the previous chapters, I identified many strategic junctures and specified the choice sets of political actors. What explained those choices? This question was the empirical focus of this book. If one compares explanations based on structural variables alone to those that look at a combination of structural and emotion resources, the latter do a much better job. I would argue that an approach that considers emotion resources not only explains variation in outcomes more effectively, but also more validly captures the reality of the conflict. Such an approach does not sanitize the conflict or create cardboard figures out of complex actors.

My approach has also focused on the interaction between local political actors and Western interveners as a dynamic process. The types of conflicts that played out in the Balkans involved rapidly changing contexts. In fact, the goal of political actors is often to change these contexts. They do so by creating emotions of anger and fear with violence and by using resentment to frame political conflicts. The focus on emotions overcomes the problems of highly context dependent survey research. Surveys can capture attitudes at one point in time, but they are not often able to understand how motivations, beliefs, and evaluation of information can rapidly change. Emotions are the mechanisms that explain such change.

Standard variable-based approaches also fail to explain the dynamic nature of the competition between Western intervener and opponent. There are problems with the validity of common variables. In particular, conceptions of political rights do not capture the basic reality of political struggle in these cases, which is often about perceptions of subordination and dominance. There are problems regarding the changing intensity of a variable's effect, or even changes in the variable's causal direction during the process. Such approaches do not easily capture how the emergence of one factor, such as the promise of EU accession in the Balkan cases, can arise to incorporate common sense conceptions that drive political behavior of both elites and nonelites.

There is a more general problem with these approaches, though. Tied to a rational choice worldview treatments that use standard variables, especially those manifested in large-N statistical works, concentrate on constraints rather than opportunities. As a central point of this work, emotions provide opportunities for political actors. Although the expansion of Europe may dominate Western Balkan politics in the long run, the political actors I observed in the Western Balkans were not heavily constrained in the short and medium run. With an assessment of their emotion resources, they often took great chances and endured heavy costs; they used their imaginations to pull off effective provocations; they calibrated their strategies. In terms of common terminology, what I have observed in the Western Balkans was agency over structural constraint.

There is a tendency in social science, perhaps unsurprisingly, to be "scientific." The meaning of that in practice has been a quasi-religious quest to show that history and culture do not matter, that everything is a matter of structural constraints or economics. Most ironically, many political scientists are driven to try to find that politics does not matter. I found something different in the Balkans. I found actors who were connected to their groups' histories, who took chances, who often committed ugly acts. Above all, they were their own, complex actors driven by emotion and reason. I have tried to develop methods to accurately understand their actions and convey their histories.

Appendix A

A Note on Names

I. PROGRESSION OF NAMES RELEVANT TO YUGOSLAVIA
AND SERBIA

1918: Kingdom of Serbs, Croats, and Slovenes

1929 (October 3): Kingdom of Yugoslavia

Communist Period: Partisan movement names country Democratic Federal Yugoslavia in 1943; renamed Federal People's Republic of Yugoslavia in 1946; renamed the Socialist Federal Republic of Yugoslavia in 1963 (SFRY)

1992 (March 27): Federal Republic of Yugoslavia (FRY)

2003 (February 4): State Union of Serbia and Montenegro

2006: (June 3): Independent Montenegro and (June 5) independent Serbia

2. MUSLIMS/BOSNIAKS

1961: Census introduces category "Muslims in the ethnic sense"

1968: Constitutional changes to designate "Muslim" as an official nationality

1993 (September): Congress of Bosniak Intellectuals introduces name "Bosniak"; some groups retain Muslim designation

Appendix B

Alternative Arguments

The "general" dependent variable of this study was very broad: the success or failure of an intervention as defined by the intervener's own goals – that is, whether the West achieved what it set out to do in each case. The second dependent variable was much more specific: the variation in provocations and tactics listed in the lower left box of Figure 1.1, repeated as Figure B.1. To review, my claim was that by adding emotions to the analysis, we can explain when opponents of intervention use bombings versus boycotts, indiscriminate killing versus discriminate killing, when they do nothing, and so on. The specific dependent variable is related to the larger one. The more success an opponent has in launching effective provocations against the intervener, the greater the chances that the intervener's mission will fail. Certainly, the overall success or failure of an intervention is determined by a combination of factors. As the case studies in this book have shown, there is no simple answer to the success and failure of intervention; there is no magic explanatory bullet.

In this note, I address how the emotions-based approach developed here challenges or complements major alternative explanations. These alternative approaches can be discussed in terms of the elements of the basic framework outlined in Figure B.1.

Explanations can be differentiated by their emphasis on one aspect of this framework over others. I have concentrated on the presence/absence of emotion resources in the upper right hand box of this diagram. The distribution of these emotion resources goes far in explaining whether opponents of intervention are able to employ the provocations in the lower left box to change or hinder the intervener's "game."

One set of approaches concentrate on the nature of the actors playing the game. Perhaps the best known of these theories discuss "spoilers." Intervention failure occurs when spoilers, who are likely to employ strategies and tactics such as violence and boycott, are allowed to play the game. Success comes from eliminating or marginalizing these bad actors. A second set of approaches address the nature of structural resources specified in the second link of the

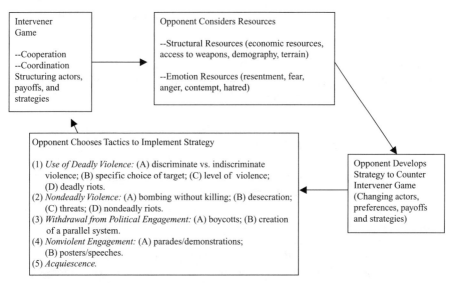

FIGURE B.1. Western Intervention and the Nature of Its Opposition (Repeated from Figure 1.1).

chain. For these explanations, intervention failure occurs when interveners lack the resources to apply the most effective sticks and carrots. A third set of approaches concentrate on the first box of the diagram. These theories stress that the intervention game must be played a specific way: the intervener must address governance issues in a specific sequence. In the best-known version of this approach, interveners fail when they attempt to install liberal democratic reforms before establishing necessary institutions that will allow those reforms to take hold. I address these alternative approaches and their relationship to the present work in turn.

I. ACTORS/SPOILERS

As mentioned in the Conclusion, the material in this book casts doubt on approaches that emphasize types of actors. Consider the categories in Stephen Stedman's typology. He distinguishes among "limited" spoilers who are willing to share power and cooperate with the intervention game, "greedy" spoilers who constantly calculate whether to cooperate or defect, and "total" spoilers who are incorrigible and will always play defection.[1] Conflicts generate spoilers because conflicts generate winners and losers, the latter likely wanting to "spoil" the result of the contest.

The Balkan cases illustrate the difficulties for interveners in categorizing actors and identifying consistent and reliable partners. At one point, the West

[1] Stephen Stedman, "Spoiler Problems in Peace Processes," *International Security* (1997) 22: 5–53. See previous discussion in Chapter 4.

surely classified Slobodan Milosevic as a greedy spoiler who could be bought off or threatened relatively easily. Indeed, in the mid-1990s Milosevic seemed to respond predictably to the West's sticks and carrots. After some limited bombings and an offer to remove sanctions, Milosevic became a signatory to the Dayton Accords that ended the Bosnian war. When the West confronted Milosevic a few short years later over Kosovo, they anticipated that this greedy actor would again quickly capitulate. The West did not anticipate the need to bomb Serbia for months. As shown by their complete lack of preparation, the West certainly did not anticipate Milosevic's ethnic cleansing campaign in Kosovo in response to Western actions. The problem, I argue, is that Milosevic had a set of emotion resources available in the Kosovo case that would work to support both confrontation and ethnic cleansing even when Serbia was in a weakened position. These resources allowed an actor who had previously behaved in a greedy fashion to act as a total spoiler.

The Kosovo case exhibits the complexity of actors in violent conflicts and how they are not easily categorized. At one point before the war, the U.S. State Department labeled the Kosovo Liberation Army a terrorist organization, presumably to isolate the group as a spoiler. Soon after, the KLA became a close partner. Moreover, the behavior of "nonspoilers" in Kosovo after the intervention was not always in line with the Western game. For instance, many of the West's closest partners worked to pressure the West through a destabilization of Kosovo during the Standards before Status period.

President Rugova (who was compared to Gandhi for his nonviolent politics of the 1990s) and other moderate Albanian leaders failed to condemn the 2004 riots. This was not surprising in light of the fact that violence was instrumental in ending the Standards before Status policy and hastening Kosovo's independence.

In addition to Rugova, consider other Kosovar Prime Ministers in the post-occupation years. Ramush Haradinaj, an American favorite, was named Prime Minister after the October 2004 elections, but served only 100 days before being indicted by the Hague for crimes against humanity. He was acquitted for lack of evidence, but in July 2010 he was rearrested on grounds of witness intimidation. As Hague Tribunal President Patrick Robinson explained in his ruling, "The trial chamber failed to appreciate the gravity of the threat that witness intimidation posed to the trial's integrity. . . . Given the potential importance of these witnesses to the prosecution's case, the error undermined the fairness of the proceedings and resulted in a miscarriage of justice."[2] In reference to another key Kosovo leader, Joe Biden stated that Hashim Thaci was the "George Washington of Kosovo." However, in 2010 a Council of Europe report, picking up on earlier claims by Carla del Ponte, accused Prime Minister Thaci of being a leader in criminal networks that have engaged in organ trafficking. Thaci's political party was also suspected of malfeasance in the 2010 elections. The voting in Thaci's strongholds had to be redone due to vote

---

[2] *BBC News*, July 21, 2010.

rigging. Whatever the merits of these various charges (which are in the process of being seriously investigated at the time of this writing), the West is relying on this set of actors to implement the rule of law and establish democratic norms within the progression of the Basic Game.

The Bosnian case has exhibited similar issues. In the late 1990s, the West was desperately seeking to marginalize Serbian nationalist total spoilers in Bosnia. The West believed they had found their alternative in the form of Milorad Dodik. In the words of one commentator:

[R]ays of hope are breaking through in Bosnia. Thanks to its youthful Prime Minister, Milorad Dodik, 39, the R.S. has abandoned its obstruction of the 1995 Dayton peace agreement and instead is working to implement it. Eager to see him succeed, the U.S. and Europe are mustering money and political preference to keep him in office. "He's a godsend," says Jacques Paul Klein, Principal Deputy High Representative, whose office is charged with implementing Dayton's civilian provisions. "To see him step out of the blue is amazing. . . . He's been very, very good and very energetic."[3]

After designating Dodik as a nonspoiler, the West went to great lengths to reward and support him. In an effort to split Bosnian Serbs into competing moderate and extremist camps, Western interveners rewarded Dodik with various carrots while punishing his more nationalist opponents with sticks.[4] The long-term result was not positive. A decade after the glowing assessment in the quoted passage, Dodik was clearly the most powerful Serb politician in Bosnia. However, in contrast to that assessment, Dodik was now considered by many Western officials as "an unabashed nationalist and the greatest threat to Bosnia's fragile, multiethnic peace."[5]

Certainly the problem of unreliable nonspoilers is not restricted to the Balkans. At the time of this writing, Western leaders were also struggling with their designated partner in Afghanistan, President Hamid Karzai, following tainted elections and corruption charges. In many cases, it is not just losers of conflicts that act like spoilers, but winners as well.

The emotion-based approach and the empirical material here suggest that "good" actors will often employ "bad" actions. Emotions, especially those stemming from violent conflict, serve as both a powerful resource and a forceful constraint. If a powerful emotion resource exists, we should expect that any ambitious political entrepreneur, regardless of previous conduct, will consider using that resource to achieve critical goals. For example, when Kosovo Albanian leaders needed to break what they saw as a stagnant Standards before

---

3 Massimo Calabresi, "Hope on the Rise: A Surprising Young Bosnian Serb Leader Brings Good News to a War-Ravaged Country," *Time Europe*, April 6, 1998. In the same article, Chris Bennett of the International Crisis Group called Dodik "the most significant political development since Dayton was signed."

4 For a detailed discussion, see Roland Paris, *At War's End: Building Peace after Civil Conflict* (Cambridge: Cambridge University Press, 2004), pp. 103–7.

5 Radio Free Europe/Radio Liberty, "Milorad Dodik – One Foot in Bosnia, but His Heart in Serbia," April 28, 2009.

Status intervention policy, they did not hesitate to use anger – and tactics related to that emotion – to achieve that goal. The existence of powerful emotions within a population also acts as a constraint. For instance, the existence of ethnic contempt will usually deter political leaders from embracing policies of integration. In the face of ethnic resentments, few political actors will wish to accept any bargain smacking of subordination. Whether Dodik was a moderate in his personal orientation, as envisioned by Western interveners, or whether he was always a secret nationalist hardliner is unknowable. Regardless of his personal nature, the power of Bosnian Serb resentments meant that any Bosnian Serb leader would find the path toward acceptance of police reform and other centralizing policies a difficult one. The existence of this emotion, rather than the spoiler/nonspoiler orientation of the leader, would seem to be the best predictor of the observed variation in outcome.

II. RESOURCES

A second set of theories concentrate on the level and nature of intervener resources. An exemplar of this approach is Doyle and Sambanis's *Making War and Building Peace*.[6] In that work, Doyle and Sambanis present a peacebuilding triangle. The three variables that constitute the triangle are the depth of the hostility of the conflict, local capacity, and international capacity. International capacity is really the only variable in the hands of the intervener. The hostility of the conflict, measured primarily by the number of deaths and displacements, captures how deep or intense the conflict was prior to the intervener entering the story. The local capacity variable, measured by per capita GDP and energy consumption, is also determined by factors inherent in the country facing the intervention. High hostility and poor local capacity will lead to low chances of intervention success. A smart intervener can compensate for these problems by increasing the level of international resources committed to the intervention – providing greater economic assistance, larger numbers of troops, and a more robust mandate. If a particular conflict has low domestic capacity and great depth of hostility, there is a greater inherent probability of failure, and this means greater international capacity will be needed to increase the probability of success. If there is high domestic capacity and small depth of hostility, the conflict has a higher inherent probability of success and lower international capacity will be needed to produce success.

Doyle and Sambanis's work merges a theory of structural constraints with a sticks and carrots approach. Depth of hostility and local capacity act as constraints but interveners can still shape the outcome if they have sufficient resources to shape incentives. As they write:

peacekeeping and peacemaking are integral parts of peacebuilding as they affect actors' incentives to support or undermine peace implementation.... We see peace as the

---

[6] This section is largely from a report written by one of my graduate research assistants, Tara Maller.

outcome of a dynamic process, which is shaped partially by the peacekeepers performance and their peacemaking and peacebuilding efforts and by the parties' reactions
to those efforts and partially by other factors, such as the level of local capacities and
the residual hostility after civil war.[7]

The empirical reality of the Balkans does cast some doubt on the idea that
international resources can compensate for deep hostility and lack of local
capacity. As mentioned at several points in the text, few cases of intervention
have ever had so many international resources poured into reconstruction.
Levels of international economic aid in both Bosnia and Kosovo have surpassed
that of the Marshall Plan; Kosovo has received 25 times as much aid per capita
as Afghanistan; 60,000 international troops deployed to Bosnia (and 10,000
civilian personnel) and 30,000 to Kosovo (the equivalent number in Iraq would
have been 526,000).[8] Yet Kosovo was not successful, and Bosnia has had at
best a mixed result. As much of this book has been devoted to illustrating how
emotion resources can be used to counter material resources, I will not further
belabor that point.

Rather, I would like to emphasize how the emotions-based work here complements Doyle and Sambanis's work in important ways. First and foremost,
the authors recognize that residual depth of hostility is a critical factor in
intervention. In other words, they would agree that the lived experiences of
individuals in conflict leave a powerful residue that shapes future outcomes.
The problem is that their conception of hostility is not very specific. The present
work shows how different types of violence lead to different types of hostility –
fear, anger, hatred. It shows how violence-related hostility combines with other
types of hostility in the form of ethnic contempt and political resentments to
form a more specific set of constraints and resources.

In contrast, Doyle and Sambanis do not really provide an answer to what
drives particular levels of violence or types of violence. They do not try to
explain how and why hostility reached the level it did during the preintervention
stage of the conflict (which often helps explain actions after intervention). Nor
do they attempt to explain why actors in high-hostility situations might use
violence after the introduction of an intervention regime. If high hostility means
a lower probability of success and requires greater capacity in compensation,
we need a better understanding of the mechanisms that drive different types
and intensities of violence in these cases. An emotions-based approach provides
a dynamic story about how political entrepreneurs may mobilize and exploit
emotional resources in the postconflict stage to undermine the efforts of the
intervener. In Michael Gilligan's review of the Doyle and Sambanis book, he
comments, "What is missing is a theoretical story about why the agents in a

---

[7] Michael W. Doyle and Nicholas Sambanis, *Making War and Building Peace* (Princeton, NJ:
Princeton University Press, 2006), p. 27.

[8] These figures are from Gordon Bardos, "Bosnian Lessons," *National Interest Online*, July 16,
2010.

civil war behave in such a way as to produce the triangle."[9] The present book tries to provide key parts of that story.

Also, Doyle and Sambanis's structure-oriented work does raise questions for further research that I was not able to address here. Specifically, a future area of research could ask how the emotion resources that I have identified here might work in combination with Doyle and Sambanis's structural variables. In other words, are certain collective emotions impacted by the local capacity in a country? Does low local capacity perhaps make it easier for opponents of intervention to exploit emotions by intensifying or magnifying certain emotional reactions such as fear?

III. SEQUENCING AND OUTBIDDING

Roland Paris's *At War's End* lays out a clear sequencing strategy in a program he terms "institutionalization before liberalization." Paris clearly and succinctly states the core principle of his argument:

What is needed in the immediate postconflict period is not quick elections, democratic ferment, or economic "shock therapy" but a more controlled and gradual approach to liberalization, combined with the immediate building of governmental institutions that can manage these political and economic reforms.[10]

Paris devotes a chapter to Croatia and Bosnia, explaining the success of the first in terms of exceptional circumstances. The problem for Paris's argument is that Western interveners took his lesson to heart in the later case of Kosovo. The main idea behind the policy of Standards before Status was a version of the institutionalization before liberalization blueprint. As detailed in the Kosovo chapters of this book, political actors could strategically use the emotions of anger and contempt to wreck that policy. The Standards before Status version of a controlled and gradual approach ended in the massive riots of 2004.

Jack Snyder's argument in *From Voting to Violence* is related to both the sequencing and spoiler issues in interventions.[11] Its focus on nationalist outbidding is relevant to both the collapse of Yugoslavia and the Western democratizing interventions in Kosovo and Bosnia.

Snyder's work lays out a specific chain of events. As along the lines of Paris's argument, the lack of a strong institutional base in the early years of democratization creates severe problems. Without established political parties and a mature and free press, holdover elites from the previous nondemocratic regime

[9] Michael Gilligan, "Making War and Building Peace *and* Sustainable Peace: Power and Democracy after Civil Wars," *Perspectives on Politics* (2007) 5: 208–10.

[10] Paris, *At War's End*, pp. 7–8.

[11] Jack Snyder, *From Voting to Violence: Democratization and Nationalist Conflict* (New York: W. W. Norton and Co., 2000). I owe much of this section on Snyder and outbidding to my graduate research assistant Sameer Lalwani.

can silence co-ethnic rivals through nationalist outbidding.[12] Rival groups often feel compelled to use the same techniques. The result is a spiraling process where politics becomes dominated by extremist nationalist mythmaking. In the worst cases, belligerent nationalist myths lead to mobilization for violence against either external or internal enemies.

Snyder's work identifies "bad actors" that arise endogenously out of the process of democratization. As Snyder's approach embodies an important conventional wisdom, it is worth citing at length:

Before democratization begins, nationalism is usually weak or absent among the broad masses of the population. Popular nationalism typically arises during the earliest stages of democratization, when elites use nationalist appeals to compete for popular support. Democratization produces nationalism when powerful groups within the nation not only need to harness popular energies to the tasks of war and economic development, but they also want to avoid surrendering real political authority to the average citizen. For those elites, nationalism is a convenient doctrine that justifies a partial form of democracy, in which an elite rules in the name of a nation yet may not be fully accountable to its people. Under conditions of partial democratization, elites can often use their control over the levers of government, the economy, and the mass media to promote nationalist ideas, and thus set the agenda for debate. Nationalist conflicts arise as a by-product of elites' efforts to persuade the people to accept divisive nationalist ideas.[13]

Snyder labels his model the elite persuasion view. If this elite persuasion model is applied to intervention, Snyder's argument implies that interveners should not provide ready opportunities for extremist nationalist elites to persuade their populations in the early years of democratization. Given the lack of mature electoral institutions and democratic parties, nationalist demagogues can often win early elections that legitimize their power. The solution is that interveners should not allow early elections. Given the lack of a developed and balanced media, democratic interveners should control speech and media in the early years of occupation until an open "marketplace for ideas" truly arises.[14] Along with scholars who argue for a sequencing of reforms, Snyder sees an inevitable erosion of the power of ethnic appeals. Over time, a more complex society will develop new economic, political, and social groups, which will create the possibility for cross-cutting cleavages and new types of coalitions that will be the basis for multiethnic democracy.[15]

---

[12] See V. P. Gagnon, *The Myth of Ethnic War: Serbia and Croatia in the 1990's* (Ithaca, NY: Cornell University Press, 2004), for a version of this theory applied to Serbia and Croatia during the collapse of Yugoslavia.

[13] Jack Snyder, *From Voting to Violence*, p. 32.

[14] Jack Snyder and Karen Ballentine, "Nationalism and the Marketplace of Ideas," *International Security* (1996) 21: 5–40.

[15] Philip Roeder and Donald Rothchild make a forceful argument for creating power-dividing, individual-based democratic institutions after civil wars. They stress that competition within the ethnic group will create incentives to reach out across ethnic lines. The result will be multiple majorities that serve to mitigate ethnic conflict. The problem for the Balkans is that Roeder and Rothchild hold that this strategy requires "a consensus among most of the leaders of the

Two points in this argument are especially relevant here – the process of outbidding and the nationalist myths that Snyder and others see as the material used by those engaged in outbidding. I address these in turn.

One of the prime goals of this book has been to explain subregional variation in the conflicts in the Balkans. It is not clear how outbidding theory can explain this subregional variation. The conditions Snyder postulates – nascent state-building and democratization, elite competition, nationalism, and partial monopolies of information – were all present during the international interventions in the Balkans in the 1990s, yet these cases produced differentiated outcomes, both in terms of types and levels of violence and in terms of responses to intervention games.

Second, outbidding theories explain escalation better than deescalation. The approach would have difficulty explaining the mitigation of resentment in Macedonia and the lack of escalation in Montenegro.

Another major weakness of the outbidding literature is the underspecification of the mechanisms. Outbidding and intraethnic competition by nature are an appeal to a domestic audience, but they cannot be accurately deployed without a sufficient understanding of the collective emotions that are available and need to be triggered or activated.

This last point leads into a question about the nationalist myths that are the stuff of outbidding strategies. How do nationalist myths actually motivate individuals? For Snyder, nationalism is an idea that gets interjected at a certain early point in the democratization process. Note that the passage implies that no one is really a nationalist at the start of the process: as stated, "nationalism is usually weak or absent for the broad masses" and elites use nationalism because it is a "convenient doctrine" for holdover elites who wish to retain power. The theory rests on the assumption that an idea that was weak or absent can suddenly be brought in by a small group of elites to motivate individuals to support violence and other high-cost actions.

The concept of nationalism is too vague and does not specify finer-grained mechanisms that would motivate individuals to make sacrifices or commit and support violence. The present work's starting point is that actual lived experiences – status reversals, violence, stigma – provide the basis to motivate action. It is the residue of this experience – emotion – that shapes action tendencies, influences the way that information is processed, and affects belief formation. Moreover, psychology and other disciplines supply sufficient knowledge to assess the way specific emotions impact actions, information collection, and belief formation in different ways. Rather than relying on reference to general nationalist myths, an emotions-based theory identifies distinct forces – fear,

main ethnic groups that together their diverse populations constitute a nation (p. 18)." This key condition simply does not hold for most of the Balkan cases. See Philip Roeder and Donald Rothchild, *Sustainable Peace: Power and Democracy after Civil Wars* (Ithaca, NY: Cornell University Press, 2005).

anger, hatred, resentment, contempt – that can predict the specific contours of political mobilization and provocation.

In both Snyder's work and the present work, elites strategically work to alter the cognitions of broader masses. The difference in the approaches lies in assumptions about how easily these cognitions can be altered. In Snyder's approach, elites can easily persuade masses through myths. In the approach of this book, elite strategies are only effective if they tie into experiences/emotions.

The Balkan cases present problems for a theory based on nationalist myths. First of all, any claim that nationalism was weak in Kosovo before democratization is off base. Conflict over Kosovo's political status went back decades. Kosovo Albanian support for Kosovo independence was early and universal. In my view, Snyder's assumption of weak or absent nationalism does not fit most of the Balkan cases. As recent research by Keith Darden convincingly shows, the claim might not fit many places in modern Eastern Europe.[16] Most fundamentally, an emotions-based approach shows that the Balkan cases do not fit well with the idea of nationalist "myths." The series of political status reversals in Kosovo was not a myth; the history of Serb–Albanian violence and ethnic cleansing was not a myth; cultural prejudices and ethnic stigmas were not myths. In most political science views, if other ideas are allowed to compete with nationalist "myths," those ideas will prevail. But in the Balkans it was not ideational myths but actual experiences and their residue that drove the course of events. If anyone had a monopoly over communication and the ability to make myths in a segmented market, it was the Yugoslav Communist regime. For decades, that regime sprouted myths about Brotherhood and Unity. In the Balkans, the rapidity of the collapse of those ideas illustrates the weakness of myths when they compete with emotions. Given the emotion resources of many Balkan cases, it is not surprising that the ideas of liberal democracy did not rapidly catch on either.

IV. MONOLITHIC ACTORS

Undoubtedly, the most predictable criticism of this book is that I have, with the exception of Montenegro, treated ethnic groups as unitary actors. One informal rule in political science is that ethnic groups should never be treated monolithically. There are always critical subgroups within the ethnic group that should be the focus of analysis. In many game theoretic treatments of ethnic conflict, the division is often between "extremists" and "moderates" or "hard-liners" and "soft-liners."[17] As previously discussed, most intervention theories identify spoilers as a key set of actors.

Why have I broken this rule? I agree that ethnic groups should not be treated as monoliths most of the time. But on some issues, conforming to the political

---

[16] See Keith Darden, *Resisting Occupation: Mass Schooling and the Creation of Durable National Loyalties* (Cambridge: Cambridge University Press, forthcoming).

[17] See Chapter 5 for some examples.

science norm obfuscates more than it enlightens. This book has concentrated on sovereignty issues in the Balkans. During my fieldwork in the Balkans, I encountered little variation within ethnic groups on these fundamental issues. In Kosovo, I never met an Albanian who wished to remain in a common political entity with Serbs; I never met a Serb who wished to live as part of a minority in an independent Kosovo. I met surprisingly few Albanians who had any remorse over the pogroms against Serbs in 2004; I met surprisingly few Serbs who expressed any remorse over the ethnic cleansing in Kosovo in 1999. At the most basic levels of political action, such as the ethnic composition of political parties, the ethnic group has been the common sense basis for participation and mobilization throughout the region.

In the Balkans, and perhaps most areas of the world, threats and perceived insults unify ethnic groups without much direction from leadership. Consider for example the reaction in Kosovo over charges that Albanian leaders were involved in organ trafficking. As one Kosovar journalist described:

It was a privilege to be in Kosovo when the report came out. It was astonishing to see a whole society uniting in such a homogenous fashion at a specific moment. I was surprised to see even trusted friends joining the chorus of support for Prime Minister Thaci. Kosovo reacted to the report as a single family unit, unanimously denouncing the report as a Serbian conspiracy.[18]

These events are occurring right after contentious local elections in Kosovo in a state that is now securely independent. Ethnic Albanian opponents of Thaci could have used this incident against him. Instead, all members of the group unified.

[18] Avni Zogiani, *Balkan Insight*, December 22, 2010.

References

AAAS [American Association for the Advancement of Science]. 2000. "Policy or Panic? The Flight of Ethnic Albanians from Kosovo, March to May 1999." American Association for the Advancement of Science, Science and Human Rights Program.

Addison, T., and S. M. Murshed. 2006. "The Social Contract and Violent Conflict." In Helen Yanacopulos and Joseph Hanlon, eds., *Civil War, Civil Peace*, pp. 137–163. Athens, OH: Ohio University Press.

Ahmetasevic, N. 2006. "Bosnian Returnees Quietly Quit Regained Homes." Institute for War and Peace Reporting, August 31.

Akhavan, P., and R. Howse. 1995. *Yugoslavia, the Former and Future: Reflections by Scholars from the Region*. Washington, DC: The Brookings Institution.

Albright, M. 2003. *Madam Secretary: A Memoir*. New York, NY: Miramax.

Ali, H. 2005. "Sectarian Violence Rocks Al-Amiriyah." Institute for War and Peace Reporting, September 13.

Aminzade, R., and D. McAdam. 2002. "Emotions and Contentious Politics." *Mobilization: An International Quarterly* 7(2): 107–109.

Andric, I. 1977. *The Bridge on the Drina*. Chicago, IL: University Of Chicago Press.

Andrijasevic, Z., and S. Rastoder. 2006. *The History of Montenegro*. Podgorica: Montenegro Diaspora Centre.

Arian, A. 2002. "Israeli Public Opinion on National Security." Jaffee Center for Strategic Studies, Tel-Aviv University.

Armon-Jones, C. 1986. "The Thesis of Constructionism." In R. Harre, ed., *The Social Construction of Emotions*, pp. 32–66. New York: Basil Blackwell.

Ashdown, P., and R. Holbrooke. 2008. "A Bosnian Powder Keg," *The Guardian*, October 22.

Atzilli, B. 2004. "Complex Spiral of Escalation: The Case of the Israeli–Palestinian Conflict." Unpublished paper.

Bakic, I., and R. Dunderovic. 1990. "Gradani Bosne I Hercegovine o medunaciconalnim odnosima." *Oslobodenje*, March 22.

Bakic-Hayden, M. "National Memory as Narrative Memory: The Case of Kosovo." In M. Todorova, ed., *Balkan Identities: Nation and Memory*, pp. 25–40. New York, NY: New York University Press.

Balkan Insight. 2010. "Inzko Calls on EU to Maintain Focus on Bosnia." *Balkan Insight*, January, 27.

Banac, I. 1984. *The National Question in Yugoslavia: Origins, History, Politics*. Ithaca, NY: Cornell University Press.

Banac, I. 1992. "The Fearful Asymmetry of War: The Causes and Consequences of Yugoslavia's Demise." *Daedalus* 121(2): 141–175.

Barbalet, J. 2001. *Emotion, Social Theory, and Social Structure: A Macrosociological Approach*. Cambridge: Cambridge University Press.

Bardos, G. 2008. "The New Political Dynamics of Southeastern Europe." *Southeast European and Black Seas Studies* 8(3): 171–188.

Bardos, G. 2010. "Bosnian Lessons," *National Interest Online*, July 16.

Bennett, C. 1995. *Yugoslavia's Bloody Collapse: Causes, Course and Consequences*. New York, NY: New York University Press.

Berkowitz, L. 1989. "Frustration–Aggression Hypothesis: Examination and Reformulation." *Psychological Bulletin* 106(1): 59–73.

Bianchini, S., J. Marko, and M. Uvalic. 2007. *Regional Cooperation, Peace Enforcement, and the Role of the Treaties in the Balkans*. Bologna: Longo Editore Ravenna.

Bieber, F. 2002. "The Instrumentalization of Minorities in the Montenegrin Dispute over Independence." European Centre for Minority Issues, Policy Brief #8.

Bieber, F. 2003. *Montenegro in Transition: Problems of Identity and Statehood*. Baden-Baden, Germany: Nomos Verlagsgesellschaft.

Bieber, F. 2005. "Local Institutional Engineering: A Tale of Two Cities, Mostar and Brcko." *International Peacekeepers* 12(3): 420–433.

Bieber, F. 2006. "Voting Day: Looking Each Other in the Eye." *Transitions on Line*, May 23.

Bieber, F. 2009. "Dayton Bosnia May Be Over – But What Next?" *Balkan Insight*, December 10.

Bieber, F., and Z. Daskalovski. 2003. *Understanding the War in Kosovo*. London, UK: Frank Cass.

Bildt, C. 2004. "Why Kosovo Must Not Submit to Violence." *Financial Times*, March 22.

Bilefsky, D. 2008. "Angry Serbs Burn Border Posts in Kosovo." *New York Times*, February 20.

Bilefsky, D. 2008. "Kosovo Declares Its Independence from Serbia." *New York Times*, February 18.

Binder, D. 1993. "U.S. Policymakers on Bosnia Admit Errors in Opposing Partition in 1992." *New York Times*, August 29.

Binnendijk, H., C. Barry, G. Cordero, L. Peterson Nussbaum, and M. Sinclair, eds. 2006. *Solutions for Northern Kosovo: Lessons Learned in Mostar, Eastern Slavonia, and Brcko*. Defense and Technology Paper 4. Washington DC: National Defense University Center for Technology and National Security Policy, August.

Blagojevic, M. 2000. "The Migration of Serbs from Kosovo during the 1970's and 1980's." In N. Popov, ed., *The Road to War in Serbia: Trauma and Catharsis*, pp. 212–243. Budapest: Central European University Press.

Bodenhausen, G., L. Sheppard, and G. Kramer. 1994. "Negative Affect and Social Judgment: The Differential Impact of Anger and Sadness." *European Journal of Social Psychology* 24(1): 45–62.

Booth, K. 2001. *The Kosovo Tragedy: The Human Rights Dimensions*. London, UK: Frank Cass.

Bose, S. 2002. *Bosnia after Dayton: Nationalist Partition and International Intervention*. London, UK: C. Hurst & Co. Publishers.

Botev, N. 1994. "Where East Meets West: Ethnic Intermarriage in the Former Yugoslavia, 1962 to 1989." *American Sociological Review* 59(3): 461–480.

Bougarel, X. 1999. "Cultural Identity or Political Ideology? Bosnian Islam since 1990." Paper presented at the Annual Convention of the Association for the Study of Nationalities, Columbia University, New York, April 15–17.

Bringa, T. 1995. *Being Muslim the Bosnian Way: Identity and Community in a Central Bosnian Village*. Princeton, NJ: Princeton University Press.

Brown, R. 2000. "Social Identity Theory: Past Achievements, Current Problems and Future Challenges." *European Journal of Social Psychology* 30(6): 745–778.

Brunnbauer, U. 2002. "The Implementation of the Ohrid Accord: Ethnic Macedonian Resentments." *Journal on Ethnopolitics and Minority Issues in Europe*, Issue Number 1.

Bueno de Mesquita, Ethan and Eric S. Dickson. 2007. "The Propaganda of the Deed: Terrorism, Counterterrorism, and Mobilization." *American Journal of Political Science* 51(2): 364–381.

Bujanovac Press Center. 2002. "Terrorist Attacks and Provocations in the Ground Safety Zone," January 8.

Burg, S., and M. Berbaum. 1989. "Community, Integration, and Stability in Multinational Yugoslavia." *American Political Science Review* 83(2): 535–554.

Burg, S., and P. Shoup. 1999. *The War in Bosnia and Hercegovina: Ethnic Conflict and International Intervention*. Armonk, NY: M.E. Sharpe.

Burns J. 2005. "Three Car Bombs Leave 18 Dead and 46 Hurt in a Shiite Suburb of Baghdad." *New York Times*, June 23.

Buza, S. 2003. "Ex-Rebel Chief Denies South Serbia Presevo Attack." *Reuters*, February 28.

Byman, D. 2000. "Forever Enemies? The Manipulation of Ethnic Identities to End Ethnic Wars." *Security Studies* 9(3): 149–190.

Calabresi, M. 1998. "Hope on the Rise: A Surprising Young Bosnian Serb Leader Brings Good News to a War-Ravaged Country," *Time Europe*, April 6.

Cante, F. 2008. Argumentacion, negociacion, racional y acuerdos. Bogota: Columbia.

Carnegie Endowment for International Peace. 1993. *The Other Balkan Wars: A 1913 Carnegie Endowment Inquiry in Retrospect*. Washington, DC: Carnegie Endowment for Peace, p. 151.

Cave, D. 2007. "Shiite's Tale: How Gulf with Sunnis Widened." *New York Times*, August 31.

Cederman, L., A. Wimmer and B. Min. 2010. "Why Do Ethnic Groups Rebel? New Data and Analysis." *World Politics* 62(1): 87–119.

Cerovic, S. 2001. "Serbia and Montenegro: Reintegration, Divorce, or Something Else?" Special Report, US Institute for Peace.

Churcher, B. 2002. "Kosovo Lindore/Preshevo 1999–2002 and the FYROM Conflict." Conflict Studies Research Centre, Ministry of Defence, UK, March.

Christia, F. 2007. "Walls of Martyrdom: Tehran's Propaganda Murals," *Centerpiece*, Winter.

Ciavarra, J. 2003. "Traveler Q and A: Is Iraq the Next Travel Hot Spot?" *National Geographic Traveler*, September 3.

Clark, H. 2000. *Civil Resistance in Kosovo*. Sterling, VA: Pluto Press.

Clore, G., and K. Gasper. 2000. "Feeling Is Believing: Some Affective Influences on Belief." In N. H. Frijda, A. S. Manstead, and S. Bem, eds., *Emotions and Beliefs: How Feelings Influence Thoughts*. Cambridge: Cambridge University Press.

Collier, P., V. Elliott, H. Hegre, A. Hoeffer, M. Reynal-Querol, and N. Sambanis. 2003. *Breaking the Conflict Trap: Civil War and Development Policy*. Washington, DC: Co-publication of the World Bank and Oxford University Press.

Collier, P., and N. Sambanis. 2005. *Understanding Civil War: Evidence and Analysis*, Volume 2. Washington, DC: World Bank Publications.

Collins, E., with M. McGovern 1999. *Killing Rage*. London, UK: Granta Books.

Collins, R. "Social Movements and the Focus of Emotional Attention." In Goodwin, Jasper, and Poletta, eds., *Passionate Politics*, pp. 27–44. Chicago, IL: University of Chicago Press.

Costalli, S., and F. Moro. "A Local-Level Analysis of Violence and Intervention in Bosnia's Civil War." Unpublished manuscript.

Cousens, E. 2002. "From Missed Opportunities to Overcompensation: Implementing the Dayton Agreement on Bosnia." In S. Stedman, D. Rothchild, and E. Cousens, eds., *Ending Civil Wars: The Implementation of Peace Agreements*, pp. 531–566. Boulder, CO: Lynne Rienner Publishers.

CRPM [Center for Research and Policy Making]. 2005. "Macedonian Ethnic Politics Post Ohrid Agreement: The Issue of the New Law on Local Government Boundaries." Center for Research and Policy Making, Policy Brief No. 1, Skopje, Macedonia, August 9.

Dahlman, C., and G. O'Tuathail. 2006. "Bosnia's Third Space? Nationalist Separatism and International Supervision in Bosnia's Brcko District." *Geopolitics* 11: 651–675.

Damasio, A. 1994. *Descartes' Error: Emotion, Reason, and the Human Brain*. New York, NY: Avon.

Damasio, A. 2001. "Fundamental Feelings." *Nature* 413(6858): 781.

Danner, M. 2005. "Taking Stock of the Forever War." *The New York Times Magazine*, 11.

Daragahi B. 2005. "Sunni, Shiite Cleric Press for Calm." *Boston Globe*, September 17.

Darmanovic, S. 2007. "Montenegro: Miracle in the Balkans?" *Journal of Democracy* 18(2): 152–159.

Dimitrijevic, N. 2000. *Managing Multiethnic Local Communities in the Countries of the Former Yugoslavia*. Budapest: Open Society Institute.

Dimitrovova, B. 2001. "Bosniak or Muslim? Dilemma of One Nations with Two Names." *Southeast European Politics* (October): 94–108.

Djilas, A. 1991. *The Contested Country: Yugoslav Unity and Communist Revolution 1919–1953*. Cambridge, MA: Harvard University Press.

Dobbins, J. 2006. "Preparing for Nation-Building." *Survival* 48(October): 3, 27–40.

Dollard, J., L. Dobb, N. Miller, O. Mowrer, and R. Sears. 1947. *Frustration and Aggression*. New Haven, CT: Yale University Press.

Donia, R., and J. Fine. 1994. *Bosnia and Hercegovina: A Tradition Betrayed*. New York, NY: Columbia University Press.

Downes, A. 2008. *Targeting Civilians in War*. Ithaca, NY: Cornell University Press.

Doyle, M., and N. Sambanis. 2006. *Making War and Building Peace: United Nations Peace Operations*. Princeton, NJ: Princeton University Press.

Dragojevic, M. "The Politics of Refugee Identity: Newcomers in Serbia from Bosnia and Herzegovina and Croatia, 1991–2009." Unpublished dissertation, Brown University.

Dumont, M., V. Yzerbyt, D. Wigboldus, and E. Gordijn. 2003. "Social Categorization and Fear Reactions to the September 11th Terrorist Attacks." *Personality and Social Psychology Bulletin* 29(12): 1509–1520.

Duridanski, D. 2009. "Old-Style Nationalism Has No Future in Macedonia." *Balkan Insight*, June 18.

Eagly, A., and S. Chaiken. 1993. *The Psychology of Attitudes*. Fort Worth, TX: Harcourt Brace Jovanovich College Publishers.

Edelstein, D. 2008. *Occupational Hazards: Success and Failure in Military Occupation*. Ithaca, NY: Cornell University Press.

Elster, J. 1998. "Emotions and Economic Theory." *Journal of Economic Literature*, 36 (1): 47–74.

Elster, J. 1999. *Alchemies of the Mind: Rationality and the Emotions*. Cambridge: Cambridge University Press.

Elster, J. 2003. "Memory and Transitional Justice." Manuscript delivered at the "Memory of War" Workshop, Massachusetts Institute of Technology, Cambridge, MA.

Elster, J. 2007. *Explaining Social Behavior: More Nuts and Bolts for the Social Sciences*. Cambridge: Cambridge University Press.

EUBusiness. 2005. September 14.

Fanon, F. 1965. *The Wretched of the Earth*. New York, NY: Grove Press.

Fearon, J., and D. Laitin. 2000. "Violence and the Social Construction of Identity." *International Organization* 54: 845–877.

Fearon, J., and D. Laitin. 2003. "Ethnicity, Insurgency, and Civil War." *American Political Science Review* 97(1): 75–90.

Fehr, E., K. Hoff, and M. Kshetramade 2008. "Spite and Development." *American Economic Review: Papers and Proceedings*, 98(2): 494–499.

Filkins, D. 2003. "Tough New Tactics by US Tighten Grip on Iraq Towns: Barriers, Detentions and Razings Begin to Echo Israels Anti-Guerilla Methods." *New York Times*, December 7.

Filkins, D. 2009. *The Forever War*. Vintage.

Finnemore, M. 2003. *The Purpose of Intervention: Changing Beliefs about the Use of Force*. Ithaca, NY: Cornell University Press.

Forbes, H. D. 1997. *Ethnic Conflict: Commerce, Culture, and the Contact Hypothesis*. New Haven, CT: Yale University Press.

Fortna, V. 2008. *Does Peacekeeping Work? Shaping Belligerents' Choices After Civil War*. Princeton, NJ: Princeton University Press.

Frank, R. 1988. *Passions within Reason: The Strategic Role of the Emotions*. New York, NY: Norton.

Franks, D., and V. Gecas. 1992. "Current Issues in Emotion Studies." In D. Franks and V. Gecas, eds., *Social Perspectives on Emotion: A Research Annual*. Greenwich, CT: JAI Press.

Frijda, N., A. Manstead, and S. Bem. 2000. *Emotions and Beliefs: How Feelings Influence Thoughts*. Cambridge: Cambridge University Press.

Frijda, N., and B. Mesquita. 2000. "Beliefs through Emotions." In N. Frijda, A. Manstead, and S. Bem, eds., *Emotions and Beliefs: How Feelings Influence Thoughts*, pp. 45–77. Cambridge: Cambridge University Press.

Gagnon, V. P. 2004. *The Myth of Ethnic War: Serbia and Croatia in the 1990's*. Ithaca, NY: Cornell University Press.

Gallagher, D., and G. Clore. 1985. "Effects of Fear and Anger on Judgments of Risk and Evaluations of Blame." Paper presented at annual meeting of the Midwestern Psychological Association, Chicago.

Gambetta, D. 2004. "Reason and Terror: Has 9/11 Made It Hard to Think Straight?" *Boston Review* 29(2).

Gamson, W. 1992. *Talking Politics*. Cambridge: Cambridge University Press.

Gardner, D. 2008. *The Science of Fear*. New York, NY: Dutton.

Gilligan, M. 2007. "Making War and Building Peace *and* Sustainable Peace: Power and Democracy after Civil Wars," *Perspectives on Politics* 5: 208–210.

Glaeser, E. 2005. "The Political Economy of Hatred." *Quarterly Journal of Economics* 120(1): 45–86.

Glassner, B. 2000. *The Culture of Fear: Why Americans Are Afraid of the Wrong Things*. New York, NY: Basic Books.

Glenny, M. 2000. *The Balkans: Nationalism, War and the Great Powers, 1804–1999*. New York, NY: Viking.

Glenny, M. 2008. *McMafia:A Journey through the Global Criminal Underworld*. New York, NY: Alfred A. Knopf.

Goldberg, J., J. Lerner, and P. Tetlock. 1999. "Rage and Reason: The Psychology of the Intuitive Prosecutor." *European Journal of Social Psychology* 29(56): 781–795.

Goodwin, J., J. Jasper, and F. Polletta. 2001. *Passionate Politics: Emotions and Social Movements*. Chicago, IL: University of Chicago Press.

Greenfeld, L. 1992. *Nationalism: Five Roads to Modernity*. Cambridge, MA: Harvard University Press.

Guardian. 2010. "US Embassy Cables: Partition of Kosovo Hardening, Warns US Ambassador." December 9.

Gurr, T. 1970. *Why Men Rebel*. Princeton, NJ: Princeton University Press.

Guzina, D. 2003. "Kosovo or Kosova – Could It Be Both?" In F. Bieber and Z. Daskalovski, eds., *Understanding the War in Kosovo*, pp. 31–52. London, UK: Frank Cass.

Hamburger, H. 1979. *Games as Models of Social Phenomena*. San Francisco, CA: WH Freeman.

Hamill, H. 2007. "Identity Signaling and Mimicry in the Northern Ireland Conflict, 1966–2007." Presented at the workshop "Mimicry in Civil Wars: The Strategic Use of Identity Signals," College de France, Paris, December 7–8.

Hamilton, D., and D. Mackie. 1993. *Affect, Cognition and Stereotyping: Interactive Processes in Group Perception*. San Diego, CA: Academic Press.

Hamzaj, B. 2000. *A Narrative about War and Freedom (Dialog with the Commander Ramush Haradinaj)*. Prishtina: Zeri.

Haraszti, M. 2004. "The Role of the Media in the March 2004 Events in Kosovo." Organization for Security and Co-operation in Europe (OSCE), Vienna.

Hardin, R. 1995. *One For All: The Logic of Group Conflict*. Princeton, NJ: Princeton University Press.

Harmon-Jones, E. 2000. "A Cognitive Dissonance Theory and Perspective on the Role of Emotion in the Maintenance and Change of Beliefs and Attitudes." In N. Frijda, A. Manstead, and S. Bem, eds., *Emotions and Beliefs: How Feelings Influence Thoughts*, pp. 185–211. Cambridge, UK: Cambridge University Press.

Harre, R. 1986. *The Social Construction of Emotions*. New York: Basil Blackwell.

Hayden, R. 1999. *Blueprints for a House Divided: The Constitutional Logic of the Yugoslav Conflicts*. Ann Arbor, MI: University of Michigan Press.

Hedges, C. 1998. "New Balkan Tinderbox: Ethnic Albanians' Rebellion against Serbs." *New York Times*, March 2.

Hehn, P. 1979. *The German Struggle against Yugoslav Guerrillas in World War II: German Counter-insurgency in Yugoslavia, 1941–1943*. Boulder, CO: East European Quarterly, distributed by Columbia University Press.

Heiberg, M., B. O'Leary, and J. Tirman. 2007. *Terror, Insurgency, and the State: Ending Protracted Conflicts*. Philadelphia: University of Pennsylvania Press.

Heinrich, M. 2001. Reuters. "Macedonia Peace Process Lurches into Crisis." *New York Times*, November 11.

Hislope, R. 2003. "Between a Bad Peace and a Good War: Insights and Lessons from the Almost-War in Macedonia." *Ethnic and Racial Studies* 26(1): 129–151.

Holbrooke, R. 1999. *To End a War*. New York, NY: Random House.

Holbrooke, R., and P. Ashdown. 2009. "A Bosnian Powder Keg." *London Guardian*, October 22.

Honig, J. W., and N. Both. 1996. *Srebrenica: Record of a War Crime*. New York, NY: Penguin Books.

Horowitz, D. 1973. "Direct, Displaced, and Cumulative Ethnic Aggression." *Comparative Politics* 6 (1): 1–16.

Horowitz, D. 2000. *Ethnic Groups in Conflict*. Berkeley, CA: University of California Press.

Horowitz, D. 2002. *The Deadly Ethnic Riot*. Berkeley, CA: University of California Press.

Human Rights Watch. 1999. "Federal Republic of Yugoslavia: Abuses against Serbs and Roma in the New Kosovo." *Human Rights Watch*, Vol. 11, No. 10, August.

Human Rights Watch. 2001. *Under Orders: War Crimes in Kosovo. Abuses after June 12, 1999*. New York: Human Rights Watch.

Huntington, S. 1968. *Political Order in Changing Societies*. New Haven, CT: Yale University Press.

Husanovic, J. 2001. "'Post-Conflict' Kosovo: An Anatomy Lesson in the Ethics/Politics of Human Rights." In K. Booth, ed., *The Kosovo Tragedy: The Human Rights Dimensions*, pp. 263–280. London, UK: Frank Cass.

Huszka, B. 2007. "The Presevo Valley of Southern Serbia alongside Kosovo: The Case for Decentralization and Minority Protection." CEPS Policy Briefs, issue 1–12.

Iacopino, V. 1999. "War Crimes in Kosovo: A Population-Based Assessment of Human Rights Violations against Kosovar Albanians." Boston: Physicians for Human Rights and Program on Forced Migration and Health, Center for Population and Family Health, The Joseph L. Mailman School of Public Health, and Columbia University.

ICG [International Crisis Group]. 1999. "Who's Killing Whom." International Crisis Group Report, November 2.

ICG. 2000. "Current Legal Status of the Federal Republic of Yugoslavia and of Serbia and Montenegro." International Crisis Group, Balkans Report No. 101, Brussells/Podgorica.

ICG. 2001. "Macedonia: Last Chance for Peace." International Crisis Group, Balkans Report No. 113, June 20.

ICG. 2001. "Peace in Presevo: Quick Fix or Long Term Solution?" International Crisis Group, Balkans Report No. 116, Pristina/Belgrade/Brussels, August 10.

ICG. 2003. "Bosnia's Brcko: Getting In, Getting On, and Getting Out." International Crisis Group, Balkans Report No. 144, June 2.

ICG. 2003. "Kosovo's Ethnic Dilemma: The Need for a Civic Contract." International Crisis Group, Balkans Report No. 143, May 28.

ICG. 2003. "No Room for Complacency." International Crisis Group, October 23.

ICG. 2003. "Southern Serbia's Fragile Peace." International Crisis Group, December 9.

ICG. 2004. "Collapse in Kosovo." International Crisis Group, Europe Report no. 155. Pristina/Belgrade/Brussels.

ICG. 2004. "Pan-Albanianism: How Big a Threat to Balkan Stability?" International Crisis Group, Europe Report No. 153, February 25.

ICG. 2005. "Bosnia's Stalled Police Reform: No Progress, No EU." International Crisis Group, Europe Report No. 164, September 6.

ICG. 2006. "Kosovo: The Challenge of Transition." International Crisis Group, February 17.

ICG. 2006. "Montenegro's Referendum." International Crisis Group, Europe Briefing No. 42, Podgorica/Belgrade, May 30.

ICG. 2006. "Southern Serbia: In Kosovo's Shadow." International Crisis Group, Europe Briefing No. 43, Belgrade/Pristina/Brussels, June 27.

ICG. 2008. "Kosovo and Pakistan: Gareth Evans Interviewed on ABC Lateline." International Crisis Group, February 18.

ICG. 2009. "Bosnia's Dual Crisis." International Crisis Group, Crisis Group Europe Briefing No. 57, November 12.

ICG. 2009. "Bosnia's Incomplete Transition: Between Dayton and Europe." International Crisis Group, Europe Report No. 198, March 9.

IDSCS [Institute of Democracy "Societas Civilis"]. 2005. "Public Opinion in Macedonia about the EU Integration Processes." Institute of Democracy "Societas Civilis," Skopje, Macedonia, November.

Ilievski, Z. 2007. "Country Specific Report: Conflict Settlement Agreement Macedonia." Eurac Research, Work Package 3, Report 5, September.

Independent International Commission on Kosovo. 2000. *Kosovo Report: Conflict, International Response, Lessons Learned*. Oxford: Oxford University Press.

IWPR [Institute for War and Peace Reporting]. 2002. "Presevo Albanians Snub Belgrade Again." Institute for War and Peace Reporting, November 11.

Iyengar, S., and W. McGuire. 1993. *Explorations in Political Psychology*. Durham, NC: Duke University Press.

Jarvis, C. 2000. "The Rise and Fall of the Pyramid Schemes in Albania." International Monetary Fund, IMF Staff Papers, Vol. 47(1): 1–29.

Jovanovic, N., and D. Solomon. 2006. "Serbs Greet Independence Vote with Shrugs." Institute for War and Peace Reporting, May 22.

Judah, T. 2000. *Kosovo: War and Revenge*. New Haven, CT: Yale University Press.

Judah, T. 2008. *Kosovo: What Everyone Needs to Know*. Oxford, NY: Oxford University Press.

Kakuk. G. 2002. "In Search of Home." *Focus Kosovo*, February.

Kakuk, G. 2002. "Unwanted People." Unpublished paper.

Kalyvas, S., and N. Sambanis. 2005. "Bosnia's Civil War: Origins and Violence Dynamics." in P. Collier and N. Sambanis, eds., *Understanding Civil War: Evidence and Analysis*, Volume 2. Washington, DC: World Bank Publications.

Kamberi, B. 2002. "Presevo Albanians Eye Autonomy." International War and Peace Reporting, Balkan Crisis Report, February 14.

Kaplan, R. 1994. *Balkan Ghosts*. Vancouver, WA: Vintage Books.

Kaplan, R. 2005. *Balkan Ghosts: A Journey Through History.* New York, NY: Picador USA.

Karpat, C. 2006. "Serbia and Montenegro: Unhappy Couple on the Way of Divorce?" AIA Balkan Section, January 16.

Kaufman, S. 2001. *Modern Hatreds: The Symbolic Politics of Ethnic War.* Ithaca, NY: Cornell University Press.

Kaufmann, C. 1996. "Intervention in Ethnic and Ideological Civil Wars: Why One Can Be Done and the Other Can't." *Security Studies* 6(1): 62–100.

Kaufmann, C. 2005. "Rational Choice and Progress in the Study of Ethnic Conflict: A Review Essay." *Security Studies* 14(1): 178–207.

Keltner, D., P. Ellsworth, and K. Edwards. 1993. "Beyond Simple Pessimism: Effects of Sadness and Anger on Social Perception." *Journal of Personality and Social Psychology* 64: 740–752.

Kemper, T. 1978. *A Social Interactional Theory of Emotions.* New York: John Wiley & Sons.

Kemper, T. 2001. "A Structural Approach to Social Movement Emotions." In Goodwin, Jasper, and Francesca Polletta, eds. *Passionate Politics: Emotions and Social Movements*, pp. 58–73.

Kennedy-Pipe, C., and P. Stanley. 2001. "Rape in War: Lessons of the Balkan Conflicts in the 1990's." In K. Booth, ed., *The Kosovo Tragedy: The Human Rights Dimensions*, pp. 67–84. London, UK: Frank Cass.

Kifner, J. 1999. "How Serb Forces Purged One Million Albanians." *New York Times*, May 29.

King, I., and W. Mason. 2006. *Peace at Any Price: How the World Failed Kosovo.* Ithaca, NY: Cornell University Press.

Kocovic, B. 1985. *Zrtve Drugog Svetskog Rata u Jugoslaviji [Casualties of WWII in Yugoslavia].* London, UK: Veritas Press Foundation.

Kostovicova, D. 2002. "Shkolla Shqipe and Nationhood: Albanians in Pursuit of Education in the Native Language in Interwar (1918–1941) and Post-autonomy (1989–98) Kosovo." In S. Schwanders-Sievers and B. J. Fischer, eds., *Albanian Identities: Myth and History*, pp. 157–171. Bloomington, IN: Indiana University Press.

Kuperman, A. 2002. "Tragic Challenges and the Moral Hazard of Humanitarian Intervention: How and Why Ethnic Groups Provoke Genocidal Retaliation." Ph.D. Dissertation, Massachusetts Institute of Technology.

Kuperman, A. 2005. "Suicidal Rebellions and the Moral Hazard of Humanitarian Intervention." *Ethnopolitics* 4(2): 149–173.

Kydd, A., and B. Walter. 2002. "Sabotaging the Peace: The Politics of Extremist Violence." *International Organization* 56(02): 263–296.

Laitin, D. 1998. *Identity in Formation.* Ithaca. NY: Cornell University Press.

Lampe, J. 1996. *Yugoslavia as History.* New York, NY: Cambridge University Press.

Latifi, S. 2003. "Alarm Bells in South Serbia." Institute for War and Peace Reporting, September 4.

Lazic, N. 2006. "Partition Demand Fuels South Serbia Tensions." *Balkan Insight*, February 16.

Lazic, N. 2009. "South Serbia Albanians Look to Kosovo," *Balkan Insight*, February 16,

Lee, A. 1983. *Terrorism in Northern Ireland.* Bayside, NY: General Hall Inc.

Lerner, J., R. Gonzalez, D. Small, and B. Fischhoff. 2003. "Effects of Fear and Anger on Perceived Risks of Terrorism: A National Field Experiment." *Psychological Science* 14(2): 144–150.

Lerner, J., and D. Keltner. 2000. "Beyond Valence: Toward a Model of Emotion-Specific Influences on Judgement and Choice." *Cognition & Emotion* 14(4): 473–493.

Lerner, J., and D. Keltner. 2001. "Fear, Anger, and Risk." *Journal of Personality and Social Psychology* 81(1): 146–159.

Lessenski, M., A. Habova, and V. Shopov. 2006. "The Process of Decentralization in Macedonia: Prospects for Ethnic Conflict Mitigation, Enhanced Representation, Institutional Efficiency and Accountability." Institute for Regional and International Studies (IRIS), Sofia, Bulgaria.

Lindblom, C. 1977. *Politics and Markets: The World's Political–Economic Systems.* New York: Basic.

Little, A. 2000. "Moral Combat: NATO at War." BBC2, March 12.

Long, W., and P. Brecke. 2003. *War and Reconciliation: Reason and Emotion in Conflict Resolution.* Cambridge, MA: MIT Press.

Lyon, J. 2007. "Serbia's South Watches Kosovo." *Balkan Insight*, November 6.

Machiavelli, N. 1947. *The Prince* (1513). T. Bergin translator and editor. Arlington Heights, IL: Croft Classics.

Mackie, D., T. Devos, and E. Smith, 2000. "Intergroup Emotions: Explaining Offensive Action Tendencies in an Intergroup Context." *Journal of Personality and Social Psychology* 79(4): 602–616.

Mackie, D. and D. Hamilton. 1993. *Affect, Cognition, and Stereotyping: Interactive Processes in Group Perception.* San Diego: Academic Press.

Malcolm, N. 1994. *Bosnia: A Short History.* New York, NY: New York University Press.

Malcolm, N. 1999. *Kosovo: A Short History.* New York, NY: New York University Press.

Maliqi, S. 1996. "Reading Writing, and Repression." *Balkan War Report*, pp. 44–45. May.

Mano, H. 1994. "Risk-Taking, Framing Effects, and Affect." *Organizational Behavior and Human Decision Processes* 57: 38.

Mansfield, E., and J. Snyder. 1995. "Democratization and War." *Foreign Affairs* 74 (3): 79–97.

Mansfield, E., and J. Snyder. 1995. "Democratization and the Danger of War." *International Security* 5–38.

Mansfield, E., and J. Snyder. 2007. "The Sequencing 'Fallacy.'" *Journal of Democracy* 18: 5–10.

Marusic, S. 2008. "Macedonia's New Government Faces Ethnic Challenge." *Balkan Insight*, July 10.

Matic, T. 2004. *Institute for War and Peace Reporting*, March 18.

Max, A. 2010. "Karadzic Asserts He Guarded Serbs from Islamic Militants." *Boston Globe*, March 2.

Mazower, M. 1998. *Dark Continent: Europe's Twentieth Century.* London: Allen Lane.

Mead, W. R. 2002. *Special Providence: American Foreign Policy and How It Changed the World.* New York, NY: Routledge.

Merton, R. 1941. "Intermarriage and Social Structure: Fact and Theory." *Psychiatry* 4: 361–77.

Mertus, J. 1999. *Kosovo: How Myths and Truths Started a War*. Berkeley, CA: University of California Press.

Moravcik, J., 1991. *Exporting Democracy: Fulfilling America's Destiny*. Washington, DC: American Enterprise Institute.

Moro, F. "Ethnicity Reconsidered. A Local-Level Quantitative Analysis of Violence in the Bosnian War." Unpublished manuscript.

Morrow, J. 1994. *Game Theory for Political Scientists*. Princeton, NJ: Princeton University Press.

Mueller, J. 2000. "The Banality of Ethnic War." *International Security* 42–70.

Mueller, J. 2006. *Overblown: How Politicians and the Terrorism Industry Inflate National Security Threats, and Why We Believe Them*. New York: Free Press.

Muguruza, C. C. 2003. "The European Union and Humanitarian Intervention in Kosovo: A Test for the Common Foreign Policy." In F. Bieber and Z. Daskalovski, eds., *Understanding the War in Kosovo*, p. 237. London, UK: Frank Cass.

Murphy, D. 2006. "Attack Deepens Iraq's Divide." *Christian Science Monitor*, February 23.

Myers, S. 2006. "Putin Unlikely to Agree on Missiles, White House Says." *New York Times*, April 6.

Myers, S. 2008. "Bush Supports Expansion of NATO Across Europe," *New York Times*, April 6.

Necak, D. 1995. "Historical Elements for Understanding the 'Yugoslav Question.'" In P. Akhavan and R. Howse eds., *Yugoslavia, the Former and Future: Reflections by Scholars from the Region*. Washington, DC: The Brookings Institution.

Newhagen, J. 1998. "Anger, Fear and Disgust: Effects on Approach–Avoidance and Memory." *Journal of Broadcasting and Electronic Media* 42: 265–276.

Nikolaidis, J. 2000. "Multiculturalism in Montenegro and the City of Ulcinj." In N. Dimitrijevic, ed., *Managing Multiethnic Local Communities in the Countries of the Former Yugoslavia*, pp. 447–457. Budapest: Open Society Institute.

Nikolic, L. 2003. "Ethnic Prejudices and Discrimination." In F. Bieber and Z. Daskalovski, eds., *Understanding the War in Kosovo*, pp. 53–76. London, UK: Frank Cass.

O'Connor, M. 1998. "Serbs in Bosnia Appear to Shun Favorite of U.S." *New York Times*, September 17.

Ohnuki-Tierney, E. 1990. *Culture through Time: Anthropological Approaches*. Stanford University Press.

Oppel, R., and S. Tavernise, with W. Jaff and L. Istifan. 2005. "Car Bombings in Iraq Kill 33, with Shiites as Targets." *New York Times*, May 24.

Ortner, S. 1990. "Patterns of History: Cultural Schemas in the Foundings of Sherpa Religious Institutions." *Culture through Time: Anthropological Approaches*, 57–93.

Ortony, A., G. Clore, and A. Collins. 1988. *The Cognitive Structure of Emotions*. Cambridge: Cambridge University Press.

OSCE [Organization for Security and Cooperation in Europe]. 1999. "Kosovo/Kosova: As Seen, as Told, an Analysis of the Human Rights Findings of the OSCE Kosovo Verification Mission October 1998 to June 1999." Warsaw, Poland: Organization for Security and Cooperation in Europe.

OSCE. 2007. "Parallel Structures in Kosovo, 2006–2007." Organization for Security and Cooperation in Europe, April 4.

Pajic, Z. 2007. "Bosnia and Hercegovina: A Statehood Crossroads." In S. Bianchini, J. Marko, and M. Uvalic, eds., *Regional Cooperation, Peace Enforcement, and the Role of the Treaties in the Balkans*, pp. 79–91. Bologna: Longo Editore Ravenna.

Pape, R. 2005. *Dying to Win: The Strategic Logic of Suicide Terrorism*. New York, NY: Random House.

Paris, R. 2004. *At War's End: Building Peace after Civil Conflict*. Cambridge: Cambridge University Press.

Pavkovic, A. 1997. "Anticipating the Disintegration: Nationalisms in the Former Yugoslavia, 1980–1990." *Nationalities Papers* 25(3): 427–440.

Pavlowitch, S. 1988. *The Improbable Survivor: Yugoslavia and Its Problems, 1918–1988*. Columbus, OH: Ohio State University Press.

Perritt, H., Jr. 2008. *Kosovo Liberation Army: The Inside Story of an Insurgency*. Urbana, IL: University of Illinois Press.

Petersen, R. 1997. "Ethnic Conflict, Social Science, and William Butler Yeats: A Commentary on Russell Hardin's *One For All: The Logic of Group Conflict*." *European Journal of Sociology* 38: 311–323.

Petersen, R. 2001. *Resistance and Rebellion: Lessons from Eastern Europe*. Cambridge: Cambridge University Press.

Petersen, R. 2002. *Understanding Ethnic Violence: Fear, Hatred, and Resentment in Twentieth-Century Eastern Europe*. Cambridge: Cambridge University Press.

Petersen, R. 2005. "Memory and Cultural Schema: Linking Memory to Political Action." In Francesca Cappolletto, ed., *Memory and Second World War: An Ethnographic Approach*, pp. 131–153. Oxford: Berg.

Petersen, R. 2008. "The Strategic Use of Emotion in Conflict: Emotion and Interest in the Reconstruction of Multiethnic States." In Freddy Cante ed., Argumentacion, negociacion, racional y acuerdos. Bogota: Columbia.

Petersen, R. and M. Dragojevic. 2007. "Who's Fooling Who? Mimicry, International Norms, and (Self) Deception." Paper prepared for the workshop "Mimicry in Civil Wars: The Strategic Use of Identity Signals." December 7–8.

Petersen, R., and V. Felbab-Brown. 2005. "United States Social Science and Counter-Insurgency Policy in Colombia." In F. Cante and L. Ortiz, eds., *Nonviolent Political Action in Colombia*. Bogota: Universidad del Rosario.

Petersen, R., and E. Liaras. 2006. "Countering Fear in War: The Strategic Use of Emotion in Thucydides." *Journal of Military Ethics* 5(4): 317–333.

Petersen, R., and S. Zukerman. "Anger, Violence, and Political Science." In M. Potegal, G. Stemmler, an C. Spielberger, eds., *A Handbook of Anger: Constituent and Concomitant Biological, Psychological, and Social Processes*. New York, NY: Springer.

Petruseva, A. 2003. "Ohrid: Two Years On. Institute for War and Peace Reporting, August 19.

Petruseva, A. 2005. "Rise and Fall of Macedonia's Nationalist Showman." Institute for War and Peace Reporting, March 17.

Phillips, J. 2004. *Macedonia: Warlords and Rebels in the Balkans*. New Haven, CT: Yale University Press.

Pinker, S. 2002. *The Blank Slate: The Denial of Human Nature in Modern Intellectual Life*. New York, NY: Viking.

Pond, E. 2006. *Endgame in the Balkans: Regime Change, European Style*. Washington, DC: Brookings Institution Press.

Popov, N. 2000. *The Road to War in Serbia: Trauma and Catharsis*. Budapest: Central European University Press.

Posen, B. R. 1993. "The Security Dilemma and Ethnic Conflict." *Survival* 35: 27–47

Posen, B. 2000. "The War for Kosovo: Serbia's Political–Military Strategy." *International Security* 24(4): 39–85.

Posen, B. 2003. "Command of the Commons: The Military Foundation of U.S. Hegemony." *International Security* 28(1): 5–46.

Potegal, M., G. Stemmler, and C. Spielberger. 2006. *International Handbook of Anger: Constituent and Concomitant Biological, Psychological, and Social Processes*. New York, NY: Springer.

Poulton, H., and S. Taji-Farouki. 1997. *Muslim Identity and the Balkan State*. New York, NY: New York University Press.

Poulton, H., and M. Vickers. 1997. "The Kosovo Albanians: Ethnic Confrontation with the Slav State." In H. Poulton and S. Taji-Farouki, eds., *Muslim Identity and the Balkan State*. New York, NY: New York University Press.

Pratto, F., J. Sidanius, L. Stallworth, and B. Malle. 1994. "Social Dominance Orientation: A Personality Variable Predicting Social and Political Attitudes." *Journal of Personality and Social Psychology* 67:741–741.

Project on Ethnic Relations. 2002. "Interethnic Relations in Montenegro." Project on Ethnic Relations Report: Third PER Roundtable: Albanians in Montenegro, July 5.

Radin, A. "Shh . . . The Locals Can Hear Us Arguing: International Reform Efforts in Post-Dayton Bosnia." Unpublished manuscript.

Radio Free Liberty. 2003. Balkan Report 5, December 5.

Radulovic, Z. 1999. "Montenegrin Public Opinion at a Turning Point." Podgorica, AIM, September 24.

Rama, S. 2001. "The Serb–Albanian War, and International Community's Miscalculations." *International Journal of Albanian Studies* 2(1): http://www.albanian.com/IJAS/vol2/is1/art1.html.

Ramet, S. 1992. *Nationalism and Federalism in Yugoslavia 1962–1991*. Bloomington, IN: University of Indiana Press.

Ramet, S. 1996. "Nationalism and the Idiocy of the Countryside: The Case of Serbia." *Ethnic and Racial Studies* 19(1): 70–87.

Ramet, S. 2005. *Thinking about Yugoslavia: Scholarly Debates about the Yugoslav Breakup and the Wars in Bosnia and Kosovo*. Cambridge: Cambridge University Press.

Richardson, L. 2006. *What Terrorists Want: Understanding the Enemy, Containing the Threat*. Random House.

Rifati, S. 2002. "The Roma and 'Humanitarian' Ethnic Cleaning in Kosovo." *Dissident Voice*, October 13.

Riker, W. 1986. *The Art of Political Manipulation*. New Haven, CT: Yale University Press.

Ringdal, K., A. Simkus, and O. Listhang. 2007. "Values in Southeastern Europe: A Comparison of Bosnia-Herzegovina and Macedonia." Paper prepared for the Tenth International Seminar "Democracy and Human Rights in Multiethnic Societies," Konjic, Bosnia-Herzegovina, July 9–13.

Roeder, P., and D. Rothchild. 2005. *Sustainable Peace: Power and Democracy after Civil Wars*. Ithaca, NY: Cornell University Press.

Rogan, J. 2000. "Facilitating Local Multiethnic Governance in Postwar Bosnia and Herzegovina." In Nenad Dimitrijevic, ed., *Managing Multiethnic Local Communities in the Countries of Former Yugoslavia*, pp. 183–206. Budapest, Hungary: Open Society Institute.

Rothschild, J. 1974. *East Central Europe between the Two World Wars*. Seattle, WA: University of Washington Press.

Royzman, E., C. McCauley, and P. Rosin. 2005. "From Plato to Putnam: Four Ways to Think about Hate." In Robert J. Sternberg, ed., *The Psychology of Hate*, pp. 3–36.

Salert, B. 1976. *Revolutions and Revolutionaries: Four Theories*. Greenwood Publishing Group.

Salihu, D. and J. Arsic. 2009. "Brain Drain Sucks Life from Southern Serbia." *Balkan Insight*, March 5.

Sartre, J. 1965. "Preface" in Frantz Fanon, *The Wretched of the Earth*, p. 18.

Schelling, T. 1985. *Micromotives and Macrobehavior*. New York, NY: Gordon and Breach.

Schwanders-Sievers, S. and B. J. Fischer. 2002. *Albanian Identities: Myth and History*. Bloomington, IN: Indiana University Press.

Schwarz, N., and G. Clore. 1983. "Mood, Misattribution, and Judgments of Well-Being: Informative and Directive Functions of Affective States." *Journal of Personality* 45(3): 513–523.

Shikaki, K. 2002. "Palestinian Public Opinion and the al Aqsa Intifada." *Strategic Assessment* 5(1): 15–20.

Sidanius, J., et al. 1993. "The Psychology of Group Conflict and the Dynamics of Oppression: A Social Dominance Perspective." In S. Inyengar and W. McGuire, eds. *Explorations in Political Psychology* 183–219.

Sidanius, J., and F. Pratto. 2001. *Social Dominance: An Intergroup Theory of Social Hierarchy and Oppression*. Cambridge: Cambridge University Press.

Sidanius, J., F. Pratto, and D. Brief. 1995. "Group Dominance and the Political Psychology of Gender: A Cross-Cultural Comparison." *Political Psychology* 16 (2): 381–396.

Simons, M. "Data on Balkan Wars Found in Home of Suspect." *New York Times*, July 10, 2010.

Sinclair, M. 2006. "Brcko: International Incubation." In H. Binnendijk, C. Barry, G. Cordero, L. Peterson Nussbaum, and M. Sinclair, eds., *Solutions for Northern Kosovo: Lessons Learned in Mostar, Eastern Slavonia, and Brcko*, pp. 41–49.

Sistek, F., and B. Dimitrovova. 2003. "National Minorities in Montenegro after the Break-Up of Yugoslavia." In F. Bieber, ed., *Montenegro in Transition: Problems of Identity and Statehood*, p. 169. Baden-Baden, Germany: Nomos Verlagsgesellschaft.

Sniderman, P. 2000. *The Outsider: Prejudice and Politics in Italy*. Princeton, NJ: Princeton University Press.

Snyder, J., and K. Ballentine, 1996. "Nationalism and the Marketplace of Ideas." *International Security* 21: 5–40.

Snyder, J. 2000. *From Voting to Violence: Democratization and Nationalist Conflict*. New York: W. W. Norton and Co.

Stedman, S. 1997. "Spoiler Problems in Peace Processes." *International Security* 22: 5–53.

Stedman, S., D. Rothchild, and E. Cousens. 2002. *Ending Civil Wars: The Implementation of Peace Agreements*. Boulder, CO: Lynne Rienner Publishers.

Stepanovic, I. 2005. "Serbs Sell Up in Presevo." *Balkan Investigative Reporting Network*, November 17.

Stern, J. 2003. *Terror in the Name of God: Why Religious Militants Kill*. New York: Ecco.

Sternberg, R., ed. 2005. *The Psychology of Hate*. American Psychological Association.

Stiglmayer, A. 1994. *Mass Rape: The War against Women in Bosnia-Hercegovina*. Lincoln, NE: University of Nebraska Press.

Stojanovic, S. 2008. *Politika*. January 23 to February 2.

Stroessner, S., and D. Mackie. 1993. "Affect and Perceived Group Variability: Implications for Stereotyping and Prejudice." In D. Hamilton and D. Mackie, eds., *Affect, Cognition, and Stereotyping: Interactive Processes in Group Perception*, pp. 63–86.

Suny, R. 2004. "Why We Hate You: The Passions of National Identity and Ethnic Violence." Berkeley Program in Soviet and Post-Soviet Studies.

Thorogood, T. 2007. "The South Serbia Programme: Lessons in Conflict Prevention and Recovery." UNDP Report. Issue Title: Conflict and Development, June.

Tirman, J. 2003/2004. "The New Humanitarianism: How Military Intervention Became the Norm." *Boston Review*, December/January.

Todorova, M. 2004. *Balkan Identities: Nation and Memory*. New York, NY: New York University Press.

Tokaca, M. *Human Losses in Bosnia-Herzegovina 1991–1995*. Sarajevo: Research and Documentation Center,

Tripp, T., and R. Bies. 2006. "'Righteous' Anger and Revenge in the Workplace: The Fantasies, the Feuds, the Forgiveness." In M. Potegal, G. Stemmler, and C. Spielberger, eds., *International Handbook of Anger: Constituent and Concomitant Biological, Psychological, and Social Processes*. New York, NY: Springer.

Tsebelis, G. 1990. *Nested Games: Rational Choice in Comparative Politics*. Berkeley, CA: University of California Press.

UNHCR/OSCE. 1999. "Overview of the Situation of Ethnic Minorities in Kosovo." United Nations High Commissioner for Refugees/Organization for Security and Cooperation in Europe, November 3.

Valentino, B., P. Huth, and D. Balch-Lindsay. 2004. "Draining the Sea: Mass Killing and Guerrilla Warfare." *International Organization* 58(2): 375–407.

Weiner, M. 1971. "The Macedonian Syndrome: A Historical Model of International Relations and Political Development." *World Politics* 23(4): 665–683.

West, R. 1994. *Black Lamb and Grey Falcon: A Journey Through Yugoslavia*. New York: Penguin Classics.

Wong E. 2006. "Blast Destroys Golden Dome of Sacred Shiite Shrine in Iraq." *New York Times*, February 22.

Woodward, S. 1995. *Balkan Tragedy: Chaos and Dissolution after the Cold War*. Washington, DC: Brookings.

Wuscht, J. 1963. *Population Losses in Yugoslavia during World War II: 1941–1945*. Bonn: Edition Atlantic Forum.

Xharra, J., and A. Anderson. 2004. *Institute for War and Peace Reporting*. March 18.

Yanacopulos, H. and J. Hanlon. 2006. *Civil War, Civil Peace*. Athens, OH: Ohio University Center for International Studies.

Zimmerman, W. 1999. *Origins of a Catastrophe: Yugoslavia and Its Destroyers*. New York, NY: Random House.

Index

Bosnians, 83
  Bosnian-Croats, 83
  Bosnian-Muslims, 83
  Bosnian-Serbs, 83
Brcko, 265–268
Bridgewatchers, 167
Bujanovac, 203, 214–215
Bulatovic, Momir, 276
Bulatovic, Rade, 275

Caglavica, 180
Carrington-Cutliero peace plan, 121
chicken game, 68–69
Christmas warning, 124
Ciganska Mahala, 131–132
Collier, Paul, 7, 36
Colombia, 95
  FARC, 95
communism, 116
Congress of Berlin, 272
Contact Group, 121, 155, 185
contempt, 42–43, 132–135, 150, 196, 295, 296
Council for the Defence, 154
Covic Plan, 210–211, 214
Covic, Nebojsa, 208
Croatia, 119
  recognition, 119–120
Croatian Defense Force, 250
Croats, 32, 83, 109, 110, 111, 114, 119, 120, 121, 123, 243, 245, 249, 250
  in Bosnia, 32
cultural schema, 44–46, 94–95, 160–161

Dayton Accord, 5, 107, 123, 126, 150, 155, 201, 243, 255, 256, 258, 259
  Annex 4, 255, 259
  Bosnian Constitution, 255
  voting and procedures, 256–257
Democratic League of Kosovo, 147
Democratic Party of Albanians, 214
Democratic Union for Integration, 237
Dickson, Eric, 87
displacement, 185–186
Djindjic, Zoran, 209
Djukanovic, Milo, 276, 277
Dodik, Milorad, 261, 263, 305
Doyle, Michael, 18, 65, 306–308

elections, 191
Elster, Jon, 30, 32
emotions, 6, 10, 13–14, 16, 23, 24–25, 297–298, 305–306

action tendency, 34
anger, 13, 27–29, 35–38, 81, 83
cognitive antecedent, 34–35
contempt, 13, 42–43, 81, 132–135, 150, 196
duration, 29–30
effects, 25–29
  formation of beliefs about, 28
  preservation of existing beliefs, 29
  rule selection, 28
  stereotyping, 28
fear, 13, 27–29, 37–40, 81
hatred, 13, 43–47, 94–95, 132–135, 197
rage, 84
resentment, 13, 25–27, 40–42, 81–82, 141–143, 183, 235, 240–246, 275–276
spite, 49–50, 81
status, 25–27
targeting, 19
Erdut Agreement, 125
ETA, 91–92
ethnic cleansing, 130, 135–161, 166
ethnic stigma, 29–34, 143–146, 206–207, 285–286, 295–296
  high ethnic stigma, 100–102
  high ethnic stigma predictions, 100–102
  low ethnic stigma, 98–100
  low ethnic stigma predictions, 98–100
European Security Strategy Statement, 294
European Union, 21, 117, 125, 127–128, 138, 187, 188, 230, 233, 234, 257, 261
  enlargement, 21
  European Agency for Reconstruction, 127
  Stability Pact for South Eastern Europe, 127
  Stabilization and Association Agreements, 127
  Treaty on the European Union, 117

FARC, 95
fear, 37–40
Fearon, James, 8, 35
  insurgency as technology, 8, 35–36
Ferhadija Mosque, 264
  incident, 264–265
First World War, 158, 273
former Yugoslavia, 107
  historical background, 107–116
  northern subsystem, 109–111
  southern subsystem, 108–109
Front de liberation national, 92
Frowick, Robert, 231

Macedonia (*cont.*)
  political parties, 237–238
  referendum boycotts, 239
  resentment, 223–224, 235, 240
  status, 223–224
  Tetovo, 229, 230
  violence, 230
  Western involvement, 230–231
Macedonians, 109, 222, 223, 225, 227, 234, 237
Machiavelli, 93–94
  The Prince, 94
March 2004 riots, 179–183, 184, 185, 190–191, 197, 199
Medvedja, 203, 215–216
Mesquita, Ethan Bueno de, 87
Military-Technical Agreement, 207
Milosevic, Slobodan, 115, 125, 160, 161, 199, 200, 256, 304
  Christmas warning, 124
  rise to power, 115
MIPT Terrorism Knowledge Base, 91, 93
Mitrovica, 130, 157, 168, 169, 189
  Ciganska Mahala, 130, 131
Mitrovica e Kosoves/Kosovska, 139
monolithic actors, 311
Montenegrins, 109, 114, 144, 271–272, 275
  in Kosovo, 144
Montenegrin-Serb relations, 275
Montenegro, 18, 104, 196, 202–271
  Albanians in Montenegro, 284
  Belgrade Agreement, 279–282
  Democratic Party of Socialists, 277
    split, 277
  ethnic stigma, 285–286
  ethnicity, 270–272
  identity, 270–272
  intermarriage, 275
  Montenegrin-Serb relations, 275–276
  neutrality in Kosovo war, 278
  population breakdown, 274, 289
  referendum on independence, 276–277, 281
  resentment, 275–276
  Ulcinj Agreement, 286
  United Nations embargo, 277
Mostar, 32
Mueller, John, 8, 287
Muslims, 32, 83
  in Bosnia, 32
Mustafa, Ragmi, 214

National Liberation Army (NLA), 128

NATO, 4, 20, 127, 137, 154, 155, 162, 209, 210, 211, 231–232, 234, 255
  bombing, 127, 134, 155, 156, 162
  Implementation Force (IFOR), 255
  Operation Deliberate Force, 123, 124, 155
Nis express bus convoy, 173
  bombing, 173
Northern Ireland, 92, 93
northern strategy, 189

Ohrid Framework Accord (OFA), 4, 107, 128, 201, 231, 232–233, 234, 236, 242
Open Cities Initiative, 260
Operation Deliberate Force, 155
Operation Essential Harvest, 231
Oric, Naser, 122
OSCE, 4, 75, 127, 154, 155, 163, 180, 187, 188, 189, 210, 211
Ottoman Empire, 107, 108
outbidding, 308–311
Owen-Stoltenberg plan, 121

Palestinian-Israeli conflict, 90–91
Paris, Roland, 18, 65, 75, 260, 308
  sequencing, 75
Party of Democratic Action, 214
Plavsic, Biljana, 260
Podujevo, 195
Poplasen, Nikola, 260
Presevo Valley, 203–204, 206, 207, 210, 214–215
  investment, 203, 204
  stigma, 206–207
prisoners' dilemma, 67–68, 164, 166, 256, 258
Pristina, 137, 138, 139, 147, 178, 188, 195
  demonstrations, 150, 178

Racak, 155
  massacre, 127, 154
Radic, Stjepan, 111
rage, 84
Rambouillet, 127, 155
  Milosevic refusal to sign, 155
Rankovic, Aleksandar, 142
Red Cross, 164
refugee flows, 156–158, 209
resentment, 25–27, 40–42, 81–82, 143, 183, 206–207, 235, 240–246, 275–276, 295–296
revenge killings, 165
Rexhepi, Bajram, 132

Beverly Silver, *Forces of Labor: Workers' Movements and Globalization since 1870*

Theda Skocpol, *Social Revolutions in the Modern World*

Austin Smith et al., *Selected Works of Michael Wallerstein*

Regina Smyth, *Candidate Strategies and Electoral Competition in the Russian Federation: Democracy Without Foundation*

Richard Snyder, *Politics after Neoliberalism: Reregulation in Mexico*

David Stark and László Bruszt, *Postsocialist Pathways: Transforming Politics and Property in East Central Europe*

Sven Steinmo, *The Evolution of Modern States: Sweden, Japan, and the United States*

Sven Steinmo, Kathleen Thelen, and Frank Longstreth, eds., *Structuring Politics: Historical Institutionalism in Comparative Analysis*

Susan C. Stokes, *Mandates and Democracy: Neoliberalism by Surprise in Latin America*

Susan C. Stokes, ed., *Public Support for Market Reforms in New Democracies*

Duane Swank, *Global Capital, Political Institutions, and Policy Change in Developed Welfare States*

Sidney Tarrow, *Power in Movement: Social Movements and Contentious Politics*

Sidney Tarrow, *Power in Movement: Social Movements and Contentious Politics, Revised and Updated Third Edition*

Kathleen Thelen, *How Institutions Evolve: The Political Economy of Skills in Germany, Britain, the United States, and Japan*

Charles Tilly, *Trust and Rule*

Daniel Treisman, *The Architecture of Government: Rethinking Political Decentralization*

Lily Lee Tsai, *Accountability without Democracy: How Solidary Groups Provide Public Goods in Rural China*

Joshua Tucker, *Regional Economic Voting: Russia, Poland, Hungary, Slovakia and the Czech Republic, 1990–1999*

Ashutosh Varshney, *Democracy, Development, and the Countryside*

Jeremy M. Weinstein, *Inside Rebellion: The Politics of Insurgent Violence*

Stephen I. Wilkinson, *Votes and Violence: Electoral Competition and Ethnic Riots in India*

Jason Wittenberg, *Crucibles of Political Loyalty: Church Institutions and Electoral Continuity in Hungary*

Elisabeth J. Wood, *Forging Democracy from Below: Insurgent Transitions in South Africa and El Salvador*

Elisabeth J. Wood, *Insurgent Collective Action and Civil War in El Salvador*